DATABASE MANAGEMENT THROUGH dBASE™

Robert T. Grauer
Maryann M. Barber
University of Miami

McGraw-Hill Book Company
New York St. Louis San Francisco Auckland Bogotá Caracas
Colorado Springs Hamburg Lisbon London Madrid Mexico
Milan Montreal New Delhi Oklahoma City Panama Paris
San Juan São Paulo Singapore Sydney Tokyo Toronto

DATABASE MANAGEMENT THROUGH dBASE™

Copyright © 1989 by McGraw-Hill, Inc. All rights reserved. Printed in the United States of America. Except as permitted under the United States Copyright Act of 1976, no part of this publication may be reproduced or distributed in any form or by any means, or stored in a data base or retrieval system, without the prior written permission of the publisher.

234567890 SEMSEM 8932109

P/N 024140-6
PART OF
ISBN 0-07-834780-7

This book was set in ITC Clearface Regular by Waldman Graphics, Inc.
The editor was Karen M. Jackson;
the designer was Caliber Design Planning Inc.;
the cover designer was Charles Carson;
the production supervisor was Leroy A. Young.
Project supervision was done by The Total Book.
Semline, Inc. was printer and binder.

Library of Congress Cataloging-in-Publication Data

Grauer, Robert T., (date).
  Database management through dBASE.

  Includes index.
  1. Data base management.   2. dBASE III PLUS
(Computer program)   I. Barber, Maryann M.   II. Title.
QA76.9.D3G719   1989   005.75′65   88-9159
ISBN 0-07-024140-6

DATABASE MANAGEMENT THROUGH dBASE™

ABOUT THE AUTHORS

ROBERT GRAUER received a Bachelor's degree in mechanical engineering from Rensselaer Polytechnic Institute in 1966 and a Ph.D. in operations research from the Polytechnic Institute of Brooklyn (now New York) in 1972. He is currently an associate professor in the department of Computer Information Systems at the University of Miami, where he has received the School of Business Distinguished Teaching Award.

Dr. Grauer is the author of a widely used textbook on microcomputer applications, as well as the author of several books on COBOL programming. He has been a consultant to several major organizations, including IBM, American Express, and Tandy.

MARYANN BARBER received a B.A. from the University of Florida in 1969 and both a Masters of business administration and a Masters of science in computer information systems from the University of Miami in 1985. She is currently a lecturer in the department of Computer Information Systems at the University of Miami, teaching courses in microcomputer applications, as well as database design and programming.

Ms. Barber is also a consultant in the Miami area, and has developed several major dBASE applications.

TO FRANK, TO JESSICA, AND TO MY PARENTS—for giving up a year;

TO OUR STUDENTS—for teaching us so much.

CONTENTS

Contents

x

Contents

xii

An alphabetical listing of the major dBASE III PLUS commands as covered in the text,
with the material on each command divided into four sections: syntax, discussion, tips, and
related topics. The Programmer's Notebook provides a convenient reference for particular
programming questions, but is not intended as a replacement for the Ashton-Tate
Technical Manuals. The table on p. xiii lists the commands covered in the Programmer's
Notebook.

■ TABLE NB.1

Commands and Functions in the Programmer's Notebook

APPEND	LIST HISTORY	SET DEVICE
APPEND FROM	LIST MEMORY	SET DOHISTORY
ASSIST	LIST STATUS	SET ECHO
AVERAGE	LIST STRUCTURE	SET ESCAPE
BOF()	LOCATE	SET EXACT
BROWSE	LOWER()	SET FIELDS
CDOW()	LTRIM()	SET FILTER
CHR()	MAX()	SET FORMAT
CLEAR	MIN()	SET FUNCTION
CLOSE	MODIFY COMMAND	SET HEADING
CMONTH()	MODIFY LABEL	SET HELP
CONFIG.DB	MODIFY QUERY	SET HISTORY
CONTINUE	MODIFY REPORT	SET INDEX
COPY	MODIFY SCREEN	SET INTENSITY
COUNT	MODIFY STRUCTURE	SET MEMOWIDTH
CREATE	MODIFY VIEW	SET MENU
CREATE LABEL	MONTH()	SET ORDER
CREATE QUERY	PACK	SET PATH
CREATE REPORT	PRIVATE	SET PRINT
CREATE SCREEN	PUBLIC	SET PROCEDURE
CREATE VIEW	QUIT	SET RELATION
CTOD()	READ	SET SAFETY
DATE()	RECALL	SET SCOREBOARD
DAY()	RECNO()	SET STATUS
DELETE	REINDEX	SET STEP
DELETED()	RELEASE	SET TALK
DIR	REPLACE	SET TYPEAHEAD
DISPLAY	REPORT FORM	SET UNIQUE
DISPLAY HISTORY	RESTORE	SET VIEW
DISPLAY MEMORY	RESUME	SKIP
DISPLAY STATUS	RETURN	SORT
DISPLAY STRUCTURE	RTRIM()	SPACE()
DO	RUN	STORE
DO CASE	SAVE	STR()
DO WHILE	@...SAY...GET	SUBSTR()
DTOC()	SEEK	SUM
EDIT	SELECT	TIME()
EJECT	SET	@...TO
EOF()	SET ALTERNATE	TRIM()
FIND	SET BELL	UPPER()
GO	SET CATALOG	USE
HELP	SET CENTURY	VAL()
IF	SET COLOR	WAIT
IIF()	SET CONFIRM	YEAR()
INDEX ON	SET CONSOLE	ZAP
INSERT	SET DATE	?
JOIN	SET DEBUG	*
LABEL FORM	SET DEFAULT	&
LEN()	SET DELETED	&&
LIST	SET DELIMITERS	

PREFACE

The recent introduction of dBASE IV should ensure Ashton-Tate's continued domination of data management software for the personal computer. Although dBASE IV contains numerous enhancements over its immediate predecessor (dBASE III Plus), it is in essence *upward compatible,* meaning that systems which ran under the older version will continue to function without modification. Hence the title of our book is *Database Management Through dBASE* (without specific mention of either dBASE III Plus or dBASE IV). At the time of writing (October, 1988) the educational version of dBASE III Plus is included with the text, with the anticipation that an educational version of dBASE IV will be provided when it becomes available.

More significantly however, *Database Management Through dBASE* is much more than a book on dBASE programming. It covers a wide range of topics which make it suitable for three distinct audiences:

(1) The less technical end user, interested primarily in applications, who needs to learn only a limited subset of the language;
(2) The CIS major, seeking to master the language, who requires supporting material on structured methodology; and
(3) The practicing programmer who needs a comprehensive dBASE reference.

Although no book can be all things to all people, these audiences are not as diverse as may first appear. Indeed we have seen countless students progress from disinterested end users sitting in a required applications course, to motivated individuals in a programming course, to proficient programmers enrolled in a projects course. The text is built on a unique combination of *business case studies,* a *convenience disk, hands-on exercises,* and a *programmer's notebook,* which enable it to achieve its stated objective.

The business case studies describe various problems in data management with which the reader can readily identify. The associated discussion presents theoretical concepts relating to data management, and develops the dBASE elements necessary for the eventual solution. The end user audience may omit some or all of the material on dBASE programming, yet still be able to appreciate the case solution (as implemented on the convenience disk). On the other hand, those interested in programming will appreciate the more technical information.

The convenience disk contains dBASE implementations of the various case studies, and may appeal more to the less technical audience interested primarily in running and/or modifying existing systems. The availability of the convenience disk makes it possible to construct assignments in which students are asked to suggest major changes to an existing system and/or implement minor ones. The subjects of program maintenance and the drafting of information requirements are seldom taught, yet these skills are as important as new development.

Hands-on exercises are found in every chapter and require the reader's participation at the computer. The exercises may ask the reader to assume the role of end user, experiment with commands from the dot prompt, or try his or her hand at command mode programming. In every situation, the reader is encouraged to explore variations in the commands to further increase his or her appreciation of dBASE.

The Programmer's Notebook is a section unto itself and appears at the end of the text. It contains a compendium of information on individual commands and serves as a valuable reference to both the experienced as well as the new dBASE programmer.

We believe *Database Management Through dBASE* to be superior to anything currently available on dBASE programming. The existing books (and there are many) suffer from a common shortcoming in that they are either too simple or too advanced, and often fall victim to poor organization. These books tend to be written primarily as reference books and are ill suited for use as text books. Nor do any dBASE books exist for the individual who manages data, drafts information requirements, assists in the installation of dBASE systems written (or purchased) for them, and suggests and/or implements modifications to existing systems. This less-technical audience is virtually untapped, yet it may ultimately prove to be larger than that of the more traditional dBASE programmer.

Above all *Database Management Through dBASE* has been written for the classroom and contains many elements associated with good teaching and sound pedagogy. Every chapter begins with a statement of objectives, and ends with a list of key words and concepts. It encourages participation by the reader at the computer, and provides abundant exercises and problems throughout (with solutions contained in a separate *Instructor's Manual*).

The text consists of 11 chapters and the Programmer's Notebook. Chapter 1 presents a completed system (consisting of some 30 programs and 5000 lines of code) which exists on the convenience disk. The reader is asked simply to execute the system, and thereby gains an immediate appreciation for what is possible with dBASE. This chapter also introduces the hands-on exercise format and describes how to install as well as load dBASE.

Chapters 2 through 6 present the most important commands from the dot prompt, giving students the ability to maintain a DBF file, as well as extract information from it. The section also contains separate chapters on the report generator, mailing labels, and query files, all of which operate from a similar menu structure.

Chapters 7 and 8 discuss structured programming and structured design, material which is essential for anyone wishing to progress beyond the dot prompt. Chapters 9 through 11 delve into serious dBASE programming and cover the screen generator, file maintenance, and relational databases, respectively.

The Programmer's Notebook presents some 150 dBASE commands in alphabetical sequence for convenient access. The material on each command is divided into four sections: syntax, discussion, tips, and related topics, and provides a convenient reference for detailed programming questions.

The authors would like to thank Karen Jackson, our sponsoring editor at McGraw-Hill, for making this book possible. We are also grateful to Kate Scheinman for transforming the manuscript into a finished book, to Chuck Carson for his inspired cover, and to Leroy Young for adhering to a tight production schedule. We would also like to thank our colleagues at the University of Miami, Joel Stutz, Raymond Frost, and Vicar Hernandez for their continued encouragement. Last, but certainly not least, we are indebted to: Harriet Cinque, Kean College, New Jersey; Nancy C. Haney, Professional Microcomputer Consulting/Training; Fred Niederman, University of Minnesota; and Thomas A. Pollack, Duquesne University, whose positive reviews and constructive criticism have made this a better book than it would otherwise have been.

Robert T. Grauer
Maryann M. Barber

DATABASE MANAGEMENT THROUGH dBASE™

■ OBJECTIVES

After reading this chapter, you should be able to:

- Install the student version of dBASE III PLUS to conform to a particular hardware configuration.

- Load dBASE III PLUS; distinguish between loading and installing a program.

- Differentiate between report generation and data entry; describe the primary data entry operations.

- List several types of data validation that may be done during data entry; describe the effects of entering improper data into a system.

Introduction

1

Overview

This book is about database management; in particular it is about database systems as they are implemented in dBASE III PLUS on the IBM PC and compatible microcomputers. Our overall objectives are to acquaint you with the potential of these systems through case studies and to enable you to design and implement these systems in dBASE. The book follows a "learn-by-doing" approach in which you are led through a series of hands-on exercises requiring your participation at the computer. We believe, in fact we are very sure, that you will derive your greatest benefit from our book during the time you spend on the computer.

Very little is assumed in the way of previous knowledge about computers, yet it is essential that you know something about the PC and its operating system. Accordingly, the chapter begins with a hands-on exercise that has you *turn on* the computer and its peripherals, *load* DOS, *install* dBASE to conform to your particular hardware configuration, and finally *load* dBASE and begin work.

We also think it important that you appreciate what dBASE can ultimately do and believe you can best achieve this by exploring a working system. Accordingly, the second half of the chapter presents a case study for Soleil America, Inc., then follows with a second hands-on exercise in which you use a fully functional system. We take you through the steps of *adding*, *deleting*, and *editing* records for the system, then assist you in the *report generation* process that derives useful information from the data you entered. Our emphasis at this time is on the nontechnical (or less technical) individual who knows what an information system is supposed to do, but who is not concerned with programming, per se.

Getting Started

The first hands-on exercise is not difficult and requires only that you turn on the computer and follow some simple startup procedures. Nevertheless, it will give you a feeling of accomplishment and set the stage for the more involved exercises that follow in later chapters.

The exercise will also take you through the procedure for *installing* dBASE, and through a second procedure for *loading* it *after* it has been installed. The installation process customizes dBASE to a particular hardware configuration, for example, on systems with and without a hard disk drive, or systems with 256K bytes or 640K bytes of memory, and so on. The loading process brings the installed version of dBASE into memory from where it is executed. dBASE (or, for that matter, any other program) is *installed* once and only once, whereas it is *loaded* into memory every time you use it.

All the hands-on exercises in the book are written for a system with two floppy disk drives, which is still the most common configuration in the classroom. (If, however, you have a hard disk drive, then follow the parenthetical comments in various parts of the exercise.) Regardless of which configuration you have, the first exercise requires four disks:

1. a DOS system disk to start the computer
2. the two dBASE III PLUS student disks
3. the convenience disk that came with this book

Note, too, that although we refer to the student version of dBASE III PLUS, our comments pertain to the complete version as well. The student version is limited only by the limited number of records it can process (31).

Hands-on Exercise 1–1:   Loading dBASE

Objective: To turn on the computer and its peripherals, answer the date and time prompts correctly, and install and load dBASE.

☐   **STEP 1: Turn on the computer and its peripherals.**

Place a DOS system disk *with the label side up and the label toward you* in drive A. Close the door on the disk drive. (On a system with a hard disk drive, leave the door open and boot directly from drive C.)

Next, turn on the computer and its peripherals. The number and location of the switches depends on the nature, make, and manufacturer of the peripherals. The easiest possible setup is when all system components are plugged into a surge protector, in which case only a single switch has to be turned on. In any case:

a. turn on the printer
b. turn on the monitor
c. turn on the system unit's power switch

☐   **STEP 2: Answer the date and time prompts.**

It takes anywhere from 15 seconds to a minute or two (depending on the amount of RAM in your computer) for something visible to happen. Be patient. Soon you will hear the "whirring" sound of the disk drive, followed by a beep, followed by a request to enter the current date:

```
Current date is Tue 1-01-1980
Enter new date:
```

Supply the current date, using either hyphens or slashes to separate the month, day, and year. 3–16–1989 and 3/16/89 are both valid entries for March 16, 1989 (year may be entered as either a two- or four-digit field).

The system will then return a message of the form:

```
Current time is: 0:00:20.00
Enter new time:
```

In this example, 20 seconds has elapsed since DOS was booted, that is, you probably took 20 seconds to enter the date. Time is expressed in *hours:minutes:seconds.hundredths* (on a 24-hour military clock). To enter the time, colons are required between hours, minutes, and seconds, and a period between seconds and hundredths of a second. Any omitted value is assumed to be zero. (It won't take long for you to realize that it is possible to bypass the date and time requests by pressing the enter key twice. We recommend, however, that you take the trouble to enter date and time.)

Eventually you will see the message:

```
The IBM Personal Computer DOS
Version 3.10 (C)Copyright IBM Corp, 1981, 1982, 1983,
1984
```

You may see a logo other than IBM's or a version other than 3.10 depending on which version of the operating system you are using. In any event you should be running with Version 2.10 or higher.

☐ **STEP 3: Install dBASE.**

The installation procedure is essentially the same for systems with and without a hard disk. Remove the DOS disk from drive A and replace it with the *first* dBASE program disk, being sure that drive A is the default disk drive. Now, from the A prompt (`A>`), enter the `INSTALL` command (to execute the INSTALL.BAT file contained on the dBASE disk). Figure 1.1 should appear on the monitor.

The installation procedure is *menu driven* and easy to follow. Enter the appropriate response for your configuration (the system will not accept an invalid entry), then follow the indicated instructions. *Note, however, that if you have only 256K bytes of RAM you cannot use any 3.X version of DOS; that is, you must use DOS 2.1.*

The installation procedure ends with instructions to reboot your computer (Ctrl, Alt, and Del).

☐ **STEP 4: Additional installation procedure (hard disk drive only).**

You will find it convenient to copy the files contained on the convenience disk onto your hard disk drive. Accordingly, place the convenience disk in drive A, and enter the `INSTALL2` command from the A prompt. This, in turn, will create a series of subdirectories on the hard disk and copy the files to the appropriate subdirectories.

Note, too, that Step 3's installation procedure created a CONFIG.SYS file on your hard disk drive's root directory. In doing so it renamed any preexisting CONFIG.SYS file, CONFIGS.OLD. In other words, you may now have two configuration files, CONFIG.SYS and CONFIGS.OLD, on your root directory. If that is the case, copy all the commands in the original CONFIGS.OLD file (except for any FILES and/or BUFFER commands which may be present) to the CONFIG.SYS file just created.

☐ **STEP 5: Load dBASE.**

Place the first dBASE disk in drive A if you are using a two-drive floppy disk

```
dBASE III PLUS SAMPLER INSTALLATION

    MEMORY AND DRIVE SELECTION

    A. 256K and 2 floppy drives
    B. More than 256k and 2 floppy drives
    C. 256k and 1 floppy drive and 1 harddisk
    D. More than 256k and 1 floppy drive and 1 harddisk

Type the letter corresponding to your computer's configuration:
```

FIGURE 1.1 dBASE Installation Menu

```
              dBASE III PLUS   version 1.0   IBM/MSDOS DEMO
      Copyright (c) Ashton-Tate 1984, 1985, 1986.  All Rights Reserved.
         dBASE, dBASE III, dBASE III PLUS, and Ashton-Tate
                     are trademarks of Ashton-Tate


      You may use the dBASE III PLUS software and  printed materials in
      the dBASE III PLUS software package under the terms  of the dBASE
      III  PLUS  Software  License Agreement.   In summary, Ashton-Tate
      grants you a paid-up,  non-transferable,  personal license to use
      dBASE III PLUS on one  microcomputer or workstation.   You do not
      become the owner of  the package,  nor do  you have  the right to
      copy or alter the software or printed materials.  You are legally
      accountable  for any violation of  the  License  Agreement  or of
      copyright, trademark, or trade secret laws.




   Command Line   ‖<B:>‖                    ‖              ‖     ‖

      Press ◄─┘ to assent to the License Agreement and begin dBASE III PLUS.
```

FIGURE 1.2 Opening dBASE screen

system. If you have a hard disk drive, however, enter the command CD\SAMPLER to change to the subdirectory containing the dBASE program files you just installed.

Enter the one-word command dBASE to load the program. Figure 1.2 should then appear on your monitor whether or not you have a hard drive. Press the Return key as instructed. You will be prompted for the second dBASE program disk (on a floppy disk system only). Figure 1.3, the dBASE Assistant, will then appear.

☐   STEP 6: Leave the dBASE Assistant.

We believe it is easier to operate initially without the dBASE Assistant (the

```
   Set Up  Create  Update  Position  Retrieve  Organize Modify Tools   03:32:55 pm
  ┌──────────────────────┐
  │ Database file         │
  ├──────────────────────┤
  │ Format for Screen     │
  │ Query                 │
  ├──────────────────────┤
  │ Catalog               │
  │ View                  │
  ├──────────────────────┤
  │ Quit dBASE III PLUS   │
  └──────────────────────┘




   ASSIST          ‖<B:>‖                ‖Opt: 1/6      ‖     ‖
   Move selection bar - ↑↓. Select - ◄─┘.  Leave menu - →. Help - F1. Exit - Esc.
                        Select a database file.
```

FIGURE 1.3 Opening dBASE Menu

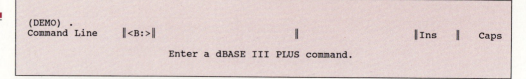

```
(DEMO) .
Command Line    ‖<B:>‖                          ‖              ‖Ins  ‖  Caps
                        Enter a dBASE III PLUS command.
```

FIGURE 1.4 The dot prompt and status line

topic is discussed further in Chapter 2), that is, with only the dBASE *dot prompt* and *status bar* present on the screen. Accordingly, press the Esc key at this time to get to the screen in Figure 1.4.

You are now at the "dot prompt," (.), the point at which all future hands-on exercises begin. The period (dot prompt) appearing at the lower left portion of the screen is dBASE's way of telling you it is waiting for a command. (The word DEMO appearing to the left of the period indicates this is the dBASE III PLUS student version.)

☐ **STEP 7: Shut the system down.**

Type QUIT to exit dBASE and end the session. You have successfully turned on the computer, installed and loaded dBASE, and issued QUIT, your first dBASE command.

Turn the power off to shut down the system. (Disks may be removed from a disk drive either before or after the power is turned off.)

There's Always a Reason

We expect you completed the hands-on exercise with little difficulty. There will be times, however, when not everything will go as smoothly as in this exercise and so we relate a favorite anecdote ("Mystery of the Month," *PC World* Magazine, April 1983). As you read our tale, remember that a computer does exactly what you tell it to do; this is not necessarily what you want it to do. It is a source of wonderful satisfaction when everything works, but also the cause of near unbelievable frustration when results are not what you expect.

Our story concerns a manager who purchased a PC and began to use it enthusiastically. Unfortunately, the feeling did not rub off on his assistant, who was apprehensive about computers in general, but who finally agreed to try the new technology.

As is frequently the case, the assistant's experience with the computer was as frustrating as the manager's was rewarding. Every time the assistant tried using the computer, an error message appeared, yet when the manager tried the same procedure it worked fine. Finally, manager and assistant went through a systematic comparison of everything they did, such as turning the machine on and off, handling disks, and using the keyboard. They could find no difference in their procedures and could not account for the repeated disk errors that plagued the assistant but left the manager alone.

Just as they were about to give up the manager noticed that his assistant was wearing a charm bracelet. He looked closely, and sure enough one of the charms was a tiny magnet containing just enough force to interfere with reading the disk. The assistant stored the bracelet in a drawer and the machine has been fine ever since.

The point of our story is that there is always a logical reason for everything a computer does or does not do, although discovering that reason may be less than obvious. You are about to embark on a wonderful journey toward the productive use of a computer, with a virtually unlimited number of potential applications. Be patient, be inquisitive, and enjoy.

Case Preview

We come now to the main portion of the chapter, presenting a completely functional system developed in dBASE III PLUS. The case study's essence is in the specification of the system requirements from the viewpoint of the end user. As you read further in the case, try to determine the information the user wants, as well as the data the system requires to provide that information. Try to visualize how data will be entered into the system and how the corresponding reports will be retrieved. Above all, note the requirement for a system that a nontechnical individual finds easy to use.

CASE STUDY:
Soleil America, Inc.

Stefan Soleil thought himself a very lucky young man. He was about to enter into a $10 million agreement with a well-known New York investment banking firm, whereby the firm would acquire a 75 percent interest in his shoe company, leaving him with the remaining 25 percent. They had also agreed to give him a 3-year employment contract to manage the company, providing him with a salary of $500,000 in year 1 and increasing by $500,000 each year to a salary of $1.5 million in year 3 (with the stipulation, of course, that all agreed-upon sales and operating income targets were met).

It was not all luck, however, as years of hard work and sound business practices did much to bring about the good fortune. Stefan had always surrounded himself with bright and trusted employees, had paid them well, and was now reaping the rewards of being an effective manager and supervisor. In the old days, he had known precisely how much every employee was earning, the date they were hired, and the date of their last salary review. This personal touch endeared him to his workers, but growth of the company in recent years had made it all but impossible to continue in this way. Accordingly, part of his plan for the transition included the Soleil Employee System, a computerized personnel information system through which he and a soon-to-be-hired personnel manager could track employee performance, promotions, and raises.

Of special importance in the new system are a series of exception reports, among them: (1) a list of employees with outstanding performance evaluations; (2) a list of employees who have not received a raise within the last year; and (3) a list of employees earning below the expected salary for their job classification. (Each job within the company is assigned a responsibility or grade level, for which a standard formula is used to compute the expected salary. Each employee's salary is computed as a percentage of the expected salary. This provides a measure of how an individual is paid compared to others with a similar job classification.)

Six months ago, Stefan hired a consultant to develop a customized, easy-to-use, menu-driven system according to his specifications. A prototype system was now in place for evaluation, after which the consultant would make final changes. Stefan hoped that the system would be simple enough to be used with relatively little training, yet sophisticated enough to provide the necessary information. He hoped that the final system would allow his personnel policies and philosophies to be kept in operation, even if he left the company at the end of his contract.

Case Solution

The case study's last paragraph refers to a prototype system used in the subsequent, hands-on exercise. Indeed, the most essential portion of the chapter is the hands-on exercise, which enables you to better appreciate an actual dBASE application. The system is fully functional and typical of systems you may be using.

The Soleil Employee System is menu driven and requires little in the way of user documentation. Although the subsequent hands-on exercise will take you through the sys-

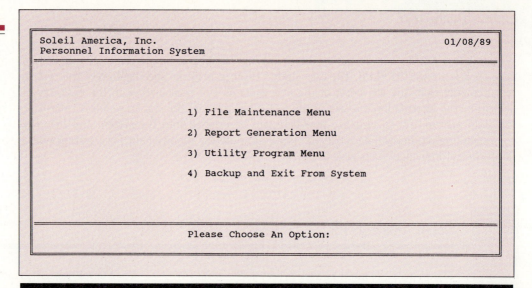

```
Soleil America, Inc.                                          01/08/89
Personnel Information System


                    1)  File Maintenance Menu

                    2)  Report Generation Menu

                    3)  Utility Program Menu

                    4)  Backup and Exit From System



                        Please Choose An Option:
```

FIGURE 1.5 Main Menu of Soleil Employee System

tem, it is useful to preview some of the screens at this time. It is helpful also to realize that the Soleil Employee System, like many others, is divided into three major components: file maintenance, report generation, and utility programs. This is apparent by examining the Main Menu shown in Figure 1.5.

The menu in Figure 1.5 requires the user to select an option by entering 1, 2, 3, or 4 (the system will not accept any other response). Each of the first three options brings up a subsidiary menu, whereas the fourth will ask about backup, then exit from the system and return you to the operating system.

Figure 1.6 shows the Main Menu's relationship to its three subsidiary menus. Figure 1.6a repeats the Main Menu from Figure 1.5, whereas Figures 1.6b, c, and d contain the File Maintenance, Report Generation, and Utility Menus.

The File Maintenance Menu in Figure 1.6b provides for *adding* a new record, *editing* (changing) an existing record, or *deleting* an existing record. It also allows you to *update* an employee's salary to reflect a raise, which is really a special type of editing operation.

The Report Generation Menu in Figure 1.6c shows that the user has several options, reflecting the information Stefan Soleil wants. It is important to emphasize however, that the information (output) the system provides is only as good as the data (input) on which it is based. No system, no matter how sophisticated, can produce valid output from invalid input, a principle aptly stated by the acronym GIGO (*Garbage In, Garbage Out*).

The Utility Menu in Figure 1.6d offers three choices (the meaning of which will become apparent as you read further in the text). In addition a backup procedure is associated with Figure 1.6a's normal exit routine to remind the user of the need for backup whenever he or she leaves the system. Suffice it to say that *it is absolutely critical to duplicate important data disks, leaving duplicate copies in different places*, that is, at home and in the office.

You should now have an overall appreciation for the Soleil Employee System's goals as well as an inkling as to its implementation. Remember, our objective at this time is for you to gain an appreciation for the power inherent within dBASE, as typified by a real application. Thus, it is not necessary now for you to be concerned with *how* the system works, only about *what* it does.

The exercise you are about to do is the very essence of the chapter. We urge you to experiment fully with the system, especially its file maintenance and report generation capabilities. Add, modify, and delete employee data, then generate several reports (before and after the various transactions). Visualize yourself as Stefan Soleil and decide whether the prototype is adequately developed for you to accept (and pay for) the system.

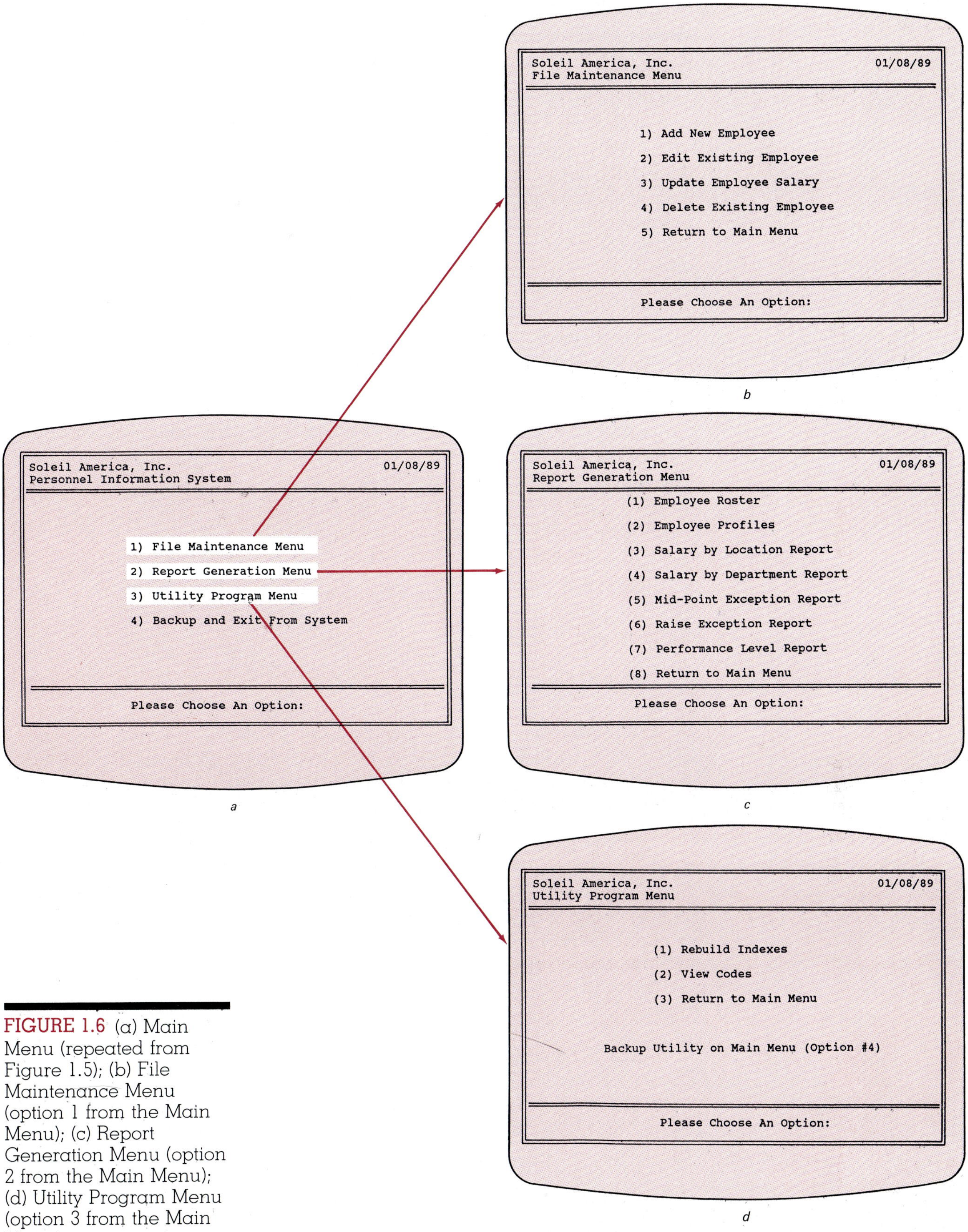

```
Soleil America, Inc.                                      01/08/89
File Maintenance Menu
_____

                    1) Add New Employee

                    2) Edit Existing Employee

                    3) Update Employee Salary

                    4) Delete Existing Employee

                    5) Return to Main Menu


_____

                    Please Choose An Option:
```
b

```
Soleil America, Inc.                                      01/08/89
Personnel Information System
_____




            1) File Maintenance Menu
            2) Report Generation Menu
            3) Utility Program Menu
            4) Backup and Exit From System


_____

            Please Choose An Option:
```
a

```
Soleil America, Inc.                                      01/08/89
Report Generation Menu
_____
                (1) Employee Roster

                (2) Employee Profiles

                (3) Salary by Location Report

                (4) Salary by Department Report

                (5) Mid-Point Exception Report

                (6) Raise Exception Report

                (7) Performance Level Report

                (8) Return to Main Menu
_____
                Please Choose An Option:
```
c

```
Soleil America, Inc.                                      01/08/89
Utility Program Menu
_____



                (1) Rebuild Indexes

                (2) View Codes

                (3) Return to Main Menu


        Backup Utility on Main Menu (Option #4)



_____

                Please Choose An Option:
```
d

FIGURE 1.6 (a) Main Menu (repeated from Figure 1.5); (b) File Maintenance Menu (option 1 from the Main Menu); (c) Report Generation Menu (option 2 from the Main Menu); (d) Utility Program Menu (option 3 from the Main Menu)

Hands-on Exercise 1–2:   The Soleil Employee System

Objective: To load the Soleil Employee System and explore its capabilities from the viewpoint of the end user. You will also verify that the system does what it is supposed to do and note any shortcomings.

☐   **STEP 1: Turn on the computer.**

Turn on the computer, place a DOS disk in drive A, and answer the date and time prompts as you did in Steps 1 and 2 for Hands-on Exercise 1–1. After turning on the computer, and if you are using a floppy disk system, place the first dBASE program disk in disk drive A and the convenience disk in disk drive B.

☐   **STEP 2: Change to the Soleil subdirectory.**

For ease of organization, a disk (floppy or hard) may be divided into *subdirectories*, with each subdirectory containing just the files of a particular system. This is precisely how the convenience disk is set up, with the dBASE files for Chapter 1 in one subdirectory, the files for Chapter 2 in another, and so on. Accordingly, you must always switch to the proper subdirectory *before* loading dBASE. Enter the appropriate command to switch to the Soleil subdirectory as follows:

```
CD B:\SOLEIL ──────────── On a floppy system
CD C:\SAMPLER\SOLEIL ────── On a hard drive
PATH C:\SAMPLER
```

The `PATH` command is necessary if you are using a hard disk drive so that DOS knows where to find the dBASE program files when you load dBASE in the next step.

☐   **STEP 3: Load dBASE.**

Enter the one word command `DBASE` (from the `A>` or `C>` prompt, depending on your system) to *load* dBASE (that is, bring the dBASE program into memory). Follow the instructions dBASE provides, ending at the dot prompt. Remember you are loading dBASE, rather than installing it (and should not repeat Steps 3 and 4 from the earlier exercise).

☐   **STEP 4: Load the Soleil Employee System.**

Enter the command `DO SOLMAIN` from the dBASE dot prompt, causing Figure 1.7 to appear on your monitor. We have taken advantage of dBASE's formatting capabilities to highlight portions of this and subsequent screens, for example, the middle portion of Figure 1.7 should be highlighted. If this is not the case, adjust your monitor's contrast knob.

Press the Return key as instructed in Figure 1.7. This takes you to the system's Main Menu, which was discussed in the case solution.

☐   **STEP 5: Enter the File Maintenance Menu.**

Enter a 1 to select the File Maintenance Menu. You should now be in a position to accomplish any of the normal file maintenance operations, that is, you can *add* a new record, or *edit* or *delete* an existing record. You can also *update* an employee's salary.

Choose the first option from the File Maintenance Menu to add a record.

☐   **STEP 6: Add a new employee.**

We will add an employee with the following data:

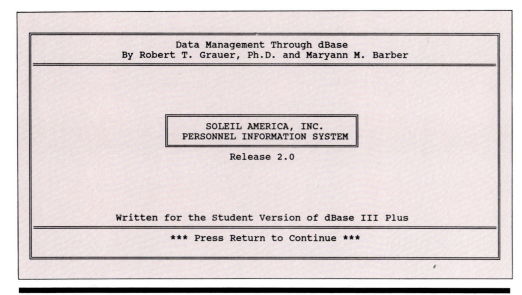

FIGURE 1.7 Opening screen for Soleil Employee System

```
                    Name: MA Coulter
   Social security number: 666-66-6666
              Birth Date: 06/22/45
               Education: Bachelor's degree
               Hire Date: November 14, 1988
                Location: Italy
                   Title: Sales representative
              Title Date: November 14, 1988
                  Salary: 25,000
             Salary Date: November 14, 1988
            Salary Grade: 5
```

The first thing the system will do is prompt for the new employee's social security number (use 666-66-6666). It will then check to make sure that an employee with this social security number has not been previously entered into the system. After the check, the screen in Figure 1.8 will appear.

Enter the data for MA Coulter, one field at a time. The system is set up so that if an entry completely fills the field, for example, the hire date, the cursor moves automatically to the next field. However, if the space for a field is not filled, for example, last name, you must press the Return key to move to the next field. You may also use the up or down arrow keys to move from field to field. (The right and left arrow keys move from character to character within a field.)

The input data for MA Coulter spells out the entries for education, location, and title, whereas the screen in Figure 1.8 requires you to enter the corresponding codes. To determine the correct codes, enter a ? as the field entry and you will see the appropriate code descriptions. (Note the message on the screen's last line.) In other words, the system provides an *online help facility* in which it exits from the current screen, displays the necessary information to help you, then returns to the earlier screen. For example, enter a single question mark in the location entry, press the Return key, and the locations and corresponding codes appear on the screen. (You can also enter two question marks and avoid pressing the Return key.)

```
Soleil America, Inc.                                          01/08/89
Personnel File Add Module
_____

            Last Name:                        Initials:

    Social Security Number: 666-66-6666       Birthdate:    /  /


    Education Code:          Hire Date:   /  /        Location Code:

         Title Code:         Title Date:    /  /

    Salary:              Salary Date:    /  /         Salary Grade:



_____
            Enter information at the cursor or blanks to quit
          Where appropriate fill field with ? to see code descriptions
```

FIGURE 1.8 Screen to add an employee record

Complete the addition for MA Coulter being careful to enter the data exactly as indicated. Note that the system contains some built-in checks for validity, for example, it will not accept a nonnumeric character in a date field. Do not, however, enter a dollar sign or comma in a salary as the system will automatically insert a comma for you. (The comma may initially appear to be in the wrong place; 10,000 will appear as 100,00. The entry will, however, correct itself when you press the Return key.) Return to the File Maintenance Menu when the entry is completed.

☐ **STEP 7: Edit an existing record.**

The File Maintenance Menu provides four types of transactions: to (1) add a new employee (as was just illustrated); (2) edit an existing employee; (3) update an existing employee's salary; and (4) delete an existing employee. Select the second option (that is, enter **2**) in Figure 1.6b's menu to edit an existing employee. The following message will appear on the screen with a place to enter the desired employee's name at the bottom:

```
Please enter name of Employee to edit below
         or press return to quit. . .


Last Name:                      Initials:
```

Enter the employee's last name for editing, for example, **Arnold**, and press the Return key. Then enter the employee's initials, for example, **JS**. (Note that if you fill the initials field, that is, you enter two initials, the system continues automatically. However, if you do not fill the field, that is you enter only a single initial, then you must press the Return key to continue.)

The system will search for Arnold's record and, if it is found, display the record on the screen as shown in Figure 1.9. In actuality you do not have to enter the initials, or even the complete last name, because the system will search for the employee based on only a partial name. In other words, you can enter **Arn** in lieu of **Arnold** in which case the system will retrieve the first employee whose last name begins with Arn. However, if you enter only a partial last name, you must press the Return key twice for the system to continue.

```
┌──────────────────────────────────────────────────────────────────┐
│ ┌────────────────────────────────────────────────────────────┐   │
│ │ Soleil America, Inc.                              01/08/89   │   │
│ │ Personnel File Edit Module                                   │   │
│ ├────────────────────────────────────────────────────────────┤   │
│ │                                                              │   │
│ │          Last Name: Arnold          Initials: JS            │   │
│ │                                                              │   │
│ │    Social Security Number: 171-77-1777   Birthdate: 03/04/45 │   │
│ │                                                              │   │
│ │  Performance Rating: 1    Title Code: 302  Title Date: 02/12/87 │ │
│ │                                                              │   │
│ │  Education Code: 4      Hire Date: 06/25/81   Location Code: 42 │ │
│ ├────────────────────────────────────────────────────────────┤   │
│ │                      Salary History                          │   │
│ │      Salary         Salary Date          Salary Grade        │   │
│ │    $ 78,000          02/17/88                  6             │   │
│ │    $ 70,000          02/12/87                  6             │   │
│ │    $ 67,000          01/10/86                  6             │   │
│ ├────────────────────────────────────────────────────────────┤   │
│ │     Press E to Edit this record, N to see Next record,       │   │
│ │       P to see Previous record, or Q to Quit:                │   │
│ └────────────────────────────────────────────────────────────┘   │
└──────────────────────────────────────────────────────────────────┘
```

FIGURE 1.9 Editing an existing employee record

After the employee record has been displayed on the screen as shown in Figure 1.9, press E to edit the record as indicated by the message at the bottom of the screen. [Alternative choices are P to display the previous record (in alphabetic sequence), N for the next record, and Q to quit the editing operation altogether.]

Use the up and down arrow keys to move about the screen, and edit any field that requires a correction. For purposes of illustration, change the title from Sales Representative to Production Coordinator. In addition, change the hire date from 6/25/81 to 5/31/80. (You can use the online help, that is, a ?, to retrieve the proper title code.) When you reach the very last field on the screen, press the enter key to see the following message:

```
Enter E to edit above information or S to save changes
                    and quit
```

Respond accordingly, then return to the File Maintenance Menu and select the salary update function.

☐   STEP 8: Update an existing salary.

It is important to clarify the difference between the edit and update functions. An edit operation replaces an existing value (and removes it from the system) because the existing value was entered incorrectly. A salary update, on the other hand, retains the old value and adds a more current value. For example, if an individual is currently earning $30,000 and receives a raise to $34,000, the previous $30,000 salary will still be retained in the system. [As per instructions from Stefan Soleil, the system maintains three salary levels: current salary, previous salary, and second previous salary. Historical data retention enables the system to calculate an individual's percent salary increase(s), a measure Mr. Soleil deemed important.]

Select the update option from the File Maintenance Menu and retrieve the employee record for Butler, that is:

```
Please enter name of Employee to update below
        or press return to quit . . .
    Last Name: Butler          Intitials:
```

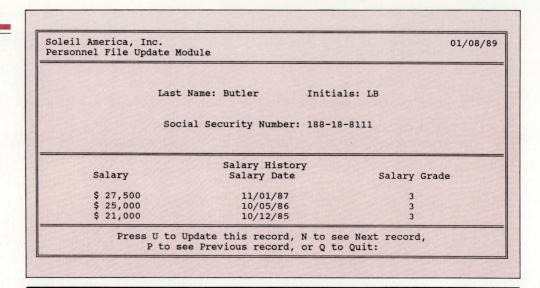

```
Soleil America, Inc.                                      01/08/89
Personnel File Update Module


             Last Name: Butler          Initials: LB


             Social Security Number: 188-18-8111


                              Salary History
         Salary               Salary Date          Salary Grade
         $ 27,500               11/01/87                 3
         $ 25,000               10/05/86                 3
         $ 21,000               10/12/85                 3

         Press U to Update this record, N to see Next record,
             P to see Previous record, or Q to Quit:
```

FIGURE 1.10 Updating an employee salary

The retrieval function works the way it does in the edit mode in that you do not necessarily have to enter the complete last name or the initials. Butler's record is displayed on the screen as shown in Figure 1.10.

Figure 1.10 displays three salaries (current, previous, and second previous) for Butler. Enter a U to update the salary and note the action on the screen. The second previous salary ($21,000) has disappeared, the two existing salaries have been moved down one level, and space is provided to enter the new current salary. Give Butler a raise to $31,000 (effective 11/1/88 with no change in grade), exit from the update, and return to the File Maintenance Menu.

☐ **STEP 9: Delete an existing employee.**

Select the fourth option from the File Maintenance Menu to delete a record and produce the message:

```
Please enter name of Employee to delete below
       or press return to quit
   Last Name:                    Initials:
```

Enter **Stutz** as the employee slated for deletion (the retrieval function works the way it did in the previous transactions). The record for Stutz appears on the screen as shown in Figure 1.11.

Enter **D** to delete the record and note the presence of the confirming message, **Are you sure? (Y/N)**, on the bottom of the screen. Answer appropriately and Stutz will be deleted.

☐ **STEP 10: Report generation.**

Although this exercise emphasizes the various file maintenance functions, file maintenance is only a means to an end. The ultimate goal of this or any other system is to provide information to the decision maker. Exit from the File Maintenance Menu (Figure 1.6b) and return to the Main Menu (Figure 1.6a), then select the Report Generation Menu (Figure 1.6c). Select one or more options from the Report Generation Menu to produce various reports.

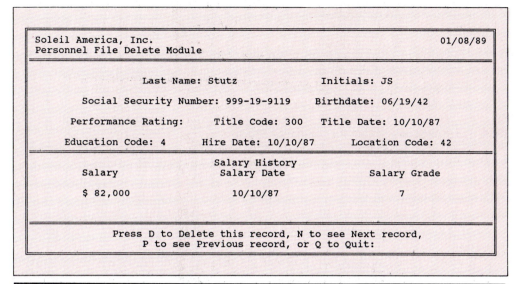

```
  Soleil America, Inc.                                          01/08/89
  Personnel File Delete Module

                    Last Name: Stutz          Initials: JS

         Social Security Number: 999-19-9119  Birthdate: 06/19/42

      Performance Rating:      Title Code: 300  Title Date: 10/10/87

      Education Code: 4    Hire Date: 10/10/87     Location Code: 42

                             Salary History
        Salary              Salary Date             Salary Grade

        $ 82,000              10/10/87                   7

          Press D to Delete this record, N to see Next record,
               P to see Previous record, or Q to Quit:
```

FIGURE 1.11 Deleting an employee

☐ **STEP 11: Experiment.**

You should now have a fair understanding of both the file maintenance and report generation functions, yet you have only begun to scratch the surface. Accordingly, we suggest that you enter several additional transactions to further appreciate the capabilities inherent in this (and other) systems. Add, delete, and modify employee records, take advantage of the online help facility and the ability to page through the employee file with the N and P options. Generate additional reports based on the data you enter.

Explore the data validation capabilities built into the system. See what happens if you select a menu option that doesn't exist, attempt to add a duplicate record, or try to edit (update) a record not in the system.

Try the Utility Menu to rebuild the system's indexes. (The meaning of this operation will become apparent as you learn about dBASE programming in later chapters. For the time being however, accept that this operation should be done periodically to avoid errors in sequencing the employee file for various reports and/or in locating individual records for editing operations.)

☐ **STEP 12: Exit the system.**

Return to the Main Menu and select the fourth option (that is, enter **4**) to exit the system. You will be asked whether or not you wish to backup your data, after which you will be returned to the operating system, that is, the DOS prompt.

☐ **STEP 13: Reset the system.**

Completing the exercise has permanently changed the original Soleil data as several employee records have been altered. In particular, you have added a new record for Coulter, changed existing records for Arnold and Butler, and deleted Stutz from the system entirely.

It is possible, however, to restore the system to what it was initially by entering the DOS command

```
COPY B:\SOLEIL\ORIGINAL.DBF B:\SOLEIL\SOLEMP.DBF
```

from the DOS prompt. Should you choose to enter this command, you can then repeat all (or part) of the hands-on exercise and obtain identical results.

The Origins of dBASE[1]

Ashton-Tate never produced a dBASE I, nor was there even a person named Ashton. The product was originally called Vulcan (after the home planet of *Star Trek's* Mr. Spock, a character known for his total recall). It was initially a commercial failure (no more than 50 copies were sold) and did not even recoup its advertising budget. At least one prominent company chose not to market the product, and its author, who had earned nothing but headaches, considered selling everything for $3000.

Today, it is the flagship product of a $200 million company. The dBASE series has been translated into French, German, Italian, Spanish, Portuguese, Danish, Dutch, Swedish, and Norwegian. The late George Tate (who died at 40 of a heart attack) and Hal Lashlee are most responsible for transforming Wayne Ratliff's Vulcan into dBASE II, and its successors dBASE III, dBASE III PLUS, and dBASE IV. Collectively, the dBASE series has sold well in excess of a million copies and continues to dominate the market for data management software.

The history of dBASE begins in 1977 with 29-year-old Wayne Ratliff, a systems designer at the Jet Propulsion Laboratory (JPL) near Pasadena, California. Ratliff was exposed to the Lab's data management and retrieval system (JPLDIS), a means of storing, retrieving, and analyzing space-gathered information. The system had been written in FORTRAN for a Univac 1108 mainframe computer.

On his own time and on his own machine (a hybrid computer built around an IMSAI 8080), Ratliff began to implement the JPLDIS commands. First came CREATE, then APPEND, LIST, EDIT, and so on, until Ratliff's version was more powerful than the original. In 1979, he began to place ads in *Byte Magazine* but faced competition from more powerful programs (among them DataStar, a product of MicroPro International Corporation). Undaunted, Ratliff released an improved Vulcan 1.6, a version that simplified editing and enabled indexing and multiple keys. Still the program didn't sell, perhaps because Ratliff was too busy to even respond to the inquiries generated by the ads in *Byte*.

Enter George Tate who, with partner Hal Lashlee, concluded that a software company offering low prices, prompt delivery, and after-sale support could be highly profitable in the emerging microcomputer industry. In January 1980, the two founded the Discount Software Group, took out ads in the leading trade journals, provided a toll-free number, and began to get results. Within a short time, the fledgling company was selling $100,000 worth of software a month, a phenomenal sum at the time (IBM would not announce the PC for another year-and-a-half).

Yet dBASE would probably not have happened were it not for the efforts of a Vulcan enthusiast who chooses to remain nameless. Tired of touting a system no one knew anything about and feeling sorry for overworked Wayne Ratliff, he began to bombard Discount Software with requests for Vulcan, a product they had never heard of. Lashlee answered most of the phone calls himself and, in August 1980, took the bait. He called Ratliff and the rest is history.

Tate and Lashlee were given exclusive rights to market Vulcan in return for a generous royalty. A new company was formed to market the product, with the intention that Ratliff would continue to improve the program. It was now known as dBASE II, a "catchy" name that implied an improvement over dBASE I which never existed. Ashton-Tate was chosen as the company name because it had a better ring than either "Tate & Lashlee" or "Lashlee & Tate."

dBASE III was announced in 1984, dBASE III PLUS in 1986, and dBASE IV in 1988. The Ashton-Tate sales have increased every year, from less than $4 million in 1981 to nearly $200 million in 1987.

---

[1]Stan Brin, "The Evolution of dBASE II," *Popular Computing Magazine*, February 1983.

Summary

We think it extremely important that you appreciate the potential inherent in dBASE to develop working systems for a variety of applications. Accordingly, the major objective of this introductory chapter was to place you in the position of end user and explore an information system implemented in dBASE III PLUS. The chapter focused on a case study for Soleil America, Inc., presented the requirements for the associated system, then asked you to explore the system on the computer.

The Soleil Employee System was shown to be completely menu driven with online help capabilities. The associated hands-on exercises took you through its file maintenance, report generation, and backup functions which typify "real world" applications. The result should be an understanding of what the system can and cannot accomplish.

Key Words and Concepts

Adding records	Exception report
Ashton-Tate	Esc key
Backup	File maintenance
CONFIG.SYS	GIGO
Data entry	Hal Lashlee
Data validation	Installing dBASE
dBASE II	Loading dBASE
dBASE III	Online help
dBASE III PLUS	QUIT
dBASE IV	Report generation
Default drive	Status bar
Deleting records	Subdirectory
DOS	George Tate
Dot prompt	Utility programs
Editing records	Vulcan
End user	Wayne Ratliff

True/False

1. The dBASE series is a product of IBM.
2. DOS requires accurate date and time information to be entered when the system is booted initially.
3. An end user requires detailed dBASE programming knowledge.
4. The dBASE series will run only on a PC manufactured by IBM.
5. A time of 23:10 indicates 10 minutes past 11 in the morning.
6. The Soleil Employee System is contained on the dBASE program disk.
7. In a two-drive floppy disk system, the dBASE program disk is normally loaded in disk drive A.
8. Additions, modifications (editing), and deletions are the typical file maintenance functions.
9. The "dot prompt" refers to the greater-than sign normally associated with PC DOS.
10. dBASE must be installed *every* time the Soleil Employee System is executed.
11. A well-designed system will produce valid output from invalid input.
12. A well-designed system will reject the attempted addition of a record already present.

1. Describe the procedure to:
   a. install dBASE
   b. load dBASE
   c. load the Soleil Employee System

2. Distinguish between:
   a. the student and full blown versions of dBASE III PLUS
   b. disk drive A and disk drive B
   c. answering and not answering the DOS request for date and time
   d. file maintenance and report generation
   e. the DOS prompt and the dBASE prompt
   f. loading and installing dBASE

3. Process the following transactions for the Soleil Employee System:
   a. Add a new employee with the following data:

```
                   Name: Small, MJ
Social security number: 787-88-7878
             Birth Date: 1/22/50
              Education: Bachelor's degree
              Hire Date: 12/12/87
               Location: Florida
                  Title: Director of Purchasing
             Title Date: 12/12/87
                 Salary: 36,000
            Salary Date: 12/12/87
           Salary Grade: 6
```

   b. Edit the following two employee records, changing the data as indicated:

   • Kinzer, JL—change education from "Other Graduate Degree" to "Master's Degree." (Use the online help facility as appropriate.)
   • Smith, RT—change birth date from 10/10/47 to 11/10/47.

   c. Update the record for SA Mellon to reflect a salary raise to $47,500 (his previous salary was $44,000) effective on 4/15/88.
   d. Delete PK Sugrue (social security number 666–77–8668) from the system.

4. A well-designed system incorporates data validation procedures within the file maintenance function in an attempt to improve the quality of data entered into the system. These procedures typically take the form of error messages that prevent the user from entering obviously incorrect transactions. With respect to the Soleil Employee System, what message (if any) will appear if you attempt to:
   a. add an employee whose record is already in the system
   b. delete an employee whose record is not in the system
   c. exit the system without backing it up
   d. enter alphabetic data in a numeric field, for example, salary
   e. enter an invalid option on a menu
   f. enter a salary raise less than the current salary
   g. enter a bad date for example, 13/25/87
   h. enter a code not contained in the system for example, a location code of 84
   Are there additional error messages you would like to see included in the system?

5. The end user is the individual ultimately responsible for providing the system specifications to a programmer or external consultant who then implements the system. The end user is also the person who ultimately accepts, and pays for, the completed system. With this in mind, are you ready to accept the Soleil Employee System as it currently exists, or are there additional functions you would like incorporated?

After reading this chapter, you should be able to:

- Define the terms field, record, file, and file structure.

- Create and/or modify a dBASE file structure; use the CREATE, MODIFY STRUCTURE, and DISPLAY STRUCTURE commands.

- Add, modify, or delete records to a file; use the APPEND, EDIT, BROWSE, DELETE, and PACK commands.

- List every record in a file or only a subset of records through variations in the DISPLAY command.

- Obtain summary information about the records in a file with the SUM, COUNT, and AVERAGE commands.

- Explain the dBASE notation and record pointer.

- Explain how to use the dBASE online help facility and the dBASE Assistant; describe the purpose of the Programmer's Notebook.

Introduction to dBase

2

OUTLINE

Overview

Chapter 1 provided an introduction to dBASE in the form of a completed system in which you assumed the role of an end user. You were made aware of inputs to the system, procedures for its operation, and desired output. In other words, you were presented with a working system with no thought whatsoever as to how it was accomplished. This chapter moves toward developing that and other systems by introducing fundamental dBASE commands.

We begin by defining basic terms in data management, then move directly into a hands-on exercise to implement these concepts in dBASE. Our approach is to get you on the computer as quickly as possible, for the sooner you begin to develop your own commands, the sooner you will truly begin the learning process. We follow the exercise with a discussion of dBASE basics, namely the *record pointer* and dBASE *notation,* then review the commands in the exercise from this viewpoint. The chapter introduces you to commands that will enable you to create a file (CREATE), enter and/or modify data in that file (APPEND, EDIT, and BROWSE), and retrieve data from that file (DISPLAY, SUM, COUNT, and AVERAGE).

The chapter also includes an introduction to the dBASE Assistant and Help facility.

The Vocabulary of Data Management

Imagine a situation in which you maintain employee data in manila folders (one folder per employee), with the entire set of folders kept in a filing cabinet. Every individual has the specifics of his or her employment (for example, social security number, name, salary, and so on) written in a folder, with the data stored in the same format in every folder.

The system just described illustrates the basics of data management terminology. The data in each manila folder is called a *record,* with the set of records (all of the folders in the file cabinet) called a *file*. Each category of information kept in a folder (social security number, name, salary, and so on) is termed a *field*. The order of fields within a record, the amount of space allocated to each field, and the type of data stored in each field is constant from record to record and is known as the *file structure*.

Figure 2.1 illustrates the terminology and is an abbreviated version of the file used in Chapter 1. Our illustrative file contains six records, with each record containing five fields.

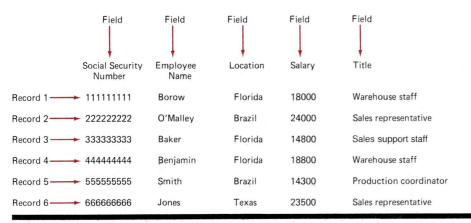

	Field	Field	Field	Field	Field
	Social Security Number	Employee Name	Location	Salary	Title
Record 1 →	111111111	Borow	Florida	18000	Warehouse staff
Record 2 →	222222222	O'Malley	Brazil	24000	Sales representative
Record 3 →	333333333	Baker	Florida	14800	Sales support staff
Record 4 →	444444444	Benjamin	Florida	18800	Warehouse staff
Record 5 →	555555555	Smith	Brazil	14300	Production coordinator
Record 6 →	666666666	Jones	Texas	23500	Sales representative

FIGURE 2.1 Data management terminology

The arrangement of fields within each record is identical (social security number is followed by name, which is followed by location, and so on) as is the allocated space for each field.

The various fields within Figure 2.1 contain different kinds of data. Salary, for example, is a *numeric* field because it contains only numbers, whereas name is a *character* field because it contains letters and special characters (for example, the apostrophe in O'Malley). (Although social security number meets the criteria of a numeric field, that is, it contains only numbers, it is more efficient to define it as a character field because it will never be used in a numeric calculation. Zip code and telephone number are two other examples of "numeric" fields which are also better defined as character fields.) The discussion in this chapter is limited to numeric and character fields; coverage of other data types is deferred to later chapters.

Merely putting data into the filing cabinet is easy; *retrieving* it in a meaningful form is quite another matter. In the course of normal business operations, you will need information about some or all of your employees. You may, for example, want the folders of only those employees who are located in Florida, or only those employees who are warehouse staff, and so on. You may need to know the total of all salaries in the company, or the total salaries for just the warehouse staff.

You will also need to *maintain* your folders to reflect on-going changes in the company. New employees will be added, necessitating the creation of new folders, whereas others may leave the company and their folders should be removed. Still others will require their folders to be updated as conditions change, for example, employees may receive a raise or transfer to a new location.

dBASE and all data management systems must provide for all these operations. There must be a way for you to define the file structure and add, modify, and delete records to an existing file. There must also be additional provisions to retrieve existing data once it has been entered. As we shall see, a specific dBASE command accomplishes each of these operations. The most basic are explained in the next section.

Elementary dBASE Commands

Our approach to teaching dBASE is to get you on the computer as quickly as possible. Accordingly, rather than cover every detail of every command, we present an overview of the most basic commands, describe their general purpose, then turn you loose with a hands-on exercise. Programming in dBASE (or any other language) is best learned by doing, and the sooner you are on the computer, the better.

■ **TABLE 2.1**
Elementary dBASE Commands

Commands affecting the file structure:
```
CREATE, DISPLAY STRUCTURE, MODIFY STRUCTURE
```

Commands for data entry:
```
APPEND, BROWSE, EDIT, DELETE, PACK
```

Commands for data manipulation:
```
DISPLAY, SUM, AVERAGE, COUNT
```

Commands to obtain assistance:
```
HELP, ASSIST
```

Miscellaneous commands:
```
QUIT, USE, SET DEFAULT
```

Table 2.1 contains 17 of the most basic dBASE commands divided into five functional categories. The very first thing you have to do is *create* a file structure to specify the order of fields within a record, as well as the length and type of data present in each field. Once the file structure has been created, you can *display* it to see if it is correct and, if not, *modify* it accordingly.

The commands for data entry allow you to add, that is, APPEND, records to an existing file. You can make changes to existing records by viewing them one at a time with the EDIT command, or several at a time with the BROWSE command. You can also remove existing records from a file, but you will need two commands to complete this task.

The DELETE command marks records for subsequent removal, but does not actually remove the records from the file (that is, dBASE gives you a chance to change your mind and recall the records slated for deletion). It is the PACK command that permanently (that is, physically) removes the records marked for deletion. (If several records are to be removed, multiple DELETE commands could and should be issued in succession before a single PACK command.)

The DISPLAY command shows some or all of the data for one or more records in the file, that is, you can display one record, every record, or only those records that meet a specified criterion (for example, employees in Florida). The SUM, COUNT, and AVERAGE commands are used for elementary arithmetic operations. SUM will total the value of a numeric field(s) for some or all records in the file, for example, it can calculate the sum of every salary or just the salaries of those records containing a title of "Warehouse Staff." COUNT, on the other hand, will produce the number of records in the file or the number of records that meet a given criterion. Similarly, the AVERAGE command can be made to apply to every record within a file, or only to a subset.

The HELP and ASSIST commands are sources of additional online information. HELP provides detailed information on any given command, whereas ASSIST initiates the dBASE III PLUS Assistant, which in turn guides you in constructing dBASE commands. Both HELP and ASSIST are discussed in detail following the exercise.

The USE command chooses (opens) an existing dBASE file for processing. The SET DEFAULT command establishes the default drive (that is, the drive dBASE searches for existing files, and the drive to which dBASE writes any new files that are created). The QUIT command exits dBASE (closing any files that were opened) and returns to DOS.

The following hands-on exercise illustrates how the data entry and data retrieval functions are implemented in dBASE. We think you will understand what the commands do from the way in which they are used in the exercise, but we include additional explanation after the exercise. You can also refer to the Programmer's Notebook for detailed information about any particular command.

Hands-on Exercise 2–1:   Elementary dBASE Commands

Objective: To create a dBASE file structure; to add, modify, and delete records to the file, and to retrieve data from that file.

☐ **STEP 1: Load dBASE.**

Load dBASE as you did in Steps 1 and 2 of Hands-on Exercise 1–2, ending at the dot prompt.

☐ **STEP 2: Define the file structure.**

We will define the file structure for the file shown in Figure 2.1. Type `CREATE` at the dot prompt. dBASE responds by asking for the name of the file you wish to create, for example, `SHOES`.

```
. CREATE
Enter the name of the new file: SHOES
```

dBASE next displays a new screen in which you are asked to enter the information for the file structure by describing each field, one field at a time. The process is interactive, easy to do, and is shown in Figure 2.2. (The upper portion of Figure 2.2 contains information on cursor control, that is, how to move from field to field within the file structure; see the Programmer's Notebook for additional information on the `CREATE` command.)

Begin by entering the name of the first field, `SOCSEC`, then press the Return key. Next, specify the type of field (character) by typing the letter `C` (recall that the social security number is defined as a character rather than a numeric field, because it will never be used in arithmetic operations). Finally, indicate the width of the field `9`, and press the Return key to move on to the next field. Repeat this procedure for all five fields. (Note that for numeric fields only, for example, `SALARY`, you will also have to specify the number of decimal places, if any.)

The upper right portion of Figure 2.2 contains information showing the number of fields entered so far and the remaining number of bytes permitted

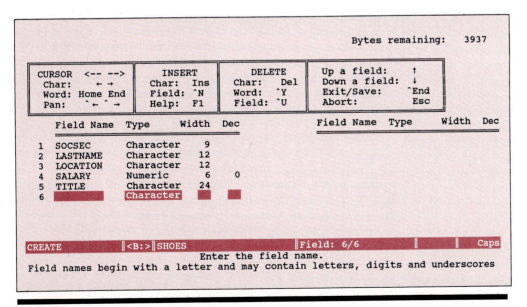

FIGURE 2.2 Defining a file structure

in the file structure. Given a maximum record length of 4000 bytes (characters), and that 63 bytes are necessary for the five fields defined so far, 3937 characters are still available.

When all of the information for the last field (in our example, TITLE) has been entered, immediately press the Return key to signify the end of the file structure. dBASE will ask you to press the Return key a second time to confirm that you are finished. It will next ask if you wish to enter data at this time. Respond N (for no), and you will be returned to the dot prompt.

☐ **STEP 3: Verify the file structure.**

The DISPLAY STRUCTURE command enables you to view the completed file structure and make sure it is correct. As Figure 2.3 shows, this command shows the field names specified during file creation, the type and width of each field, and the order in which the fields appear within a record. It also shows the number of records in the file (none to this point), and the date of the last file update, in this case the date on which the file structure was created. (The importance of responding to the date and time prompts when initially booting DOS becomes apparent, as dBASE uses this information in conjunction with its file structure.)

Verify that the file structure is exactly as you intend it to be. (Do not be concerned that the total number of positions in the record, 64 in our example, is one more than the sum of the individual field lengths; dBASE uses this extra position for its internal file management.) If you discover an error, for example, an extra or omitted field, an incorrect data type, or wrong size field, you can change the file structure through the MODIFY STRUCTURE command as described in the Programmer's Notebook.

☐ **STEP 4: Adding records.**

Type APPEND (at the dot prompt) to begin entering data, bringing Figure 2.4's *input template* into view. (APPEND is an example of a *full-screen* command because it first clears the screen of any previous output.) The input template in Figure 2.4 displays the file structure's field names and field widths for subsequent data entry. (This screen's upper portion also contains information on cursor control; it is further explained in the Programmer's Notebook.)

Enter data as it appears in Figure 2.1, beginning with the first field for the first record. As a general rule, after entering the data press the Return Key to move to the next field. The only exception is if the data completely fills the field width as happens with the social security number. In this case dBASE automatically takes you to the next field *without* pressing the Return key. In other words, completing the social security number automatically positions

```
. DISPLAY STRUCTURE
Structure for database : B:SHOES.DBF
Number of data records :        0
Date of last update    : 11/19/87
Field  Field name  Type       Width    Dec
    1  SOCSEC      Character      9
    2  LASTNAME    Character     12
    3  LOCATION    Character     12
    4  SALARY      Numeric        6       0
    5  TITLE       Character     24
** Total **                      64
```

FIGURE 2.3 Verification of the file structure

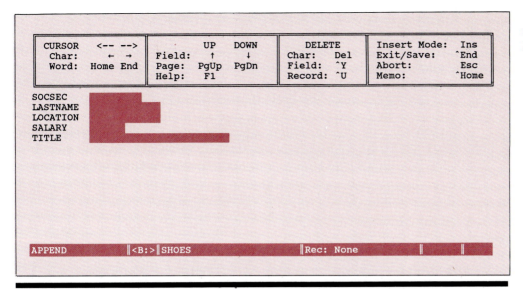

FIGURE 2.4 Input template for data entry

you in the first position of the last name field. You will, however, have to press the Return key after entering a short last name, in order to move to the location field.

Should you make a mistake during data entry, for example, typing a letter in a numeric field, dBASE will beep to inform you of the error and at the same time ignore the invalid character. dBASE also beeps when you come to the end of a field (for example, social security number), to let you know you are at the end of a field and that the next character entered will be taken as part of the next field.

When you have entered data for the last field in record 1, press the Return key to move on to record 2. After completing the field entries for O'Malley, press the Return key to bring up a blank input screen for the third record, and enter data for this record as well. Enter data for the remaining records in Figure 2.1, then press Ctrl End to terminate data entry. (You should, however, press Ctrl End while still in record 6, that is, before record 7 comes up, otherwise a blank record will be appended to the file.)

☐ **STEP 5: Modify data in existing records.**

Erroneous data can be corrected two ways. You can *edit* an individual record or you can *browse* the entire file. All that is required in either mode is to retype the field(s) in error, rather than retype the entire record.

The specific record affected by the EDIT command depends on the position of the *record pointer*, a concept discussed further at the end of the exercise. For the time being, however, enter the following from the dot prompt and observe what happens:

. 3————— *Positions the record pointer at the third record*
. EDIT
. 1————— *Positions the record pointer at the first record*
. EDIT

Typing in a 3 at the dot prompt positions the record pointer at the third record (Baker), so that the subsequent EDIT command brings up that record for modification. Similarly, entering a 1 before the second EDIT command will bring us to Borow.

Screens for the EDIT and BROWSE commands are shown in Figures 2.5a and 2.5b. EDIT, like APPEND, is a full-screen command in which one record at a time is placed on the screen for modification. The EDIT command displays a template with each field's current value, enabling you to change (edit) any or all fields in much the same way data was entered initially. The PgUp and PgDn keys will display the previous and following records, and allow you to continue editing.

The BROWSE command in Figure 2.5b displays several records simultaneously, as opposed to the EDIT command which views only a single record. Experiment using the cursor keys to move from field to field, and from record to record.

Press Ctrl End to return to the dot prompt.

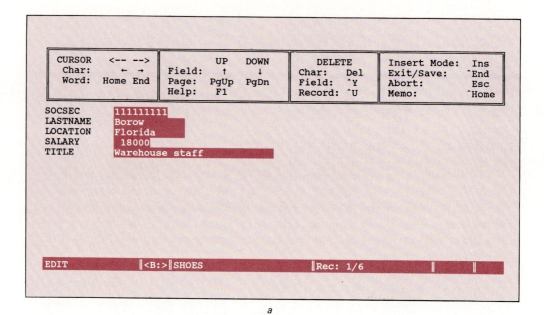

FIGURE 2.5 Data modification: (a) the EDIT command; (b) the BROWSE command

☐ **STEP 6: Delete a record.**

Two commands, `DELETE` and `PACK`, are needed to remove a record from a file. The `DELETE` command marks a record for deletion, but does not actually remove the record from the file (that is, the record is logically, but not physically, deleted). In other words, dBASE enables you to change your mind and subsequently "undelete" the record if you want to (see the `RECALL` command in the Programmer's Notebook). Executing the `PACK` command permanently, that is, physically, removes records marked for deletion.

Figure 2.6 shows the sequence of commands. The `DELETE` command marks record 6 (Jones) for deletion. This is followed by a `DISPLAY ALL` command. It confirms that the record has been logically deleted by showing the record with an asterisk. The `PACK` command permanently, that is, physically, deletes the record, while the final `DISPLAY ALL` command indicates the physical deletion has, in fact, been accomplished.

Follow the command sequence in the figure. After you have completed it, your file will contain five records (Borow, O'Malley, Baker, Benjamin, and Smith).

☐ **STEP 7: Demonstrate the `USE` and `SET DEFAULT` commands.**

The `USE` command opens, that is uses, an existing database file and is normally the first or second command issued when dBASE is initially loaded. Although the SHOES file is currently in use, and the default drive is already set to B (that is, the commands are *not* necessary at this time), we will illustrate them anyway. Consider the following for Figure 2.7:

The `USE` command searches the default drive for the file named SHOES.DBF. Only the file name (SHOES) however, need be specified in the `USE` command. This is because dBASE restricts its search to files with a DBF extension. (dBASE automatically assigns a DBF extension as part of the creation process for a file structure.)

☐ **STEP 8: Displaying individual record(s).**

The `DISPLAY` command can show a single record, every record, or only those

```
                    ┌─ Positions the record pointer to the sixth record
. 6
. DELETE
      1  record deleted
. DISPLAY ALL
Record#  SOCSEC      LASTNAME      LOCATION   SALARY  TITLE
      1  111111111  Borow         Florida    18000   Warehouse staff
      2  222222222  O'Malley      Brazil     24000   Sales representative
      3  333333333  Baker         Florida    14800   Sales support staff
      4  444444444  Benjamin      Florida    18800   Warehouse staff
      5  555555555  Smith         Brazil     14300   Production coordinator
      6 *666666666  Jones         Texas      23500   Sales representative

                                   └─ Record has been marked for subsequent deletion
. PACK
      5  records copied
. DISPLAY ALL
Record#  SOCSEC      LASTNAME      LOCATION   SALARY  TITLE
      1  111111111  Borow         Florida    18000   Warehouse staff
      2  222222222  O'Malley      Brazil     24000   Sales representative
      3  333333333  Baker         Florida    14800   Sales support staff
      4  444444444  Benjamin      Florida    18800   Warehouse staff
      5  555555555  Smith         Brazil     14300   Production coordinator
```

FIGURE 2.6 Deleting a record

```
. SET DEFAULT TO B
. USE SHOES
. DISPLAY STRUCTURE
Structure for database : B:SHOES.DBF
Number of data records :      5
Date of last update    : 11/19/87
Field  Field name  Type       Width      Dec
    1  SOCSEC      Character      9
    2  LASTNAME    Character     12
    3  LOCATION    Character     12
    4  SALARY      Numeric        6        0
    5  TITLE       Character     24
** Total **                     64
```

FIGURE 2.7 The `SET DEFAULT` and `USE` commands

records meeting a specified condition, as illustrated in Figure 2.8. `DISPLAY`, with no additional parameters, will show only the record at the current position of the record pointer. `DISPLAY ALL`, on the other hand, shows every record in the file, regardless of where the record pointer may be located.

Including the `FOR` parameter limits the displayed records to those meet-

```
                    Moves the record pointer to the second record
. 2
. DISPLAY
Record#  SOCSEC     LASTNAME    LOCATION    SALARY  TITLE
      2  222222222  O'Malley    Brazil      24000   Sales representative


. 5              Displays whatever record corresponds to the current position of the record pointer
. DISPLAY
Record#  SOCSEC     LASTNAME    LOCATION    SALARY  TITLE
      5  555555555  Smith       Brazil      14300   Production coordinator


                 Displays every record
. DISPLAY ALL
Record#  SOCSEC     LASTNAME    LOCATION    SALARY  TITLE
      1  111111111  Borow       Florida     18000   Warehouse staff
      2  222222222  O'Malley    Brazil      24000   Sales representative
      3  333333333  Baker       Florida     14800   Sales support staff
      4  444444444  Benjamin    Florida     18800   Warehouse staff
      5  555555555  Smith       Brazil      14300   Production coordinator

                                         Shows only those records meeting
                                         a specified condition
. DISPLAY FOR LOCATION = 'Florida'
Record#  SOCSEC     LASTNAME    LOCATION    SALARY  TITLE
      1  111111111  Borow       Florida     18000   Warehouse staff
      3  333333333  Baker       Florida     14800   Sales support staff
      4  444444444  Benjamin    Florida     18800   Warehouse staff


. DISPLAY FOR TITLE = 'Warehouse staff'
Record#  SOCSEC     LASTNAME    LOCATION    SALARY  TITLE
      1  111111111  Borow       Florida     18000   Warehouse staff
      4  444444444  Benjamin    Florida     18800   Warehouse staff


. DISPLAY FOR LOCATION = 'Florida' .AND. TITLE = 'Warehouse staff'

Record#  SOCSEC     LASTNAME    LOCATION    SALARY  TITLE
      1  111111111  Borow       Florida     18000   Warehouse staff
      4  444444444  Benjamin    Florida     18800   Warehouse staff
```

FIGURE 2.8 Displaying individual record(s)

```
.  SUM SALARY
        5 records summed
   SALARY
    89900


.  AVERAGE SALARY
        5 records averaged
   SALARY
    17980


.  AVERAGE SALARY FOR TITLE = 'Warehouse staff'
        2 records averaged
   SALARY
    18400


.  COUNT FOR LOCATION = 'Florida' .AND. TITLE = 'Warehouse staff'
        2 records
```

FIGURE 2.9 The `SUM`, `AVERAGE`, and `COUNT` commands

ing the designated condition. Hence, you can display the employees located in Florida, or the employees whose title is "Warehouse staff," or the employees who work in Florida *and* have the title "Warehouse staff." (The latter is an example of a *compound* condition, in which the logical operators, AND, OR, and NOT, are used to combine simple conditions.)

☐ **STEP 9: Obtaining summary information.**

The `SUM`, `AVERAGE`, and `COUNT` commands obtain summary information about the file as a whole, or about those records meeting a specified condition. Figure 2.9 illustrates the commands.

☐ **STEP 10: Exit dBASE.**

Type `QUIT` at the dot prompt to exit dBASE. You will see a brief message from Ashton-Tate, thanking you for using the program, after which you will be returned to DOS. It is extremely important for you to exit properly (by typing `QUIT`) so that your files are saved correctly to disk.

The Basics of dBASE

The exercise you just completed provides an intuitive appreciation for many commands as they are given from the dot prompt, but in no way suffices as an adequate introduction to dBASE. Indeed, we expect that the exercises have created at least as many questions as they have answered, especially with respect to how specific commands work.

In this section we begin our detailed dBASE study presenting two very basic concepts, the *record pointer* and *dBASE notation*. As we shall see, these concepts apply to all commands and provide a firm foundation for a more formal study of the language.

The Record Pointer

The records within a DBF file are numbered consecutively, beginning with 1. The first record is record 1, the second record is record 2, and so on. dBASE keeps track of its position within a file by maintaining a *record pointer* that is updated continually as commands are executed. Even when dBASE is searching through an entire file (for example, when a DISPLAY ALL command is executing), it continually changes the record pointer as it processes each record.

The record pointer's importance becomes apparent as you review individual commands from the hands-on exercise. The EDIT and DISPLAY commands, for example, affect only a single record, but how is the specific record chosen? Will the same record always be selected with either of these commands? The answer is that dBASE processes whichever record is indicated by the position of the record pointer.

You can move the record pointer with the GO command, for example, GO 2, or simply 2 (entered at the dot prompt), moves the record pointer to record number 2. Enter the DISPLAY command at this point and dBASE shows record number 2. Similarly the GO TOP and GO BOTTOM commands move the pointer to the first and last records, respectively. Other commands also affect the record pointer's value. The USE command for example opens, that is, uses, an existing DBF file and positions the record pointer to the first record.

Because dBASE knows where it is within a DBF file at any given instant, it is also important for you to know this information. Accordingly, you should always be thinking of the record pointer as you execute individual commands.

The dBASE Notation

dBASE uses a simple notation that implicitly explains all the variations allowed within a given command. Consider, for example, the DISPLAY command and how it would appear in a reference manual or text:

```
DISPLAY [<scope>] [<expression list>] [FOR <condition>]
        [WHILE <condition>] [OFF] [TO PRINT]
```

The notation consists of four distinct elements: uppercase letters, lowercase letters, angle brackets, and square brackets. *Uppercase letters* denote a dBASE term (for example, DISPLAY, FOR, WHILE, and so on) which must be spelled exactly as it appears within the command. *Lowercase letters* and/or *angled brackets* (⟨ ⟩), indicate user-supplied information, for example, field names as they were defined within a file structure. *Square brackets* ([ ]) imply optional portions of the command, that is, clauses which may or may not be included, depending on the user's objectives.

The *scope* of a command refers to the records within a file that the command affects. Omitting this parameter results in a *default* value which, in the case of DISPLAY, is one record, the record on which the record pointer is positioned. A scope of ALL means the command is to apply to every record in the file, whereas a scope of NEXT 5 applies to only the next five records (including the one at the record pointer's current position).

The *expression list* indicates which fields within the file structure are to be displayed. Omitting this parameter means that every field is to be shown, whereas including it states explicitly only those fields that will appear (for example, SOCSEC and LASTNAME). Specifying OFF causes records to be displayed *without* the record numbers, whereas TO PRINT directs output to the printer.

The FOR *condition* further limits which records are to appear (for example, only those records whose location is Florida). The condition parameter works in conjunction with the scope because all records within the scope are considered, but only those meeting the condition are displayed. Note, too, that the condition itself may be a *simple* or *compound* condition. The former imposes only a single requirement (LOCATION = 'Florida'), whereas the latter joins two or more requirements with the logical operations AND, OR, and NOT (for example, FOR LOCATION = 'Florida' .AND. TITLE = 'Warehouse Staff'). Syntactically, dBASE requires a logical operator (AND, OR, and NOT) to be set off with periods.

Figure 2.10 shows variations in the DISPLAY command.

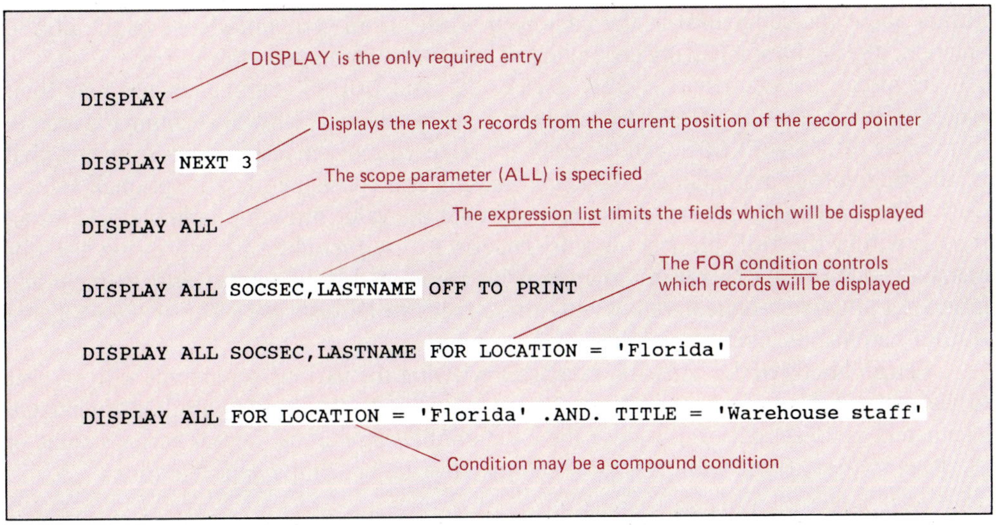

DISPLAY ─── DISPLAY is the only required entry

DISPLAY `NEXT 3` ─── Displays the next 3 records from the current position of the record pointer

DISPLAY `ALL` ─── The scope parameter (ALL) is specified

─── The expression list limits the fields which will be displayed

DISPLAY ALL `SOCSEC,LASTNAME` `OFF` `TO PRINT` ─── The FOR condition controls which records will be displayed

DISPLAY ALL SOCSEC,LASTNAME `FOR LOCATION = 'Florida'`

DISPLAY ALL `FOR LOCATION = 'Florida' .AND. TITLE = 'Warehouse staff'`

─── Condition may be a compound condition

FIGURE 2.10 Variations in the `DISPLAY` command

More About the Basic Commands

Recall that a table of basic commands, accompanied by a cursory explanation of the individual commands, preceded the hands-on exercise. Table 2.2 is an expanded version of that earlier table, with the formal dBASE syntax included for each command. Were we to say nothing

■ **TABLE 2.2**
Syntax of Elementary dBASE Commands

Comands affecting the file structure:
```
CREATE <new file>
MODIFY STRUCTURE
DISPLAY STRUCTURE [TO PRINT]
```

Commands for data entry:
```
APPEND
BROWSE [FIELDS <field list>]
EDIT [<scope>] [FOR <condition>]
DELETE [<scope>] [FOR <condition>]
PACK
```

Commands for data manipulation:
```
DISPLAY [<scope>] [<expression list>] [FOR <condition>]
          [OFF] [TO PRINT]
SUM [<expression list>] [<scope>] [FOR <condition>]
AVERAGE [<scope>] [<expression list>] [FOR <condition>]
COUNT [<scope>] [FOR <condition>]
```

Commands to obtain assistance:
```
HELP <command name>
ASSIST
```

Miscellaneous commands:
```
QUIT
USE <filename>
SET DEFAULT TO <drivename>
```

further about the commands in the table, you would, from your knowledge of the dBASE notation, already have a fair understanding of how these commands work.

Consider, for example, the SUM, AVERAGE, and COUNT commands and how their syntax is similar to the DISPLAY command just explained. Only the command names themselves (SUM, AVERAGE, and COUNT) are required in their respective commands, that is, all other entries are enclosed in square brackets and consequently are optional. Hence, SUM with no scope and no expression list, will total the value of each numerical field for all records within the DBF file (the default scope is ALL). Including an expression list (for example, SUM SALARY), causes only the fields mentioned to be totaled, just as including it in a DISPLAY statement causes only those fields to be displayed. The AVERAGE and COUNT commands function similarly.

Return briefly to the hands-on exercise, reviewing the various commands with respect to the syntax Table 2.2 presents. Try to determine why we selected (or omitted) individual parameters as we sought to introduce the basic dBASE commands. Repeat perhaps some of the steps in the exercise with additional command variations you would like to try.

Getting Help

As you work with dBASE, questions will inevitably arise about the syntax and/or capabilities of individual commands which go beyond the material in Table 2.2. Accordingly, we describe three additional sources of information, the online help facility, the dBASE Assistant, and the Programmer's Notebook, to which you may refer.

The dBASE HELP Facility

To enter the online help facility, simply type HELP at the dot prompt. The system returns the opening *HELP Main Menu* of Figure 2.11a which prompts you for one of six possible responses. Entering a 6, for example, produces the *Commands and Functions Menu* of Figure 2.11b. Enter a number from 1 to 5 to obtain additional information as indicated.

Figure 2.11c contains a list of the *Starter Set Commands,* many of which should look familiar. It was obtained by entering a 1 in the previous menu. At this point, you can enter any number from 1 to 44 to obtain detailed information on the command in question. Figure 2.11d, for example, shows the help screen associated with the DISPLAY command. (A shortcut to obtaining help on a particular command is to type HELP, followed by the name of the command at the dot prompt, that is, HELP DISPLAY, after which Figure 2.11d would appear immediately.)

The dBASE Assistant

The dBASE Assistant is a menu-driven feature intended to simplify the construction of individual commands. Type ASSIST in response to the dot prompt and you will be presented with Figure 2.12a's opening Assistant Menu. The figure should look familiar, as this screen comes up automatically whenever dBASE is loaded initially (you first saw the menu in Figure 1.3).

You can make the Assistant disappear by pressing the Esc key (as you were directed to do in Chapter 1), and reappear by typing ASSIST at the dot prompt. Once the Assistant is active (that is, ASSIST has been typed at the dot prompt), the left and right arrow keys will switch from one menu to the next, whereas the up and down keys go from option to option within a menu.

Use the left and right arrow keys to highlight the Update Menu of Figure 2.12b, then use the up and down arrow keys to highlight a command with which you are familiar (for

```
                              Help Main Menu
                              ══════════════


                      1 - Getting Started
                      2 - What Is a ...
                      3 - How Do I ...
                      4 - Creating a Database File
                      5 - Using an Existing Database File
                      6 - Commands and Functions






 HELP             ║<B:>║SHOES              ║Rec: 1/5       ║        ║
      Position selection bar - ↑↓. Select - ◄┘. Exit with Esc or enter a command.
                      ENTER >
```

a

```
                                                    COMMANDS/FUNCTIONS

            dBASE III PLUS Commands and Functions
            ══════════════════════════════════════


            1 - Commands (Starter Set)
            2 - Commands (Advanced Set)
            3 - Functions
            4 - SET TO Commands
            5 - SET ON/OFF Commands








 HELP             ║<B:>║SHOES              ║Rec: 1/5       ║        ║
      Position selection bar - ↑↓. Select - ◄┘. Previous menu - F10. Exit - Esc.
                      ENTER >
```

b

```
                                                    STARTER

            dBASE III PLUS Commands --- Starter Set
            ═══════════════════════════════════════

    1 - ?           12 - DELETE FILE   23 - LABEL      34 - REPORT
    2 - APPEND      13 - DIR           24 - LIST       35 - SCREEN
    3 - AVERAGE     14 - DISPLAY       25 - LOCATE     36 - SEEK
    4 - BROWSE      15 - DO            26 - MODIFY     37 - SET
    5 - CHANGE      16 - EDIT          27 - PACK       38 - SKIP
    6 - CLEAR       17 - ERASE         28 - QUERY      39 - SORT
    7 - CONTINUE    18 - EXPORT        29 - QUIT       40 - STORE
    8 - COPY        19 - FIND          30 - RECALL     41 - SUM
    9 - COUNT       20 - GO/GOTO       31 - RELEASE    42 - TOTAL
   10 - CREATE      21 - IMPORT        32 - RENAME     43 - TYPE
   11 - DELETE      22 - INDEX         33 - REPLACE    44 - USE


 HELP             ║<B:>║SHOES              ║Rec: 1/5       ║        ║
      Enter the name of a menu option. Finish with ◄┘. Previous menu - F10.
                      ENTER >
```

c

FIGURE 2.11 dBASE help screens: (a) opening Help Menu (entered by typing HELP at the dot prompt); (b) Commands and Functions Menu (option 6 from the opening Help Menu); (c) Starter Set Menu (option 1 from the Commands and Functions Menu); (d) DISPLAY Help screen (option 14 from the Starter Set Menu)

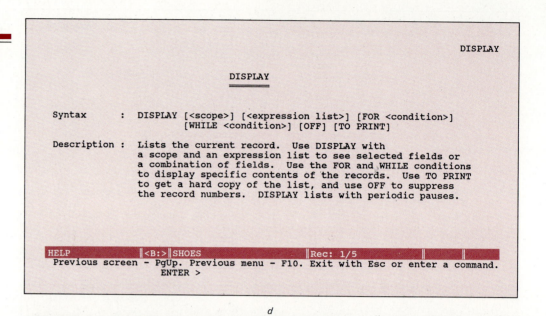

```
                                                              DISPLAY


                              DISPLAY
                              =======


    Syntax      :  DISPLAY [<scope>] [<expression list>] [FOR <condition>]
                           [WHILE <condition>] [OFF] [TO PRINT]

    Description :  Lists the current record.  Use DISPLAY with
                   a scope and an expression list to see selected fields or
                   a combination of fields.  Use the FOR and WHILE conditions
                   to display specific contents of the records.  Use TO PRINT
                   to get a hard copy of the list, and use OFF to suppress
                   the record numbers.  DISPLAY lists with periodic pauses.




 HELP           ‖<B:>‖SHOES              ‖Rec: 1/5        ‖         ‖        ‖
    Previous screen - PgUp. Previous menu - F10. Exit with Esc or enter a command.
                      ENTER >
```

d

FIGURE 2.11 dBASE help screens (Cont'd)

example, APPEND, EDIT, or BROWSE). Press the Return key and you will be presented with one of the earlier screens from the hands-on exercise to add new records and/or modify data in existing records.

The Assistant's major advantage is its ability to guide you in the step-by-step construction of various commands as they would be entered from the dot prompt. Figure 2.12c illustrates this. The Return key has been pressed after selecting the DISPLAY command

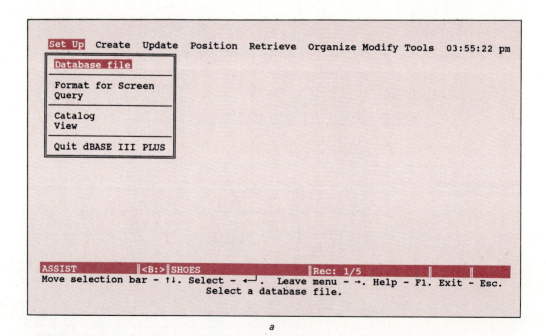

```
 Set Up   Create  Update  Position  Retrieve  Organize Modify Tools   03:55:22 pm
 ┌────────────────────┐
 │ Database file      │
 ├────────────────────┤
 │ Format for Screen  │
 │ Query              │
 ├────────────────────┤
 │ Catalog            │
 │ View               │
 ├────────────────────┤
 │ Quit dBASE III PLUS│
 └────────────────────┘





 ASSIST          ‖<B:>‖SHOES              ‖Rec: 1/5        ‖         ‖        ‖
 Move selection bar - ↑↓. Select - ⏎.  Leave menu - →. Help - F1. Exit - Esc.
                      Select a database file.
```

a

FIGURE 2.12 The dBASE Assistant: (a) the Assistant's Opening Menu (entered by typing ASSIST at the dot prompt); (b) the Assistant's Update Menu; (c) the Assistant's Retrieve Menus

from the Retrieve Menu. A second menu (box) appears at the right of the figure with "Spe-cify scope" highlighted. It, in turn, produces the last menu at the bottom right of the figure. You could now use the up and down arrow keys to choose the desired scope; for example, ALL and press the Return key.

The end result of the selections made from the series of Assistant Menus is the construction of the command DISPLAY ALL, which appears in the lower left portion of Figure 2.12c. Many people find the Assistant especially helpful because it cuts down on typing, eliminates spelling errors, and "painlessly" teaches the command syntax. Our personal preference, however, is not to use it. We find it easier and faster to type in complete commands at the dot prompt, rather than constructing them piecemeal via the Assistant. We leave you to your own conclusions.

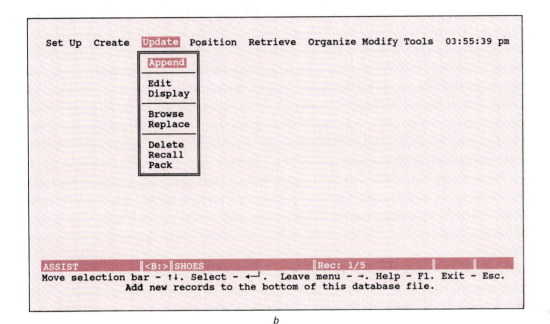

b

c

The Programmer's Notebook

The Programmer's Notebook is an independent *reference* section at the end of this book. Unlike the dBASE Help and Assistant facilties which display their information on the monitor, the Notebook provides a written copy of its suggestions and is therefore more convenient for study. In addition, the Notebook provides substantially more information than either of the other two sources.

We expect you will use the Notebook to supplement what you learn in class and/or what you learn from the body of the text. It is especially helpful for answering specific questions about individual commands, which are listed alphabetically in the Notebook.

Summary

The essence of the chapter is in the hands-on exercise and all that accompanied it. Mastering the exercise will enable you to define (and modify) a dBASE file structure; to add, edit, and/or delete records in the associated file; and to obtain summary information about the file. The exercise also introduced you to 15 specific dBASE commands (`CREATE`, `MODIFY` and `DISPLAY STRUCTURE`, `APPEND`, `BROWSE`, `EDIT`, `DELETE`, `PACK`, `DISPLAY`, `SUM`, `AVERAGE`, `COUNT`, `QUIT`, `USE`, and `SET DEFAULT`).

Of greater importance, however, was the discussion of generalized dBASE concepts, namely the record pointer and dBASE notation which develop the foundation for future study. In addition, we discussed three further sources of information: the online HELP and ASSIST facilities, and the Programmer's Notebook.

Key Words and Concepts

`APPEND`	File
`ASSIST`	File structure
`AVERAGE`	Full-screen command
`BROWSE`	`GO BOTTOM`
Byte	`GO TOP`
Character field	`HELP`
Compound condition	Input template
Condition	`MODIFY STRUCTURE`
`COUNT`	Numeric field
`CREATE`	`OFF`
Ctrl End	`PACK`
Data entry	Programmer's Notebook
DBF extension	`QUIT`
`DELETE`	Record
`DISPLAY`	Record pointer
`DISPLAY STRUCTURE`	Scope
Dot prompt	`SET DEFAULT TO`
`EDIT`	`SUM`
Expression list	`TO PRINT`
Field	`USE`

True/False

1. There is no limit to a dBASE record's maximum size.
2. A file structure cannot be changed after it has been created and saved.
3. The DELETE command deletes a record permanently.
4. The EDIT command displays multiple records simultaneously on the screen.
5. A file contains one or more records.
6. A record contains one or more fields.
7. Ctrl End writes changes made during editing to disk.
8. The prompt characters for DOS and dBASE are the same.
9. The APPEND command always adds records to the beginning of a file.
10. Every record within a file has the same number of fields.
11. Output of the DISPLAY command can be directed to the printer.
12. Records listed by the DISPLAY command must be shown with their record numbers.
13. The USE command establishes the default drive.
14. Specific information on the DISPLAY command can be obtained with the command HELP DISPLAY.
15. The PACK command physically deletes all records marked for deletion.
16. The ASSIST facility must be used to create a DBF file.
17. The SUM and COUNT commands are equivalent.
18. The SUM command must include values from *every* record in the file in computing a total.
19. The USE command positions the record pointer to the first record within a file.
20. Most commands operate *independently* of the record pointer.

Exercises

1. Supply the dBASE command(s) to:
   a. correct individual records
   b. display multiple records on the screen while simultaneously allowing you to correct any of the displayed records
   c. create (modify) a file structure
   d. add records to the end of an existing data file
   e. mark a record for subsequent removal
   f. physically remove records marked for deletion
   g. save changes and exit from the edit or browse modes
   h. position the record pointer at the first record in a file
   i. deactivate the dBASE Assistant
   j. obtain additional information on the EDIT command
2. Distinguish between:
   a. data entry and data retrieval
   b. operating with and without the dBASE Assistant
   c. editing and browsing
   d. DISPLAY and DISPLAY ALL
   e. a field and a file
   f. upper- and lowercase letters within the dBASE syntax
   g. the DOS prompt and the dBASE prompt
   h. the SUM and COUNT commands
   i. use of PgUp and PgDn keys when editing records
   j. character fields and numeric fields

k. `GO TOP` and `GO BOTTOM`
l. the `HELP` and `ASSIST` commands

3. Perhaps the best source of information about dBASE is dBASE itself; that is to find out the effect of a particular command or parameter, execute the command from the dot prompt and draw your own conclusions. With this in mind, execute the following sets of commands, pausing at the end of each set to answer the associated questions.

Set 1:

```
. DISPLAY OFF
. DISPLAY SOCSEC,LASTNAME
. DISPLAY ALL LASTNAME,SOCSEC
. DISPLAY
. DISPLAY STRUCTURE TO PRINT
```

a. What is the effect of including the field names of only two of the five fields? Does the order of the field names in the command make any difference?
b. What is the effect of the `TO PRINT` parameter? the `OFF` parameter?
c. What is the difference between `DISPLAY`, `DISPLAY ALL`, and `DISPLAY STRUC-TURE`?
d. What happens to the record pointer after a `DISPLAY ALL` command has been executed?
e. What is the default scope of the `DISPLAY` command? What is the effect of `ALL`?

Set 2:

```
. 3
. EDIT
. GO TOP
. EDIT
. BROWSE
```

f. Which record is edited as a result of the first `EDIT` command? the second `EDIT` command? Why were different records edited?
g. What is the difference between the `EDIT` and `BROWSE` commands? How many records are on the screen (at one time) as a result of the two commands?

Set 3:

```
. GO 2
. DELETE
. DISPLAY ALL
. PACK
. DISPLAY ALL
```

h. How many records are displayed by the first `DISPLAY ALL` command? by the second `DISPLAY` command?
i. Which record is missing? How was it deleted?

Set 4:

```
. SUM
. SUM ALL
. COUNT FOR TITLE = 'Warehouse staff'
. AVERAGE SALARY
. AVERAGE SALARY FOR TITLE = 'Warehouse staff'
```

j. What is the difference between `SUM` and `SUM ALL`? What is the `SUM` command's default scope?
k. What is the difference between `AVERAGE SALARY` and `AVERAGE SALARY FOR TITLE = 'Warehouse staff'`?

■ OBJECTIVES

After reading this chapter, you should be able to:

- Describe how indexing makes it possible to list records in multiple sequences.

- Distinguish between files with extensions of NDX and DBF; describe how to access the DOS directory from within dBASE.

- Differentiate between a master and an active (open) index; describe how the distinction is made in dBASE.

- Distinguish between the INDEX ON and SET INDEX TO commands.

- Define and build a concatenated index.

- Describe how to list records in ascending, as well as descending, sequence and how to index on a calculated field.

3

Indexing

OUTLINE

Overview

The importance of *indexing* is best appreciated by recalling that the records in Chapter 2 were entered, and subsequently listed, in social security sequence. There will be many times however when data is more meaningful if it is presented in a different sequence, for example, alphabetically or in order of increasing or decreasing salary. Indexing makes this possible.

The chapter begins with a conceptual discussion of indexing, then introduces the necessary dBASE commands (`INDEX ON`, `SET INDEX TO`, `USE with INDEX`, and `CLOSE INDEXES`) for implementation. We distinguish between *master* and *open* (active) indexes, then describe how indexes are updated automatically during maintenance to a DBF file. We also cover finer points of indexing including using a *concatenated* key, a key based on a *calculated* numeric field, and how to process records in either *ascending* or *descending* sequence.

The chapter contains three hands-on exercises, all of which are essential if you are to truly understand the all-important concept of indexing.

The Concept of Indexing

Figure 3.1a depicts an employee file, consisting of five records, that we created in Chapter 2. The records appear in *physical* sequence, that is, in the order in which they were originally entered into the SHOES.DBF file in Chapter 2. You might wish, however, to access the records in a different *logical* sequence, for example, alphabetically or in order of increasing salary.

Assume, for example, that the five employee records are to be retrieved alphabetically. A person looking at the file of Figure 3.1a would know to list the records in the sequence Baker, Benjamin, Borow, O'Malley, and Smith. In other words, rather than retrieving records in the *physical* order in which they are stored (that is, records 1, 2, 3, 4, and 5), the person would present them in the *logical* sequence beginning with record 3 (Baker), then record 4 (Benjamin), then records 1, 2, and 5 (Borow, O'Malley, and Smith). The logical sequence in which records are retrieved is known as an *index*; the field on which the index is based is termed a *key*.

Figures 3.1b, c, and d contain an alphabetic, salary, and social security index respectively; all are associated with the file of Figure 3.1a. Each index specifies a different logical sequence in which records in the DBF file may be processed. Thus, records would be listed alphabetically according to Figure 3.1b's last name index, they would be listed in increasing order of salary in conjunction with Figure 3.1c's salary index, and by social security number according to Figure 3.1d's index. (The last example is trivial at this time, because the social security index's logical sequence matches the physical order in which records appear in the DBF file. That situation is, of course, subject to change should additional records be added to the DBF file.)

As you can see in the figure, an index does not contain any fields other than the one on which the index is based, together with the corresponding record number in the DBF file. In other words, the index provides the sequence in which records are to be retrieved from the associated DBF file. For example, to retrieve records alphabetically according to the index in Figure 3.1b, dBASE would first retrieve record 3 (Baker), then record 4 (Benjamin), then records 1, 2, and 5 (Borow, O'Malley, and Smith, respectively).

You can make a good analogy between a book's index and a dBASE index. Both are arranged according to a key phrase or field, and both indicate where the corresponding information may be found by providing the page number in the book or record number in the file. In addition, just as a book's index is kept in a separate section, an index in dBASE is stored as a separate (NDX) file.

Given this conceptual view of indexing, we proceed to the dBASE INDEX ON command which creates the actual index(es).

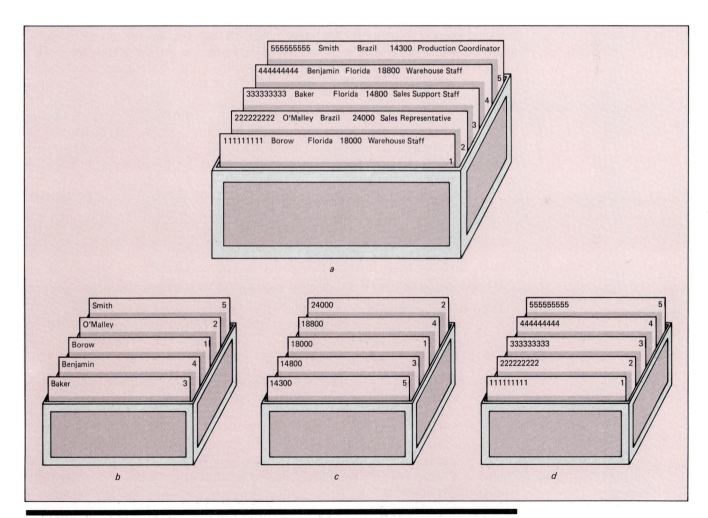

FIGURE 3.1 A file and its indexes: (a) data file; (b) alphabetic index; (c) salary index; (d) social security number index

INDEX ON

The INDEX ON command creates an index (NDX) file which, in turn, is associated with the open DBF file. (Use of this command assumes that a DBF file has been previously opened with a USE command.) Consider:

Syntax:
```
INDEX ON field expression TO filename
```

Examples:

INDEX ON LASTNAME TO LASTNAME
INDEX ON SALARY TO SALARY
INDEX ON SOCSEC TO SOCSEC

Fieldname

Filename with NDX extension

In the command syntax the *field expression* specifies the *key* on which the index is based, for example, LASTNAME, SALARY, or SOCSEC. (The key may be a single field in the file or derived from a combination of fields within the file structure, a feature discussed later in the chapter.) The *filename* denotes the name of the generated index file, that is, the dBASE created to hold the index. It is given the extension NDX.

We find it convenient to give the index file the same name as the field on which it is based, for example, INDEX ON LASTNAME TO LASTNAME, but this is not a requirement. In this example, the first occurrence of LASTNAME corresponds to the field within the file structure of the associated DBF file, whereas the second occurrence is the name of the index file (LASTNAME.NDX). Using this convention makes it easy to remember the sequence associated with each index file.

Any time an index is created via the INDEX ON command, it is made the master index and brought into effect in conjunction with the open DBF file. This means that all subsequent commands, for example, DISPLAY ALL, will access the file according to the master index's logical order. Note that should another INDEX ON command be issued, a new master index automatically comes into effect.

Hands-on Exercise 3–1 implements these concepts in dBASE. It is a short exercise, but it effectively demonstrates the capabilities inherent in indexing.

Hands-on Exercise 3–1:   Creating Index Files

Objective: To show how a single DBF file can be accessed in multiple sequences through indexing; demonstrate the INDEX ON command to create new indexes.

☐   STEP 1: Load dBASE.
Load dBASE and retrieve the SHOES.DBF file created in Chapter 2. Display the file structure and list all records in the file as indicated in Figure 3.2.

☐   STEP 2: Index the file.
Enter the commands in Figure 3.3 to create the last name, salary, and social security number indexes. (The latter index may appear superfluous at this time, since records in the SHOES.DBF file are already in social security sequence. Its necessity, however, will be demonstrated in Hands-on Exercise 3–2 when new records are added to the DBF file.)

A DISPLAY ALL command follows each INDEX ON command and lists the records according to the index just created. In each instance the DISPLAY command also shows the dBASE record numbers.

```
. USE SHOES
. DISPLAY STRUCTURE
Structure for database : B:SHOES.DBF
Number of data records :      5
Date of last update    : 11/19/87
Field  Field name  Type       Width    Dec
    1  SOCSEC      Character       9
    2  LASTNAME    Character      12
    3  LOCATION    Character      12
    4  SALARY      Numeric         6        0
    5  TITLE       Character      24
** Total **                      64

. DISPLAY ALL
Record#  SOCSEC     LASTNAME      LOCATION    SALARY  TITLE
      1  111111111  Borow         Florida     18000   Warehouse staff
      2  222222222  O'Malley      Brazil      24000   Sales representative
      3  333333333  Baker         Florida     14800   Sales support staff
      4  444444444  Benjamin      Florida     18800   Warehouse staff
      5  555555555  Smith         Brazil      14300   Production coordinator
```

FIGURE 3.2 The SHOES.DBF file

```
. INDEX ON LASTNAME TO LASTNAME
      5 records indexed
. DISPLAY ALL
Record#  SOCSEC     LASTNAME      LOCATION    SALARY  TITLE
      3  333333333  Baker         Florida     14800   Sales support staff
      4  444444444  Benjamin      Florida     18800   Warehouse staff
      1  111111111  Borow         Florida     18000   Warehouse staff
      2  222222222  O'Malley      Brazil      24000   Sales representative
      5  555555555  Smith         Brazil      14300   Production coordinator
```

a

```
. INDEX ON SALARY TO SALARY
      5 records indexed
. DISPLAY ALL
Record#  SOCSEC     LASTNAME      LOCATION    SALARY  TITLE
      5  555555555  Smith         Brazil      14300   Production coordinator
      3  333333333  Baker         Florida     14800   Sales support staff
      1  111111111  Borow         Florida     18000   Warehouse staff
      4  444444444  Benjamin      Florida     18800   Warehouse staff
      2  222222222  O'Malley      Brazil      24000   Sales representative
```

b

```
. INDEX ON SOCSEC TO SOCSEC
      5 records indexed
. DISPLAY ALL
Record#  SOCSEC     LASTNAME      LOCATION    SALARY  TITLE
      1  111111111  Borow         Florida     18000   Warehouse staff
      2  222222222  O'Malley      Brazil      24000   Sales representative
      3  333333333  Baker         Florida     14800   Sales support staff
      4  444444444  Benjamin      Florida     18800   Warehouse staff
      5  555555555  Smith         Brazil      14300   Production coordinator
```

c

FIGURE 3.3 Creation of indexes: (a) Last name index; (b) salary index; (c) social security number index

☐ **STEP 3: View the file directory.**

The DOS directory can be accessed from within dBASE by entering the command DIR *.* from the dot prompt. Enter this command and you should see the SHOES.DBF file, in addition to the three index files (LASTNAME.NDX, SALARY.NDX, and SOCSEC.NDX) just created. (dBASE automatically assigns the extension NDX to index files, analogous to the way it assigns DBF as the extension for data files.)

Note, too, that the DIR *.* command views *all* files on the directory. Alternatively, DIR *.NDX could have been used to view just the index files. The DIR command, entered with no parameters, displays just the DBF files.

☐ **STEP 4: Exit dBASE.**

Type QUIT to exit dBASE.

Master versus Open (Active) Indexes

In computing, it is a fundamental truth that a file's contents will change continually. New records will be added, existing records will be modified, while still other records will be deleted. It is absolutely critical, therefore, that the indexes associated with a file change in parallel with the file itself.

Figure 3.4 continues our earlier example of a single DBF file with three indexes (last name, salary, and social security number). A sixth record, Brown, has been appended at the end of Figure 3.4a, which in turn produces changes in the indexes of Figures 3.4b, 3.4c, and 3.4d.

As you can see in Figure 3.4a, Brown is *physically* the sixth (last) record in the DBF file, whereas his name is *logically* the fourth record when the file is processed alphabetically. In other words, the index in Figure 3.4b has been adjusted to reflect the addition of the new record and to maintain the alphabetic sequence (Baker, Benjamin, Borow, *Brown*, O'Malley, and Smith). Similarly, the indexes in Figures 3.4c and 3.4d have also been updated to maintain the salary and social security sequences. (You should be able to trace through any of the indexes in Figure 3.4 and retrieve all six records in alphabetic, salary, or social security order.)

As indicated, adding or deleting any record to or from the file in Figure 3.4a requires corresponding adjustments to the various indexes. Fortunately, dBASE provides commands to adjust these indexes automatically and hence frees you from any manual changes. You must, however, understand the difference between a *master* and an *open* (active) index.

As we have seen, multiple indexes may be associated with the same DBF file. At any given time however, there can be only one *master* index, that is, the index that determines the logical sequence in which the records are accessed. A new master index may be designated as often as necessary, but at any given instant records are processed according to the current master index, that is, by last name, *or* by salary, *or* by social security number.

Several indexes may be *open* (active) simultaneously, however, meaning that they will be updated automatically (by dBASE) should the DBF file change. The commands to designate a master index and/or open additional indexes are discussed in the next section.

SET INDEX TO

The SET INDEX TO command designates an existing index as the master index and opens it as well. Although the INDEX ON command also makes the newly created index the master index, the creation process can be time consuming, especially with large files. Accordingly,

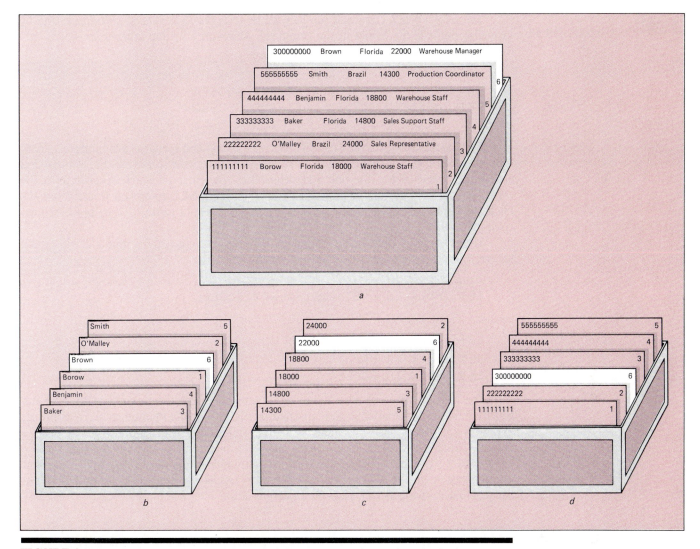

FIGURE 3.4 Adding records to an indexed file: (a) data file; (b) alphabetic index; (c) salary index; (d) social security number index

INDEX ON should *not* be used to select the master index; SET INDEX TO is the preferred command. Consider:

Syntax:
```
SET INDEX TO filename-1 [,filename-2, filename-3 ...]
```

Examples:
```
SET INDEX TO LASTNAME
SET INDEX TO SALARY
SET INDEX TO SOCSEC
```

These examples select the last name, salary, and social security indexes, respectively, as the master index. Each command designates a new master index while implicitly closing any previously open indexes. Thus, SET INDEX TO SALARY makes salary the master index, but closes the last name index. Similarly, SET INDEX TO SOCSEC designates social security as the master index while closing the salary index. Hence, if all three commands were executed in succession one after another, illogical as that may be, only the social security index would be left open, and that index would be the master index.

The SET INDEX command can be used to *open multiple indexes simultaneously* by including multiple file names in the command. Although all three indexes are open, only one will be the master index, for example:

First index listed is the master index
```
SET INDEX TO LASTNAME,SALARY,SOCSEC
SET INDEX TO SALARY,LASTNAME,SOCSEC
```
All three indexes are open, salary is the master index

Both commands *open* the existing salary, last name, and social security indexes. There is a difference between them, however, because the first index listed in the command is always the *master* index, the one that determines the order in which records from the corresponding DBF file will be processed. Hence, the first SET command would cause the file to be processed alphabetically, whereas the second would cause it to be processed according to salary.

There is also a tremendous difference between a single SET command with three indexes and three commands each with one index. Consider:

Opens all three indexes, making last name the master index
```
SET INDEX TO LASTNAME,SALARY,SOCSEC
```

versus

```
SET INDEX TO LASTNAME
SET INDEX TO SALARY
SET INDEX TO SOCSEC
```
Social security index is opened, closing the salary index

The first command opens three indexes (with last name the master index), enabling all three indexes to be automatically updated in subsequent file maintenance. By contrast, the other commands open one index at a time, implicitly closing any previously opened indexes. Thus, SET INDEX TO SALARY opens the salary index (closing last name), while SET INDEX TO SOCSEC opens the social security index (closing salary). Any subsequent maintenance operations will update only the open (social security) index, resulting in potential problems with the last name and salary indexes.

USE with INDEX

The USE with INDEX command does the same thing as separate USE and SET INDEX commands. Consider:

Syntax:
```
USE filename-1 [INDEX filename-2, filename-3 ... ]
```

Example 1: (USE with INDEX)
```
USE SHOES INDEX LASTNAME,SALARY,SOCSEC
```

Example 2: (Separate USE and SET commands)
```
USE SHOES
SET INDEX TO LASTNAME,SALARY,SOCSEC
```

Examples 1 and 2 are equivalent. Example 1 combines the USE and SET commands into a single statement. It simultaneously opens the SHOES.DBF file, and the last name, salary, and social security indexes, with last name as the master index. Example 2 uses a SET INDEX command to open the index files after the preceding USE command first opened the associated DBF file.

CLOSE INDEXES

CLOSE INDEXES closes all open indexes so that any subsequent command will process records according to the physical sequence of the DBF file. The SET INDEX TO command, with no files specified, also closes all open indexes.

Hands-on Exercise 3–2: Updating Index Files

Objective: To demonstrate how open indexes are automatically updated when records are added to a DBF file; differentiate between master and open (active) indexes.

☐ **STEP 1: Load dBASE.**

Load dBASE. Open (use) the existing SHOES.DBF file from Hands-on Exercise 3–1.

☐ **STEP 2: Choose a master index.**

The SET command opens an existing index and is used after the index has been created. Enter the command SET INDEX TO LASTNAME as shown in Figure 3.5, followed by a DISPLAY ALL command. The records should appear in alphabetic order.

The result of these two commands is almost identical to the earlier use of INDEX ON LASTNAME TO LASTNAME followed by DISPLAY ALL. This time, however, the index file was merely activated in lieu of being created. Accordingly, SET INDEX executes faster than INDEX ON (especially with large files), as the latter physically creates an index file.

Enter the second SET and DISPLAY combination shown in Figure 3.5 to list records in order of increasing salary.

```
. SET INDEX TO LASTNAME
. DISPLAY ALL
Record#   SOCSEC      LASTNAME     LOCATION    SALARY   TITLE
      3   333333333   Baker        Florida     14800    Sales support staff
      4   444444444   Benjamin     Florida     18800    Warehouse staff
      1   111111111   Borow        Florida     18000    Warehouse staff
      2   222222222   O'Malley     Brazil      24000    Sales representative
      5   555555555   Smith        Brazil      14300    Production coordinator
```

a

```
. SET INDEX TO SALARY
. DISPLAY ALL
Record#   SOCSEC      LASTNAME     LOCATION    SALARY   TITLE
      5   555555555   Smith        Brazil      14300    Production coordinator
      3   333333333   Baker        Florida     14800    Sales support staff
      1   111111111   Borow        Florida     18000    Warehouse staff
      4   444444444   Benjamin     Florida     18800    Warehouse staff
      2   222222222   O'Malley     Brazil      24000    Sales representative
```

b

FIGURE 3.5 The SET INDEX TO statement: (a) last name index is the master index; (b) salary index is the master index

```
. CLOSE INDEXES
. DISPLAY ALL
Record#   SOCSEC     LASTNAME      LOCATION    SALARY TITLE
      1   111111111  Borow         Florida     18000  Warehouse staff
      2   222222222  O'Malley      Brazil      24000  Sales representative
      3   333333333  Baker         Florida     14800  Sales support staff
      4   444444444  Benjamin      Florida     18800  Warehouse staff
      5   555555555  Smith         Brazil      14300  Production coordinator
```

FIGURE 3.6 The CLOSE INDEXES statement

☐ **STEP 3: Close indexes.**
Enter the CLOSE INDEXES command as shown in Figure 3.6 to close the open index. The records in the SHOES.DBF file will now be processed in the order in which they were physically entered.

☐ **STEP 4: Add a record.**
Any open index will be automatically updated during the subsequent addition (or deletion) of records to the associated DBF file. Accordingly, type either of the command sequences shown below to open the SHOES.DBF file, together with the three existing indexes.

```
USE SHOES INDEX SOCSEC,LASTNAME,SALARY
```

or

```
USE SHOES
SET INDEX TO SOCSEC,LASTNAME,SALARY
```

Enter the APPEND command from the dot prompt and Figure 3.7 will come into view. Enter data for Brown as shown, but do *not* press the Return key after completing his title. Press Ctrl End instead, to save the record and return to the dot prompt.

☐ **STEP 5: Verify that the indexes have been updated.**
Enter the SET INDEX commands in Figure 3.8 to verify that the existing indexes have been updated to accommodate the addition of Brown's record. Each of the SET INDEX commands in the figure opens all three existing indexes (in the event of additional file maintenance) and differs only in the master index designation.

☐ **STEP 6: Exit dBASE.**
Type QUIT to exit dBASE and return to the DOS prompt.

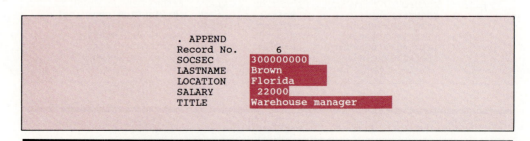

FIGURE 3.7 Input template for data entry

```
. SET INDEX TO LASTNAME,SOCSEC,SALARY
. DISPLAY ALL
Record#   SOCSEC      LASTNAME    LOCATION    SALARY   TITLE
      3   333333333   Baker       Florida     14800    Sales support staff
      4   444444444   Benjamin    Florida     18800    Warehouse staff
      1   111111111   Borow       Florida     18000    Warehouse staff
      6   300000000   Brown       Florida     22000    Warehouse manager
      2   222222222   O'Malley    Brazil      24000    Sales representative
      5   555555555   Smith       Brazil      14300    Production coordinat
```

a

```
. SET INDEX TO SALARY,LASTNAME,SOCSEC
. DISPLAY ALL
Record#   SOCSEC      LASTNAME    LOCATION    SALARY   TITLE
      5   555555555   Smith       Brazil      14300    Production coordinat
      3   333333333   Baker       Florida     14800    Sales support staff
      1   111111111   Borow       Florida     18000    Warehouse staff
      4   444444444   Benjamin    Florida     18800    Warehouse staff
      6   300000000   Brown       Florida     22000    Warehouse manager
      2   222222222   O'Malley    Brazil      24000    Sales representative
```

b

```
. SET INDEX TO SOCSEC,LASTNAME,SALARY
. DISPLAY ALL
Record#   SOCSEC      LASTNAME    LOCATION    SALARY   TITLE
      1   111111111   Borow       Florida     18000    Warehouse staff
      2   222222222   O'Malley    Brazil      24000    Sales representative
      6   300000000   Brown       Florida     22000    Warehouse manager
      3   333333333   Baker       Florida     14800    Sales support staff
      4   444444444   Benjamin    Florida     18800    Warehouse staff
      5   555555555   Smith       Brazil      14300    Production coordinat
```

c

FIGURE 3.8 Updating of indexes: (a) updated last name index; (b) updated salary index; (c) updated social security number index

Finer Points of Indexing

The indexes we have been using were each derived from a single field within the file structure (for example, last name, social security number, and salary). However, it is also possible to derive an index from a *combination* of fields, and/or to list records in *descending* (high to low) rather than *ascending* (low to high) sequence. Figure 3.9 illustrates these concepts.

Figure 3.9b contains an index based on a *concatenated* key in which the location and last name fields are combined to produce a new index, listing employees by location, and alphabetically within each location. The index in Figure 3.9c is based on the *calculated* values of percent salary increase, a field not found in the file structure. It is calculated from other fields (salary and old salary) which are found in the file structure. (The DBF file in Figure 3.9a has been expanded to include an old salary field so that the percent increase may be computed.) Finally, Figure 3.9d sequences employees in *descending* order of salary, created by multiplying the value of salary by -1.

The syntax of the INDEX ON command specifies only that the index be derived from a *field expression*, that is, INDEX ON field expression TO filename, which up to now has consisted of a single field within the file structure. As we shall see, the field expression (key) in each of Figure 3.9's examples is a bit more involved.

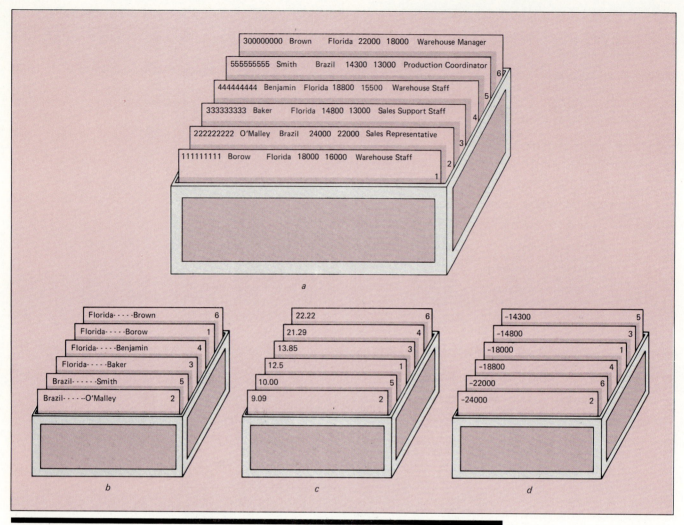

FIGURE 3.9 Finer points of indexing: (a) data file; (b) location and last name index; (c) percent salary increase index; (d) salary index—descending order

Indexing on a Concatenated Key

The index in Figure 3.9b lists employees by location and alphabetically within each location. In other words, the index is based on a combination of the location and last name fields as follows:

⌐*Concatenated key*

INDEX ON LOCATION+LASTNAME TO LOCATION

The "addition" of two or more fields in this way is known as a *concatenated key,* and consists (in this example) of the characters in the location field followed immediately by those in the last name field. As you can see in Figure 3.9b, the concatenated key results in all the Brazilian employees appearing together (in alphabetic order), followed by all the Florida employees (also in alphabetic order). We say that location is the more important or *primary* field, whereas name is the less important or *secondary* field.

Indexing on a Calculated Numeric Field

An index may also be based on a *calculated* numeric key, that is, a field not contained in the DBF file per se, but one which is computed from other fields that are. Assume, for example, that the original SHOES.DBF file has been expanded to include an old salary field (as is shown in Figure 3.9a) and that records are to be processed in order of *percent salary increase*. (Percent salary increase is computed by taking the difference between the current and old salaries, dividing by the old salary, and multiplying the result by 100.) The command to create such an index would be:

———— Calculated key

```
INDEX ON 100*(SALARY-OLDSALARY)/OLDSALARY TO INCREASE
```

The index in Figure 3.9c contains the calculated values of the percent salary increase and the corresponding record numbers in the DBF file. Note, however, that the results of the calculation are used only to sequence records within the index file (Figure 3.9c) and are *not* stored in the DBF file.

Indexing in Descending Sequence

The keys in a dBASE index are always listed in *ascending* (low to high) sequence. Records can, however, be made to appear in *descending* (high to low) sequence, by including a *negative* value in the field expression as shown in Figure 3.9d. Consider:

↙ Salary field is multiplied by −1 to produce a "descending" index

```
INDEX ON -SALARY TO SALARY
```

A "descending" index is actually a special case of a calculated numeric field in that the key value is multiplied by −1. The concept applies to numeric fields only.

Hands-on Exercise 3–3:   Finer Points of Indexing

Objective: To demonstrate the finer points of indexing by creating indexes based on a concatenated key, a calculated field, and one that will list records in descending sequence.

☐   STEP 1: Modify the file structure.
Load dBASE, then open (use) the SHOES.DBF file. Enter the `MODIFY STRUC-TURE` command so that the OLDSALARY field can be added to the file structure. Figure 3.10 will appear on your monitor.

Position the cursor on the line containing the `TITLE` field, then press Ctrl N to add the new field. Enter the field name, type, and length (OLDSALARY, Numeric, and 6, respectively), then press Ctrl End to save these changes in the file structure. You will be asked to press the Return key to confirm the changes, after which the message "6 records added" will appear. This indicates that the six existing records have been modified to accommodate the new field.

☐   STEP 2: Add the new salary data.
Type `GO TO P`. Type `BROWSE` to enter the browse mode in order to add the old salary values to the existing records. Enter the data as shown in Figure 3.11, then press Ctrl End to save the modifications.

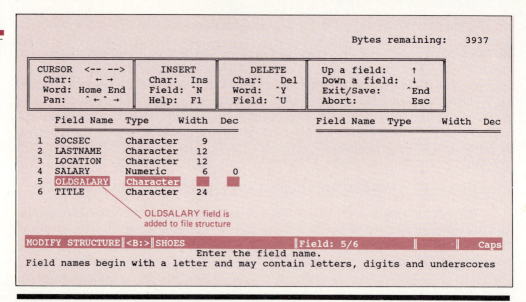

Bytes remaining: 3937

CURSOR <-- -->	INSERT	DELETE	Up a field: ↑
Char: ← →	Char: Ins	Char: Del	Down a field: ↓
Word: Home End	Field: ^N	Word: ^Y	Exit/Save: ^End
Pan: ^ ← ^ →	Help: F1	Field: ^U	Abort: Esc

	Field Name	Type	Width	Dec		Field Name	Type	Width	Dec
1	SOCSEC	Character	9						
2	LASTNAME	Character	12						
3	LOCATION	Character	12						
4	SALARY	Numeric	6	0					
5	OLDSALARY	Character							
6	TITLE	Character	24						

OLDSALARY field is
added to file structure

MODIFY STRUCTURE ‖<B:>‖SHOES   ‖Field: 5/6   ‖   ‖   Caps
Enter the field name.
Field names begin with a letter and may contain letters, digits and underscores

FIGURE 3.10 MODIFY STRUCTURE command

☐   **STEP 3: Create the new index files.**
Enter the INDEX ON and associated DISPLAY ALL commands in Figure 3.12c
to illustrate the finer points of indexing just discussed. Figure 3.12a displays
the records alphabetically within location, Figure 3.12b shows them in increasing order of percent salary increase, and Figure 3.12c displays them in
decreasing order of salary.

The commands to create these indexes parallel what you have already
seen and should not pose any difficulty. Observe, however, that since the
value of a calculated index is not stored in the DBF file per se, the DISPLAY
ALL statement in Figure 3.12b includes a specification of the calculated field.

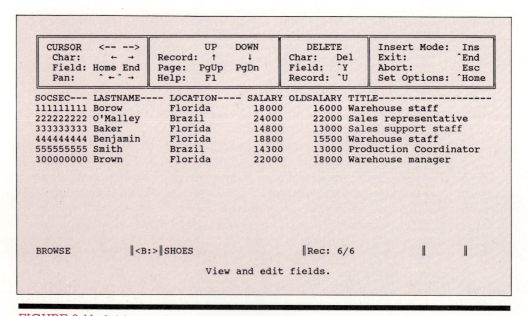

CURSOR <-- -->	UP DOWN	DELETE	Insert Mode: Ins
Char: ← →	Record: ↑ ↓	Char: Del	Exit: ^End
Field: Home End	Page: PgUp PgDn	Field: ^Y	Abort: Esc
Pan: ^ ← ^ →	Help: F1	Record: ^U	Set Options: ^Home

SOCSEC---	LASTNAME----	LOCATION----	SALARY	OLDSALARY	TITLE------------------
111111111	Borow	Florida	18000	16000	Warehouse staff
222222222	O'Malley	Brazil	24000	22000	Sales representative
333333333	Baker	Florida	14800	13000	Sales support staff
444444444	Benjamin	Florida	18800	15500	Warehouse staff
555555555	Smith	Brazil	14300	13000	Production Coordinator
300000000	Brown	Florida	22000	18000	Warehouse manager

BROWSE   ‖<B:>‖SHOES   ‖Rec: 6/6   ‖   ‖
View and edit fields.

FIGURE 3.11 Addition of previous salaries

```
. INDEX ON LOCATION+LASTNAME TO LOCATION
  100% indexed           6 Records indexed

. DISPLAY ALL SOCSEC,LASTNAME,LOCATION,SALARY
Record#   SOCSECNUM LASTNAME    LOCATION    SALARY
      2   222222222 O'Malley    Brazil      24000
      5   555555555 Smith       Brazil      14300
      3   333333333 Baker       Florida     14800
      4   444444444 Benjamin    Florida     18800
      1   111111111 Borow       Florida     18000
      6   300000000 Brown       Florida     22000
```
a

```
. INDEX ON 100*(SALARY-OLDSALARY)/OLDSALARY TO INCREASE
  100% indexed           6 Records indexed
. DISPLAY ALL LASTNAME,SALARY,OLDSALARY,100*(SALARY-OLDSALARY)/OLDSALARY
Record#   LASTNAME    SALARY OLDSALARY 100*(SALARY-OLDSALARY)/OLDSALARY
      2   O'Malley    24000  22000                             9.09
      5   Smith       14300  13000                            10.00
      1   Borow       18000  16000                            12.50
      3   Baker       14800  13000                            13.85
      4   Benjamin    18800  15500                            21.29
      6   Brown       22000  18000                            22.22
```
b

```
. INDEX ON -SALARY TO SALARY
SALARY.ndx already exists, overwrite it? (Y/N) Yes
  100% indexed           6 Records indexed
. DISPLAY ALL SOCSEC,LASTNAME,LOCATION,SALARY,OLDSALARY
Record#   SOCSEC     LASTNAME    LOCATION    SALARY OLDSALARY
      2   222222222  O'Malley    Brazil      24000   22000
      6   300000000  Brown       Florida     22000   18000
      4   444444444  Benjamin    Florida     18800   15500
      1   111111111  Borow       Florida     18000   16000
      3   333333333  Baker       Florida     14800   13000
      5   555555555  Smith       Brazil      14300   13000
```
c

FIGURE 3.12 Finer points of indexing: (a) a concatenated index; (b) indexing on a calculated field; (c) records in descending salary sequence

Note too, that since SALARY.NDX already exists (albeit, in ascending sequence), Figure 3.12c includes a warning message asking whether the index should be overwritten.

☐ **STEP 4: Exit dBASE.**
Type QUIT to exit dBASE and return to DOS.

Summary

The chapter began with a conceptual discussion of indexing, showing how the presence of multiple indexes makes it possible to list a file in varying sequences. It continued by presenting the necessary dBASE commands for implementation. The INDEX ON command creates an index (NDX file), whereas SET INDEX *opens* (one or more) existing indexes as well as designates a single *master* index. The USE with INDEX command was shown to do the same thing, while CLOSE INDEXES closes all open indexes.

The chapter stressed the importance of opening all indexes associated with a DBF file so that any subsequent file maintenance operations will automatically update the associated indexes. The difference between an *open* and a *master* index was also emphasized.

The chapter ended with a presentation of finer points associated with indexing. We showed how to create a *concatenated* index based on two or more fields, how to list records in *descending* as well as *ascending* sequence, and how to index on a *calculated* field.

Key Words and Concepts

Active index	Master index
Ascending sequence	MODIFY STRUCTURE
Calculated field	NDX extension
CLOSE INDEXES	Open index
Concatenated index	Primary field
Descending sequence	Secondary field
DIR	SET INDEX TO
DIR *.*	USE filename
INDEX ON	USE filename INDEX indexname

True/False

1. It is possible for a given file to have several indexes associated with it.
2. The DOS directory cannot be accessed from within dBASE.
3. The same field can be used to create an index in ascending sequence, and another in descending sequence.
4. A single SET INDEX command can open multiple indexes.
5. A single SET INDEX command can designate multiple master indexes.
6. An index must be created just before being used.
7. The SET INDEX command closes as well as opens existing indexes.
8. The DIR command (with no parameters) will display DBF and NDX files.
9. An index may be created based on several fields within a file structure.
10. The command CANCEL INDEXES closes all open index files.
11. Adding records via the APPEND command will automatically update the associated index file(s).

Exercises

1. Supply the dBASE commands to:
   a. open a DBF file together with its existing index(es)
   b. view the file directory from within dBASE
   c. create an index for an existing DBF file
   d. change the master index for a DBF file
   e. close all index files
   f. create a concatenated index

2. Distinguish between:
   a. `DIR` and `DIR *.*` as entered from the dBASE prompt
   b. the command `USE SHOES INDEX SALARY`
   and `USE SHOES`
   `INDEX ON SALARY TO SALARY`
   c. the two occurrences of `SALARY` in the command
   `INDEX ON SALARY TO SALARY`
   d. the command `INDEX ON`
   and `SET INDEX TO`
   e. the command `SET INDEX TO SOCSEC,LASTNAME`
   and `SET INDEX TO LASTNAME,SOCSEC`
   f. the command `INDEX ON SALARY TO SALARY`
   and `INDEX ON -SALARY TO SALARY`
   g. an open index and a master index
   h. the command `SET INDEX TO SOCSEC,LASTNAME`
   and `SET INDEX TO SOCSEC`
   `SET INDEX TO LASTNAME`
   i. the command `INDEX ON LASTNAME TO LASTNAME`
   and `INDEX ON LASTNAME+FIRSTNAME TO LASTNAME`
   j. the command `INDEX ON LOCATION+LASTNAME TO EMPLOYEES`
   and `INDEX ON LASTNAME+LOCATION TO EMPLOYEES`

3. Consider the command sequence in Figure 3.13 in which a seventh record for Jones is added to the existing SHOES.DBF file. Explain why the record does *not* appear as a result of the subsequent `LIST OFF` command.

4. Begin with the SHOES.DBF file (as it exists in Figure 3.11) and do the following:
   a. Add a new record for Rudolph (with social security number 400000000, located in Chicago, with salaries of 24,000 and 21,000, and a job title of Sales Representative).
   b. Delete the existing record for Benjamin.
   c. Be sure that the five existing indexes (last name, social security, salary, location, and salary increase) are properly updated. List the file in each of these sequences after the addition and deletion have been accomplished.

5. Create a file structure to hold the data in Figure 3.14, then enter the data into the file structure. Create whatever indexes are necessary, then enter the required commands to produce the lists of students shown below. List all fields in the file structure in every

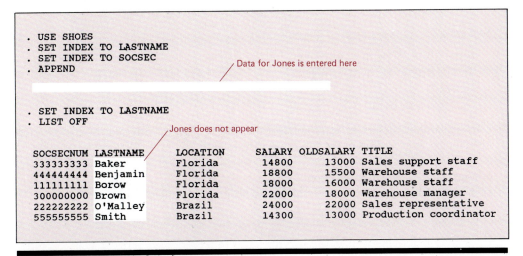

FIGURE 3.13 Commands for Exercise 3

Student Name	Major	Quality Points Earned	Credits Taken
Alan Moldof	Business	60	20
Joel Stutz	Business	180	50
Marion Milgrom	Education	140	38
Jessica Grauer	Business	96	28
Adam Moldof	Education	160	84
John Smith	Business	180	75
Eleanor Rudolph	Education	140	75
Benjy Grauer	Business	96	50
Toni Essman	Business	120	38
Karen Levine	Business	180	85
Michael Essman	Education	140	66
Jessica Blatt	Business	60	28

FIGURE 3.14 Data for Exercise 5

report. In addition, the students' grade point average (quality points earned/credits taken) is to appear as well.

a. a master list of all students in alphabetic order

b. a list of those students on the dean's list (grade point average of 3.00 or higher) in decreasing order of grade point average

c. an alphabetic list of students on academic probation (grade point average less than 2.00)

d. a master list of all students by major and alphabetically within major

6. What is the difference (if any) between the following command sequences? What problems (if any) do you see in any of the sequences?

Sequence 1:

```
. USE SHOES INDEX SOCSEC,LASTNAME
. APPEND
     (3 records are added)
```

Sequence 2:

```
. USE SHOES
. SET INDEX TO SOCSEC,LASTNAME
. APPEND
     (3 records are added)
```

Sequence 3:

```
. USE SHOES INDEX SOCSEC
. SET INDEX TO LASTNAME
. APPEND
     (3 records are added)
```

7. Establish a file structure to accommodate the data in Figure 3.15, and then enter data. List employees according to the following indexes:

a. alphabetically within location

b. ascending salary within location

c. by date of hire (employees with longest seniority are to appear first)

We expect you to have no difficulty with part *a*, but we do anticipate some difficulty in part *b*. In particular, there will be a problem in creating the concatenated index in that salary and location are of different data types (numeric and character, respectively). The problem can be resolved, however, by referring to the `INDEX ON` command in the Programmer's Notebook which discusses the subtleties involved.

```
Employee name      Location      Salary      Date Hired
-------------------------------------------------------
Fitzgerald         New York      $28,000     01/01/86
Friedel            Boston        $30,000     01/01/87
Davis              Atlanta       $29,000     02/04/86
Cordell            Atlanta       $28,000     02/04/87
Tillberg           Boston        $35,000     05/14/79
Kendrick           Boston        $24,000     09/02/84
Martineau          New York      $23,000     01/01/83
Grauer             New York      $32,000     02/14/83
Ferraro            New York      $29,000     09/24/82
Pattishall         Atlanta       $40,000     05/16/70
```

FIGURE 3.15 Data for Exercise 7

■ OBJECTIVES

After reading this chapter, you should be able to:

- Distinguish between data and information and describe how one is converted into the other.

- Use the dBASE report generator to create and/or modify report forms; discuss the relationship among DBF, NDX, and FRM files in conjunction with the report generator.

- Access the dBASE help facility to determine variations in the REPORT FORM command.

- Distinguish between the LIST and DISPLAY commands.

- Describe the dBASE record pointer and discuss how various commands alter its position within a file.

Report Generation

OUTLINE

Overview

The chapter opens with a new example with which we are all familiar, the United States of America. We present a table containing data on all 50 states and describe various reports that present the data in a more useful fashion.

The dBASE-specific material focuses on the *report generator,* describes how to create and modify *report forms,* and gives you an opportunity to review earlier material on *indexing* and the *record pointer.* The chapter also reviews the help facility and indexing, and distinguishes between the LIST and DISPLAY commands.

We begin, however, with a brief discussion on the difference between *data* and *information,* describing how one is converted into the other. Finally, and perhaps most importantly, we discuss the importance of viewing computer output critically.

United States Example

Figure 4.1 lists the United States alphabetically and includes the year a state entered the Union, its population in 1980, and its area in square miles. Figure 4.2 contains four reports derived from these data listing the original 13 states, the 10 smallest states according to area, the 10 largest states according to population, and the 10 states with the highest population density.

The two figures effectively illustrate the difference between *data* and *information.* Data refers to a fact or facts about a person, place, or thing, and in our example (Figure 4.1), includes items such as the state name, year admitted to the Union, area, and population. Information, on the other hand, is data that has been rearranged into a form perceived as useful by the recipient, for example, the 10 states with the highest population density (population/area). Put another way, data is the raw material, whereas information is the finished product. Information can be used to make decisions, raw data cannot.

The distinction between data and information is often difficult to discern. In general, however, data is seen as something less than information, although what one person perceives as data may be viewed as information by another. The alphabetic listing of all 50 states, with every state's associated facts, may be viewed as information by one person, and as raw data by someone else.

Data is converted to information through *calculation* (computation), *selection* (listing only a subset of the records in a file), and *indexing* (presenting records in a different sequence). As you view the reports of Figure 4.2, try to determine which operations were

State Name	Entered Union	Population in 1980	Area sq mi
ALABAMA	1819	3893888	51609
ALASKA	1959	401851	589757
ARIZONA	1912	2718215	113909
ARKANSAS	1836	2286435	53104
CALIFORNIA	1850	23667902	158693
COLORADO	1876	2889964	104247
CONNECTICUT	1788	3107576	5009
DELAWARE	1787	594338	2057
FLORIDA	1845	9746324	58560
GEORGIA	1788	5463105	58876
HAWAII	1959	964691	6450
IDAHO	1890	943935	83557
ILLINOIS	1818	11426518	56400
INDIANA	1816	5490224	36291
IOWA	1846	2913808	56290
KANSAS	1861	2363679	82264
KENTUCKY	1792	3660777	40395
LOUISIANA	1812	4205900	48523
MAINE	1820	1124660	33215
MARYLAND	1788	4216975	10577
MASSACHUSETTS	1788	5737037	8257
MICHIGAN	1837	9262078	58216
MINNESOTA	1858	4075970	84068
MISSISSIPPI	1817	2520638	47716
MISSOURI	1821	4916686	69686
MONTANA	1889	786690	147138
NEBRASKA	1867	1569825	77227
NEVADA	1864	800493	110540
NEW HAMPSHIRE	1788	920610	9304
NEW JERSEY	1787	7364823	7836
NEW MEXICO	1912	1302894	121666
NEW YORK	1788	17558072	49576
NORTH CAROLINA	1789	5881766	52586
NORTH DAKOTA	1889	652717	70665
OHIO	1803	10797630	41222
OKLAHOMA	1907	3025290	69919
OREGON	1859	2633105	96981
PENNSYLVANIA	1787	11863895	45333
RHODE ISLAND	1790	947154	1214
SOUTH CAROLINA	1788	3121820	31055
SOUTH DAKOTA	1889	690768	77047
TENNESSEE	1796	4591120	42244
TEXAS	1845	14229191	267338
UTAH	1896	1461037	84916
VERMONT	1791	511456	9609
VIRGINIA	1788	5346818	40817
WASHINGTON	1889	4132156	68192
WEST VIRGINIA	1863	1949644	24181
WISCONSIN	1848	4705767	56154
WYOMING	1890	469557	97914

FIGURE 4.1 United States data (USSTATES.DBF)

needed for their creation. The rest of the chapter introduces the necessary dBASE commands to convert data (as it exists in a DBF file) to informational reports (for example, Figure 4.2) along the lines just discussed.

The dBASE Report Generator

The reports in Figure 4.2 were produced with the dBASE report generator, a powerful menu-driven facility we shall describe in depth. Each report is based on its own *report form* and is associated with a different index (the states are listed in different sequences in each report).

A report form can be thought of as an empty report, or *template*. It contains the

```
  The 13 Original States
  (By year of admission)

       State           Year
  =============        ====

     DELAWARE          1787
     NEW JERSEY        1787
     PENNSYLVANIA      1787
     CONNECTICUT       1788
     GEORGIA           1788
     MARYLAND          1788
     MASSACHUSETTS     1788
     NEW HAMPSHIRE     1788
     NEW YORK          1788
     SOUTH CAROLINA    1788
     VIRGINIA          1788
     NORTH CAROLINA    1789
     RHODE ISLAND      1790
```

a

```
    The 10 Smallest States
      (in terms of area)

      State            Area
                     (sq miles)
   =============    ==========

   RHODE ISLAND        1214
   DELAWARE            2057
   CONNECTICUT         5009
   HAWAII              6450
   NEW JERSEY          7836
   MASSACHUSETTS       8257
   NEW HAMPSHIRE       9304
   VERMONT             9609
   MARYLAND           10577
   WEST VIRGINIA      24181
```

b

```
     The 10 Largest States
    (in terms of population)

      State          Population
   =============    ===========

   CALIFORNIA         23667902
   NEW YORK           17558072
   TEXAS              14229191
   PENNSYLVANIA       11863895
   ILLINOIS           11426518
   OHIO               10797630
   FLORIDA             9746324
   MICHIGAN            9262078
   NEW JERSEY          7364823
   NORTH CAROLINA      5881766
```

c

```
       The 10 States With Highest Population Density

        State       Population    Area    Density
                      (1980)     (sq mi)
     =============  ==========   =======  =======

     NEW JERSEY       7364823      7836      940
     RHODE ISLAND      947154      1214      780
     MASSACHUSETTS    5737037      8257      695
     CONNECTICUT      3107576      5009      620
     MARYLAND         4216975     10577      399
     NEW YORK        17558072     49576      354
     DELAWARE          594338      2057      289
     OHIO            10797630     41222      262
     PENNSYLVANIA    11863895     45333      262
     ILLINOIS        11426518     56400      203
```

d

FIGURE 4.2 Data versus information: (a) the thirteen original states; (b) the ten smallest states; (c); the ten most populated states; (d) the ten most densely populated states

report's title, formatting characteristics (for example, margins and spacing), column headings, and so on, but no data. An actual report is produced by merging the United States DBF file (sequenced by the desired index) with the designated report form as shown in Figure 4.3.

As you can see, all four reports are derived from the same DBF file. The report form, however, is different in every instance; that is, one report contains the state name and year of admission to the Union, another the state name and area, and so on. Accordingly, four distinct *report forms* are required, each of which must be created separately. Note, too, that the order in which the states are listed is different in every report, so that four different indexes are also necessary.

The report forms are created through the dBASE report generator, a menu-driven process illustrated in Hands-on Exercise 4–1. The report generator is initiated by the CREATE REPORT command and results in a FRM file which can be used repeatedly. The report form can, if necessary, be subsequently modified through the MODIFY REPORT command. We expect that you will be able to use the report generator with just the expla-

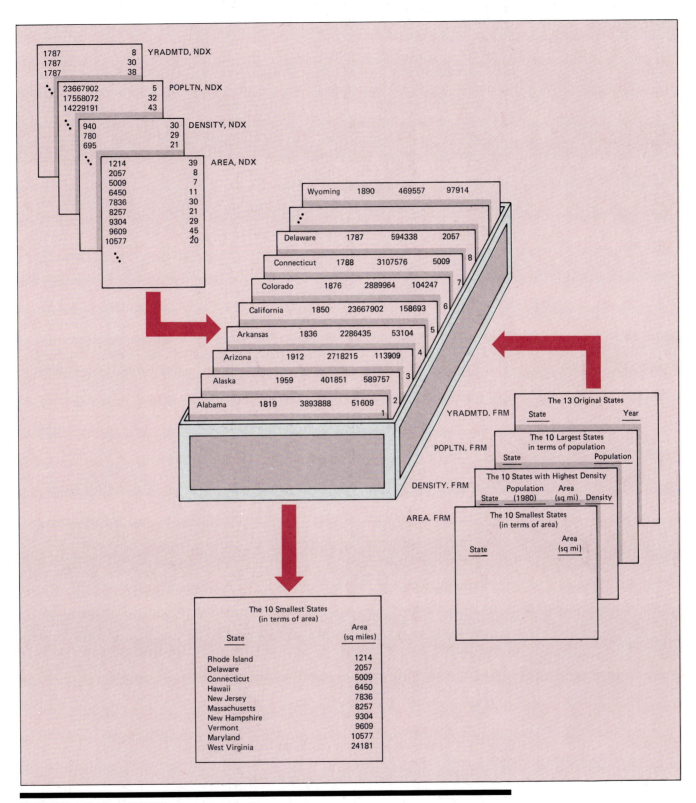

FIGURE 4.3 The dBASE report generator

nation provided in the exercise, but direct you to the Programmer's Notebook for additional information.

The exercise begins with the creation of the four required indexes (year of admission, area, population, and density). It then introduces the report generator and shows how to create the first report form in detail. You are asked to create the three remaining report forms, and then to merge the individual report forms with the associated indexes to produce the actual reports. Finally, you are asked to view the directory, and verify the presence of the nine required files (one DBF file, four NDX files, and four FRM files).

Hands-on Exercise 4–1: The dBASE Report Generator

Objective: To introduce the dBASE report generator; describe how to create report forms and produce reports using combinations of DBF, NDX, and FRM files.

☐ **STEP 1: Log into the proper subdirectory.**

The student version of dBASE III Plus is *limited to 31 records, and as such is not suitable for the United States example.* Thus if you are using the student (as opposed to the full blown) version you must do this exercise with a *different* set of data than given in Figure 4.1. We have therefore developed an alternate DBF file which lists 30 arbitrarily chosen countries of the world, as shown on page 83. Accordingly:

With the *full blown* dBASE III Plus:

```
CD B:\USSTATES ——————————  With a floppy disk system (convenience disk
                            should be placed in drive B:)
CD C:\SAMPLER\USSTATES ——  With a hard disk drive
PATH C:\SAMPLER
```

With the *student version:*

```
CD B:\WORLD ——————————————  With a floppy disk system (convenience disk
                            should be placed in drive B:)
CD C:\SAMPLER\WORLD ——————  With a hard disk drive
PATH C:\SAMPLER
```

Load dBASE after you have logged into the proper subdirectory.

☐ **STEP 2: Open the DBF file**

Enter the appropriate USE command (depending on your choice of DBF file), and then display the structure of the DBF file you have opened.

```
. USE USSTATES ——————————  Alternatively USE WORLD
. DISPLAY STRUCTURE
```

Note, however, that the field names are identical regardless of which DBF file you are using. Accordingly, all other steps in this exercise apply equally to both files, with no further modifications necessary.

☐ **STEP 3: Create the necessary indexes.**

Enter the commands shown in Figure 4.5 to create the four index files for year admitted, area, population, and density. Where possible, the index file is given the same name as the field on which it is based, that is, the first occurrence of YRADMTD is the name of a field within the file structure, whereas the second occurrence is the name of the index file itself (YRADMTD.NDX).

```
         Structure for database : B:USSTATES.dbf
         Number of data records :      50
         Date of last update    : 11/12/87
         Field  Field name  Type       Width    Dec
             1  NAME        Character     14
             2  YRADMTD     Numeric        4
             3  POPLTN      Numeric       10
             4  AREA        Numeric        8
             5  REGION      Character     15

         ** Total **                     52
```

FIGURE 4.4 The USSTATES file structure

The minus signs preceding POPLTN and POPLTN/AREA in the third and fourth commands create indexes that sequence the records from the DBF file in *descending* order, that is, from high to low according to the indicated field.

The DIR command at the end of Figure 4.5 verifies the presence of the index files on the current directory.

☐   STEP 4: Create a report form.

Enter the command CREATE REPORT YRADMTD to initiate the report generator. YRADMTD, the field name in the file structure, is chosen as the report name just as it was used earlier as the index file name. This convention makes it easier to associate the report form with the proper index.

dBASE next supplies a series of screens to guide you through the process of building a report form. The first of these is shown in Figure 4.6 and contains a *menu bar* across the top of the screen. It lists five possible selections: Options,

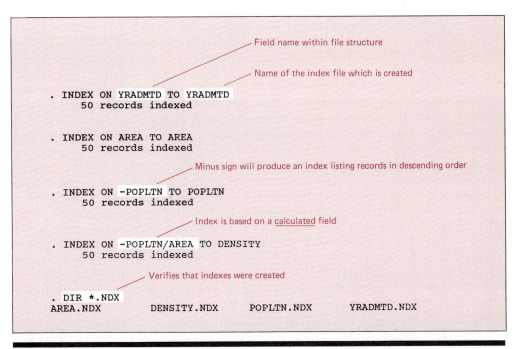

FIGURE 4.5 Creation of index files

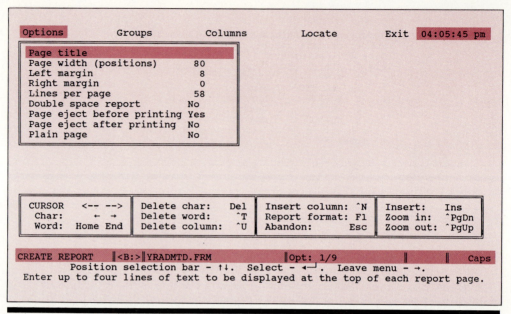

```
Options            Groups         Columns         Locate          Exit  04:05:45 pm

  Page title
  Page width (positions)    80
  Left margin                8
  Right margin               0
  Lines per page            58
  Double space report      No
  Page eject before printing Yes
  Page eject after printing  No
  Plain page                No




  CURSOR    <-- -->   Delete char:    Del   Insert column: ^N   Insert:    Ins
    Char:     ← →     Delete word:     ^T   Report format: F1   Zoom in:  ^PgDn
    Word:  Home End   Delete column:   ^U   Abandon:      Esc   Zoom out: ^PgUp

 CREATE REPORT  ║<B:>║YRADMTD.FRM          ║Opt: 1/9        ║      ║  Caps
              Position selection bar - ↑↓.   Select - ◄┘.   Leave menu - →.
        Enter up to four lines of text to be displayed at the top of each report page.
```

FIGURE 4.6 Initial screen for the report generator

Groups, Columns, Locate, and Exit. The *left and right arrow keys* are used to move from selection to selection. Press either key and observe what happens.

In Figure 4.6 the Options selection is highlighted, and hence the box in the upper left portion of the screen reflects the choices available with this selection. The options in the highlighted box reflect standard page formatting defaults, for example, a page width of 80 positions, 58 lines per page, and so on. All are acceptable as set initially. Indeed the only parameter you need to change at this time is the page title. Use the *up and down arrow keys* to select page title, *then press the Return key*. Enter the title as desired (up to four lines are available). You must, however, enter all four lines, even if a line is blank (press the Return key). *Do not worry about centering the title; it is done automatically*. When you finish entering the title, press the right arrow key until the Columns option is highlighted in the menu bar.

☐ STEP 5: Enter column information.

Remember that this entire exercise is concerned with producing a report on the first 13 states admitted to the Union and that the report contains columns for the state name and year of admission. Now use the up and down arrow keys to highlight Contents, and press the Return key once more. Enter the field name for the first column *as it appears in the file structure* (that is, enter NAME), and again press the Return key. At this point, dBASE knows that the contents of the first column in the report are to be taken from the NAME field in the data file. You must now tell dBASE the heading for that column.

Use the up and down arrow keys to highlight Heading and press the Return key. Type State as the heading's first line and press the Return key; type = = = = = = = = = = for the second line and press the Return key; then press the Return key twice more indicating that the heading's third and fourth lines are blank. Press the PgDn key to move on to the next column and repeat the process for the YRADMTD column, entering the data shown in Figure 4.7.

Figure 4.7 shows the report generation screen for the second column, after the necessary information has been entered. The box at the top of the figure indicates that the column's contents are to be taken from the YRADMTD

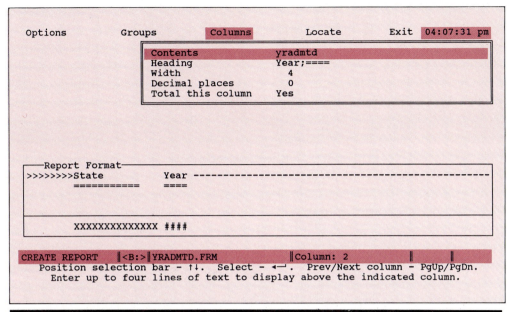

```
  Options          Groups          Columns           Locate        Exit  04:07:31 pm

                    ┌──────────────────────────────────────────────────────┐
                    │ Contents              yradmtd                          │
                    │ Heading               Year;====                        │
                    │ Width                    4                             │
                    │ Decimal places           0                             │
                    │ Total this column      Yes                             │
                    └──────────────────────────────────────────────────────┘




      ┌─Report Format───────────────────────────────────────────────────────────┐
      │>>>>>>>>State          Year ----------------------------------------------- │
      │        ===========    ====                                                │
      │                                                                           │
      ├───────────────────────────────────────────────────────────────────────── ┤
      │       XXXXXXXXXXXXXX ####                                                  │
      └───────────────────────────────────────────────────────────────────────── ┘

  CREATE REPORT    ║<B:>║YRADMTD.FRM              ║Column: 2            ║        ║
      Position selection bar - ↑↓.  Select - ◄─┘.  Prev/Next column - PgUp/PgDn.
      Enter up to four lines of text to display above the indicated column.
```

FIGURE 4.7 Report generator with two columns completed

field in the data file, and that a two-line heading (consisting of `Year` and `===`) will be used. The column width is four positions, there are no decimal places within the field, and there is no total for this column. (To suppress the total, use the up and down arrow keys to highlight "Total this column" and press the Return key to change the value to No.) Note too that the box at the bottom of Figure 4.7 shows how the completed report will appear, based on all columns entered so far.

You can move between columns at any time by using the PgUp key to return to a previous column and/or PgDn to move to a subsequent column. You could, for example, return to a previous column to better center a heading and/or add an additional heading line. After you have completed the report specifications, that is, when no more fields or modifications are necessary, highlight the Exit option (use the left and right arrow keys), select Save (with the up and down arrow keys), and press the Return key.

☐ **STEP 6: List the original 13 states.**
Completing Steps 4 and 5 has produced the report form file YRADMTD.FRM, but has not generated a report per se. In order to produce the actual report, you must merge the data in the DBF file with the report template just created; further you want to access the records in a specified sequence. Figure 4.8a shows the necessary commands together with the generated report in Figure 4.8b.

The `SET INDEX TO` command designates YRADMTD.NDX as the master index, that is, the index currently in effect for the USSTATES.DBF file. The `REPORT FORM` command specifies the name of the report form to be used and merges it with records in the open DBF file. Specifying the `NEXT 13` parameter includes only 13 records (that is, the first 13 states) in the report as opposed to every record in the file.

☐ **STEP 7: Generate the remaining reports.**
The procedure to generate the three remaining reports (for area, population, and density) parallels Steps 4, 5, and 6 above, the only differences being in

```
. SET INDEX TO YRADMTD
. REPORT FORM YRADMTD NEXT 13
```

a

```
Page No.      1
11/26/86
                        The 13 Original States
                        (By year of admission)

    State           Year
    ===========     ====

    DELAWARE        1787
    NEW JERSEY      1787
    PENNSYLVANIA    1787
    CONNECTICUT     1788
    GEORGIA         1788
    MARYLAND        1788
    MASSACHUSETTS   1788
    NEW HAMPSHIRE   1788
    NEW YORK        1788
    SOUTH CAROLINA  1788
    VIRGINIA        1788
    NORTH CAROLINA  1789
    RHODE ISLAND    1790
```

b

FIGURE 4.8 Report produced by dBASE report generator: (a) command sequence to print report; (b) generated report

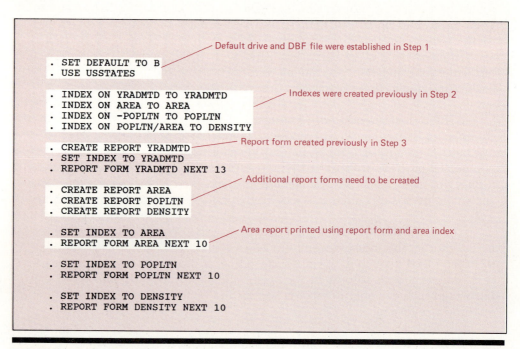

FIGURE 4.9 Generation of additional reports

the report titles and the designated fields. Each report requires its own report form and is associated with a different index. Refer to Figure 4.2 as you create these forms for the report titles, fields, and column headings to be included. The density report uses a field expression (POPLTN/AREA) for the column contents in column 4.

Figure 4.9 shows the necessary commands to generate the four reports. Some of the commands are repeated from earlier steps to help you review the overall process. The figure implies the use of consecutive commands to create the additional report forms in lieu of printing the reports one at a time.

☐   STEP 8: Experiment.

Four illustrative reports have been developed, but the possibilities are endless. Practice makes perfect, so experiment away, creating additional reports of your own design.

You might also view the directory with the command **DIR *.*** which should now contain a total of nine files. There is the original DBF file, the four report forms (each with extension FRM), and the four index files (each with extension NDX).

Type **QUIT** to exit dBASE when you are finished.

Commands Affecting the Record Pointer

The reports just produced list the records in different sequences, depending on the master index. Recall that dBASE remembers its position within a file by maintaining a *record pointer* which is set to the record number of the current record. The record numbers themselves are assigned consecutively as records are appended to the file; that is, the first record within a DBF file is record 1, the second is record 2, and so on. Thus, in the USSTATES.DBF file, Alabama is record 1, Alaska is record 2, and Wyoming is record 50. The importance of the record pointer will become apparent as we consider additional reports.

Various commands affect the record pointer's position as illustrated in Figure 4.10. The USE statement opens the file and positions the record pointer at the first record in the file, that is, Alabama. At this point, no index is in effect and the states would be listed in the order in which they appear in the DBF file itself.

The SET INDEX TO POPLTN command opens the population index and positions the record pointer at the first record in the population sequence. (Recall that POPLTN.NDX was based on the *negative* value of population and thus sequenced states in *decreasing* order of population.) The ensuing DISPLAY command shows the record for California because it has the largest population, and appears first according to the (descending) population index.

The DISPLAY NEXT 5 command lists the next five states, *according to the population index*, beginning with the state where the record pointer is currently located. California is the first state listed in both the DISPLAY and DISPLAY NEXT commands because the record pointer does not move as a consequence of the initial DISPLAY command as it was issued with no other parameters. Observe also that the record numbers are those assigned to the records in the USSTATES.DBF file.

A similar example is provided for the area index. The SET INDEX TO AREA command changes the master index and positions the record pointer at the first record according to the new index. The initial DISPLAY command shows Rhode Island as the first state in the area sequence, whereas the DISPLAY NEXT 5 command lists the first five states according to area (in ascending order).

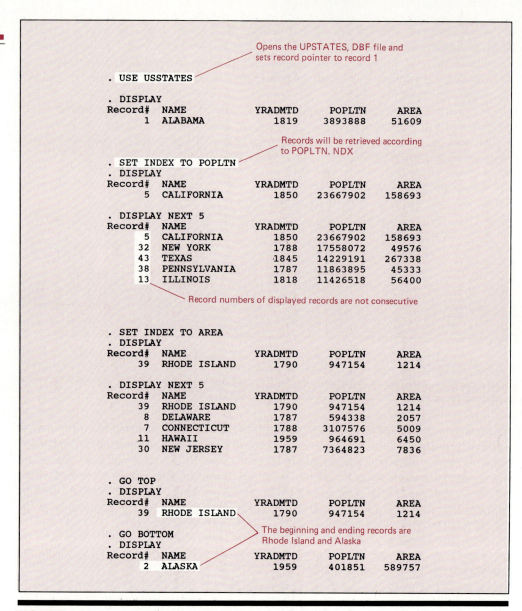

FIGURE 4.10 The dBASE record pointer

The figure also introduces the GO TOP and GO BOTTOM commands. They position the record pointer at the beginning and end of the file, again according to the active index. As you would expect, Rhode Island and Alaska are shown to be the smallest and largest states respectively.

DISPLAY versus LIST

DISPLAY ALL and LIST are similar commands. They show selected records on the monitor or printer (both commands can include a TO PRINT option). The difference is in the amount of information shown at one time and is illustrated in Figure 4.11.

The DISPLAY ALL command shows only as many records as will fit on the monitor at one time, whereas LIST (or LIST ALL) shows all the records within a DBF file through continuous scrolling operations. In other words, the DISPLAY ALL command pauses periodically with the message "Press any key to continue" when the screen is full. LIST, on the other hand, lists the entire file without the intervening messages or pauses.

```
. USE USSTATES
                    ┌── DISPLAY by itself shows a single record
. DISPLAY ─┘
Record#  NAME           YRADMTD      POPLTN       AREA
      1  ALABAMA           1819     3893888      51609

. DISPLAY ALL
Record#  NAME           YRADMTD      POPLTN       AREA
      1  ALABAMA           1819     3893888      51609
      2  ALASKA            1959      401851     589757
                 .
                 .
                 .
     19  MAINE             1820     1124660      33215
Press any key to continue
     20  MARYLAND          1788     4216975      10577
     21  MASSACHUSETTS     1788     5737037       8257
                 .              One screen of information is
                 .              displayed at a time
                 .
     39  RHODE ISLAND      1790      947154       1214
Press any key to continue
     40  SOUTH CAROLINA    1788     3121820      31055
     41  SOUTH DAKOTA      1889      690768      77047
                 .
                 .
                 .
     50  WYOMING           1890      469557      97914
                  ┌── All 50 states appear without intervening message
. LIST ALL ─┘
Record#  NAME           YRADMTD      POPLTN       AREA
      1  ALABAMA           1819     3893888      51609
      2  ALASKA            1959      401851     589757
                 .
                 .
                 .
     50  WYOMING           1890      469557      97914
                  ┌── LIST is equivalent to LIST ALL
. LIST ─┘
Record#  NAME           YRADMTD      POPLTN       AREA
      1  ALABAMA           1819     3893888      51609
      2  ALASKA            1959      401851     589757
                 .         All 50 states appear without intervening message
                 .
                 .
     50  WYOMING           1890      469557      97914
```

FIGURE 4.11 DISPLAY versus LIST

Another difference is in the implied scope; DISPLAY has an implied scope of one whereas LIST implies ALL. In other words the commands DISPLAY and LIST (both with no parameters) display one and all of the records respectively. Finally DISPLAY with no parameters does *not* alter the record pointer's position, whereas LIST by itself positions the record pointer just beyond the end of the file.

Use and Abuse of the Computer

The reports we have been discussing are simple and straightforward, and easily produced without error. Unfortunately, that statement is a bit too optimistic because students and professionals alike make all too many careless errors when using the computer and are far too accepting of reports produced by others. Consider, for example, Figure 4.12, which contains two erroneous attempts at producing the report listing the original 13 states. It is

State	Year
ALABAMA	1819
ALASKA	1959
ARIZONA	1912
ARKANSAS	1836
CALIFORNIA	1850
COLORADO	1876
CONNECTICUT	1788
DELAWARE	1787
FLORIDA	1845
GEORGIA	1788
HAWAII	1959
IDAHO	1890
ILLINOIS	1818

a

State	Year
RHODE ISLAND	1790
VERMONT	1791
KENTUCKY	1792
TENNESSEE	1796
OHIO	1803
LOUISIANA	1812
INDIANA	1816
MISSISSIPPI	1817
ILLINOIS	1818
ALABAMA	1819
MAINE	1820
MISSOURI	1821
ARKANSAS	1836

b

FIGURE 4.12 Use and abuse of the computer: (a) wrong index; (b) record pointer in wrong position

important to say that these examples are *not* contrived, but were reproduced from student assignments. The errors seem obvious now, but nevertheless went undetected by students who submitted the reports for a grade.

Figure 4.12a lists the first 13 states in the USSTATES.DBF file, rather than the first 13 admitted. The report was produced by using the DBF file *without* the associated YRADMTD index.

The error in Figure 4.12b is more subtle and is *caused by failing to reset the record pointer*. The REPORT FORM command alters with a NEXT parameter the position of the record pointer; this must be recognized or else the wrong states will be processed. Consider:

```
USE USSTATES
SET INDEX TO YRADMTD
REPORT FORM YRADMTD NEXT 13
```

Given that the report form, data file, and associated index are the ones desired, these statements will properly produce the report in question. However, after the REPORT FORM YRADMTD NEXT 13 command has been initially executed, the record pointer remains on the 13th record in the year-admitted sequence (Rhode Island). Thus, if you were to repeat the statement, REPORT FORM YRADMTD NEXT 13, without resetting the record pointer (that is, without specifying GO TOP), states 13 through 25 would appear on the subsequent report. In all probability, the student who submitted the report in Figure 4.12b was dissatisfied with a heading in the report form and/or the paper alignment, made the proper adjustment, then reran the report without resetting the record pointer.

Our point is simply that most individuals are not critical enough when viewing computer output. Beginning students and/or first-time computer users especially are often so happy when they produce output that they automatically assume it to be correct. Nothing could be further from the truth.

More About Report Forms

The online dBASE Help facility provides the quickest access to additional information. Enter the command HELP REPORT from the dot prompt and the following will appear:

```
REPORT FORM report form file [scope]
   [FOR condition] [PLAIN] [HEADING 'character string']
   [NOEJECT] [TO PRINT] [TO FILE file]
```

The dBASE notation (originally introduced in Chapter 2) is used to explain variations in the REPORT FORM command. Every entry except for the name of the report form, is enclosed in square brackets meaning that these entries are optional. Consider:

Example 1:
```
USE USSTATES INDEX AREA
REPORT FORM AREA ————————————————— Lists all states
```

Example 2:
```
USE USSTATES INDEX AREA
REPORT FORM AREA FOR AREA < 30000 ——— Lists all states with area less
                                        than 30,000 square miles
```

Example 3:
```
USE USSTATES INDEX AREA
REPORT FORM AREA NEXT 10 ———————————— Lists only the first 10 states in
                                        the report
```

Obtaining Subtotals

The United States is often divided into sections according to history or geographic region for convenience in studying the country. Figure 4.13 lists the states by geographic region, and alphabetically within region, with population subtotals computed for each region. The figure also illustrates a new capability of the report generator, namely to group records and produce subtotals.

There are, however, two things that must be done to produce Figure 4.13. A new index, sequencing states *by region and alphabetically within each region* needs to be created, and the existing population report form has to be modified. Both items will be accounted for in Hands-on Exercise 4–2.

Hands-on Exercise 4–2:   Additional Capabilities

Objective: To change the appearance of a report by modifying an existing report form and to introduce subtotals into a report.

☐   STEP 1: Open the appropriate DBF file

Place the convenience disk in drive B: and log into the proper subdirectory (depending on whether you have the student or full-blown version of dBASE III Plus) as described in Step 1 of Hands-on Exercise 4-1. Load dBASE, and then use either USSTATES.DBF or WORLD.DBF as appropriate. As in the previous exercise, the field names are indentical in both file structures, so that the rest of the exercise applies equally to either file.

☐   STEP 2: Create a concatenated index.

The states within the subtotal report are listed by region, and alphabetically within region, necessitating the use of both fields in creating the associated index file. Accordingly enter the command:

```
INDEX ON REGION+NAME TO REGION
```

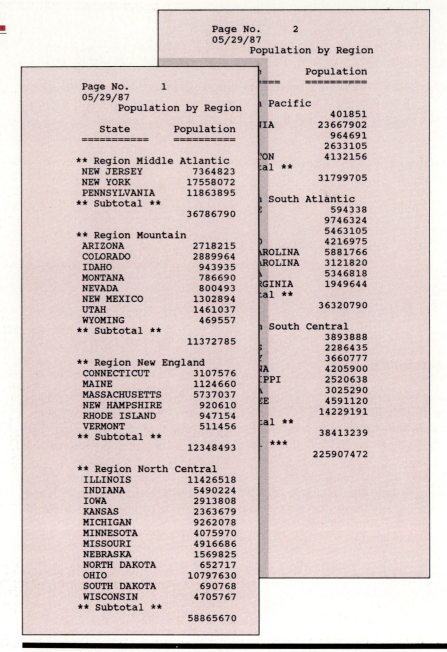

```
                              Page No.      2
                              05/29/87
                                 Population by Region

                                           Population
                         ====              ==========
                       Pacific
                                              401851
                    NIA          23667902
                                              964691
                                             2633105
                    ON                       4132156
                   al **

                                            31799705

                   South Atlantic
                                              594338
                                             9746324
                                             5463105
                                             4216975
                  AROLINA          5881766
                  AROLINA          3121820
                                             5346818
                  RGINIA           1949644
                  al **

                                            36320790

                   South Central
                                             3893888
                                             2286435
                                             3660777
                  A                          4205900
                  PPI                        2520638
                                             3025290
                  EE                         4591120
                                            14229191
                  al **

                                            38413239
                  · ***

                                           225907472
```

```
              Page No.      1
              05/29/87
                 Population by Region

           State          Population
       ============       ==========

       ** Region Middle Atlantic
       NEW JERSEY         7364823
       NEW YORK          17558072
       PENNSYLVANIA      11863895
       ** Subtotal **

                         36786790

       ** Region Mountain
       ARIZONA            2718215
       COLORADO           2889964
       IDAHO               943935
       MONTANA             786690
       NEVADA              800493
       NEW MEXICO         1302894
       UTAH               1461037
       WYOMING             469557
       ** Subtotal **

                         11372785

       ** Region New England
       CONNECTICUT        3107576
       MAINE              1124660
       MASSACHUSETTS      5737037
       NEW HAMPSHIRE       920610
       RHODE ISLAND        947154
       VERMONT             511456
       ** Subtotal **

                         12348493

       ** Region North Central
       ILLINOIS          11426518
       INDIANA            5490224
       IOWA               2913808
       KANSAS             2363679
       MICHIGAN           9262078
       MINNESOTA          4075970
       MISSOURI           4916686
       NEBRASKA           1569825
       NORTH DAKOTA        652717
       OHIO              10797630
       SOUTH DAKOTA        690768
       WISCONSIN          4705767
       ** Subtotal **

                         58865670
```

FIGURE 4.13 A report with subtotals

to create the index file REGION.NDX. The plus sign in the **INDEX ON** command indicates a concatenated key, that is, a key based on two or more fields. Region is the more important field, it is listed first in the command, and it is designated the *major* or *primary* field. The name field is less important; it is listed second in the command and is designated the *minor* or *secondary* field.

☐　**STEP 3: Modify the existing report form.**
The existing population report form has to be changed to indicate that subtotals are required. Enter the command **MODIFY REPORT POPLTN** to retrieve the report form, then use the left and right arrow keys to highlight the Groups option. Figure 4.14 should appear on your monitor.

Use the up and down arrow keys to highlight Group On Expression, then press the Return key. Enter the field on which to compute the subtotals; in this

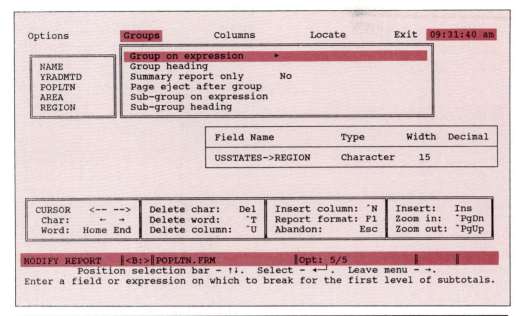

FIGURE 4.14 Generation of subtotals

case, region. Press the F10 function key to bring up the box on the left of the figure (containing the field names as they appear within the file structure), use the up and down arrow keys to highlight REGION, and press the Return key. REGION has been entered as the Group On Expression.

That's all there is to it. Note that the master index must have Region as its primary (or only) key because when the actual report is generated, dBASE begins a new grouping (subtotal) each time it encounters a different value in this field. In other words, the master index must be consistent with the field specified in the Group On Expression.

Save the modified report form with the exit option. Enter the command REPORT FORM POPLTN to produce the actual report. Exit dBASE and return to the DOS prompt.

Summary

The chapter began with a discussion of the differences between data and information, and the processes by which one is converted to the other. The material was presented within the context of an extended example, based on data for the United States, which was used throughout the chapter. The chapter also made you aware of the limitations of computer-generated information and stressed the importance of critically viewing computer output.

The dBASE *report generator*, in conjunction with various index files, was used to prepare four sample reports. Additional discussion reviewed the *record pointer* and indexing, and differentiated between the LIST and DISPLAY commands.

Additional capabilities within the report generator were also discussed. We indicated that a given report could be made to include only a designated number of records (REPORT FORM . . . NEXT) as well as an indeterminate number of records which meet a given criterion (`REPORT FORM . . . FOR`). We also saw that the output could be directed to either the printer (`REPORT FORM . . . TO PRINT`) or a disk file (`REPORT FORM . . . TO FILE file`) in addition to the monitor. Finally, we discussed how to modify an existing report form and how to include subtotals within a report.

Key Words and Concepts

Ascending sequence	`LIST`
Concatenated index	`LIST ALL`
`CREATE REPORT`	Menu bar
Descending sequence	`MODIFY REPORT`
`DISPLAY`	`MODIFY STRUCTURE`
`DISPLAY ALL`	Record pointer
F10 function key	`REPORT FORM`
`GO BOTTOM`	Report generator
`GO TOP`	`SET INDEX TO`
Group On Expression	Subtotal
`INDEX ON`	Template

True/False

1. `LIST`, with no additional parameters, does *not* move the record pointer.
2. `DISPLAY`, with no additional parameters, does *not* move the record pointer.
3. `DISPLAY ALL` positions the record pointer *after* the last record in the file.
4. A report form cannot be modified after it has been created and saved.
5. A sophisticated data management system will produce correct reports from invalid data.
6. The output of the `REPORT FORM` command can be directed to the monitor or printer.
7. The order in which records appear in a given report is most likely immaterial.
8. The `REPORT FORM` command must include every record in the associated DBF file.
9. The `REPORT FORM` command *cannot* be used in conjunction with an index file.
10. A file may not be indexed on any field not present in its file structure.
11. Major key and primary key are synonymous.
12. Minor key and secondary key are synonymous.

Exercises

1. Supply the dBASE command(s) to:
   a. modify an existing report form
   b. position the record pointer at the first logical record within a file
   c. display the first five records in a file
   d. display the next five records (from the current position of the record pointer)
   e. access the online help facility to obtain available information on the `REPORT FORM` command
   f. direct the output of the `REPORT FORM` command to the printer
2. Distinguish between:
   a. an ascending and a descending index
   b. the YRADMTD.FRM and YRADMTD.NDX files
   c. `GO TOP` and `GO BOTTOM`

d. DISPLAY and DISPLAY ALL
e. CREATE REPORT and MODIFY REPORT
f. HELP and HELP REPORT
g. DISPLAY ALL and LIST ALL
h. LIST and LIST ALL
i. REPORT FORM . . . NEXT and REPORT FORM . . . FOR
j. use of the PgUp and PgDn keys in modifying a report

3. Figure 4.15 contains various attempts at producing a report of the 10 states with highest population density. Indicate the problem with each of the indicated reports.

State	Population (1980)	Area (sq mi)	Density (pers/mi)
==========	==========	=======	=========
NEW JERSEY	7364823	7836	940
RHODE ISLAND	947154	1214	780
MASSACHUSETTS	5737037	8257	695
CONNECTICUT	3107576	5009	620
MARYLAND	4216975	10577	399
NEW YORK	17558072	49576	354
DELAWARE	594338	2057	289
OHIO	10797630	41222	262
PENNSYLVANIA	11863895	45333	262
TEXAS	14229191	67338	211

a

State	Population (1980)	Area (sq mi)	Density (pers/mi)
==========	==========	=======	=========
ALASKA	401851	589757	1
WYOMING	469557	97914	5
MONTANA	786690	147138	5
NEVADA	800493	110540	7
SOUTH DAKOTA	690768	77047	9
NORTH DAKOTA	652717	70665	9
NEW MEXICO	1302894	121666	11
IDAHO	943935	83557	11
UTAH	1461037	84916	17
NEBRASKA	1569825	77227	20

b

State	Population (1980)	Area (sq mi)	Density (pers/mi)
==========	==========	=======	=========
NEW JERSEY	7364823	7836	939.870
RHODE ISLAND	947154	1214	780.193
MASSACHUSETTS	5737037	8257	694.809
CONNECTICUT	3107576	5009	620.398
MARYLAND	4216975	10577	398.693
NEW YORK	17558072	49576	354.165
DELAWARE	594338	2057	288.934
OHIO	10797630	41222	261.939
PENNSYLVANIA	11863895	45333	261.705
ILLINOIS	11426518	56400	202.598
*** Total ***			
			4803.304

c

FIGURE 4.15 (a) First erroneous report; (b) second erroneous report; (c) third erroneous report

4. Given the following two command sequences:

Sequence 1:

```
. USE B:USSTATES
. SET DEFAULT TO B

. INDEX ON AREA TO AREA
. CREATE REPORT AREA
. REPORT FORM AREA NEXT 10
. INDEX ON -POPLTN TO POPLTN
. CREATE REPORT POPLTN
. REPORT FORM POPLTN
```

Sequence 2:

```
. SET DEFAULT TO B
. USE USSTATES

. INDEX ON AREA TO AREA
. INDEX ON -POPLTN TO POPLTN

. CREATE REPORT AREA
. CREATE REPORT POPLTN

. SET INDEX TO AREA
. REPORT FORM AREA NEXT 10

. SET INDEX TO POPLTN
. REPORT FORM POPLTN
```

a. Are the two sets of commands equivalent?
b. With respect to the first report in the first sequence:
   • How many states will appear in the report?
   • In which order will the states be listed?
c. With respect to the second report in the second sequence:
   • How many states will appear in the report?
   • In which order will the states be listed?
d. Specify all files (and extensions) that exist as a consequence of the first command sequence.
e. What problems, if any, do you see with the following command sequence? (Assume that the necessary index files and report forms exist on the default disk.)

```
. USE USSTATES INDEX AREA
. REPORT FORM AREA NEXT 10
. REPORT FORM POPLTN
```

5. Figure 4.16 contains statistical data for 30 arbitrarily chosen countries. The data have been entered on the convenience disk in the WORLD.DBF file, within the WORLD subdirectory. Use the dBASE report generator to prepare reports that:
   a. List the 10 largest countries in terms of area; do *not* total the area.
   b. List the 10 largest countries in terms of population; compute the total population for the listed countries.
   c. List the five countries with the highest population density; do *not* total the density.
   d. List the first 20 countries admitted to the United Nations.
   e. Obtain group totals for population by continent.

Country	Area (sq miles)	Population (1984 est)	Year Admitted	Region
Algeria	918497	21300000	1962	Africa
Argentina	1065189	29627000	1945	South America
Bangladesh	55598	96539000	1974	Asia
Brazil	3286470	131305000	1945	South America
Burma	261288	35480000	1948	Asia
Canada	3851809	25142000	1945	North America
China	3691521	1022054000	1945	Asia
Congo	132046	1694000	1960	Africa
Egypt	385201	45809000	1945	Africa
Finland	130119	4850000	1955	Europe
France,	210040	54872000	1945	Europe
Germany, East	41825	16724000	1973	Europe
Germany, West	96011	61493000	1973	Europe
Ghana	92098	13367000	1957	Africa
Hungary	35919	10691000	1955	Europe
India	1269420	730572000	1945	Asia
Israel	8219	3958000	1949	Asia
Japan	147470	119896000	1945	Asia
Kenya	224081	18580000	1963	Africa
Mexico	761604	75702000	1945	North America
Portugal	36390	10008000	1955	Europe
Spain	195988	38234000	1955	Europe
Sweden	179896	8331000	1946	Europe
Switzerland	15941	6500000	1945	Europe
Togo	21853	2838000	1960	Africa
USSR	8649490	272500000	1945	Asia
United Kingdom	94222	56023000	1945	Europe
United States	3615123	234249000	1945	North America
Vietnam	127207	57612000	1977	Asia
Zaire	905063	31250000	1960	Africa

FIGURE 4.16 Statistical data for 30 countries (WORLD.DBF)

■ OBJECTIVES

After reading this chapter, you should be able to:

- Use the mailing label facility in dBASE; describe the CREATE LABEL, MODIFY LABEL, and LABEL FORM commands.

- Implement a mail-merge operation by combining the dBASE COPY command and a word processor.

- Discuss elementary file design considerations.

- Differentiate between character, numeric, date, and logical fields as they are used within a file structure.

- Describe the use of the SET and CLEAR FIELDS commands.

- Discuss the use of the up and down arrow keys from the dot prompt.

5

Mailing Labels

OUTLINE

Overview

This chapter introduces a new case study on The Dade County Metro Zoo. It focuses on the dBASE capability to support the generation of form letters and the associated mailing labels. We discuss how to create and access *label forms* and show how this parallels the report form process discussed in Chapter 4. The coverage includes material on using the COPY command to produce a file suitable for use with a mail-merge facility, the TRIM function to improve the appearance of the mailing labels, and the LABEL FORM, CREATE LABEL, and MODIFY LABEL commands.

Although the chapter's emphasis is on the *mail-merge* operation, the case solution raises several issues about the design of the *file structure*. We discuss which fields should and should not be included, as well as consider *field type* and *field size*. The case solution gives you an opportunity to review commands associated with data manipulation (SUM, COUNT, AVERAGE, and LIST). We also introduce the use of the SET and CLEAR FIELDS commands to improve the appearance of displayed information.

Case Preview

The case you are about to read centers around the development of a fund raising system for the Dade County Metro Zoo. Karen Johnson, the recently appointed Director of Special Programs, has been given the task of building a mailing list, soliciting donations, and monitoring contributions as they are received. Solving the case requires preparing form letters to solicit donations, generating mailing labels to use in conjunction with the form letters, and analyzing contributions as they come in. You will see that Ms. Johnson is interested in knowing the average contribution, the number of people contributing, and so on.

As you read the case study try to determine precisely what information is required from the system, and what data input is necessary to generate that information. Since our solution begins with the file structure design, we suggest that you develop your own file structure before viewing ours. Think carefully about which fields to include, and what the field length and data type should be for each field included in the file structure.

Karen Johnson was feeling very good about her new position as Director of Special Programs for the Dade County Metro Zoo, one of the most popular and exciting attractions in southern Florida. Already she had plans for week-long summer camps for elementary and junior high school students, picnic dinners under the stars, special seminars, and so on. She realized, however, that those functions would have to wait until there were sufficient funds to finance them. There had been a substantial cost overrun opening the last exhibits, and there was little money left for new programs.

Karen settled quickly into one of her primary functions, that of fund raising, and was determined to make her first project a very successful one. She knew she needed a clever basis for the appeal and was stymied for two days, until the idea of an "Adopt An Animal" campaign popped into her head during her daily five-mile run through the zoo's nature trail. She could solicit contributions on three levels: $25 to "adopt" a reptile, $50 to "adopt" a bird, and $100 to "adopt" a mammal. Adoptive "parents" would receive a personalized adoption certificate, a picture of their animal, and educational information about the zoo. Karen realized that the guest book maintained at the zoo entrance would be a wonderful source of potential donors, and she hoped that those people who had already visited the zoo would be as excited as she was about the zoo's potential.

Feeling good about her proposal, she approached Mr. Marder, the zoo's director. He gave her idea enthusiastic approval, but cautioned her about the need to maintain strict records.

Luckily, Karen had been exposed to application software as an undergraduate business major, and to dBASE III PLUS in particular. The zoo provided access to an IBM PC, and she knew that it, along with dBASE III PLUS, would be an invaluable tool in organizing and producing the information she needed to follow the progress of the fund raising campaign.

Karen had already determined that her first task would be to generate a series of form letters and associated mailing labels to use in conjunction with her appeal. She recognized the need to update her records to reflect contributions as they were received and to prepare reports reflecting the source and amount of the donations. She also wanted the system to be capable of future mailings, and hence wanted to record the date on which a donation was received. Karen took out a yellow legal pad and began to list the reports she wanted:

1. A set of personalized letters to solicit donations and a set of mailing labels to accompany these letters.
2. A set of personalized thank-you notes to individuals who contributed to the campaign and a set of mailing labels to accompany the thank-you notes; a list of people who contributed but who had not yet been sent thank-you notes.
3. A master list (in alphabetic order) of people who contributed to the campaign. Also, summary information on the total amount of money raised, the number of people who contributed, and the amount of the average contribution.

[1]Although the case study is based on the Dade County Metro Zoo in Dade County, Florida, it is in fact a simplification of programs that actually exist. Ms. Johnson and Mr. Marder are products of the authors' imagination.

Case Solution

We begin our solution by discussing the file structure in detail, the first consideration of which is to reconcile the necessary *input* with the desired *output*. You must be absolutely certain that the data entered into a system will be sufficient to provide all necessary information. Otherwise the system is almost guaranteed to fail from the beginning.

Unfortunately, the design of the file structure is often taken for granted, and consequently is done quickly and poorly. We have seen too many instances of clients requesting additional reports only to be told that extensive (and expensive) programming changes would be necessary, or worse, that the system did not contain sufficient data to provide the information they requested. Accordingly, we cannot overemphasize the need for careful design of the file structure.

Designing the File Structure

Figure 5.1 contains our suggested file structure; it may or may not correspond to what you envisioned as you read the case study. Indeed, whether or not our solution is the same as yours is not really important because there are many satisfactory answers. What is essential, however, is that the chosen structure contain all necessary data so that the required reports can be generated.

Suffice it to say that there are many acceptable solutions, and that there is no single "right" or "wrong" answer. Nevertheless, the design of the *file structure is the single-most important step in system development,* and consequently we will discuss it at length. Figure 5.1 may seem obvious upon presentation, but it does reflect the results of many decisions, all of which affect the eventual success of a system. These decisions include:

1. the fields to be included
2. the size of each field
3. the data type of each field
4. the order of the fields within a record

Consider, for example, how these questions affect the most "obvious" field, a person's name. No one will contest that a field for name is necessary, or further that the system should include an individual's first and last name, and a prefix (for example, Mr. or Ms.) for that name. It is less obvious what the size of the name field should be, and/or if that name should be one field or divided into three separate fields as was done in Figure 5.1.

What would be wrong for example, if name were treated as a single field (31 positions in all), consisting of the prefix, first name, and last name, in that order? Consider the consequences of a single field (instead of the three in the figure), in light of the following names:

Dr. Joel Stutz
Mr. Philip Glassman
Ms. Helen Rumsch

Whether you realize it or not, these names were listed in alphabetic order, and therein lies the problem. dBASE sequences a file beginning with the *leftmost position* of the key in question (in this case, name) which creates the rather unusable "alphabetic" sequence. It should be apparent, therefore, that last name requires its own field if records are to appear alphabetically.

Because separating the last name is necessary, is it also necessary for the prefix to be treated as yet another field as opposed to its being part of the first name? In this case, the answer is also yes, because the case description alludes to the need for both solicitation letters and thank-you notes. Perhaps we will eventually choose salutations in the form of "Dear Joel" as opposed to the more formal "Dr. Stutz," both of which would require the

Field	Field Name	Type	Width
1	LASTNAME	Character	16
2	FIRSTNAME	Character	12
3	PREFIX	Character	3
4	STREET	Character	24
5	CITY	Character	18
6	STATE	Character	2
7	ZIPCODE	Character	5
8	DONATION	Numeric	3
9	DONOR_DATE	Date	8
10	ADOPT	Character	1
11	THANK_YOU	Logical	1

FIGURE 5.1 Suggested file structure

prefix to be separate from the first name. This may or may not always be the case, but it costs nothing at this point to opt for the separate fields.

Consider also what other decisions were made with respect to including (or omitting) fields within Figure 5.1's file structure. We use two lines for the address (consisting of street on line one, and city, state, and zip code on line two) instead of three (omitting a line for company name). The shorter address requires less storage, and also simplifies programming for both report forms and mailing labels. It does, however, preclude a business affiliation. Two lines were chosen in this instance only after examining the potential data and finding that residential addresses appeared almost exclusively.

Regardless of whether you go with two or three line addresses, zip code must be stored as a separate field so that you can index on this field and thereby take advantage of bulk mail (which requires presorting by zip code). The length of the zip code should not, however, be automatically set to five positions in every application, as some systems may require the newer "zip + 4" designation. Five positions were deemed suitable in our system because of the preponderance of residential addresses.

The size of the first and last name fields is more arbitrary. Sixteen positions were specified for the last name, but 15 or 17 would have sufficed equally well. Does that mean that lengths of 12 or 24 positions are also acceptable? Probably not. Our experience has been that 12 is generally too small, and 24 too large. The allotted space should be large enough to contain the names in the file, but not so large as to waste space when only shorter names are present. Accordingly, we have settled on a length of 16 positions and use that in virtually all our systems.

Even with the specification of *field type*, things are not always as they seem. Zip code is designated as a character field rather than a numeric field, because dBASE processes characters more efficiently than numbers, and because arithmetic is never performed on zip code. In other words, the numeric data type is best used only with fields that will appear in calculations, rather than for all fields composed of digits. Similarly, a social security number or a phone number (when called for) should also be defined as a character field.

The case description intimated that future (or repeated) mailings might be possible; hence a *date field* (DONOR_DATE) is included within the file structure. Knowing when a donation was received will ensure that individuals who do contribute will not be solicited too often (for example, more than once a year).

The adoption field (ADOPT) illustrates the use of a one-position *code* to designate the type of animal adopted (R, B, and M for reptile, bird, and mammal, respectively) as opposed to spelling out the animal's name completely. Use of codes rather than expanded values in a file structure results in saving considerable storage space on disk, and also results in more efficient, and less error-prone, processing.

The final field in the file structure, THANK_YOU, is an example of a *logical field*, that is, a field with only two possible values, true or false. They may be entered as T, F, t, f, Y, N, y, or n). The purpose of this field in our example is to indicate whether or not a thank-you note has been sent. Although a one-position character field would appear to satisfy this requirement equally well, dBASE processes logical fields far more efficiently, and hence its use at this time.

The result of these deliberations has produced the file structure shown earlier in Figure 5.1. As you can infer from the discussion, there are no hard and fast rules for designing a file structure. The decisions made as to the fields needed, their sizes and types, must reflect the needs of the current (and future) system, and are often subjective. As you proceed through the text you will be exposed to many different applications which will help you develop the necessary experience to design your own systems.

The Mail-Merge Operation

A *mail-merge* operation combines an "empty" *form letter* with a file of names and addresses to produce a series of personalized letters. In essence, it creates the "same letter" many times by merging the form letter with the set of names and addresses, changing only the personalized information from letter to letter. The process is depicted in Figure 5.2. It contains a *form letter* (Figure 5.2a), a file of names and addresses (Figure 5.2b), and the individual letters created as a result of the mail-merge operation (Figure 5.2c).

Realize, however, that data within a dBASE DBF file cannot be directly read by a word processor but must first go through a conversion process. The file of names and addresses in Figure 5.2b is *not* a DBF file per se, but an ASCII file created from a DBF file by using the dBASE COPY command as discussed later in the chapter.

The illustration in Figure 5.2 is for WordStar and its associated mail-merge program, but the concepts are applicable to any word processor. The *dot commands* embedded within the form letter of Figure 5.2a relate to the mail-merge operation and/or page-formatting instructions. The first such command, .OP, omits the page numbers and is necessary to suppress the automatic page-numbering feature of the word processing program (it makes no sense for the second person to see page number 2 on the bottom of his or her letter). The .PA command, appearing at the bottom of the letter, produces a page break and causes each subsequent letter to begin on the top of a new page.

The remaining dot commands pertain to the mail-merge operation itself. The .DF command specifies the name of the file, APPEAL.TXT in this example, containing the names and addresses to be used in the mail-merge operation. (The APPEAL.TXT file itself is an ASCII file created from the original DBF file using the dBASE COPY command.) The .RV command lists the field (variable) names in the order in which they appear in APPEAL.TXT.

The fields in the data file of Figure 5.2b (APPEAL.TXT) are separated by commas as is required by the WordStar mail-merge program. Note the correspondence between the data in Figure 5.2b and the variable definition statement (the .RV command line) in Figure 5.2a that is, the numerical position of the field name in the .RV statement matches exactly the numerical position of the corresponding element in the data file.

The ampersands appearing at the beginning and end of several words in the form letter are WordStar's way of indicating that a value is to be taken from a data file and substituted in its place. When WordStar encounters a variable name (that is, a field beginning and ending with an ampersand), it obtains the value for that variable from the data file, reading in the data element from the file that is in a corresponding position to that of the field name in the .RV statement. WordStar proceeds record by record, using one record for each form letter. Thus, the letters are prepared one at a time, with each letter containing a different name and address.

Mailing Labels

Completing the form letters solves only part of the problem, as *mailing labels* are required to address the envelopes that will contain the letters. dBASE is truly at its best in this regard for its mailing label facility is both fast and easy to use.

Figure 5.3 contains a set of "two up" mailing labels (the labels are printed in two columns per page) for use in conjunction with the form letters in Figure 5.2. The labels were produced in *zip code* sequence (to take advantage of bulk mail rates) and match the sequence in which the form letters were produced.

Mailing labels are generated in much the same way as reports were in Chapter 4. A *label form* (analogous to a report form) contains the characteristics of the mailing labels (for example, the number of lines per label, the number of labels across a page, the fields within a label, and so on), but no actual data. A set of mailing labels is produced by merging a DBF file (sequenced according to the desired master index) with the designated label form as shown in Figure 5.4.

The label form itself is created via a menu-driven process that functions similarly to the report generator. It is initiated with the command CREATE LABEL, and creates a permanent label form with an extension LBL. The label form can, if necessary, be subse-

```
.OP
.DF appeal.txt
.RV prefix,firstname,lastname,address,city,state,zipcode
                                        November 24, 1988
&prefix& &firstname& &lastname&
&address&
&city&, &state&    &zipcode&

Dear &firstname&,

We invite you to join our family and become a "zoo parent" for
as little as $25 in the Adopt-an-Animal Program.

It's so easy...No diapers, no schools, just the warm feeling of
sharing and the pride of your "wild child".  When you become a
parent you provide for the animal's food and care.  Most
importantly, you will have the satisfaction of knowing that you
are helping to support the growing animal collection at Metrozoo.

You receive a personalized adoption certificate, a picture of
your animal, and educational information about the zoo.  You
adopt for one year.  The option to renew is yours.

Additional information about our zoo and the Adopt-an-Animal
program is enclosed.  Thank you for your consideration.

                        Sincerely,

.PA
```

a

```
"Mr.","Eric","Manin","2362 NW 122 Drive","Coral Springs","FL","33065"
"Ms.","Sarah","Moldof","2606 Nassau Bend","Coconut Creek","FL","33066"
"Ms.","Helen","Rumsch","2801 Victoria Way","Coconut Creek","FL","33066"
"Mr.","Chris","Anderson","8137 NW 2nd Court","Coral Springs","FL","33071"
"Ms.","Jessica","Grauer","2133 NW 102 Terrace","Coral Springs","FL","33071"
"Mr.","Eric","Kenoyer","729 NW 82 Avenue","Coral Springs","FL","33071"
"Mr.","Adam","Moldof","297 NW 104 Avenue","Coral Springs","FL","33071"
"Ms.","Linda","Neider","18240 SW 78 Place","Coral Springs","FL","33071"
"Mr.","Frank","Barber","13601 79 Avenue","Miami","FL","33176"
"Dr.","Joel","Stutz","12738 SW 69 Terrace","Miami","FL","33183"
"Mr.","Philip","Glassman","1254 SW 66 Terrace","Plantation","FL","33317"
"Ms.","Stella","Palumbo","6190 Woodlands Blvd.","Tamarac","FL","33319"
"Ms.","Lorraine","William","5104 White Oak Lane","Tamarac","FL","33319"
"Ms.","Joan","Milgrom","261 NE 8 Street","Ft. Lauderdale","FL","33334"
"Ms.","Tobi","Cohen","7110 High Sierra Circle","West Palm Beach","FL","33411"
"Mr.","Jack","Hill","Century Village","Deerfield Beach","FL","33441"
```

b

```
                                        November 24, 1988
Ms. Helen Rumsch
2801 Victorian Way
Coconut Creek, FL     33066

Dear Helen,
```

```
                                        November 24, 1988
Ms. Sarah Moldof
2606 Nassau Bend
Coconut Creek, FL     33066

Dear Sarah,
```

```
                        November 24, 1988
Mr. Eric Manin
2362 NW 122 Drive
Coral Springs, FL     33065

Dear Eric,

We invite you to join our family and become a "zoo parent" for
as little as $25 in the Adopt-an-Animal Program.

It's so easy...No diapers, no schools, just the warm feeling of
sharing and the pride of your "wild child".  When you become a
parent you provide for the animal's food and care.  Most
importantly, you will have the satisfaction of knowing that you
are helping to support the growing animal collection at Metrozoo.

You receive a personalized adoption certificate, a picture of
your animal, and educational information about the zoo.  You
adopt for one year.  The option to renew is yours.

Additional information about our zoo and the Adopt-an-Animal
program is enclosed.  Thank you for your consideration.

                        Sincerely,
```

c

FIGURE 5.2 Mail-merge operation: (a) the form letter; (b) dBASE generated file of names and addresses; (c) merged letters

FIGURE 5.3 Two up mailing labels

quently modified with a MODIFY LABEL command. After the label form has been created the LABEL FORM command generates the actual labels, just as reports were generated through the REPORT FORM command. Consider:

Syntax:
```
LABEL FORM label-file-name [scope][SAMPLE][TO PRINT]
        [FOR/WHILE condition][TO FILE filename]
```

Examples:
```
LABEL FORM APPEAL
LABEL FORM APPEAL SAMPLE TO PRINT
LABEL FORM APPEAL FOR DONATION > 0
LABEL FORM APPEAL FOR ZIPCODE = '33065'
```

Many of the options in the LABEL FORM command have been covered earlier in conjunction with the REPORT FORM and other commands. For example, output can be directed to either the printer or a file. The SAMPLE option is quite helpful as it allows a sample label to be printed, enabling you to check spacing before printing the actual labels.

It is also possible to produce subsets of mailing labels from a given DBF file; for example, labels for individuals who have contributed, labels for individuals living in a certain zip code, and so on. Selecting which records to include is done by including the FOR parameter in the label generation process (for example, LABEL FORM . . . FOR DONATION > 0).

Required dBASE Commands

The production of form letters and mailing labels requires knowledge of two more dBASE commands. The TRIM command eliminates trailing blanks after various fields; the COPY command converts data within a dBASE DBF file to a form understandable by a word processor. Both commands are explained in detail.

TRIM

The appearance of the addresses within the mailing labels is unremarkable because they appear exactly as we would like them to. There is, for example, no inordinate amount of

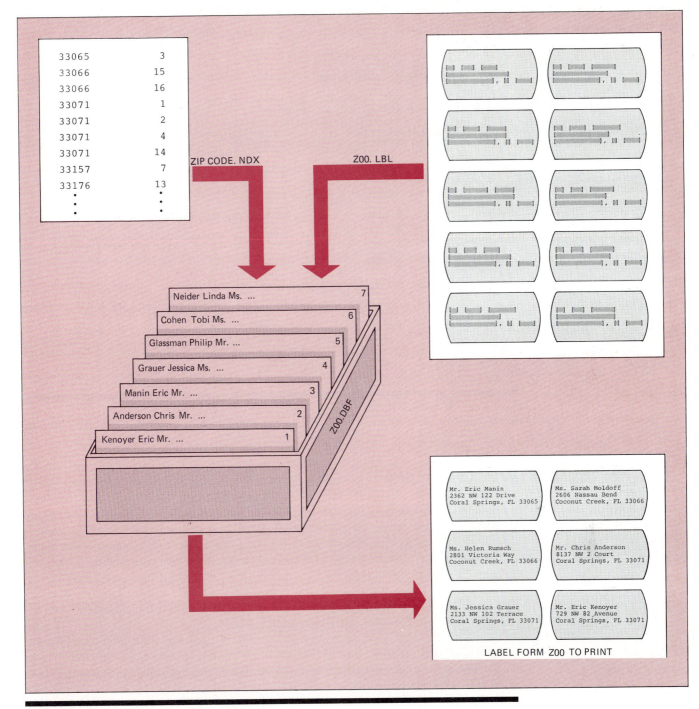

FIGURE 5.4 Creation of mailing labels

space between the first and last name, nor between the city and state. In addition, a comma appears between the city and state, for example, "Coral Springs, Florida," which is as it should be. We make these observations, only because the nicely appearing addresses require additional dBASE statements.

It is important to recognize the significance of *fixed-length* fields as they are defined in a file structure. First name, for example, is defined as a 12-position character field. This means it requires 12 positions for output whenever it appears in a LIST, or DISPLAY statement, regardless of the length of the first name itself. In other words, if first name and last name were to appear together in a DISPLAY statement for Chris Anderson, for example

Example 1: Mailing label as it would appear with no trim function

    Mr. Chris   Anderson
    8137 NW 2nd Court
    Coral Springs   FL 33071

Example 2: Automatic trim as implemented by dBASE mailing label

    Mr. Chris Anderson   prefix,lastname,firstname
    8137 NW 2nd Court   street
    Coral Springs FL 33071   city,state,zipcode

                                    Commas separate fields in mailing label

Example 3: Insertion of a comma

    Mr. Chris Anderson   prefix,lastname,firstname
    8137 NW 2nd Court   street
    Coral Springs   ,FL   33071   city+","+state+"   "+zipcode

                                    Plus signs indicate concatenation

Example 4: Use of TRIM function

    Mr. Chris Anderson   prefix,lastname,firstname
    8137 NW 2nd Court   street
    Coral Springs, FL   33071   TRIM(city)+", "+state+"   "+zipcode

                                    TRIM function is introduced

FIGURE 5.5 The TRIM function

DISPLAY FIRSTNAME,LASTNAME,DONATION the output would appear as "Chris Anderson   " followed by the amount of the donation. Twelve positions are used to display the first name; five for Chris, followed by seven trailing blanks. Similarly, 16 positions are used for the last name, eight for Anderson, and eight for the trailing blanks.

Fortunately, dBASE provides a TRIM function to eliminate trailing blanks, for example, DISPLAY TRIM(FIRSTNAME)+LASTNAME. In addition, the mailing label facility itself includes an automatic trim function as well. Figure 5.5 illustrates these capabilities.

Example 1 shows a mailing label as it would appear with no trim function in effect. Extra spaces exist between the first and last name fields as was explained, and between the city (defined as an 18-position character field) and state.

Example 2 depicts the same mailing label as it is created using the *default* trim function of the mailing label facility. Any field followed by a comma (for example, city and state in the last line of the address) is automatically stripped of its trailing blanks, with a single blank inserted between adjacent fields.

Although the label in Example 2 looks reasonable, its look could be improved by inserting a comma between the city and state, and by spaces between the state and zip code. Example 3 shows the first attempt at this enhancement and uses plus signs to *concatenate* (join together) the city, state, and zip code fields with both a comma and additional spaces. As you can see, however, concatenation removes the implied trim function which had previously removed the trailing blanks after city.

Example 4 completely resolves this problem. It uses the TRIM function in combination with concatenation to produce the last line of the address. The entry, TRIM(city), prints only the nonblank characters within the city field (that is "Coral Springs" as opposed to "Coral Springs   ") and is then concatenated with the comma, the state and the additional spaces.

As indicated, data within a DBF file cannot be read directly by a word processor. The dBASE `COPY` command, however, can be used to copy all (or part of) a DBF file to a second file in a form suitable for use with a mail-merge operation. Consider:

Syntax: (abbreviated)
```
COPY TO new file [FIELDS field list][FOR condition]
[DELIMITED]
```

Example 1:
```
USE ZOO
COPY TO APPEAL DELIMITED
```

Example 2:
```
USE ZOO INDEX ZIPCODE
COPY TO APPEAL2 FIELDS      —Entered as one line
     PREFIX,FIRSTNAME,LASTNAME,STREET,CITY,STATE,ZIPCODE
     DELIMITED
```

Example 3:
```
USE ZOO INDEX ZIPCODE
COPY TO DONOR FIELDS      —Entered as one line
     PREFIX,FIRSTNAME,LASTNAME,STREET,CITY,STATE,ZIPCODE
     DELIMITED FOR DONATION > 0 .AND. .NOT. THANK_YOU
```

Example 1 copies every field in every record within the ZOO.DBF file to a new file, APPEAL.TXT (TXT is automatically assigned as the file extension when the DELIMITED option is used). Specifying the `DELIMITED` parameter also encloses the character fields in the new file within quotation marks and separates the fields with commas (a requirement of WordStar and many other mail-merge programs).

Example 2 copies only the specified fields to the new file, (APPEAL2.TXT), while still copying every record in the original ZOO.DBF file. Note, too, that the DBF file was opened with a zip code index, so that the TXT file has its records in zip code order. By contrast, the records in the first example's TXT file (where no index was active) are in the same order as the DBF file itself.

Finally, Example 3 copies only the designated fields for a limited number of records, that is, only those people who contributed (`DONATION > 0`), but who have not yet been thanked (`.NOT.THANK_YOU`). The records in this file will also be in zip code order.

Hands-on Exercise 5–1 implements the mail-merge operation and illustrates the mailing label facility.

Hands-on Exercise 5–1:   Mailing Labels

Objective: To use the `COPY` command to produce a file of names and addresses for subsequent use in a mail-merge operation; use the mailing label facility to create a set of mailing labels.

☐   STEP 1: Log onto the ZOO subdirectory.
Place the convenience disk in drive B:, log onto the ZOO directory, then load dBASE with the proper procedure for your configuration.

```
CD B:\ZOO ——————— With a floppy disk system
CD C:\SAMPLER\ZOO ——— With a hard disk drive
PATH C:\SAMPLER
```

☐ **STEP 2: Open the file structure.**

Execute the following commands from the dot prompt to open the existing DBF file, create a zip code index, and display the file structure.

```
. USE ZOO
. INDEX ON ZIPCODE TO ZIPCODE
. DISPLAY STRUCTURE
```

The zip code index is necessary so that both the file containing the names and addresses, and the mailing labels themselves, are produced in zip code order.

☐ **STEP 3: Create the file of names and addresses.**

Enter the **COPY** command shown below (the command is entered on one line) to produce the file of names and addresses (APPEAL.TXT) for use in the eventual mail-merge operation. Recall that the **DELIMITED** option inserts commas between fields as required by most word processors.

— Command is entered on one line

```
COPY TO APPEAL FIELDS
PREFIX,FIRSTNAME,LASTNAME,STREET,CITY,STATE,ZIPCODE
DELIMITED
```

☐ **STEP 4: Enter the mailing label facility.**

The procedure to build a label form parallels that for generating a report form, as described in Chapter 4. The command **CREATE LABEL** initiates the mailing label facility, after which dBASE prompts for the label file name.

```
. CREATE LABEL
Enter label file name: ZOO
```

dBASE next supplies a series of screens that guide you through the process of building the label form, the first of which is shown in Figure 5.6.

Figure 5.6 contains a *menu bar* across the top of the screen with three possible choices: Options, Contents, and Exit. The *left and right arrow keys* are used to move from option to option, with the up and down arrow keys used to select choices within an option.

Use the appropriate keys to highlight Predefined size, under Options, noting how the initial labels are 3½ inches wide by $^{15}/_{16}$ inches long, and 1 column per page. Now, press the Return key repeatedly, observing how the predefined label size changes (3½ × $^{15}/_{16}$ × 2, then 3½ × $^{15}/_{16}$ × 3, and so on until the choices repeat. When the desired label size (3½ × $^{15}/_{16}$ × 2) appears again, proceed to Step 5.

☐ **STEP 5: Complete the label form.**

Use the left and right-arrow keys to highlight the Contents option, whereupon a screen resembling Figure 5.7 comes into view. The contents of each line is specified by indicating the appropriate field names from the original file structure. Multiple fields entered on the same line of the label (for example, prefix, firstname, lastname) are separated by commas, causing a space to be inserted between the fields when they are printed. The **TRIM** function and the

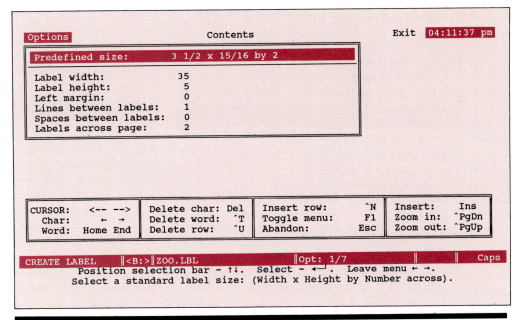

FIGURE 5.6 Initial screen in label generation

plus signs for concatenation can be used to provide more customized spacing between fields.

The label in Figure 5.7 provides a maximum of five lines of which only three are used. In completing the label you must, however, press the Return key after every line, including lines 4 and 5. Note too, that the left-hand side of the figure contains a box with the field names as they were defined in the file structure (brought up by pressing the F10 function key). This is extremely convenient as it enables the field names to be entered automatically (by using the up and down arrow keys to highlight the appropriate field and then press-

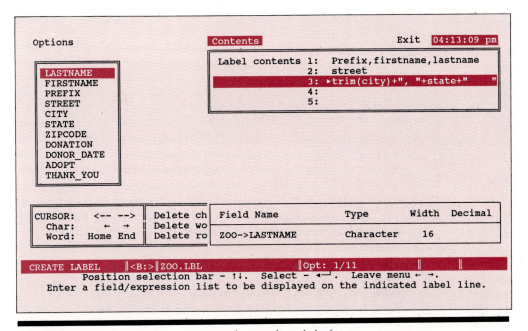

FIGURE 5.7 Entering the contents of a mailing label

ing the Return key). It also guarantees that the field names will be entered correctly.

☐   **STEP 6: Save the label form.**
When you have finished entering the contents of the mailing label, use the left and right arrow keys to select the Exit option from the menu bar. Use the up and down arrow keys to highlight the Save option and press the Return key.

☐   **STEP 7: Generate the labels.**
The actual printing of the mailing labels takes place when the label form is merged with the DBF file via a `LABEL FORM` command. Accordingly:

- `USE ZOO`
- `SET INDEX TO ZIPCODE`
- `LABEL FORM ZOO`

Repeating the `USE` and `SET INDEX` commands is not necessary, but is shown to emphasize that labels are generated from the ZOO file in zip code sequence. The `LABEL FORM` command merges the label form just created, with the DBF file (in zip code sequence). (The process is analogous to producing a report from a report form.)

If you are in any way unsatisfied with the labels (for example you want the labels printed one rather than two across), you can change the existing label form with the `MODIFY LABEL` command. Enter the label facility, make any desired changes, and resave the label form.

You might also try generating labels for only a subset of records within the DBF file; for example, only for those individuals who have contributed. The latter is accomplished by including the FOR parameter within the label command, for example `LABEL FORM ZOO FOR DONATION > 0.`

☐   **STEP 8: Exit dBASE.**
Type `QUIT` to exit dBASE.

Beyond Mailing Labels

Creating form letters and the associated mailing labels from a given DBF file in no way, shape, or form precludes using that file for other purposes. The initial case solution stressed the design of the file structure and the importance of including additional fields (beyond the name and address), so that the system could produce the desired reports.

In particular, the case presentation indicated a requirement to know the total amount of money raised, the average contribution, the number of people who contributed, the names of those contributing, and so on. There is also an implied requirement to maintain the system, that is, to add records as the mailing list expands, update existing records to reflect contributions received, and delete records no longer current.

The commands needed to meet these requirements have nothing to do with mailing labels per se, and have, in fact, been presented in previous chapters. Nevertheless, the current case gives you an excellent opportunity for review, and so, Hands-on Exercise 5–2 includes the `LIST`, `SUM`, `AVERAGE`, `COUNT`, and `SET INDEX` commands covered earlier. We will also present two new commands, `SET` and `CLEAR FIELDS`, used to improve the appearance of displayed output.

SET FIELDS

The LIST and/or DISPLAY commands normally show *every* field in each record they display. While this is not a problem in records with a limited (in size) file structure, it is a problem in larger structures because the fields from one record "wrap around" from one line to the next, making the output difficult to read.

The SET FIELDS command acts as a filter and limits the fields as the result of subsequent commands to only those specified in the field list. Consider:

Syntax:
SET FIELDS TO [field list]

Example:
SET FIELDS TO LASTNAME,DONATION

In this example, only the last name and donation fields will appear as the result of a subsequently issued DISPLAY or LIST command. Note, too, that once a SET FIELDS command has been issued it remains in effect throughout a session until turned off by the CLEAR FIELDS command.

Hands-on Exercise 5–2: Beyond Mailing Labels

Objective: To review commands from earlier chapters associated with reporting requirements (LIST, SUM, AVERAGE, and COUNT); demonstrate the SET and CLEAR FIELDS commands; explore the use of the up and down arrow keys from the dot prompt.

☐ STEP 1: Open the ZOO.DBF file.
Place the convenience disk in drive B:, load dBASE, and open the ZOO.DBF file as in the first exercise. Create a second index on LASTNAME as indicated:

```
. USE ZOO
. INDEX ON LASTNAME TO LASTNAME
```

☐ STEP 2: Demonstrate the SET FIELDS command.
Enter the following commands to show the effect of the SET FIELDS command:

LIST OFF ——— *All fields will be shown*
SET FIELDS TO LASTNAME,FIRSTNAME,DONATION,DONOR_DATE,THANK_YOU
LIST OFF ——— *Only fields specified in the SET FIELDS command will be shown*

The output produced by the first LIST command (OFF is included to suppress the record numbers) is difficult to read because the fields *wrap around* the screen. This is because LIST, with no additional parameters, shows *every field* for every record.

Because this exercise is not concerned with the fields that produce the address, the SET FIELDS command can be used to suppress their appearance. The second LIST command produces the output of Figure 5.8, which is the basis for the rest of the exercise and contains the ZOO.DBF file as it currently exists on your convenience disk. The records are displayed alphabetically by last name (since LASTNAME was made the active index in Step 1).

```
      LASTNAME          FIRSTNAME       DONATION DONOR_DATE THANK_YOU
      Anderson          Chris               100 11/13/88    .F.
      Barber            Frank                   /   /       .F.
      Cohen             Tobi                    /   /       .F.
      Glassman          Philip                  /   /       .F.
      Grauer            Jessica              50 10/16/88    .T.
      Hill              Jack                 25 10/16/88    .T.
      Kenoyer           Eric                 50 11/08/88    .T.
      Manin             Eric                 25 11/30/88    .F.
      Milgrom           Joan                    /   /       .F.
      Moldof            Adam                 50 11/14/88    .F.
      Moldof            Sarah                   /   /       .F.
      Neider            Linda                   /   /       .F.
      Palumbo           Stella               25 10/28/88    .T.
      Rumsch            Helen                50 10/19/88    .T.
      Stutz             Joel                100 10/14/88    .T.
      William           Lorraine                /   /       .F.
```

FIGURE 5.8 Illustrative zoo donor file (ZOO.DBF)

```
                              ─── Total value of all donations

 . SUM DONATION
      16 records summed
 DONATION
      475

                              ─── Average donation (includes zero values)

 . AVERAGE DONATION
      16 records averaged
 DONATION
      30

                              ─── Average donation (includes only non-zero values)

 . AVERAGE DONATION FOR DONATION > 0
      9 records averaged
 DONATION
      53

                              ─── Names of contributing individuals
                                  (Displayed fields are controlled by SET FIELDS command)

 . LIST FOR DONATION > 0 OFF

 LASTNAME          FIRSTNAME       DONATION DONOR_DATE THANK_YOU
 Anderson          Chris               100 11/13/88    .F.
 Grauer            Jessica              50 10/16/88    .T.
 Hill              Jack                 25 10/16/88    .T.
 Kenoyer           Eric                 50 11/08/88    .T.
 Manin             Eric                 25 11/30/88    .F.
 Moldof            Adam                 50 11/14/88    .F.
 Palumbo           Stella               25 10/28/88    .T.
 Rumsch            Helen                50 10/19/88    .T.
 Stutz             Joel                100 10/14/88    .T.

                              ─── Names of individuals who contributed but not yet acknowledged

 . LIST FOR DONATION > 0 .AND. .NOT. THANK_YOU OFF
 LASTNAME          FIRSTNAME       DONATION DONOR_DATE THANK_YOU
 Anderson          Chris               100 11/13/88    .F.
 Manin             Eric                 25 11/30/88    .F.
 Moldof            Adam                 50 11/14/88    .F.

                              ─── Number of individuals who contributed but not yet acknowledged

 . COUNT FOR DONATION > 0 .AND. .NOT. THANK_YOU
      3 records
```

FIGURE 5.9 Reporting requirements

☐ STEP 3: Generate the required reports.

Figure 5.9 contains various combinations of the LIST, SUM, AVERAGE, and COUNT commands being used to extract some of the required information. (Report forms could also have been created to produce the equivalent information.) The commands in the figure are a review of material covered earlier in Chapter 2 and should not pose any difficulty.

Do note, however, the difference between the two AVERAGE commands. The first computes the average donation for *all* 16 records in the file, whereas the second includes only those individuals making a contribution (their names are displayed in the subsequent LIST command).

☐ STEP 4: Use the up and down arrow keys.

dBASE maintains a command buffer that stores the last 20 commands entered from the dot prompt. You can bring any of these commands back to the dot prompt in order to edit and/or reissue the command (and thus avoid retyping the command) by pressing the up arrow key the appropriate number of times. Pressing the up arrow key once retrieves the previous command, pressing it again retrieves the second previous command, and so on.

Assume, for example, that you are at the dot prompt *after* the last command (COUNT) in Figure 5.9 has been executed. Press the up arrow key to retrieve the COUNT command, then press it a second time to retrieve the LIST command. Now press the Return key to reexecute the LIST command just retrieved.

The down arrow key works in reverse as it displays the next command in the buffer (after a previous command has been retrieved). Experiment with the *up and down arrow* keys until you are comfortable with their function.

☐ STEP 5: Reset the displayed fields.

Enter both the CLEAR and SET FIELDS commands shown in Figure 5.10. The CLEAR FIELDS negates the effects of the SET FIELDS command issued in Step 2, after which the subsequent SET FIELDS command defines a new set of fields. Now list the first four records in the ZOO.DBF file, in both alphabetic and zip code sequence, according to the SET INDEX and LIST commands in Figure 5.10.

☐ STEP 6: Exit dBASE.

Type QUIT to exit dBASE and return to DOS.

Summary

The chapter introduced the dBASE mailing label facility and showed how it can be used in conjunction with a word processor to generate both form letters and the associated mailing labels. All necessary dBASE commands were covered including COPY, TRIM, CREATE and MODIFY LABEL, and LABEL FORM. The parallel nature of *label* and *report forms* was also stressed.

The importance of properly *designing the file structure* was emphasized as was the need to reconcile reporting requirements with available input. The chapter also reviewed the LIST, SUM, AVERAGE, and COUNT commands, introduced the SET and CLEAR FIELDS commands, and discussed the use of the up and down arrow keys from the dot prompt.

```
                                    Cancels the previous SET FIELDS command
  . CLEAR FIELDS
                                    Indicates new list of fields to be listed
  . SET FIELDS TO LASTNAME,STREET,CITY,STATE,ZIPCODE


  . SET INDEX TO LASTNAME
  . LIST OFF NEXT 4

LASTNAME          STREET                  CITY              STATE ZIPCODE
Anderson          8137 NW 2nd Court       Coral Springs     FL    33071
Barber            13601 79 Avenue         Miami             FL    33176
Cohen             7110 High Sierra Circle West Palm Beach   FL    33411
Glassman          1254 SW 66 Terrace      Plantation        FL    33317

                                  Zipcode is made the active index
  . SET INDEX TO ZIPCODE
  . LIST OFF NEXT 4

LASTNAME          STREET                  CITY              STATE ZIPCODE
Manin             2362 NW 122 Drive       Coral Springs     FL    33065
Moldof            2606 Nassau Bend        Coconut Creek     FL    33066
Rumsch            2801 Victoria Way       Coconut Creek     FL    33066
Anderson          8137 NW 2nd Court       Coral Springs     FL    33071
```

FIGURE 5.10 The `CLEAR FIELDS`, `SET FIELDS`, and `SET INDEX` commands

Key Words and Concepts

Character field
CLEAR FIELDS
COPY
CREATE LABEL
Data type
Date field
DELIMITED
Down arrow key
Fixed length field
Form letter
LABEL FORM
Logical field
Mail-merge

Mailing label
Menu bar
MODIFY LABEL
Numeric field
PgDn key
PgUp key
SET FIELDS TO
SET INDEX TO
Trailing blanks
TRIM function
Two-up labels
Up arrow key
Word processor

True/False

1. A logical field always has a field length of 1.
2. Last name, first name, and middle initial should generally be defined as separate fields as opposed to being grouped together.
3. Zip code is usually defined as a separate field, as opposed to including it in a larger address field.
4. Zip code contains only numbers, and hence should be defined as a numeric field.
5. A two-line address will suffice in all applications.

6. Report forms and label forms are created with essentially the same procedure(s).
7. A file created by the dDBASE COPY command cannot be input directly to a word processor.
8. WordStar is the *only* word processor capable of a mail-merge operation.
9. Pressing the down arrow key will retrieve the last command issued from the dot prompt.
10. The SET FIELDS command can be used in conjunction with either the DISPLAY or LIST commands.

Exercises

1. Distinguish between:
   a. a mailing label and mail-merge operation
   b. a character field and a logical field
   c. a COPY statement, with and without the DELIMITED option
   d. AVERAGE DONATION and AVERAGE DONATION FOR DONATION > 0
   e. the file extensions LBL and FRM
   f. pressing the up and down arrow keys at the dot prompt
   g. use of the left and right arrow keys versus the up and down arrow keys when creating a label form
   h. field length and field type

2. As indicated in the chapter, careful attention must be given to designing the file structure, or else the resulting system will not perform as desired. Consider the following:
   a. An individual's age may be calculated from his or her birth date which in turn can be stored as a field within a record. An alternative technique would be to store age directly in the record and thereby avoid the calculation. Which field, that is, age or birth date, would you use? Why?
   b. Social security number is typically chosen as a record key in lieu of a person's name. What attribute does the social security number possess which often makes it the superior choice?

3. The following *erroneous* set of commands is intended to create a file of names and addresses (THANKYOU.TXT) which can be subsequently input into a word processor's mail-merge facility. In addition, the commands are to create a series of mailing labels for envelopes to address the thank-you notes. (Only people who have contributed but have not yet been thanked are to receive a thank-you note.)

```
. USE ZOO                    — Command entered on one line
. COPY TO THANKYOU FIELDS
      PREFIX,FIRSTNAME,CITY,STATE,ZIPCODE
      FOR THANKYOU .AND. DONATION > 0 DELIMITED
. CREATE LABEL THANKYOU
```

   (Instructions to create mailing labels for thank-you notes go here)

```
. SET INDEX TO ZIPCODE
. LABEL FORM THANKYOU
```

   Identify the various errors in the command sequence. In so doing, it will be helpful to determine: (a) for which records (and in what sequence) is the set of names and addresses being prepared; (b) are all necessary fields included; and (c) for which records (and in what sequence) are the mailing labels being prepared?

4. Indicate exactly how each of the following would appear as the result of a DISPLAY command. Answer for Chris Anderson.

```
a. TRIM(Lastname)+", "+TRIM(Firstname)+" "+Prefix
b. TRIM(Lastname)+", "+Prefix+TRIM(Firstname)
c. Prefix+TRIM(Firstname)+TRIM(Lastname)
d. Prefix+Firstname+Lastname
e. Prefix+" "+TRIM(Firstname)+" "+TRIM(Lastname)
```

5. The error messages dBASE displays are often difficult to understand, as typified by the following command and the associated error message:

```
. LABEL FORM THANKYOU          —— Error message returned by dBASE
Syntax error in contents expression.
```

dBASE is indicating that something is wrong with the label form THANKYOU.LBL, but provides no additional help. Your only recourse is to modify the label form (with the command MODIFY LABEL THANKYOU), examine the contents of the various fields, and try to determine the cause of the error. Accordingly, consider Figure 5.11 and indicate the necessary modification(s) to the appropriate fields. (Hint: Refer to the file structure in Figure 5.1.)

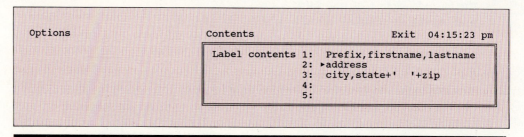

FIGURE 5.11 Erroneous label form

After reading this chapter, you should be able to:

- Use the FIND, LOCATE, and CONTINUE commands to move to individual records within a DBF file; describe the differences among these commands.

- Explain why a DISPLAY or EDIT command is often used in conjunction with a FIND, LOCATE, or CONTINUE command.

- Use the SET FILTER TO command to establish a filter condition; explain how the existence of a filter condition affects a DBF file.

- Differentiate between the SET FIELDS and SET FILTER commands; explain how to negate the effects of both commands.

- Describe the relational and logical operators that may be present in a dBASE condition.

- Describe the use of the date conversion function DTOC( ).

- Create a dBASE query file.

6

Query Files and Related Topics

Overview

Implicit in the Metro Zoo case study in Chapter 5 is the requirement to update the existing DBF file to reflect incoming donations as well as other changes to the data. There may also be a need to select groups of records for other mailings, for example, a thank-you note to acknowledge those individuals who made a donation, a limited mailing to people living in specific zip codes near the zoo, a future mailing to solicit additional contributions from previous donors, and so on.

All of these requirements are addressed with new commands covered in this chapter. We begin by presenting the FIND, LOCATE, and CONTINUE commands to identify individual records for editing, then continue with the SET FILTER command to isolate a group of records within the file that meet a specified *condition*. This, in turn, leads to a discussion of how to build dBASE conditions and how to use *relational* and *logical* operators. The use of date conversion functions in a condition is also covered.

The final topic is the development of *query* files, a specialized dBASE file that permanently stores a filter condition, thereby enabling it to be retrieved later. We take you through the process of building a query file in detail, showing how it parallels the development of report forms and mailing label forms.

Metro Zoo Revisited

Figure 6.1 contains the ZOO.DBF file as it exists on the convenience disk at the end of Chapter 5. (A SET FIELDS command is in effect to limit the fields displayed on the screen to those most pertinent to the current discussion.) The figure reflects the file as it might appear some time after the initial mailing; contributions have been recorded and thank-you notes have been sent to some, but not all of the people who contributed.

Let us assume that additional events have transpired and that the file in Figure 6.1 has to be updated to reflect the following:

1. New contributions have been received from Joan Milgrom and Tobi Cohen for $100 and $50, respectively. Both donations were received on 12/01/88. Their records should be updated accordingly.
2. The envelope addressed to Sarah Moldof has come back from the post office with an indication that she has moved with no known forwarding address. Her record should be deleted.
3. Thank-you notes are to be sent to all individuals who have contributed but who have not yet been thanked, after which the file should be updated to reflect the thank-you notes.

LASTNAME	FIRSTNAME	DONATION	DONOR_DATE	THANK_YOU
Anderson	Chris	100	11/13/88	.F.
Barber	Frank		/ /	.F.
Cohen	Tobi		/ /	.F.
Glassman	Philip		/ /	.F.
Grauer	Jessica	50	10/16/88	.T.
Hill	Jack	25	10/16/88	.T.
Kenoyer	Eric	50	11/08/88	.T.
Manin	Eric	25	11/30/88	.F.
Milgrom	Joan		/ /	.F.
Moldof	Adam	50	11/14/88	.F.
Moldof	Sarah		/ /	.F.
Neider	Linda		/ /	.F.
Palumbo	Stella	25	10/28/88	.T.
Rumsch	Helen	50	10/19/88	.T.
Stutz	Joel	100	10/14/88	.T.
William	Lorraine		/ /	.F.

FIGURE 6.1 Illustrative zoo donor file (ZOO.DBF) (reproduced from Figure 5.8)

Required dBASE Commands

To accomplish these operations we need to identify individual records within the DBF file (for example, Cohen Milgrom, and Moldof) so that the records can be updated. We must also be able to isolate the group of people who are to receive thank-you notes.

The FIND, LOCATE, and CONTINUE commands focus on individual records whereas the SET FILTER command pinpoints a group of records. Each command is discussed in detail.

FIND

The FIND command is the fastest way to locate individual records in a database (DBF) file. Use of the command *requires the DBF file to have been opened with an index* as it attempts to match a specified character string to the value of the key field. Consider:

Syntax:
```
FIND character-string
```

Example:
```
SET INDEX TO LASTNAME ——— FIND requires an active index
FIND Moldof
```

A successful find operation positions the record pointer at the *first* record containing a value of the index key that matches the character string. The command positions the record pointer but does not display the record; thus the latter operation requires a separate DISPLAY or EDIT command.

The command FIND Moldof, will always position the record pointer at the *same* record, that is, at the first Moldof in the file. To find the next Moldof (if one exists) you must issue a SKIP command to move the record pointer to the second Moldof, another SKIP to go to the next Moldof, and so on until the condition is no longer satisfied or until the end-of-file is reached. Note that the SKIP command merely moves the record pointer to the next record in indexed order, which will be the second Moldof, if there is one.

Note, too, there is a difference between the commands FIND Moldof and FIND MOLDOF in that dBASE distinguishes between upper and lower case (MOLDOF will not be found in the existing ZOO.DBF file). In other words, the value of the character string in a

FIND command must exactly match the value in the DBF file. Failure to find the specified character string, for example MOLDOF, causes a "No find" message to be displayed. Quotation marks are not required around the character string unless it is to be entered with leading blanks, that is, "   Moldof" is different than "Moldof".

The nuances associated with finding or not finding records underscore the importance of proper data entry. In other words, inadvertently entering uppercase letters where lowercase letters were intended, misspelling a name, including extra blanks where they don't belong, and so on, will invariably cause problems in the system's operation.

LOCATE

The LOCATE command is also used to find specific records in a database file, but unlike the FIND command, it does *not* require an index. The lack of an index, as we shall see, offers both advantages and disadvantages. Consider:

Syntax:
LOCATE FOR condition

Example:
LOCATE FOR lastname = 'Moldof'

A successful locate operation moves the record pointer to the *first* record matching the specified condition. As with the FIND command LOCATE positions the record pointer but does not display the record. LOCATE also differentiates between upper- and lowercase letters.

Another similarity between the two commands is that LOCATE always returns the first record meeting the specified condition. Accordingly, it is often followed by a CONTINUE command which moves the record pointer to the next record meeting the condition (just as FIND is followed by SKIP). Repeated execution of a CONTINUE command will step through the file, retrieving each record which meets the condition specified in the most recently executed LOCATE command, until no more records can be found, at which point the message "End of locate scope" appears.

The difference between the two commands is that LOCATE searches *sequentially,* whereas FIND goes *directly* to the desired record. The difference between the commands FIND Moldof and LOCATE FOR lastname = 'Moldof' may not be apparent from the existing ZOO.DBF file because it is so small (only 16 records) and execution is quick in both instances. The difference will, however, become obvious in larger files associated with real systems.

The fact that LOCATE does not use an index can be advantageous because it enables a search on a condition for which no key exists, that is, the condition in the LOCATE command permits the use of inequalities, whereas the FIND command always searches for a matching (that is, equal) key. Thus, if you needed to retrieve the first record for which a donation was received you could enter the command LOCATE FOR DONATION > 0, whereas no comparable command exists with the FIND operation.

SET FILTER Command

The SET FILTER command enables you to look at a group of records (as opposed to individual records retrieved with the FIND and LOCATE commands) by limiting the view of a database to those records meeting a specified condition. Consider:

Syntax:
SET FILTER TO <condition>

Examples:

```
SET FILTER TO DONATION > 0
SET FILTER TO ZIPCODE = '33071'
SET FILTER TO DONATION > 0 .AND. ZIPCODE = '33071'
SET FILTER TO
```

Once a filter condition is set, it is as though the file in use consists of only those records meeting the designated condition. The effect of the command is shown in Figure 6.2. Figure 6.2a shows a file with no filter condition in effect, whereas Figure 6.2b depicts a filtered view that includes only those records where a donation has been made. Note, however, that the DBF file contains the same number of records in both instances. In other words, the nondonating records have *not* been deleted but are treated as though they weren't there. Figures 6.2c and 6.2d contain additional examples for individuals whose zip code is 33071, and for individuals who have contributed *and* whose zip code is 33071.

After a filter condition has been established, it remains in effect until another filter condition takes its place or the filter is turned off entirely. The latter is accomplished by entering a SET FILTER TO command *without* a condition.

Use of a filter condition saves keystrokes and reduces the chance for error which can best be demonstrated by example. Consider the procedure for sending out thank-you notes, which first requires isolation of those individuals who have contributed but who have not yet been thanked. We must then perform a series of operations on these records, and only these records, as indicated:

1. List the individuals meeting this condition.
2. Generate a file of names and addresses for input into a mail-merge operation so that personal thank-you notes may be written.
3. Produce a corresponding set of mailing labels.
4. Update the file to reflect that the thank-you notes have been written.

Figure 6.3 contains two equivalent sets of commands (with and without a filter condition) to accomplish these operations. In essence, the absence of a filter in Figure 6.3a requires the condition to be repeated in every command (LIST, COPY, LABEL FORM, and LOCATE). This approach is tedious to say the least, as well as error prone, because the identical condition is retyped from command to command. By contrast, using a filter in Figure 6.3b enables the condition to be entered only once.

Another advantage of the filter condition occurs during the maintenance process and may not be apparent from the commands as they are written. Conceptually, we need to update (EDIT) the record of every individual meeting the current condition. This requires you to position the record pointer at the beginning of the file, then move from record to record as appropriate.

The unfiltered file of Figure 6.3a mandates repeated execution of both the CONTINUE and EDIT commands. The filtered file, however, logically contains *only* those records meeting the filter condition. Accordingly, you need to issue the EDIT command only once, after which you can use the PgDn key to go to the next record(s) meeting the filter condition.

A word of explanation about the condition is also in order. Consider:

———— Periods set off logical operators

```
DONATION > 0 .AND. .NOT. THANK_YOU
```

We need to identify individuals who have contributed (DONATION > 0), *and* who have not yet been thanked (.NOT. THANK_YOU). The value of both the DONATION and THANK_YOU fields can be tested in the same condition, by including the AND operator (dBASE requires that it be set off by periods) in the condition.

DONATION was defined as a numeric field, and hence it can be compared directly to zero to see if a contribution was recorded. THANK_YOU, on the other hand, was defined as a logical field meaning it can assume only the values "true" or "false." The name of the variable (THANK_YOU) was assigned to reflect the "true" condition, and the NOT operator

LASTNAME	ZIPCODE	DONATION	DONOR_DATE	THANK_YOU
Anderson	33071	100	11/13/88	.F.
Barber	33176		/ /	.F.
Cohen	33411		/ /	.F.
Glassman	33317		/ /	.F.
Grauer	33071	50	10/16/88	.T.
Hill	33441	25	10/16/88	.T.
Kenoyer	33071	50	11/08/88	.T.
Manin	33065	25	11/30/88	.F.
Milgrom	33334		/ /	.F.
Moldof	33071	50	11/14/88	.F.
Moldof	33066		/ /	.F.
Neider	33071		/ /	.F.
Palumbo	33319	25	10/28/88	.T.
Rumsch	33066	50	10/19/88	.T.
Stutz	33183	100	10/14/88	.T.
William	33319		/ /	.F.

a

LASTNAME	ZIPCODE	DONATION	DONOR_DATE	THANK_YOU
Anderson	33071	100	11/13/88	.F.
Barber	33176		/ /	.F.
Cohen	33411		/ /	.F.
Glassman	33317		/ /	.F.
Grauer	33071	50	10/16/88	.T.
Hill	33441	25	10/16/88	.T.
Kenoyer	33071	50	11/08/88	.T.
Manin	33065	25	11/30/88	.F.
Milgrom	33334		/ /	.F.
Moldof	33071	50	11/14/88	.F.
Moldof	33066		/ /	.F.
Neider	33071		/ /	.F.
Palumbo	33319	25	10/28/88	.T.
Rumsch	33066	50	10/19/88	.T.
Stutz	33183	100	10/14/88	.T.
William	33319		/ /	.F.

b

LASTNAME	ZIPCODE	DONATION	DONOR_DATE	THANK_YOU
Anderson	33071	100	11/13/88	.F.
Barber	33176		/ /	.F.
Cohen	33411		/ /	.F.
Glassman	33317		/ /	.F.
Grauer	33071	50	10/16/88	.T.
Hill	33441	25	10/16/88	.T.
Kenoyer	33071	50	11/08/88	.T.
Manin	33065	25	11/30/88	.F.
Milgrom	33334		/ /	.F.
Moldof	33071	50	11/14/88	.F.
Moldof	33066		/ /	.F.
Neider	33071		/ /	.F.
Palumbo	33319	25	10/28/88	.T.
Rumsch	33066	50	10/19/88	.T.
Stutz	33183	100	10/14/88	.T.
William	33319		/ /	.F.

c

```
LASTNAME    ZIPCODE  DONATION  DONOR_DATE  THANK_YOU
--------    -------  --------  ----------  ---------
Anderson    33071    100       11/13/88    .F.
Barber      33176                /  /      .F.
Cohen       33411                /  /      .F.
Glassman    33317                /  /      .F.
Grauer      33071    50        10/16/88    .T.
Hill        33441    25        10/16/88    .T.
Kenoyer     33071    50        11/08/88    .T.
Manin       33065    25        11/30/88    .F.
Milgrom     33334                /  /      .F.
Moldof      33071    50        11/14/88    .F.
Moldof      33066                /  /      .F.
Neider      33071                /  /      .F.
Palumbo     33319    25        10/28/88    .T.
Rumsch      33066    50        10/19/88    .T.
Stutz       33183    100       10/14/88    .T.
William     33319                /  /      .F.
```

d

FIGURE 6.2 The SET FILTER command: (a) entire ZOO.DBF file; (b) SET FILTER TO DONATION > 0; (c) SET FILTER TO ZIPCODE = '33071'; (d) SET FILTER TO DONATION > 0 .AND. ZIPCODE = '33071'

```
. LIST OFF FOR DONATION > 0 .AND. .NOT. THANK_YOU
                                    Condition is repeated from command to command

. COPY TO THANKYOU FOR DONATION > 0 .AND. .NOT. THANK_YOU
        FIELDS PREFIX,FIRSTNAME,LASTNAME,STREET,CITY,STATE,ZIPCODE

. LABEL FORM THANKYOU FOR DONATION > 0 .AND. .NOT. THANK_YOU
                                    Condition is repeated from command to command

. LOCATE FOR DONATION > 0 .AND. .NOT. THANK_YOU
. EDIT
. CONTINUE          EDIT and CONTINUE commands must be issued repeatedly
```

```
.SET FILTER TO DONATION > 0 .AND. .NOT. THANK_YOU

.LIST OFF                     Condition is entered once in SET FILTER command

. COPY TO THANKYOU
        FIELDS PREFIX,FIRSTNAME,LASTNAME,STREET,CITY,STATE,ZIPCODE

. LABEL FORM THANKYOU

. EDIT            PgDn key will move to the next record in the filtered database
```

FIGURE 6.3 Sending thank-you notes: (a) without a filter condition; (b) with a filter condition

(set off by periods) is necessary to test for the "false" condition, that is, individuals who have not yet contributed. Conditions are further explained following the hands-on exercise.
Hands-on Exercise 6–1 implements these concepts in dBASE.

Hands-on Exercise 6–1: Finding (Locating) Individual Records

Objective: To demonstrate the use of the FIND, LOCATE, and CONTINUE commands in identifying individual records; to illustrate the SET FILTER command in isolating a group of records.

☐ **STEP 1: Open the existing ZOO.DBF file.**
Place the convenience disk in drive B:, boot DOS, then log onto the ZOO subdirectory as follows:

```
CD B:\ZOO ─────────────────────────── With a floppy disk system

CD C:\SAMPLER\ZOO ─────────────────── With a hard disk drive
PATH C:\SAMPLER
```

Load dBASE using the appropriate procedure for your configuration. Enter the commands to open the existing ZOO.DBF file, then limit the fields that will be displayed on the screen, that is:

```
.USE ZOO
.SET FIELDS TO LASTNAME,FIRSTNAME,DONATION,DONOR_DATE,THANK_YOU
```

☐ **STEP 2: Update the records for Cohen and Milgrom.**
Enter the SET INDEX and FIND commands as shown in Figure 6.4, so that the appropriate editing may take place. The FIND command requires an active index; hence the SET INDEX command is included in the figure.

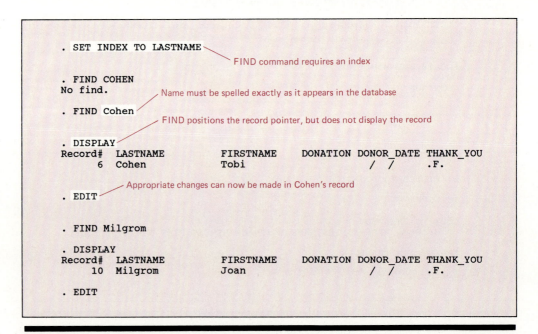

FIGURE 6.4 The FIND command

(Should you attempt to find a record without first opening an index, dBASE returns the error message, "Database is not indexed".)

Note, too, the difference between the commands FIND COHEN and FIND Cohen and how the former was unsuccessful. In other words, you must enter the value for which you are searching exactly as it appears in the file. Remember also that the FIND command merely positions the record pointer, but does not display the found record. Accordingly, note the use of both DISPLAY and EDIT after the record for Cohen has been found.

Enter the appropriate information for Cohen (a $50 contribution received on 12/01/88), then repeat the entire process for Milgrom (a $100 donation received on 12/01/88). Press Ctrl End to save these changes and return to the dot prompt.

☐ **STEP 3: Delete the record for Sarah Moldof.**

Enter the LOCATE command as shown in Figure 6.5, after which dBASE returns the message "Record = 14". This means that the search was successful (that is, a record satisfying the condition in the LOCATE command has been identified), and that the record pointer has been moved accordingly.

Recall, however, that LOCATE (like FIND) merely moves the record pointer but does not display the record in question. Accordingly, a DISPLAY command is issued to view the record before actually deleting it. As you can see, the wrong Moldof (Adam instead of Sarah) was found, so that an additional search is necessary.

Enter the CONTINUE command as shown in Figure 6.5 to continue the search, starting with the *current* position of the record pointer. (If you were to erroneously use another LOCATE command instead of CONTINUE, you would again wind up on Adam Moldof's record because the results of a given LOCATE command are always the same. The CONTINUE command, however, initiates the search from the current position of the record pointer, and so it returns the next record meeting the condition.)

The DISPLAY command confirms that the record for Sarah Moldof has been found, and the subsequent DELETE command marks her record accordingly. (Remember too, that the record is logically rather than physically deleted, and that a subsequent PACK command would be required to physically remove it from the file.)

FIGURE 6.5 The LOCATE and CONTINUE commands

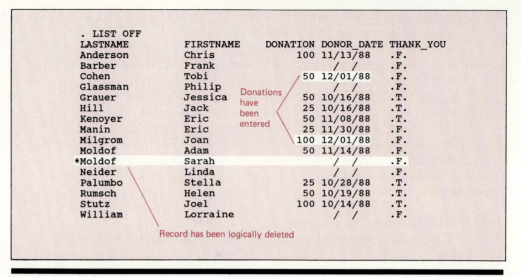

```
. LIST OFF
LASTNAME           FIRSTNAME      DONATION DONOR_DATE THANK_YOU
Anderson           Chris               100 11/13/88   .F.
Barber             Frank                   /  /       .F.
Cohen              Tobi                 50 12/01/88   .F.
Glassman           Philip                  /  /       .F.
Grauer             Jessica              50 10/16/88   .T.
Hill               Jack                 25 10/16/88   .T.
Kenoyer            Eric                 50 11/08/88   .T.
Manin              Eric                 25 11/30/88   .F.
Milgrom            Joan                100 12/01/88   .F.
Moldof             Adam                 50 11/14/88   .F.
*Moldof            Sarah                   /  /       .F.
Neider             Linda                   /  /       .F.
Palumbo            Stella               25 10/28/88   .T.
Rumsch             Helen                50 10/19/88   .T.
Stutz              Joel                100 10/14/88   .T.
William            Lorraine                /  /       .F.
```

Donations have been entered

Record has been logically deleted

FIGURE 6.6 Updated ZOO.DBF file

☐ **STEP 4: Verify the file maintenance operations.**
A simple `LIST OFF` (or `DISPLAY ALL OFF`) command confirms the results of the preceding steps as shown in Figure 6.6. Note that only five fields are shown for each record because of the `SET FIELDS` command issued at the beginning of the exercise.

☐ **STEP 5: The SET FILTER command.**
The `SET FILTER` command limits the view of the database to those records meeting the designated condition. Enter the command as shown in Figure 6.7 to list only those individuals who have contributed (`DONATION > 0`), but who have not yet received a thank-you note (`.NOT. THANK_YOU`).

☐ **STEP 6: Prepare the file of names and addresses.**
Enter the command `COPY DELIMITED` as shown in Figure 6.8a, being sure to spell the field names correctly, with commas between the fields. The initial `COPY` command will *not* execute however, because the `SET FIELDS` command which is in effect restricts the view of the DBF file to the fields shown in Figure 6.7, and does not include the fields for prefix and address.

The `CLEAR FIELDS` command makes all fields available once more, after which the `COPY` command can be reexecuted. (Use the up arrow key to retrieve the earlier `COPY` command from the command buffer, rather than retyping the entire command.) This time the `COPY` will be successful, as in-

```
. SET FILTER TO DONATION > 0 .AND. .NOT. THANK_YOU
. LIST OFF
LASTNAME           FIRSTNAME      DONATION DONOR_DATE THANK_YOU
Anderson           Chris               100 11/13/88   .F.
Manin              Eric                 25 11/30/88   .F.
Cohen              Tobi                 50 12/01/88   .F.
Milgrom            Joan                100 12/01/88   .F.
Moldof             Adam                 50 11/14/88   .F.
```

FIGURE 6.7 The SET FILTER command

Command is entered on one line

```
. COPY TO THANKYOU FIELDS
        PREFIX,FIRSTNAME,LASTNAME,STREET,CITY,STATE,ZIPCODE DELIMITED
Variable not found.
```

dBASE is unable to find the field name PREFIX

Negates the effect of the existing SET FIELDS command

```
. CLEAR FIELDS
```

Use the Up arrow key to retrieve command, rather than retyping it

```
. COPY TO THANKYOU FIELDS
        PREFIX,FIRSTNAME,LASTNAME,STREET,CITY,STATE,ZIPCODE DELIMITED
   5 records copied
```

The TXT extension is automatically assigned by dBASE

```
. TYPE THANKYOU.TXT
```

a

```
"Mr.","Chris","Anderson","8137 NW 2nd Court","Coral Springs","FL","33071"
"Ms.","Tobi","Cohen","7110 High Sierra Circle","West Palm Beach","FL","33411"
"Mr.","Eric","Manin","2362 NW 122 Drive","Coral Springs","FL","33065"
"Ms.","Joan","Milgrom","261 NE 8 Street","Ft. Lauderdale","FL","33334"
"Mr.","Adam","Moldof","297 NW 104 Avenue","Coral Springs","FL","33071"
```

b

FIGURE 6.8 Generating the file of names and addresses: (a) commands to create the file; (b) contents of THANKYOU.TXT

dicated by the message "5 records copied". (The SET FILTER command is still in effect limiting the records copied to those that match the filter condition, that is, individuals who have contributed, but who have not been thanked.) The TYPE command displays the names and addresses in the newly created file, THANKYOU.TXT.

☐   **STEP 7: Generate the mailing labels.**
Enter the command LABEL FORM ZOO, to create the mailing labels shown in Figure 6.9. (The label form ZOO.LBL, was created in Chapter 5 and should

```
Mr. Chris Anderson          Ms. Tobi Cohen
8137 NW 2nd Court           7110 High Sierra Circle
Coral Springs, FL   33071   West Palm Beach, FL   33411


Mr. Eric Manin              Ms. Joan Milgrom
2362 NW 122 Drive           261 NE 8 Street
Coral Springs, FL   33065   Ft. Lauderdale, FL   33334


Mr. Adam Moldof
297 NW 104 Avenue
Coral Springs, FL   33071
```

FIGURE 6.9 Mailing labels

still be on your convenience disk.) The `SET FILTER` command is still in effect so that only five mailing labels are created, which in turn match the names and addresses in Figure 6.8.

☐ **STEP 8: Edit the filtered records.**

Implicit in the requirement for sending out thank-you notes is the need to update the ZOO.DBF file for these individuals, indicating that the thank-you notes were, in fact, sent. Accordingly, enter the following commands:

```
.GO TOP
.EDIT
```

The `GO TOP` command positions the record pointer at the top of the file (according to the master index on last name), and is necessary because the `LABEL FORM` command just issued moved the record pointer to the end of the file. The `EDIT` command will bring up Chris Anderson's record, at which point you could change the value in the THANK_YOU field from `F` to `T` indicating that a thank-you note was sent. *Do not, however, change Anderson or any subsequent records at this time, as we wish the database to stay intact for the next hands-on exercise in the chapter.*

The PgDn key brings up the next record in the database according to the `SET FILTER` condition which is still in effect. Thus, *the next record you see will be the next one meeting the filter condition,* just as the previous `COPY` and `LABEL FORM` commands processed only the filtered records. In other words, you can use the PgDn key to step quickly through the ZOO.DBF file, landing on *only* those records that need editing (Anderson, Cohen, Manin, Milgrom, and Adam Moldof).

Press Ctrl End to return to the dot prompt at the conclusion of editing.

☐ **STEP 9: Exit dBASE.**

Type `QUIT` to exit dBASE and return to the dot prompt.

Conditions

The use of a condition is fundamental to almost every dBASE command, because it defines records on which the command is to operate. Although many conditions are simple in appearance (and have been used implicitly since the beginning of the book), other conditions grow quite complex and require additional explanation. Accordingly, the next several pages describe in detail how conditions are developed.

Relational Operators

Table 6.1 shows the *relational operators* permitted within a condition.

A relational operator compares a character string to a character string, or a number to a number, but cannot compare a character string directly to a number (unless the number is converted to a character string). The compared values may be either constants or variables.

A relational operator may *not* be used with a logical field, as the logical field in and of itself, is considered a condition. In other words, specifying a logical variable, for example, THANK_YOU, implies that the value of the logical variable is true.

A relational operator can be used in conjunction with a date, provided a suitable conversion has taken place. Accordingly, dBASE provides the `DTOC` (<u>D</u>ate <u>to</u> <u>C</u>haracter)

■ **TABLE 6.1**
dBASE Relational Operators

Operation	Operator
Less than	<
Greater than	>
Equal to	=
Not equal to	<> or #
Less than or equal to	<=
Greater than or equal to	>=

function to convert the value in a date field to a character string, so that a comparison can take place.

Table 6.2 contains both valid and invalid examples of relational operators, including the use of the DTOC function. (The examples assume that LASTNAME, DONATION, THANK_YOU, and DONOR_DATE have been defined as character, numeric, logical, and date fields, respectively.)

Logical Operators

The logical operators AND, OR, and NOT (set off by periods) are used to combine two or more simple conditions into a multiple (compound) condition. Consider:

```
DONATION > 0 .AND. LASTNAME = 'Anderson'
DONATION > 100 .OR. DTOC (DONOR_DATE) > '01/01/88'
```

The results of the condition (whether it is considered true or false) depend on the sequence in which the logical operators are evaluated. Consider what happens in the following example depending on which operator takes precedence, the AND or the OR.

```
DONATION > 100 .OR. DTOC (DONOR_DATE) > '01/01/88'
.AND. ZIPCODE = '33065'
```
————AND is evaluated before OR

dBASE provides a *hierarchy of operations* so that a condition may be evaluated without ambiguity. NOT is evaluated first, followed by AND, and then OR. Hence, for the above condition to be true, either the donation must be greater than 100, *or* both the donation date must be after 1/1/88 and the zip code is 33065.

■ **TABLE 6.2**
The Relational Operators

Example	Comments
LASTNAME = 'Anderson'	Valid.
LASTNAME = "Anderson"	Valid.
LASTNAME = Anderson	Invalid; character field requires either quotation marks or apostrophes.
DONATION < 100	Valid.
DONATION>0	Valid; spaces before and after the relational operator are not required.
DONATION > '100'	Invalid; numbers must appear without enclosing marks.
THANK_YOU = 'T'	Invalid; logical fields may not be used with relational operators.
THANK_YOU	Valid.
DTOC (DONOR_DATE) > '01/01/88'	Valid; condition is true if the date is after January 1, 1988.
DONOR_DATE > '01/01/88'	Invalid; dates may not be compared directly to a character string.

Parentheses can also be used to clarify (and sometimes alter) the normal hierarchy of operations. Consider:

Parentheses do not change the order of operations

```
DONATION > 100 .OR. (DTOC(DONOR_DATE) > '01/01'88'
.AND. ZIPCODE = '33065')
```

Parentheses have changed the original condition

```
(DONATION > 100 .OR. DTOC(DONOR_DATE) > '01/01/88')
.AND. ZIPCODE = '33065'
```

Query Files

The conditional powers of dBASE enable reports to be generated for various subsets of records within a file, that is, for records satisfying many different conditions. As we have seen conditions can become quite complex, and continually retyping the same condition is both tedious and error prone. The use of a filter condition helps somewhat, but does not solve the problem completely because the condition must still be entered initially every time the filter is invoked, for example, from session to session, or when switching back and forth between filters within the same session.

Fortunately, there is a better way. A filter condition can be permanently stored in a special type of file, known as a *query file,* which can be retrieved at any time to filter the view of the database. A query file is created and saved in much the same way as report forms and label forms. You are presented with a query menu, which uses the left and right arrow keys to move across the top of the screen, and the up and down arrow keys to select an option from within a submenu. The CREATE QUERY and MODIFY QUERY commands function just as their counterparts do for report forms and mailing labels.

Hands-on Exercise 6–2 demonstrates the use of query files.

Hands-on Exercise 6–2:   Query Files

Objective: To create a query file corresponding to the filter condition DONATION > 0 .AND. .NOT. THANK_YOU for those individuals who have contributed but who have not yet been thanked.

☐   STEP 1: Open the existing ZOO.DBF file.
Open the ZOO.DBF file as you did in Hands-on Exercise 6–1, then issue the SET INDEX and SET FIELDS commands as indicated:

```
. USE ZOO
. SET INDEX TO LASTNAME
. SET FIELDS TO                           — Command entered on one line
LASTNAME,FIRSTNAME,DONATION,DONOR_DATE,THANK_YOU
```

☐   STEP 2: Create the query file.
Enter the command CREATE QUERY THANKYOU to begin creating the query file. (THANKYOU was chosen as the name of the query file.) The Query Menu in Figure 6.10 will come into view, with the Set Filter option highlighted.

☐   STEP 3: Select the first field.
Use the up and down arrow keys to highlight Field Name, and press the Return key. A second box will come into view showing the fields in the file structure, as shown in Figure 6.11. Highlight DONATION and press the Return key.

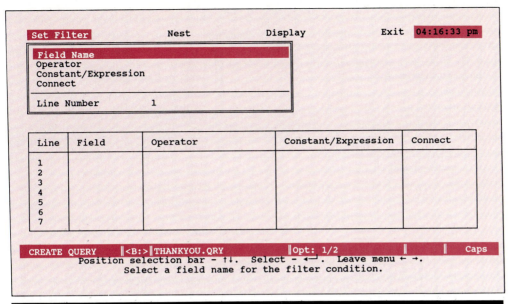

```
┌─────────────────────────────────────────────────────────────────┐
│ Set Filter          Nest          Display          Exit  04:16:33 pm│
│ ┌───────────────────────────────────────────┐                    │
│ │ Field Name                                 │                    │
│ │ Operator                                   │                    │
│ │ Constant/Expression                        │                    │
│ │ Connect                                    │                    │
│ ├───────────────────────────────────────────┤                    │
│ │ Line Number        1                       │                    │
│ └───────────────────────────────────────────┘                    │
│                                                                   │
│ ┌──────┬────────┬──────────────┬────────────────────┬──────────┐ │
│ │ Line │ Field  │ Operator     │ Constant/Expression │ Connect  │ │
│ ├──────┼────────┼──────────────┼────────────────────┼──────────┤ │
│ │ 1    │        │              │                    │          │ │
│ │ 2    │        │              │                    │          │ │
│ │ 3    │        │              │                    │          │ │
│ │ 4    │        │              │                    │          │ │
│ │ 5    │        │              │                    │          │ │
│ │ 6    │        │              │                    │          │ │
│ │ 7    │        │              │                    │          │ │
│ └──────┴────────┴──────────────┴────────────────────┴──────────┘ │
│ CREATE QUERY    <B:> THANKYOU.QRY          Opt: 1/2        Caps   │
│      Position selection bar - ↑↓.  Select - ◄┘.  Leave menu ← →.  │
│           Select a field name for the filter condition.           │
└─────────────────────────────────────────────────────────────────┘
```

FIGURE 6.10 Query Menu

☐ **STEP 4: Select the first relational operator.**
Use the up and down arrow keys to highlight the Operator option, then press
the Return key to bring the relational operators into view as shown in Figure
6.12. Use the up and down arrow keys to highlight the greater than sign and
press the Return key.

☐ **STEP 5: Complete the first condition.**
The first field name and relational operator have been chosen, meaning that
you must now enter the appropriate constant to complete the condition. Use
the up and down arrow to highlight Constant/Expression, press the Return

```
┌─────────────────────────────────────────────────────────────────┐
│ Set Filter          Nest          Display          Exit  04:17:49 pm│
│ ┌───────────────────────────────────────────┐  ┌──────────────┐  │
│ │ Field Name                    ▶           │  │ LASTNAME     │  │
│ │ Operator                                   │  │ FIRSTNAME    │  │
│ │ Constant/Expression                        │  │ DONATION     │  │
│ │ Connect                                    │  │ DONOR_DATE   │  │
│ ├───────────────────────────────────────────┤  │ THANK_YOU    │  │
│ │ Line Number        1                       │  └──────────────┘  │
│ └───────────────────────────────────────────┘                    │
│                                                                   │
│ ┌────────────────┬─────────┬───────┬─────────┬──────────┬───────┐ │
│ │ Field Name     │ Type    │ Width │ Decimal │ ant/Expression │ Connect │
│ ├────────────────┼─────────┼───────┼─────────┼──────────┼───────┤ │
│ │ ZOO->DONATION  │ Numeric │   3   │    0    │          │       │ │
│ │ 3              │         │       │         │          │       │ │
│ │ 4              │         │       │         │          │       │ │
│ │ 5              │         │       │         │          │       │ │
│ │ 6              │         │       │         │          │       │ │
│ │ 7              │         │       │         │          │       │ │
│ └────────────────┴─────────┴───────┴─────────┴──────────┴───────┘ │
│ CREATE QUERY    <B:> THANKYOU.QRY          Opt: 3/5        Caps   │
│      Position selection bar - ↑↓.  Select - ◄┘.  Leave menu ← →.  │
│           Select a field name for the filter condition.           │
└─────────────────────────────────────────────────────────────────┘
```

FIGURE 6.11 Field names

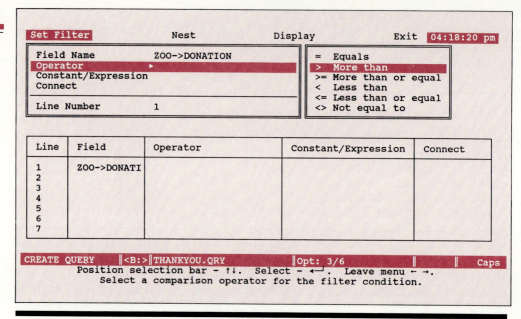

FIGURE 6.12 Relational operators

key, enter the value zero, and press the Return key once more. The first part of the condition (`DONATION > 0`) is now complete.

Now highlight the Connect option, press the Return key, and the connecting operators appear as shown in Figure 6.13. Choose Combine with .AND. as the connector and press the Return key.

☐ STEP 6: Complete the condition.

Repeat Steps 3 through 5 above for the second field, `THANK_YOU`, and proceed as before. The only difference is that since `THANK_YOU` was defined as a logical field (with permissible values of only T or F), its only available operators will be Is True and Is False (as opposed to the relational operators

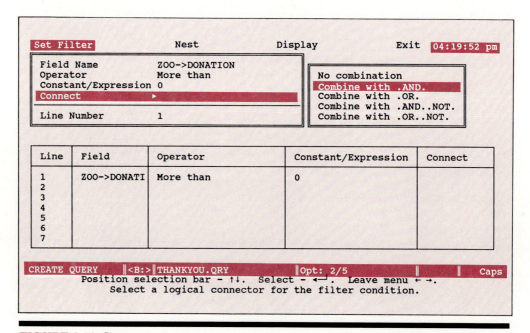

FIGURE 6.13 Connect choices

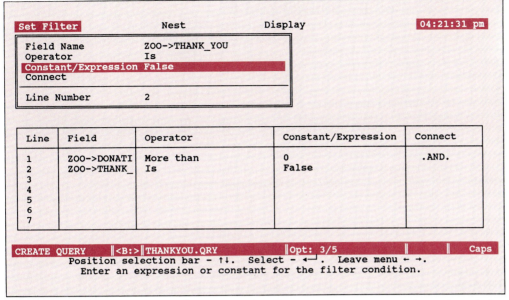

```
Set Filter              Nest           Display              04:21:31 pm

  Field Name           ZOO->THANK_YOU
  Operator             Is
  Constant/Expression  False
  Connect

  Line Number          2
```

Line	Field	Operator	Constant/Expression	Connect
1	ZOO->DONATI	More than	0	.AND.
2	ZOO->THANK_	Is	False	
3				
4				
5				
6				
7				

```
CREATE QUERY     <B:> THANKYOU.QRY           Opt: 3/5                    Caps
        Position selection bar - ↑↓.  Select - ◄┘.  Leave menu ← →.
        Enter an expression or constant for the filter condition.
```

FIGURE 6.14 Completed condition

permitted with numerical fields). You should end with a completed condition equivalent to `DONATION > 0 .AND. .NOT. THANK_YOU`, as shown in Figure 6.14.

☐ **STEP 7: Display the records meeting the filter condition.**
Remain in the Query Menu to display the records meeting the filter condition. Use the left and right arrow keys to highlight the Display option, press the Return key, and Figure 6.15 should appear on your monitor. Chris Anderson, the first record meeting the filter condition, is displayed. Press the PgDn key to see the next record (Eric Manin), and so on.

```
  Set Filter              Nest         Display           Exit  04:22:11 pm

  LASTNAME    Anderson
  FIRSTNAME   Chris
  DONATION    100
  DONOR_DATE  10/13/88
  THANK_YOU   F
```

Line	Field	Operator	Constant/Expression	Connect
1	ZOO->DONATI	More than	0	.AND.
2	ZOO->THANK_	Is	False	
3				
4				
5				
6				
7				

```
CREATE QUERY     <B:> THANKYOU.QRY           Rec: 2/16
     Next/Previous record - PgDn/PgUp.  Toggle query form - F1.  Leave option ← →.
        Display records in the database that meet the query condition.
```

FIGURE 6.15 Display after creation of the query

☐ **STEP 8: Save the completed query file.**

Use the left and right arrow keys to highlight the Exit option, then the up and down arrow keys to highlight the Save option. Press the Return key and the query file THANKYOU.QRY is saved on disk (THANKYOU was the file name assigned in Step 3, whereas QRY is the extension supplied by dBASE).

☐ **STEP 9: Turning filters off and on.**

Enter the commands in Figure 6.16 to turn the filter condition off and on. The command SET FILTER TO, entered without a condition, negates the effect of any existing filter, as shown in Figure 6.16a. By contrast, the command shown in Figure 6.16b, SET FILTER TO FILE THANKYOU, retrieves the query file just created and activates the associated filter condition.

☐ **STEP 10: Exit dBASE.**

Type QUIT to exit dBASE and return to DOS.

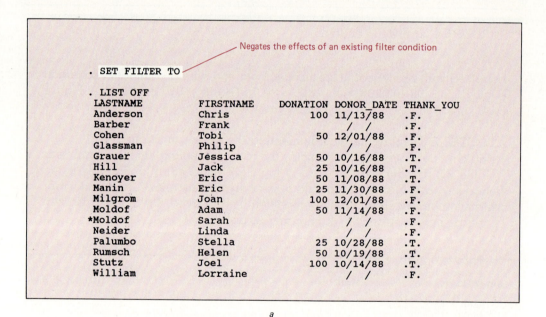

FIGURE 6.16 Turning filters on and off: (a) turning off a filter condition; (b) turning on a filter condition

Summary

The chapter began with a discussion of the `FIND`, `LOCATE`, and `CONTINUE` commands to identify individual records within a DBF file, then continued with the `SET FILTER` command to isolate a group of records meeting a specified condition. We discussed the rules associated with dBASE conditions, covering both relational and logical operators.

The second half of the chapter dealt with query files, a special type of dBASE III PLUS file that permanently stores a filter condition. The procedure to create a query file was covered in detail.

Key Words and Concepts

`AND`	Mailing labels
`CLEAR FIELDS`	`MODIFY QUERY`
Compound condition	`NOT`
`CONTINUE`	`OR`
`COPY`	Query file
`CREATE QUERY`	Relational operators
`DTOC ( )`	`SET FIELDS`
Filter condition	`SET FILTER`
`FIND`	
`LOCATE`	
Logical operators	

True/False

1. The `LOCATE` command requires an index.
2. The `FIND` command requires an index.
3. The `FIND` command can be expected to execute quicker than the corresponding `LOCATE` command.
4. `SET FILTER` may not be used in conjunction with `SET FIELDS`.
5. A given condition may not include more than one `AND`, `OR`, or `NOT` relational operator.
6. Using the `SET FILTER` command requires the existence of a corresponding query file.
7. The `FIND` and `LOCATE` commands move the record pointer, but do not display the associated record.
8. A date field may not appear in a dBASE condition.
9. The `SET FILTER` command physically deletes all records from the database not meeting the filter condition.
10. The `REMOVE FILTER` command negates the effect of a preexisting filter condition.
11. A query file permanently stores a filter condition.
12. Several filters may be stored in the same query file.

Exercises

1. Distinguish between:
   a. a query file and a filter condition
   b. `SET FIELDS` and `SET FILTER`

```
SOCSECNUM  LASTNAME----  LOCATION----  SALARY  OLDSALARY  TITLE----------------

111111111  Borow         Florida       18000   16000      Warehouse staff
222222222  O'Malley      Brazil        24000   22000      Sales representative
300000000  Brown         Florida       22000   18000      Warehouse manager
333333333  Baker         Florida       14800   13000      Sales support staff
444444444  Benjamin      Florida       18800   15500      Warehouse staff
555555555  Smith         Brazil        14300   13000      Production coordinator
```

FIGURE 6.17 Employee file for Exercises 2 and 3 (shown earlier as Figure 3.13)

  c. a LOCATE command and a FIND command

  d. a LOCATE command and a CONTINUE command

  e. the commands SET FILTER TO THANKYOU

          SET FILTER TO FILE THANKYOU

2. Figure 6.17 contains the SHOES.DBF file as it existed at the end of Chapter 3. Indicate the employees who meet the following conditions, then develop and implement the corresponding dBASE commands to produce an actual list of the employees.

  a. employees earning more than $18,000

  b. employees earning more than $18,000 and who work in Florida

  c. employees earning more than $18,000 or employees who work in Florida

  d. employees whose current salary is at least $2,000 more than their previous salary

  e. employees whose salary increase was less than 10 percent

  f. any employee whose title is not "Warehouse staff"

  g. all "Warehouse staff" employees earning at least $15,000

3. Assume that the command USE SHOES INDEX LASTNAME has been issued in conjunction with the SHOES.DBF file in Figure 6.17. Indicate the effect, together with any dBASE messages that might appear, of the following commands:

  a. FIND SMITH

  b. LOCATE FOR LASTNAME = 'SMITH'

  c. FIND Smith

  d. LOCATE FOR LASTNAME = 'Smith'

  e. FIND 555555555

  f. LOCATE FOR SOCSECNUM = '555555555'

  g. LOCATE FOR SALARY > 20000

  h. CONTINUE (issued immediately after part g above)

4. Examine Figure 6.6, which shows the ZOODONOR.DBF file after it has been updated. Is the update complete? Are there any other fields in the file structure whose values are known, but have not been updated?

After reading this chapter, you should be able to:

• Describe the requirements of a menu-driven program.

• Define structured programming; explain what is meant by the "one entry point/one exit point" philosophy.

• Define pseudocode; list two conventions to follow in writing pseudocode.

• List the dBASE statements used to implement the basic building blocks of structured programming.

• Distinguish between the dBASE interactive and command modes.

• Discuss why coding standards are necessary in dBASE; suggest at least three standards to follow in writing dBASE programs.

• Define debugging; state how this is accomplished in dBASE.

• Discuss the need for proper program documentation; describe several elements used in program documentation.

7

Menu-Driven Programs

Overview

Although we were pleased with the reports produced in previous chapters, and said nothing to the contrary, the methodology is, in reality, quite primitive. The requirement for entering commands one at a time via the keyboard is severely limiting, and results in having to retype command sequences. To say the least, this is an inefficient and error-prone procedure. Perhaps of even greater consequence is the requirement for the person entering the commands to be trained in dBASE. The solution is to permanently store the set of necessary commands as a *program* that can be recalled (executed) at any time. Accordingly, the major objective of this chapter is to develop a *menu-driven* program capable of producing a variety of reports based on those in the United States example in Chapter 4.

The chapter begins with the requirements of the menu-driven program. We develop the logic necessary to write the program and in so doing, discuss both *structured programming* and *pseudocode*. We introduce a variety of new dBASE statements, show how they are applicable to the problem at hand, and finally implement the program via a hands-on exercise. The chapter concludes with a brief discussion of programming standards and documentation.

A Menu-Driven Program

Let us return to the four reports on the United States produced in Chapter 4, remembering how they were created in the hands-on exercises. In particular, recall how commands were continually entered from the dot prompt to produce the various reports. Wouldn't it be simpler if you could simply call up a program that asked you, in English, which report(s) you wanted?

Figure 7.1 demonstrates that capability exactly. Figures 7.1a, b, and c request information about the type of report desired (area, population, year of admission, or density), the sequence in which states are to be listed (ascending or descending), and the number of states to be included. The program collects all three responses and then produces the report shown in Figure 7.1d. Imagine how much easier this menu-driven program is to use than the method in Chapter 4.

Implicit in these screens is a *data validation* capability in that the program will reject invalid responses. In other words, the program is expecting a response of A, B, C, or D to indicate the type of report desired, and it must be smart enough to reject any response which is invalid (that is, a response other than A, B, C, or D). Similarly, the program should validate the desired sequence (either an A or D) and the number of states to include in the report (from 1 to 50). Once valid responses have been obtained, the report can be generated.

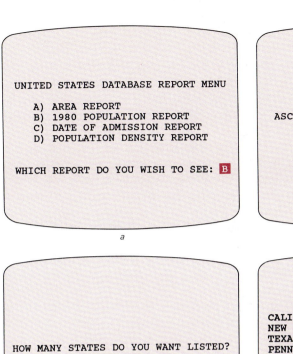

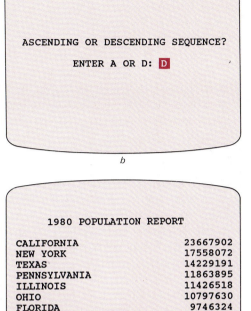

FIGURE 7.1 Output of interactive dBASE program: (a) first prompting message (answer B has been entered); (b) second prompting message (answer D has been entered); (c) third prompting message (answer 10 has been entered); (d) output produced by the program

It is also important to recognize the *generality* implied by the input screens of Figure 7.1. We could just as easily have asked for a report listing the states in ascending order of admission, descending order of population, and so on. Hence, the menu-driven system is not only easy to use, but flexible as well in terms of its ability to generate a large number of reports.

Figure 7.1 effectively establishes the requirements for the menu-driven program, namely that it be:

1. Able to produce four types of reports (area, population, year of admission, or density), listing a variable number of states for each report in either ascending or descending sequence.
2. Capable of validating the user's inputs for the type of report, sorting sequence, and number of states.
3. Easy to use and not require any knowledge of programming languages or data management systems.

The entire chapter is aimed at developing a menu-driven program with these capabilities. As you shall see, much of the discussion will not be concerned with dBASE per se, but with the underlying program logic. Accordingly, it will be necessary to specify what types of processing statements need to be included in the program and the sequence in which those statements are executed. That, in turn, leads us to a discussion of programming methodology, a discipline known as *structured programming*.

Much time and effort has been devoted to finding the best way to write programs. The outcome of that research has given rise to a discipline known as *structured programming* which applies to any language, be it dBASE, BASIC, or COBOL. The discipline aims to produce logically correct programs, easily read and maintained by someone other than the original author.

The theory we are about to discuss may seem somewhat abstract, without any immediate application. It is, however, the basis for good programming and its relevance will become apparent as the menu-driven program is developed. Accordingly, you may find it useful to merely skim this section now and return to it later as you code the program in dBASE.

The logic in a structured program can be viewed as a set of basic building blocks, put together in various combinations to solve a problem. Only three types of building blocks are necessary: *sequence, selection* (a decision), and *iteration* (a loop). The fact that these structures are sufficient to express any desired logic was first postulated in a now-classic paper by Bohm and Jacopini.[1]

The elementary building blocks of structured programming are shown graphically in Figure 7.2. Each building block is expressed as a *flowchart* or pictorial representation of programming logic. Flowcharts use special symbols to communicate information. A rectangle indicates a processing statement, a diamond indicates a decision, and a small circle connects portions of the flowchart. Each of the building blocks in the figure have one key feature in common: a *single entry point* and a *single exit point*.

The sequence block of Figure 7.2a implies that program statements are executed sequentially, that is, in the order in which they appear. The two blocks, A and B, could denote anything from single statements to complete programs.

The selection block of Figure 7.2b shows the choice between two actions. A condition, which can be either true or false, is tested and if the condition is true, block A is executed; if it is false, block B is executed. The condition is a *single entry* point to the structure and both paths meet in a single exit point.

Iteration (or looping) in Figure 7.2c calls for the repeated execution of one or more statements. A condition is tested and, if it is true, block A is executed and the condition retested. If, however, the condition is false, control passes to the next sequential statement after the iteration structure. Again, there is exactly *one entry* point and *one exit* point from the structure.

Figure 7.2d contains a fourth type of building block, known as the *case* structure, which expresses a multibranch situation. Although case is really a special instance of selection, it is convenient to extend the definition of structured programming to include this fourth type of building block. The case construct evaluates a condition which can have several values and branches to one of several paths depending on the value of the condition. As with the other fundamental building blocks, there is one entry point and one exit point.

Sufficiency of the Basic Structures

Structured programming theory says simply that an appropriate combination of the elementary building blocks may be derived to solve any problem in logic. This is possible because an entire structure (sequence, selection, iteration, or case) may be substituted in Figure 7.2 anywhere block A or B appears. Figure 7.3 shows a combination of the basic structures illustrating this point.

Figure 7.3 is essentially a selection structure. However, instead of specifying a single

[1]Bohm and Jacopini, "Flow Diagrams, Turning Machines and Languages with Only Two Formation Rules," *Communications of the ACM,* May 1966.

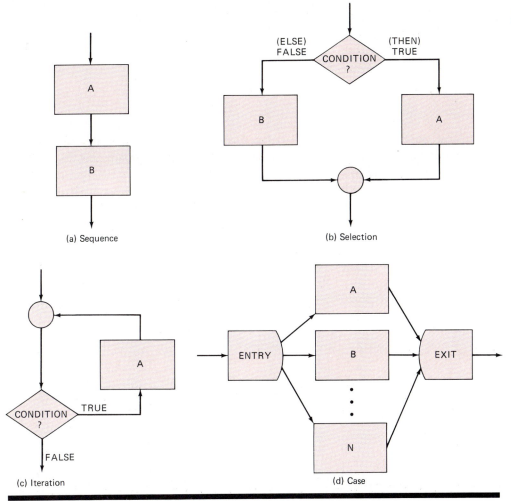

(a) Sequence

(b) Selection

(c) Iteration

(d) Case

FIGURE 7.2 The building blocks of structured programming

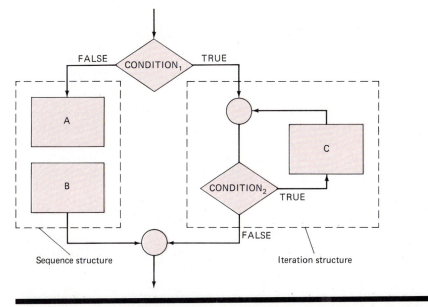

Sequence structure

Iteration structure

FIGURE 7.3 Sufficiency of the basic structures

statement for the true and false branches, as was done in Figure 7.2b, a complete building block is used instead. Thus, if condition 1 is true, an iteration structure is entered, whereas, if it is false, a sequence structure is executed. Both the iteration and sequence structures meet at a single point; this in turn, becomes the exit point for the initial selection structure.

Pseudocode

Although small flowcharts of the type drawn in Figures 7.2 and 7.3 are useful, their popularity has dropped significantly in recent years. The decline may be attributed to many factors. Flowcharts are time consuming to draw, difficult to follow and maintain, and stretch over several pages for realistic problems. More importantly perhaps, is the fact that flowcharts were rarely used for their intended purpose, which was as a development aid in writing programs. Whereas, in theory, you were supposed to draw a flowchart *before* writing a program, in practice it was often drawn *after* the fact.

Programmers did, however, willingly and often, write notes to themselves before coding a program. Formalization of this "neat notes to oneself" came to be known as *pseudocode*. Because people do this anyway, it has gained considerable acceptance.

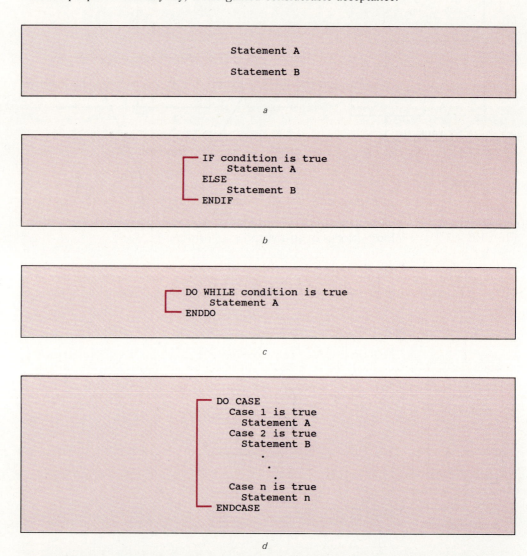

FIGURE 7.4 Structured programming in pseudocode

Pseudocode uses Englishlike statements similar to computer instructions to describe logic. The technique has a very distinct block structure that is extremely conducive to structured programming. An example of pseudocode, corresponding to the flowcharts in Figure 7.2 is shown in Figure 7.4.

Pseudocode is not bound by formal syntactical rules as is a programming language. Nor is it bound by indentation which is done strictly at your discretion. We suggest, however, certain conventions to make pseudocode easier to read. We like to indent as shown in Figure 7.4 and to use vertical lines to indicate the extent of the selection, iteration, and case constructs. We also use the words ENDIF, ENDDO, and ENDCASE to further highlight the range of the elementary building blocks.

With practice, pseudocode can be written quickly and easily. The only real limitation is a restriction to the elementary building blocks (sequence, selection, iteration, and case) that causes the pseudocode to flow easily from the top down. Good pseudocode should be sufficiently precise to be a real aid in writing a program, while informal enough to be intelligible to nonprogrammers. The very nature of the technique prohibits establishing exact rules; that would imply a formalism pseudocode does not possess. Nevertheless, we suggest you take a second look at Figure 7.4, and try to adhere to our suggestions for indentation and the use of vertical lines.

The next several pages use both structured programming and pseudocode in developing the menu-driven program.

Developing the Menu-Driven Program

Thus far we have shown that the basic building blocks of structured programming are sufficient to develop the logic to solve any problem and we have chosen pseudocode as the preferred method for expressing that logic. Now we are ready to apply these concepts to the problem at hand.

Review the requirements of the menu-driven program postulated earlier. You can see that the eventual program will consist of two major sections, *user input* and *report generation*. The input portion will accept and validate input parameters from the user, after which the report generation segment will create a report based on the input provided. Thus, in very general terms, the program will execute statements in *sequence* to:

1. Obtain the report type (area, population, date of admission, or density).
2. Obtain the report sequence (ascending or descending).
3. Obtain the number of states to include in the report.
4. Generate the report.

Now realize the detail implied in the user input portion of the program. The user is asked to input a response, for example the report type. The program then checks the validity of that response and, if invalid, asks the user to once again enter the report type desired. The new response must also be validated, and the process should continue until a proper answer has been obtained. Similar sets of statements must then be executed to obtain the other responses, that is, the report sequence and the number of states to include in the report. You can begin to see how the basic building blocks will be used to describe a procedure for obtaining a valid response.

The logic for the user input portion of the menu-driven program is expressed in the pseudocode in Figure 7.5. The figure contains three parallel sets of instructions for each of the three responses, that is, report type (area, population, year of admission, or density), report sequence (ascending or descending), and number of states (1 to 50).

Consider the logic to obtain the report type, that is, Figure 7.5a. A loop is established in which the user is continually asked for a response until a valid response is obtained. The execution of that loop is controlled by a *switch,* that is, a variable which assumes one of two

```
              Set valid-report-switch to 'no'
           ┌ DO WHILE valid-report-switch = 'no'
           │    Get user's response
           │  ┌ IF user's response is valid
           │  │     Set valid-report-switch to 'yes'
           │  │ ELSE
           │  │     Tell user to input a valid report type
           │  └ ENDIF
           └ ENDDO
```

a

```
              Set valid-sequence-switch to 'no'
           ┌ DO WHILE valid-sequence-switch = 'no'
           │    Get user's response
           │  ┌ IF user's response is valid
           │  │     Set valid-sequence-switch to 'yes'
           │  │ ELSE
           │  │     Tell user to input a valid report sequence
           │  └ ENDIF
           └ ENDDO
```

b

```
              Set valid-number-switch to 'no'
           ┌ DO WHILE valid-number-switch = 'no'
           │    Get user's response
           │  ┌ IF user's response is valid
           │  │     Set valid-number-switch to 'yes'
           │  │ ELSE
           │  │     Tell user to input a valid number of states
           │  └ ENDIF
           └ ENDDO
```

c

FIGURE 7.5 Pseudocode for data entry portion: (a) obtaining the report type; (b) obtaining the report sequence; (c) obtaining the number of states

values (yes or no). The switch is initially set to no (indicating that a valid response has not yet been obtained) and the loop is entered. The user supplies a response. If the response is valid, the switch is set to yes and the loop is terminated. If, on the other hand, an invalid response is supplied, the switch remains set to no, which causes the loop to be repeated. The user is again asked for a response, the response is checked, and so on. The process continues an indeterminate number of times, until a valid response is obtained. Figures 7.5b and c contain similar logic to obtain the remaining user responses.

Figure 7.6 depicts the logic to create a particular report once the three valid user inputs have been received. The report generation process begins with a case structure to evaluate the user's choice of report type and, based on this value, writes an appropriate heading, then opens the file with the appropriate index. (Implicit in this logic is the assumption that the four distinct indexes, on area, population, year of admission, and density, have been previously created.)

Next, we see the logic that determines whether the states in a report are to be listed in ascending or descending sequence. If the user chooses ascending sequence, states will be listed by starting at the beginning of the index and moving forward; they will be listed in descending sequence by starting at the end of the index and moving backward. [Implicit in this logic is the assumption that the indexes were established in ascending order, for example

```
        ┌─ DO CASE
        │      CASE 1: Write report heading for Area report
        │             Open file and use area index
        │      CASE 2: Write report heading for Population report
        │             Open file and use population index
        │      CASE 3: Write report heading for Admission report
        │             Open file and use admission index
        │      CASE 4: Write report heading for Density report
        │             Open file and use density index
        └─ ENDCASE


        ┌─ IF report sequence is ascending
        │      Start with first state in index (and move forward)
        │  ELSE
        │      Start with last state in index (and move backward)
        └─ ENDIF


           SET COUNTER TO ZERO
        ┌─ DO WHILE counter < number of states
        │  ┌─ DO CASE
        │  │      CASE 1: Write detail line for Area report
        │  │      CASE 2: Write detail line for Population report
        │  │      CASE 3: Write detail line for Admission report
        │  │      CASE 4: Write detail line for Density report
        │  └─ END CASE
        │
        │  ┌─ IF report sequence is ascending
        │  │      Go to next state
        │  │  ELSE
        │  │      Go to previous state
        │  └─ ENDIF
        │
        │      INCREMENT COUNTER BY 1
        └─ ENDDO
```

FIGURE 7.6 Pseudocode for report generation portion

the index on area begins with Rhode Island, and continues to Alaska. Thus, if the user requested that states be listed in descending order (the largest state first), we would go to the end of the index, that is, Alaska, and move backward to Texas, California, and so on.]

The DO WHILE loop at the end of Figure 7.6 writes the proper number of detail lines (one for each state in the report). A counter, initialized to zero outside the loop and incremented by 1 within the loop, controls the loop. When the proper number of lines have been written, the value of the counter will be equal to the desired number of states. This terminates the loop and ends the program.

Depending on the report type chosen, the case construct within the DO WHILE loop writes the appropriate line. (Detail lines for the various reports contain different fields; for example the area report contains the state name and area, the population report has the name and population, and so on.) Observe also the IF statement within the loop that determines whether the record pointer is moved to the next or previous record.

The logic for the menu-driven program is complete as depicted in the pseudocode in Figures 7.5 and 7.6. These figures do not contain dBASE statements per se, and must therefore be converted to dBASE syntax so that the program can be run on the computer. This, in turn, leads to a discussion of dBASE programming.

Implementation in dBASE

There are essentially two ways to teach dBASE programming. The first is to devote considerable time to explaining all the nuances associated with the necessary dBASE statements, and then, and only then, write a program. The second is to plunge right in with only an intuitive understanding of the various statements, and leave the details for later. We are firm advocates of the latter approach, and believe strongly that quick exposure to programming helps remove the mystical aura that too often surrounds the subject.

Review, for a moment, what you have accomplished so far. The early chapters have acquainted you with various dBASE statements issued at the dot prompt, in which individual commands were executed immediately when they were entered. Thus, you already have a good understanding of how a large number of dBASE statements function individually. The current chapter has presented the requirements of a generalized menu-driven program, developed the necessary logic via the building blocks of structured programming, and expressed the logic in pseudocode. It remains to convert that logic to dBASE syntax, which in turn requires the introduction of several new dBASE commands.

However, in keeping with our philosophy of a quick entry into programming, we present only the bare essentials of the necessary dBASE commands, and suggest you refer to the Programmer's Notebook for additional information. We suggest also that you skip back and forth between the discussion and the completed program as you read.

Statements for Structured Programming

The implementation of structured programming in dBASE must accommodate the building blocks. Sequence is trivial because dBASE statements appear in a program in the order in which they are to be executed. Selection is implemented by the dBASE IF statement, iteration by the dBASE DO WHILE statement, and case by the dBASE DO CASE statement. As we shall see, the dBASE syntax closely resembles the pseudocode shown earlier in Figure 7.4.

The IF statement tests a condition that allows conditional execution of a set of commands; it also provides an optional alternative path (ELSE) which is executed if the condition tests false. An IF statement *must* terminate with ENDIF.

The DO WHILE statement repeatedly tests a condition, executing a set of commands as long as the stated condition is true. A DO WHILE statement *must* end with ENDDO.

Finally, DO CASE permits the execution of one of several possible paths (cases), including one alternative or error checking condition. A DO CASE statement *must* end with an ENDCASE.

We defer discussing these statements further until we present the completed program.

Input/Output Statements

Any program must make provision to receive input and generate output. Figure 7.1, for example, displayed various messages asking the user for information on which to base a report; it subsequently displayed the resulting report.

The dBASE @...SAY command is used to display a message(s) on the screen, while the @...GET command (in conjunction with a READ command) makes it possible to obtain and store information. (Refer to the Programmer's Notebook for additional information.) As you can see, both commands contain row and column coordinates enabling you to specify precisely where on the screen the information is to be obtained or displayed. Finally the ? command is used to print lines in the report.

Statements Affecting the Record Pointer

The USE statement, in conjunction with the INDEX parameter, opens the file and designates the master index; for example, USE USSTATES INDEX AREA causes the states to be processed in order of area.

The GO or GOTO statement positions the record pointer to a specific record number. GO TOP and GO BOTTOM position the pointer at the first and last records, respectively, *according to the master index,* for example, to Rhode Island and Alaska, respectively, if area is the master index.

SKIP +1 moves the record pointer one state forward in the file, according to the order of the active index. Similarly, SKIP −1 moves one state backward, also according to the order of the active index. Thus, the statements:

```
USE USSTATES INDEX AREA
GO TOP ———————————————— Positions record pointer at Rhode Island
DISPLAY
SKIP +1 ——————————————— Moves record pointer forward to Delaware
DISPLAY
```

will display first Rhode Island and then Delaware, whereas the statements:

```
USE USSTATES INDEX AREA
GO BOTTOM ————————————— Positions record pointer at Alaska
DISPLAY
SKIP −1 ——————————————— Moves record pointer backward to Texas
DISPLAY
```

will display Alaska and Texas.

The Completed Program

Figure 7.7 shows the completed menu-driven program as implemented in dBASE. (The vertical lines in the figure are drawn only to highlight the overall program logic and are not part of the program.) Your objective at this time should be to conceptually understand the program as opposed to becoming bogged down with dBASE details. We do expect you, however, to be able to follow the overall flow, noting especially how the building blocks of structured programming are incorporated.

The program is divided into two segments, *user input* and *report generation.* Figure 7.7a contains the input portion that obtains the user's responses; Figure 7.7b depicts the report generation segment that writes the desired report (based on the user-supplied inputs).

The first three statements in Figure 7.7a (CLEAR, SET BELL OFF, and SET TALK OFF) clear the screen, suppress the bell at the end of a user response, and prevent dBASE messages from appearing on the screen during program execution. The effects of the latter two statements are best illustrated by coding the program with and without them in Hands-on Exercise 7–1.

The next several statements obtain the user's response concerning the type of report desired, by first prompting for an appropriate response. The messages displayed on the screen are generated via @...SAY statements; they specify the row and column on the screen where the message is to begin. Thus, the statement, @ 3,23 SAY 'UNITED STATES DATABASE REPORT MENU' displays its message beginning in row 3, column 23 of the monitor. Note the *beginning and ending* apostrophes surrounding the message. Remember, too, that the program rejects invalid responses (that is, a report type other than A, B, C, or D), and must continue to reject invalid responses until a proper value is received.

The dBASE *memory variable,* mrepmenu, controls the data validation loop. (A memory variable temporarily stores data which is not part of a DBF file.) The value of mrepmenu is originally set to no with a STORE statement. dBASE then obtains the value of another memory variable, mselect, which stores the choice of report type, and checks whether the choice is valid. If the report type is other than A, B, C, or D (that is, the value of mselect is less than A or greater than D), the report type is invalid and the message "Please choose

```
CLEAR                                      ── suppresses bell at end of a user response
SET BELL OFF
SET TALK OFF                               ── prevents dBASE messages from echoing on the screen
@ 3,23 SAY 'UNITED STATES DATABASE REPORT MENU'
@ 6,23 SAY '   A) AREA REPORT '
@ 7,23 SAY '   B) 1980 POPULATION REPORT'
@ 8,23 SAY '   C) DATE OF ADMISSION REPORT'
@ 9,23 SAY '   D) POPULATION DENSITY REPORT'
@ 13,23 SAY ' WHICH REPORT DO YOU WISH TO SEE: '
STORE 'no ' TO mrepmenu
DO WHILE mrepmenu = 'no '
     STORE ' ' TO mselect             ── initializes a memory variable
     @ 13,57 GET mselect PICTURE 'A'
     READ
     @ 18,20 SAY SPACE(50)            ── blanks out columns 20 to 69 in line 18
     STORE UPPER(mselect) TO mselect
     IF mselect < 'A' .OR. mselect > 'D'
          @ 18,20 SAY 'Please choose one of the options listed!'
     ELSE
          STORE 'yes' TO mrepmenu     ── memory variable controls validation loop
     ENDIF
ENDDO
CLEAR
@ 9,25 SAY 'ASCENDING OR DESCENDING SEQUENCE?'
@ 11,25 SAY '          ENTER A OR D: '
STORE 'no ' TO msequence
DO WHILE msequence = 'no '
     STORE ' ' TO mseq
     @ 11,47 GET mseq PICTURE 'A'
     READ
     STORE UPPER(mseq) TO mseq        ── converts lower case to upper case
     @ 18,27 SAY SPACE(50)
     IF mseq = 'A' .OR. mseq = 'D'
          STORE 'yes' TO msequence
     ELSE
          @ 18,27 SAY 'Please enter A or D only!'
     ENDIF
ENDDO
CLEAR
@ 9,23 SAY 'HOW MANY STATES DO YOU WANT LISTED?'
@ 11,23 SAY '          ENTER NUMBER: '
STORE 'no ' TO mnumber
DO WHILE mnumber = 'no '
     STORE 0 TO mnum
     @ 11,46 GET mnum PICTURE '99'
     READ
     @ 18,23 SAY SPACE(50)
     IF mnum <1 .OR. mnum > 50
          @ 18,23 SAY 'Enter a number from 1 to 50 only!'
     ELSE
          STORE 'yes' TO mnumber
     ENDIF
ENDDO
```

a

```
CLEAR
DO CASE                                    ── appropriate index is opened
     CASE mselect = 'A'
          STORE '        AREA REPORT        ' TO mheading
          USE usstates INDEX area
     CASE mselect = 'B'
          STORE ' 1980 POPULATION REPORT   ' TO mheading
          USE usstates INDEX popltn
     CASE mselect = 'C'
          STORE ' DATE OF ADMISSION REPORT ' TO mheading
          USE usstates INDEX yradmtd
     CASE mselect = 'D'
          STORE 'POPULATION DENSITY REPORT' TO mheading
          USE usstates INDEX density
ENDCASE
? '                        ',mheading
? ' '                                      ── ? statements displays heading
IF mseq = 'A'
     GO TOP
ELSE                                       ── record pointer is positioned at beginning (end) of index
     GO BOTTOM
ENDIF
STORE 0 TO mcounter
DO WHILE mcounter < mnum
     DO CASE
          CASE mselect = 'A'
               ? '             ',name,'        ',area
          CASE mselect = 'B'
               ? '             ',name,'        ',popltn
          CASE mselect = 'C'
               ? '             ',name,'        ',yradmtd
          CASE mselect = 'D'
               ? '             ',name,'   ',popltn/area
     ENDCASE
     STORE mcounter + 1 TO mcounter
     IF mseq = 'A'
          SKIP
     ELSE
          SKIP -1
     ENDIF
ENDDO
CLOSE DATABASES
RETURN
```

b

FIGURE 7.7 Menu-driven program in dBASE: (a) user input portion of the menu-driven program; (b) report generation portion of the menu-driven program

one of the options listed" appears. If, however, the report type is valid, the switch controlling the loop (that is, mrepmenu) is set to yes and the loop is terminated.

A similar procedure is followed to obtain the report sequence and number of states. The memory variable msequence controls the data validation loop for the former, and the sequence selected (ascending or descending) is stored in mseq. Similarly, mnumber controls the final data validation routine, with the user-supplied parameter stored in mnum.

The relationship of the coordinates in the @...SAY and @...GET statements in Figure 7.7a merits attention. Consider, for example, the statement @ 13,23 SAY 'WHICH REPORT DO YOU WISH TO SEE: ' which begins in column 23 and ends in column 56 and prompts the user to enter a report type. It makes sense for the cursor to remain positioned at the end of the message while waiting for the user's input, which is accomplished by using the proper row and column coordinates in the @...GET statement.

The statement, @ 13,57 GET mselect PICTURE 'A' displays an input template for the memory variable mselect (the memory variable that stores the report type) in row 13, column 57 of the screen. In other words, the ending position of the @...SAY statement's prompting message is coordinated with the user input position in the corresponding @...GET statement. The PICTURE clause in the @...GET statement indicates the type and length of the memory variable expected in the user response. A picture of 'A' indicates a one-character *alphabetic* response whereas 'AA' would imply a two-character alphabetic response. Similarly, a picture clause of '99' implies a two-digit numeric response. It is used in connection with the number of states. Attempting to enter the improper type of response (for example alphabetic when numeric is called for) causes dBASE to "beep," thereby alerting you of the error.

Neither DOS nor dBASE distinguishes between commands entered in upper- or lowercase, for example, DOS accepts both DIR and dir as equivalent directory commands. Similarly, we would like our program to accept either upper- or lowercase responses for report type (A, B, C, and D in addition to a, b, c, and d). Because the internal representation of upper- and lowercase letters is different (that is, A is not the same as a), the STORE UPPER statement converts the value (that is, the user-supplied choice of report type) to its uppercase value before validating the response.

The user input portion of the program ends with valid responses having been supplied for the memory variables mselect (the type of report), mseq (ascending or descending sequence), and mnum (the number of states). The report generation program in Figure 7.7b will create the desired report based on the values of these parameters.

Report generation begins by clearing the screen. Next a DO CASE statement is entered. It stores, but does not write, the appropriate report heading in a memory variable, based on the desired report type. Observe also that the USSTATES DBF file with its appropriate index is opened within the case structure, enabling the chosen report to appear in proper sequence, for example, the area report lists states in area sequence, the population report lists them in population sequence, and so on.

The IF statement positions the record pointer at the beginning (TOP) or end (BOTTOM) of the master index according to whether ascending or descending sequence was chosen. We are now in a position to print the detail lines in the report by moving the record pointer forward in the file beginning at the top (if ascending sequence was selected) or backward from the bottom (for descending sequence).

The memory variable mnum contains the number of states that are to appear in the completed report. We can generate a report with the proper number of detail lines by establishing a loop to print the detail line, and then executing that loop mnum times. A counter (mcounter) is used to accomplish this. It is initialized to zero *outside* the loop and incremented by one *inside* the loop.

The loop itself contains a CASE statement to write the proper detail line for the report selected. The loop also contains a selection structure which moves the record pointer forward to the next record (SKIP +1) or backward to the previous record (SKIP −1) so that the states will appear in proper sequence. The program ends with statements to close all files (CLOSE DATABASES) and return to DOS.

Hands-on Exercise 7–1: Menu-Driven Programs

Objective: To demonstrate the dBASE command mode by developing a structured, menu-driven program.

☐ **STEP 1: Create the menu-driven program using a word processor.**
The first, and longest, step in this exercise is to create a file containing the menu-driven program of Figure 7.7. Although dBASE contains its own program editor, it is easier to use a word processor to create the program file. (You may, however, want to use the dBASE facility when you need to make program modifications; see the Programmer's Notebook for information on `MODIFY COMMAND`.)

Use the *nondocument* mode of your word processor to create a file named MENU.PRG (dBASE uses the PRG extension for its program files) and type in the program in Figure 7.7. Copy the MENU.PRG file to the appropriate subdirectory, `B:\USSTATES` (for a floppy disk system) or `C:\SAMPLER\USSTATES` (for a hard disk drive).

Recall that the dBASE student version is limited to a DBF file with 31 records and is insufficient for the USSTATES.DBF file. Accordingly, if you are using the student version, modify the program to use the data on countries of the world (WORLD.DBF) as you did in Chapter 4.

☐ **STEP 2: Log into the USSTATES subdirectory.**
Log into the USSTATES subdirectory with the appropriate command, then load dBASE according to the procedure for your configuration:

```
CD B:\USSTATES

CD C:\SAMPLER\USSTATES
PATH C:\SAMPLER
```
Substitute WORLD for USSTATES if appropriate

☐ **STEP 3: Create the necessary index files.**
The program in Figure 7.7 requires four index files in addition to the DBF file. Accordingly create them at this time via the commands:

```
. USE USSTATES
. INDEX ON YRADMTD TO YRADMTD
. INDEX ON AREA TO AREA
. INDEX ON POPLTN TO POPLTN
. INDEX ON POPLTN/AREA TO DENSITY
```
Enter USE WORLD instead, if this is the DBF file you are using

You may already have some or all of the index files on your data disk from previous exercises in Chapter 4. (Remember, however, that in this exercise all indexes are to be in ascending order and hence you may have to recreate (overwrite) the indexes on population and density.)

Verify that the necessary files are on your data disk by entering the command `DIR *.*` from the dot prompt. Your directory should contain the appropriate DBF file, four index files (YRADMTD.NDX, AREA.NDX, POPLTN.NDX, and DENSITY.NDX), and the program file (MENU.PRG) created in Step 1. Remember the significance of the different extensions: DBF (data file), NDX (index file), and PRG (program file).

☐ **STEP 4: Execute the program.**
Enter the command `DO MENU` at the dBASE dot prompt, whereupon your

program will take over. If all goes well, you will see the prompting messages in Figure 7.1 appear on the screen one by one; after you have entered the appropriate responses, dBASE generates the requested reports. It is more than likely, however, that you will have made one or more errors in entering your program, which in turn will cause problems when you attempt to execute your program.

A mistake in a program is known as a "bug," hence "debugging" is the process of detecting and correcting programming errors. (The term is attributed to Grace Hopper who found a moth trapped in the relay of an early computer, causing the machine to short-circuit. The problem was entered in the machine's log book as "a case of a bug being found," and the term has stuck ever since.)

Step 5 discusses debugging.

☐ **STEP 5: Debugging.**

dBASE, like all programming languages, has a rigidly prescribed syntax that must be followed exactly. In other words, failure to enter statements in the precise format expected by dBASE will result in various error messages.

Consider, for example, Figure 7.8. Figure 7.8a contains a portion of the original program in which several statements were deliberately altered to produce three syntactical errors. Figure 7.8b shows the resulting dBASE messages when execution was attempted.

The first error, Unterminated string, indicates that a closing quotation mark was omitted at the end of a character string in our program. The second error, File does not exist, implies dBASE is unable to find either a DBF or index file on the default disk. The error resulted because we specified an incorrect filename, using USE UNITED as opposed to USE USSTATES. Finally, the last error, Variable not found, happened because the memory variable name mhead was indicated in the print statement whereas we had previously defined it as *mheading*.

The message, Cancel, Ignore, or Suspend? (C, I, or S), appearing at the bottom of the screen follows each error. It is dBASE's way of asking what action you wish to take as a result of the error. A response of C (Cancel) returns you to the dot prompt and prevents any further program execution. I (Ignore) disregards the error and continues execution, whereas S (Suspend) temporarily halts program execution and returns you to the dot prompt. From there you can enter additional commands, after which execution may be resumed by issuing the RESUME command.

We suggest that you initially ignore the error messages and continue execution as long as it is productive. Make sure to write down all errors for subsequent correction in the program file. Eventually you will be returned to the dot prompt, either through the program's termination or the cancel command. At that point you can use either the dBASE MODIFY COMMAND (see Programmer's Notebook) or your word processor to make the necessary program corrections and try again.

You may be quite confused in your first confrontation with dBASE error messages. You may even think that dBASE is a bit unreasonable in its demands for precision and that it should be smart enough to know what you mean even if you make a mistake. Unfortunately, that is not the case. dBASE will only do what you tell it to do; this is not necessarily what you want it to do. Just be patient, and try to remain calm and collected. Reflect a moment and the error often becomes quickly apparent. Remember too that experience is the best teacher and that you will get better with practice.

```
        DO CASE
           CASE mselect = 'A'
              STORE '        AREA REPORT          TO mheading
              USE united INDEX area
           CASE mselect = 'B'
              .
                 .
                    .
        ENDCASE
        ? '                              ',mhead
```

a

```
        Unterminated string.          First Error Message
                                                              ?
              STORE '        AREA REPORT          TO mheading
        Called from - B:menu.prg
                                                    Ending quote missing

             Cancel, Ignore, or Suspend? (C, I, or S)


                                      Second Error Message
        File does not exist.
                            ?
              USE united INDEX area
        Called from - B:menu.prg
                                 File name should be usstates
             Cancel, Ignore, or Suspend? (C, I, or S)


                                   Third Error Message
        Variable not found.
        ? '                              ',mhead
        Called from - B:menu.prg                ?
                                         Variable should be mheading

             Cancel, Ignore, or Suspend? (C, I, or S)
```

b

FIGURE 7.8 Debugging in dBASE: (a) erroneous statements in MENU.PRG; (b) error messages produced by dBASE

Coding Standards

We expect that you were successful in the hands-on exercise, and that our intuitive explanation of the program makes more sense to you now than it did before. We suggest that you return now to Figure 7.7, and review the individual dBASE statements. In particular, we want to make you aware of several *coding standards* (conventions) we follow to make our programs easier to read.

dBASE does not require the conventions we are about to discuss, but uses them to make programs easier to follow and maintain. Indeed, you will best appreciate the significance of this section if you are ever called on to read and/or modify someone else's program. Our suggestions are:

- *Indent detail lines under* IF, DO WHILE, *and* DO CASE *statements:* Indentation, by a consistent amount (for example, three spaces) is a tremendous aid in showing the scope associated with these basic building blocks. Thus, the statement:

```
IF mchoice = 'A'
   GO TOP
ELSE
   GO BOTTOM
ENDIF
```

is inherently easier to read than:

```
IF mchoice = 'A'
GO TOP
ELSE
GO BOTTOM
ENDIF
```

Similar examples can be constructed for the DO WHILE and DO CASE statements. Proper indentation is perhaps the most important convention to follow in writing programs.

- *Use upper- and lowercase to differentiate between dBASE commands and programmer-supplied variables:* We follow the general convention of uppercase letters denoting dBASE reserved words whereas lowercase letters imply programmer chosen names. Thus, we code USE usstates INDEX area, as opposed to either USE USSTATES INDEX AREA or use usstates index area.

     Although implementing this guideline is a bit tedious (especially if your keyboard does not have a Caps Lock indicator), it is followed almost universally and hence is recommended strongly.

- *Use spaces before and after operational symbols:* We believe that the appearance of a program is improved significantly by proper spacing within a line. Thus, we prefer the statements:

```
CASE select = 'A'
```

and

```
STORE mcounter + 1 TO mcounter
```

as opposed to:

```
CASE select='A'
```

and

```
STORE mcounter+1 TO mcounter
```

- *Spell out all dBASE words in full:* Most dBASE statements can be abbreviated to the first four letters, for example, STOR is acceptable in lieu of STORE. It is well worth your effort, however, to spell out all commands.

Program Documentation

In addition to following the coding standards just described, accompany your program with written documentation to provide further description of its function. Unfortunately, documentation is something most programmers do poorly, if at all. Nevertheless, the individuals who do the poorest job of documentation are generally the ones who yell the loudest when maintaining someone else's programs.

Proper documentation does require time and effort. Documentation, per se, is not fun, but it is part of the programming function. Hence it should be done, and done well. Although there is no common agreement on precisely what constitutes proper documentation, we suggest that the following elements be present:

- *Pseudocode:* Given that individuals naturally write notes to themselves before coding, the pseudocode is essentially done and should not pose a burden. This is perhaps the most essential piece of documentation.

- *Program narrative:* The narrative is a verbal description of the program's overall function and is helpful as a prelude to viewing the program.

- *File description(s):* You should include a list of all DBF files and their associated file structure; you should also list all associated index files together with the field on which they are indexed.

- *Data dictionary:* The data dictionary lists all memory variables in the program, together with a description of the intended purpose and possible values.

Program Narrative: MENU.PRG

  MENU.PRG is a menu driven program capable of generating four distinct report types, based on user supplied input. The program is divided into two main modules, *user input* in which user responses are requested on the screen, and *report generation* in which the reports are created based on the inputs furnished.

  The user input portion begins with the display of three successive menus to determine: (1) the type of report, (2) the sequence of records within the report, and (3) the number of states to appear within the report. Each user response is checked for validity; i.e., the program will continue to ask for user responses until valid choices are supplied.

  The report generation segment creates a heading and opens the data file and appropriate index, based on the report type selected by the user. The record pointer is positioned at the top or bottom of the file, depending on whether an ascending or descending report sequence was selected. A loop is then entered to print the proper number of detail lines according to a user-specified number. Each time the loop is executed, a report line is generated with the content of the detail line dependent on the report type. The record pointer is moved to either the next or previous record, depending on the user-specified sequence.

Database file(s): USSTATES.DBF

Structure:

1 NAME	Character	14	(Name of state)
2 YRADMTD	Numeric	4	(Year of admission to union)
3 POPLTN	Numeric	10	(Population in 1980)
4 AREA	Numeric	8	(Area in square miles)
5 REGION	Character	15	(Region of country)

Index file(s):

YRADMTD.NDX	- key:	YRADMTD of USSTATES.DBF
POPLTN.NDX	- key:	POPLTN of USSTATES.DBF
AREA.NDX	- key:	AREA of USSTATES.DBF
DENSITY.NDX	- key:	POPLTN/AREA of USSTATES.DBF

Memory variables:

mrepmenu	- keeps "report type menu" on screen; assumes value of "yes" or "no"
mselect	- user supplied value to indicate report type; assumes value of "A", "B", "C", or "D"
msequence	- keeps "sequence menu" on screen; assumes value of "yes" or "no"
mseq	- user supplied value to indicate report sequence; assumes value of "A" or "D"
mnumber	- keeps "number of states menu" on screen; assumes value of "yes" or "no"
mnum	- user supplied value to indicate number of states: assumes value of 1 to 50
mheading	- first line of report heading
mcounter	- counter to control the number of states in the report; will eventually equal mnum at which point report is finished

FIGURE 7.9 Program documentation

Figure 7.9 shows the documentation for the menu-driven program. (The pseudocode appeared earlier in Figures 7.5 and 7.6 and hence is not repeated.)

Summary

The chapter revolved around a generalized menu-driven program, the data for which was introduced in Chapter 4. The program's requirements for ease of use, flexibility, and data validation were stressed. The chapter covered *structured programming* theory and discussed how programming logic could be expressed in *pseudocode*. Considerable time was also spent developing the underlying logic for the menu-driven program within the context of structured programming.

The second half of the chapter dealt with implementing the menu-driven program in dBASE. The necessary dBASE statements were presented, and a hands-on exercise covered the actual machine implementation. We also touched on debugging, the importance of program documentation, and the need for coding standards.

Key Words and Concepts

@...GET	Grace Hopper
@...SAY	IF
Ascending sequence	Ignore
Bohm and Jacopini	Iteration
Bug	Memory variable
Cancel	Menu-driven program
Case structure	MODIFY COMMAND
CLEAR	PICTURE 'A'
Coding standards	PICTURE 'AA'
Data dictionary	PICTURE '99'
Data validation	Pseudocode
Debugging	READ
Descending sequence	Report generation
DO CASE	Selection structure
DO WHILE	Sequence structure
Documentation	SKIP +1
ELSE	SKIP -1
ENDCASE	STORE
ENDDO	STORE UPPER ( )
ENDIF	Structured programming
Flowchart	Suspend
GO TOP	Switch
GO BOTTOM	User friendly

True/False

1. A structured program is guaranteed not to contain logical errors.
2. Structured programming can be implemented in a variety of languages.

3. The logic of any program can be expressed as a combination of only three types of logic structures.
4. The "one entry/one exit" philosophy is essential to structured programming.
5. The case construct is one of the three basic logic structures.
6. `SKIP` and `SKIP+1` are equivalent statements.
7. Pseudocode has precise syntactical rules.
8. A dBASE program file can be created with an ordinary word processor.
9. The output of a dBASE program can be directed to either the monitor or the printer.
10. Indentation is not important when writing dBASE programs.
11. dBASE requires MENU.PRG as the name of a menu-driven program.
12. The dBASE `IF` statement requires an `ELSE` clause.
13. A person using a menu-driven system needs a detailed knowledge of data base programming.
14. Pseudocode makes no provision for an unconditional branch.

Exercises

1. The following problem pertains neither to dBASE nor to a common business application. It is a problem with which you are totally unfamiliar, and consequently a problem for which you have no preexisting bias toward a solution. Nevertheless, the exercise demonstrates the applicability of both structured programming and pseudocode to virtually any physical setting.

    A robot is sitting on a chair, facing a wall a short distance away. The objective is to: (1) develop the necessary logic (restricted to the basic building blocks of structured programming) to have the robot walk to the wall and return to its initial position; and (2) to express that logic in pseudocode. The robot understands the following commands which are to be used in your solution:

    ```
    STAND
    SIT
    TURN ────── Turns right ninety degrees
    STEP
    ```

    In addition, the robot can raise its arms and sense the wall with its fingertips. (However, it cannot sense the chair on its return trip, since the chair is below arm level.) Accordingly, the robot must count the number of steps to the wall or chair using the following commands:

    ```
    ADD ───────────────── Increments counter by 1
    SUBTRACT ──────────── Decrements counter by 1
    ZERO COUNTER ──────── Sets counter to zero
    ARMS UP
    ARMS DOWN
    ```

    The wall is assumed to be an integer-number of steps away. It is highly recommended that various student solutions be presented in class. Select a volunteer to act as the robot and see whether the submitted solutions actually accomplish the objective.

2. Use the following program fragment to answer parts a through f below. [`EOF ( )` is a dBASE variable that will assume a true value when the end-of-file is reached. In other words, `EOF ( )` is a switch used to control the loop in the program.]

```
USE B:EMPLOYEE
INDEX ON SALARY TO SALARY
DO WHILE .NOT. EOF()
    ? NAME,SALARY
    SKIP +1
ENDDO
```

   a. What is the name of the DBF file in use? On which drive is it located?

   b. What is the name of the index file in use? On which drive is it located?

   c. What is the record key? In which order (ascending or descending) will the records be listed?

   d. What would happen if the SKIP+1 statement were replaced by SKIP−1?

   e. What would happen if the SKIP+1 statement were eliminated entirely?

   f. What changes would have to be made for records to list in the opposite order from part c above? (Do not create any additional indexes.)

3. Assume that the USSTATES.DBF file has been modified to contain an additional field containing the 1970 population of each state. Modify the program in Figure 7.7 to include a fifth permissible report type: the percentage of population growth from 1970 to 1980. Is this change(s) difficult to make? Can you see how well-written programs facilitate program maintenance?

4. Several improvements can be made to the program in Figure 7.7 to enhance the user interface. Accordingly, supply the necessary modifications to:

   a. Produce a "beep" when the user inputs an erroneous response, for example, a report type other than A, B, C, or D. [The dBASE statement ? CHR(7) produces the desired beep.]

   b. Allow the user to direct program output to the printer. (The dBASE SET PRINT ON statement directs all subsequent output to the printer.)

   c. Enhance the appearance of the menus in Figure 7.1, for example, surround each set of messages with a box of asterisks. (This is accomplished via additional @...SAY statements to display the asterisks at designated points on the screen.)

5. It is often very useful to examine the contents of memory variables during program execution. Accordingly, Figure 7.10 was produced by placing the DISPLAY MEMORY statement two lines from the end of the program in Figure 7.7. (The "priv" entry following each memory variable indicates the variable is private and can be used only by the MENU program. The concept of private versus public variables will be explained further in Chapter 10.)

   Use the information in Figure 7.10 to determine the report requested by the user (that is, work backward and determine the user responses from the data input portion).

6. Figure 7.11a contains a modified and *erroneous* section of code for the original program in Figure 7.7. Figure 7.11b contains the error messages produced by dBASE. Indicate the necessary corrections.

```
MREPMENU     priv  C   "yes"
MSELECT      priv  C   "B"
MSEQUENCE    priv  C   "yes"
MSEQ         priv  C   "D"
MNUMBER      priv  C   "yes"
MNUM         priv  N   12
MCOUNTER     priv  N   12
MHEADING     priv  C   "  1980 POPULATION REPORT  "
```

FIGURE 7.10 Contents of memory variables

```
DO WHILE mcounter < mnum
   DO CASE
      CASE mselect = 'A'
         ? '                      ',name'              ',area
      CASE mselect = 'B'
   .
      .
         .
   ENDCASE
   STORE mcounter + 1
   IF mseq = A
      SKIP
   ELSE
      SKIP -1
   ENDIF
ENDDO
```

a

```
                                                    First Error
Unrecognized phrase/keyword in command.
                                          ?
         ? '                      ',name'              ',area
Called from - B:menu.prg

   Cancel, Ignore, or Suspend? (C, I, or S)


                                                    Second Error
Unrecognized phrase/keyword in command.
                           ?
   STORE mcounter + 1
Called from - B:menu.prg

   Cancel, Ignore, or Suspend? (C, I, or S)


                        Third Error
Variable not found.
                     ?
   IF mseq = A
Called from - B:menu.prg

   Cancel, Ignore, or Suspend? (C, I, or S)
```

b

FIGURE 7.11 Program and error messages for Exercise 6: (a) modified code for Exercise 6; (b) error messages for Exercise 6

■ **OBJECTIVES**

After reading this chapter, you should be able to:

- Show how various management concepts apply to both organizations and information systems.

- Differentiate between structured programming and structured design.

- Describe how a hierarchy chart is developed; discuss three criteria for evaluating a completed hierarchy chart.

- State how a system may be tested before its programs are completed; describe what is meant by top-down testing.

- Describe the dBASE statements used to pass control from one program to another within a system.

8

Design and Implementation

The United States example in Chapter 7 introduced the dBASE command mode, and demonstrated the flexibility inherent in a menu-driven program. However, powerful as that example might have been, it consisted of only a single program, whereas an *information system* contains multiple programs which are related to one another. The Soleil Employee System introduced in Chapter 1, for example, contains approximately 40 programs and 5000 lines of code.

Rest assured that we will not take you through the detailed coding for all 40 programs. We think it is important, however, that you understand how the programs are related to one another and how the overall system is tested and developed. This, in turn, leads to a discussion of *structured design,* a methodology which goes beyond the structured programming concepts of Chapter 7.

We begin with a review of the Soleil Employee System, then present a *hierarchy chart* listing the major programs in that system. We develop the logic necessary to relate those programs to one another and express that logic in pseudocode. The most important portion of the chapter, however, deals with how a system is implemented and tested. Accordingly, we discuss the use of *program stubs* (partially completed programs) to enable testing to begin before a system is fully completed. We also introduce dBASE commands that pass control from one program to another within a system.

CASE STUDY:
Soleil America, Inc., Revisited

Return briefly to the case description and hands-on exercises associated with Soleil America, Inc., in Chapter 1. Recall, in particular, the menu-driven nature of the system as shown in Figure 8.1.

The opening menu on the left side of the figure enables you to choose between four major functions: file maintenance, report generation, utilities, and leaving the system (with appropriate backup). More specific choices are provided in the subordinate menus (shown in the middle of the figure) displayed when any of these options are

chosen. For example, a response of 1 to the opening menu brings up the File Maintenance Menu to add, edit, update, or delete an employee record. Similarly, a response of 2 returns the Report Generation Menu allowing a choice of one of seven reports. The Utilities Menu allows for additional functions.

The flow of the overall system is easily understood if you view Figure 8.1 (and perhaps repeat some or all of Chapter 1's hands-on exercises). Entry into the system presents you with the opening menu (shown in the left-most portion of the figure),

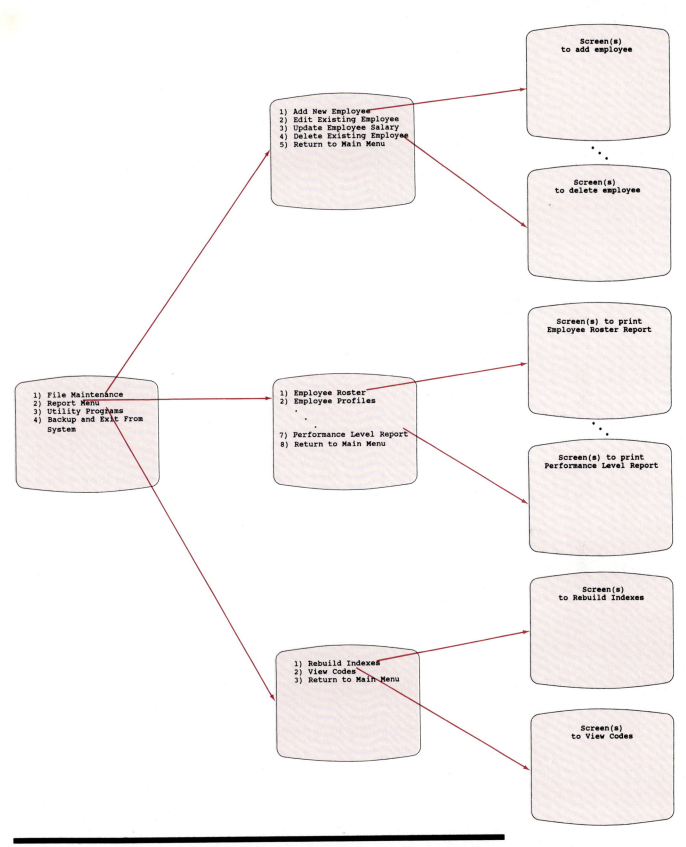

FIGURE 8.1 Overall view of the Soleil Employee System

from where you go to one of three subordinate menus (shown in the middle) that lead eventually to additional screens (shown on the right).

Control of the system passes continually from menu to menu within Figure 8.1. Initially, it flows from left to right (for example, from the Opening Menu to the File Maintenance Menu, given a response of 1, to the screen to add a new record, given a second response of 1). After the addition is completed, control switches from right to left, that is, back to the File Maintenance Menu, which in turn goes back to the opening menu, and then the process begins anew. It is also possible to stop at an intermediate menu and reverse direction, rather than going all the way back to the opening menu.

Hence, after completing the addition, another file maintenance function (editing, updating, or deleting) could be selected from the File Maintenance Menu in lieu of returning to the Opening Menu.

Although it is theoretically possible to develop a single program capable of the function implied by Figure 8.1, such a program would be extremely unwieldy. It is necessary, therefore, to develop a system of programs. This is indeed a major undertaking. In other words, our concern is with developing several programs and the relationship of these programs to one another. That, in turn, leads to a discussion of *structured design* which forms the bulk of this chapter.

Structured Design

Structured design is a methodology that ensures individual programs fit properly together to form a system. It embodies a series of techniques that identify the tasks a system is to accomplish, then relates those tasks to one another hierarchically. In essence, this has already been accomplished for the Soleil Employee System by the menu descriptions of Figure 8.1.

Use your imagination to turn Figure 8.1 on its side (rotate it 90° to the right so that the main menu is on top of the page). Imagine also that each part of the figure no longer represents a computer screen, but a person in an organization together with his or her job description. Thus, the "person" at the top of the organizational chart (the organization's chief executive) is in charge of displaying the main menu. He or she has three subordinates who display the File Maintenance, Report, and Utility menus, respectively. Each of these middle managers has several lower-level subordinates for the more elementary functions, for example, adding a record, preparing the employee roster report, rebuilding indexes, and so on.

We have, in effect, turned Figure 8.1 into a *hierarchy chart* of the kind used in structured design, and have redrawn it as such in Figure 8.2. The hierarchy chart is the primary tool of structured design and is analogous to a company's organizational chart. The *blocks* in a hierarchy chart represent programs in a system, just as blocks in an organizational chart correspond to positions in a company. The *levels* within the hierarchy chart describe the relationships between programs in a system, just as levels in an organizational chart describe manager-subordinate relationships among positions.

The program at the top of the hierarchy chart is the system's "boss," just as the person at the top of an organizational chart runs the company. The programs on any level (except the first) are *called from* a program on the next higher level, and in turn *call* programs on the next lower level in the hierarchy chart. In much the same way, people in an organizational chart report to the individual on the level immediately above them while people on lower levels report to them.

With respect to the hierarchy chart of Figure 8.2, DISPLAY-MAIN-MENU will, at different times, call DISPLAY-MAINTENANCE-MENU, DISPLAY-REPORT-MENU, and DISPLAY-UTILITY-MENU. DISPLAY-MAINTENANCE-MENU will call ADD-EMPLOYEE-RECORD, EDIT-EMPLOYEE-RECORD, UPDATE-EMPLOYEE-SALARY, or DELETE-EMPLOYEE-RECORD. Similarly, the other middle managers, DISPLAY-REPORT-MENU and DISPLAY-UTILITY-MENU, will call one of their lower level subordinates. Eventually, the lowest level "worker" (program) completes its function, returns control to its middle manager, who in

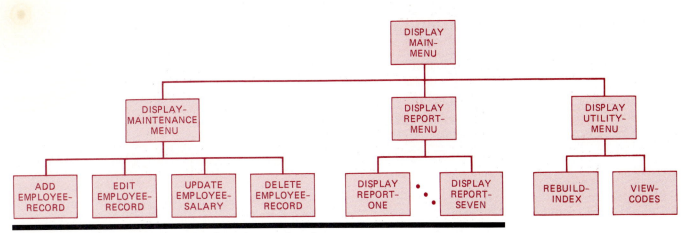

FIGURE 8.2 The Soleil America, Inc., hierarchy chart

turn returns control to the overall system boss. The process continues indefinitely with control passing back and forth among the various programs.

The hierarchy chart is by far structured design's most important tool. It is useful both as a design aid *before* programs are written and as a documentation aid to facilitate maintenance *after* the system is completed.

Creating the Hierarchy Chart

A hierarchy chart is created in levels, beginning at the top and working down to the bottom. It might help initially to imagine the entire system as consisting of a single, albeit very complex, program at the top of the chart. Given the impracticality of coding such a complex program, we choose instead to subdivide it into primary functions placed on the next lower level of the hierarchy chart. We then further subdivide those functions into their primary functions, and continue the process until the functions can no longer be logically subdivided. In other words, the system is repeatedly divided into smaller and smaller programs, until eventually the lowest level programs can be coded without difficulty. At that stage the design phase is complete and the programming phase can begin.

The earlier analogy between a system's hierarchy chart and a corporation's organizational chart is applicable to this discussion as well. Consider, for example, that when an individual is sufficiently motivated to create a new company, he or she proceeds from the *top* of the organization down. More than likely, the entrepreneur installs him- or herself as president, then hires vice-presidents for engineering, finance, marketing, and so on. Eventually, *when the top of the organization is in place,* assembly line workers, sales personnel, and so on, are hired at the bottom of the organization to make and sell the product.

In much the same way the development of a system's hierarchy chart is begun by recognizing the major functions the system is to accomplish, and placing these directly under the main program (on level 1). Each of these primary tasks is divided into more elementary programs which are placed on lower levels (level 2 and beyond) of the hierarchy chart. The decision as to how many programs to include and how they should be related to one another is necessarily subjective. Sooner or later, however, you will reach a point where the lower level functions cannot be further subdivided and the hierarchy chart is finished. It must then be reviewed for effectiveness.

As already indicated, the design of a hierarchy chart is somewhat subjective. Nevertheless, there are certain guidelines that can be applied to this procedure which result in selecting one design over another. In particular, we consider the following criteria:

1. Are the modules (programs) functional?
2. Is the hierarchy chart complete?
3. Is there proper subordination?

Each of these is discussed in turn.

Functionality

A well-designed hierarchy chart consists entirely of *functional modules*. A functional module may be defined as a program that does one, and only one job, the nature of which is apparent from the module's name. Again, the analogy to a corporation is appropriate in that individuals who try to do too many different things are generally ineffective (that is, a "jack of all trades, but a master of none"). Similarly, a single program that attempts to perform many functions is also a cause for concern.

As indicated a module's function should be clear from examining its name. Note, for example, that the name of every program in Figure 8.2 consists of a verb, an adjective or two, and a noun, for example, DISPLAY-MAINTENANCE-MENU or ADD-EMPLOYEE-RECORD. Naming programs in this fashion is an ideal way to ensure that a system consists entirely of functional programs; indeed if a program cannot be named in this way, its function is probably not clearly defined and the hierarchy chart should be redone.

Another way of expressing the need for functional modules is to strive for module independence; that is, the internal workings of one program should not affect those of another. Perhaps you have already been associated with a working system in which changes were implemented, only to have some other, apparently unrelated, portion of the system no longer work properly. The problem may be due in part to programs in the system being unnecessarily dependent on one another.

What we are saying is that in an ideal situation, changes made to one program should not affect the results of any other. In a practical sense programs have to be somewhat related otherwise they would not be parts of the same system; however, the amount of interdependence between programs should be minimized to the greatest extent possible. With respect to Figure 8.2, for example, a change in the procedure for adding an employee record should not affect how employee salaries are updated. This is because the modules, ADD-EMPLOYEE-RECORD and UPDATE-EMPLOYEE-SALARY are each functional in their own right, and consequently independent of one another.

Again the analogy to a corporate organization pertains here. An accountant does not want to hear from a marketing manager how to do his or her job, and vice versa. Nor should the marketing manager's actions have any effect on how the accountant balances the books. What we are saying is that people in a company (or programs within a system) should be as autonomous as possible.

Completeness

The next criteria in evaluating a hierarchy chart is to verify its completeness, that is, the hierarchy chart should provide for every function the system requires. You test for completeness level by level, again starting at the top, and working down.

With respect to Figure 8.2, for example, ask yourself whether the three functions on level 1, DISPLAY-MAINTENANCE-MENU, DISPLAY-REPORT-MENU, and DISPLAY-UTILITY-MENU do everything their boss module (DISPLAY-MAIN-MENU) implies? That is to say, are these the only functions necessary to carry out the tasks called for in the main menu?

Next drop to level 2 and repeat the process. Do the modules ADD-EMPLOYEE-RECORD, EDIT-EMPLOYEE-RECORD, UPDATE-EMPLOYEE-SALARY, and DELETE-EMPLOYEE-RECORD fulfill all the functions associated with DISPLAY-MAINTENANCE-MENU? Do the various DISPLAY-REPORT modules complete the functions associated with DISPLAY-REPORT-MENU, and so on.

Subordination

Proper subordination implies that every lower level module reports to an appropriate higher level module. It would be wrong for example in Figure 8.2, to have DISPLAY-REPORT-MENU report to DISPLAY-MAINTENANCE-MENU instead of DISPLAY-MAIN-MENU. It may seem obvious in this example, but mistakes are often made in practice.

Proper subordination also implies that a given module have only a single manager, although that module can (and does) have multiple subordinates. Thus, DISPLAY-MAINTENANCE-MENU reports to a single manager (DISPLAY-MAIN-MENU), but has four subordinates (ADD-EMPLOYEE-RECORD, EDIT-EMPLOYEE-RECORD, UPDATE-EMPLOYEE-SALARY, and DELETE-EMPLOYEE-RECORD).

Finally, proper subordination has to do with *span of control,* the number of subordinates reporting to a manager. Consider, for example, the organizational chart in Figure 8.3a which depicts the Hatfield family business. The president, A. Hatfield, has been complaining of falling profits since he brought his children, B. and C. Hatfield, into the company.

It doesn't take an extensive management background to realize that the Hatfield organization is top heavy. A. Hatfield does nothing other than manage B. Hatfield, who in turn controls C. Hatfield, whose role in life is to manage I. Milgrom. Milgrom, on the other hand, is overloaded because 21 people report to him. The problems are related to *span of control,* that is, the number of subordinates reporting directly to a manager. Milgrom has too many, whereas each member of the Hatfield family has too few.

The McCoy family in Figure 8.3b exhibits a better structure. Here the president manages three vice-presidents, who in turn each manage seven subordinates. Profits have continued to rise, even after introducing the McCoy offspring, and the company appears to be well run. This does not imply that every organization needs to have exactly three vice-presidents, nor must every vice-president have exactly seven subordinates. It does say, however, that there is a more effective span of control in the McCoy organization than in the Hatfield organization.

Similar criteria can be applied to a system's hierarchy chart. Systems with ineffective spans of control (too many or too few) can generally be said to be poorly designed and, hence, are difficult to follow and/or maintain.

Structured Design versus Structured Programming

Structured design is a *functionally* oriented technique whereas structured programming is *procedural* in nature. The difference is significant as both methodologies are required in the process of system development. You begin by creating the hierarchy chart for a system using structured design. You then link the programs together within the context of structured programming, presenting this logic in pseudocode.

To put it another way, the hierarchy chart indicates *what* functions are necessary, but not when (or how often) they are to be performed. It contains no decision-making logic whatsoever, nor does it imply anything about the order or frequency in which various

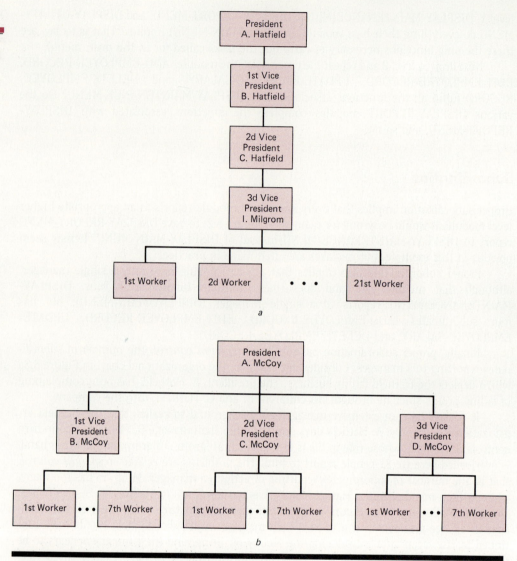

FIGURE 8.3 Span of control within an organization: (a) Hatfield Organization (improper span of control); (b) McCoy Organization (proper span of control)

programs within a system are executed. The pseudocode, on the other hand, depicts the sequence in which the functions (programs) are executed using only the fundamental blocks of sequence, selection, iteration, and case.

The hierarchy chart in Figure 8.2 indicates that the highest level program in the system, DISPLAY-MAIN-MENU, calls three subordinate programs, DISPLAY-MAINTENANCE-MENU, DISPLAY-REPORT-MENU, and DISPLAY-UTILITY-MENU. It does not, however, specify how often these programs will be called, nor does it indicate the conditions for calling one subordinate in lieu of another. That, in turn, is specified within the logic of the DISPLAY-MAIN-MENU program, developed according to the building blocks of structured programming, first expressed in pseudocode, and eventually converted to program syntax (in this case, dBASE).

The DISPLAY-MAIN-MENU Program

Review the operation of the Soleil Employee System as evidenced by the hands-on exercises and other experimentation in Chapter 1. The system displayed an opening menu which led to other menus for the file maintenance, reporting, and utility functions. You selected a subservient function, completed the associated requirements, and were eventually returned to the opening menu, whereupon the process began again. The cycle repeated itself an indeterminate number of times until you elected to exit the system entirely, but at no time were you allowed to input an invalid selection in response to the opening menu. The DISPLAY-MAIN-MENU program, located at the top of the hierarchy chart, implements these capabilities.

Pseudocode for the DISPLAY-MAIN-MENU program is displayed in Figure 8.4. It contains an outer loop to continually display the opening menu and an inner loop that requests input until a valid response is received. In other words, the outer loop redisplays the main menu after the system returns from a lower level program, and thus enables the user to select another function. The inner loop guarantees that the user will always input a valid response.

The outer loop is controlled by the variable mainloop. It is set to true and remains at that setting until the user elects to exit from the system by entering a 4 in response to the Opening Menu. That, in turn, causes mainloop to be set to false which terminates the outer loop and exits the system. The inner loop is controlled by the variable menuloop. It, too, is set to true and remains set to true until a valid response (1, 2, 3, or 4) is entered. When this occurs, menuloop is set to false and the appropriate lower level program is called.

Remember, too, that while pseudocode contains the logic inherent in a program, it is not an actual programming language and consequently must be translated into dBASE syntax. The latter contains precise commands that include input/output statements, that is, the ability to display information on the screen for the user and to receive user responses via the keyboard.

The completed program is shown in Figure 8.5. It contains little that is new in the way of dBASE commands other than the DO statements used to call the lower level programs. The program begins with three SET statements to (1) eliminate the bell on data input; (2) suppress the intermediate dBASE messages; and (3) erase the dBASE status bar. The mainloop and menuloop variables control the outer and inner loops as was explained before.

The initial statements in the outer loop clear the screen, display the date and title information, then display the opening menu. The inner loop is executed repeatedly until a valid response is obtained from the user. Note the use of the various @...SAY statements

```
              Set mainloop to true
          ┌─ DO WHILE mainloop is true
          │     Clear screen
          │     Display menu choices
          │     Set menuloop to true
          │  ┌─ DO WHILE menuloop is true
          │  │     Get user's menu choice
          │  │  ┌─ DO CASE
          │  │  │     CASE 1: Call file maintenance program
          │  │  │                Set menuloop to false
          │  │  │     CASE 2: Call report program menu
          │  │  │                Set menuloop to false
          │  │  │     CASE 3: Call utility program menu
          │  │  │                Set menuloop to false
          │  │  │     CASE 4: Display backup information
          │  │  │                Set menuloop to false
          │  │  │                Set mainloop to false
          │  │  │     OTHERWISE: Display error message
          │  │  └─ ENDCASE
          │  └─ ENDDO
          └─ ENDDO
              Exit system and return to DOS
```

FIGURE 8.4 Pseudocode for DISPLAY-MAIN-MENU

```
***SOLMAIN.PRG
***This program maps the main menu
***
CLEAR
SET TALK OFF
SET STATUS OFF
STORE 'T' TO mainloop
DO WHILE mainloop = 'T'
   CLEAR                            ── Displays system date
   @ 2,70 SAY DATE()
   @ 2,2 SAY 'Soleil America, Inc.'
   @ 3,2 SAY 'Personnel Information System'
   @ 4,2 SAY 'Release 1.0'
   @ 09,27 SAY '1) File Maintenance'
   @ 11,27 SAY '2) Report Menu'
   @ 13,27 SAY '3) Utility Programs'
   @ 15,27 SAY '4) Backup and Exit From System'
   @ 21,27 SAY 'Please Choose An Option: '
   STORE 'T' TO menuloop
   DO WHILE menuloop = 'T'
      STORE ' ' TO opt
      @ 21,52 GET opt PICTURE '9'
      READ
      DO CASE
         CASE opt='1'                 ── Call to lower level program
            DO SOLFILE.PRG
            STORE 'F' TO menuloop
         CASE opt='2'                 ── Call to lower level program
            DO SOLREP.PRG
            STORE 'F' TO menuloop
         CASE opt='3'                 ── Call to lower level program
            DO SOLUTIL.PRG
            STORE 'F' TO menuloop
         CASE opt='4'
            STORE 'F' TO menuloop
            DO SOLBKUP.PRG           ── Call to lower level program
            @ 14,27 SAY '*** Exit from system ***'
            STORE 1 TO x
            DO WHILE x < 40          ── Delay loop to leave message on screen
               STORE 1 + x TO x
            ENDDO
            STORE 'F' TO mainloop
      OTHERWISE                      ── "Beep" for invalid response
         ? CHR(7)
         @ 23,17 SAY '*** Please Choose One of the Options Listed! ***'
      ENDCASE
   ENDDO
ENDDO
QUIT ───── Exists dBASE and returns to DOS
```

FIGURE 8.5 Soleil Main Menu program

to display information on the screen, and the combination of the `@...GET` and `READ` statements to obtain user input via the keyboard.

The `DO CASE` statement within the inner loop directs control to the appropriate lower level program according to the value of the variable *opt* (obtained via the preceding `GET` statement). A simple `DO` statement in the form, `DO program name`, transfers control to the lower level program. For example, if the user responded 1 initially (that is he or she requested the file maintenance function from the main menu), control would pass from the main menu program in Figure 8.5 to the SOLFILE.PRG program. The lower level program executes in its entirety, then returns control to the main menu program at the statement immediately below the `DO` statement that transferred control in the first place. (You'll best appreciate the continual transfer of control from one program to another after completing Hands-on Exercise 8–1.)

The `DO CASE` statement also prevents the system from accepting an invalid value (that is, a number other than 1, 2, 3, or 4). Should an invalid response be entered, the `?`

CHR(7) statement causes the system to beep and the @...SAY statement displays an error message. The inner loop is reexecuted and the system once again prompts for a proper response, allowing the user to input his or her choice.

Eventually, the user will elect to leave the system by responding 4 to the opening menu; this causes several things to happen. Control will first be passed to the SOLBKUP.PRG program, then returned to the @...SAY statement that displays the message "*** Exit from system***." The latter will remain briefly on the screen while the delay loop (DO WHILE X < 40) is executed. Finally, mainloop is set to false, the outer loop terminates, and the QUIT statement is executed, returning control to DOS.

We hope that you were able to follow our discussion, and that the listing in Figure 8.5 is in fact, perfectly clear. Do not be concerned, however, if you are unsure about the operation of one or more statements. Proceed to the next section on top-down implementation and its associated hands-on exercise. Remember dBASE programming is best learned by doing, and thus completing the hands-on exercise will go a long way in helping you to understand the commands in Figure 8.5.

Top-Down Implementation

Completion of the Soleil Employee System requires you to eventually write a program for every box in the hierarchy chart of Figure 8.2. Our intent, however, is not to spend an undue amount of time in programming per se, but rather to provide an appreciation for the system development process. Accordingly, we describe how the system would be implemented and tested, omitting the detailed program listings.

Realize also that while the process of creating attractive menus (with respect to the placement of rows and columns on the screen) is time consuming, it is not very difficult. Far more important is the logic that accepts the user's response, and then determines which program within the system is executed next. In other words, our initial concern should be that the system guarantees a valid user response, rather than deciding if the message requesting that response should appear in row 18 or row 20.

Unfortunately, many students mistakenly develop the screen layouts first, leaving the more complex portions of the system for later. By contrast, the *top-down* philosophy requires simply that the more important programs in a system (those at or near the top of the hierarchy chart) be developed first, with the details left for later. The concept is simple, even obvious, yet one ignored too often in practice.

Again the analogy between a system's hierarchy chart and a corporate organizational chart is appropriate. A new company begins with the president and not the janitor, so why not begin system development at the top as well. Moreover, the higher a person appears on an organizational chart, the more responsible his or her position. In much the same way, programs appearing near the top of a hierarchy chart are generally more important (that is, they contain more complex logic) than those near the bottom.

The top-down philosophy espouses that testing begin as soon as possible, *even before all of the programs in a system have been completed*. Although this may sound implausible, it is easily accomplished by supplying partially completed programs, known as *program stubs*, for the lower level programs in the system.

Consider, for example, the DISPLAY-MAIN-MENU program of Figure 8.5, which requires four additional programs (SOLFILE, SOLREP, SOLUTIL, and SOLBKUP) before testing can begin. What if, however, we initially developed very simple versions of these programs as shown in Figure 8.6. We could then proceed to test the DISPLAY-MAIN-MENU program fully. The results of the early testing will indicate that the subordinate programs are called in proper sequence. It will also provide a sense of how the completed system will operate.

```
***SOLFILE.PRG
CLEAR
@10,16 SAY 'The file maintenance menu would be located here'
@12,10 SAY 'The user would add, edit, update, or delete employee records'
WAIT
RETURN
```

a

```
***SOLREP.PRG
CLEAR
@10,16 SAY 'The report menu would be located here'
@12,13 SAY 'The user would choose one of several reports'
WAIT
RETURN
```

b

```
***SOLUTIL.PRG
CLEAR
@10,16 SAY 'The utility menu would be located here'
@12,15 SAY 'The user would choose a utility function'
WAIT
RETURN
```

c

```
***SOLBKUP.PRG
***
CLEAR
@10,16 SAY 'The backup procedure would be described here'
WAIT
RETURN
```

d

FIGURE 8.6 Level 1 programs stubs: (a) file maintenance program stubs; (b) report menu program stubs; (c) utility menu program stubs; (d) backup procedure program stub

The program stubs in Figure 8.6 are easy to code, trivial in nature, and consist of four types of statements:

1. A CLEAR statement to erase the screen.
2. @...SAY statements to print a message indicating that the programs have been called.
3. A WAIT statement requiring only that the user press any key to continue (this signifies he or she has read the message).
4. A RETURN statement to return control to the calling program, in this case the DISPLAY-MAIN-MENU program.

The availability of the stub programs enables you to test the DISPLAY-MAIN-MENU program confirming that it is performing correctly. Recall that the purpose of the DISPLAY-MAIN-MENU program is to display an opening menu (shown in Figure 8.7), request that the user enter a response to the menu, validate that response (that is, check that it is 1, 2, 3, or 4), and then transfer control to an appropriate lower level program corresponding to the user's answer to the opening menu.

Once testing of the DISPLAY-MAIN-MENU program has been completed you will know that it interacts properly with its subordinate programs, and that it is also capable of rejecting invalid user responses. You will not know if the lower level programs are working, only that they have been called correctly. Nevertheless, the accomplishment is significant as you will appreciate by completing Hands-on Exercise 8–1.

Hands-on Exercise 8–1:   Top-Down Testing/1

Objective: To illustrate top-down testing through development of program stubs.

☐   **STEP 1: Create the necessary programs for testing.**

We suggest that you do *not* use the convenience disk for this exercise in order to avoid confusion between the completed system (which exists on the convenience disk) and the program stubs you will create in this exercise. Accordingly, place a *newly formatted data disk* in drive B (or log onto a new subdirectory on a hard drive) at this time.

Use either a word processor or the dBASE MODIFY COMMAND capability to create the main menu program of Figure 8.5 and the *four* program stubs of Figure 8.6. (See the Programmer's Notebook for specifics on the MODIFY COMMAND.) Name the file containing the main menu program SOLMAIN.PRG (PRG is the dBASE extension used to indicate a program file). Similarly, the files containing the program stubs should all have the PRG extension, with file names corresponding to the DO statements in the SOLMAIN program. Thus, when you are finished, the data disk in drive B should contain five files: SOLMAIN.PRG, SOLFILE.PRG, SOLREP.PRG, SOLUTIL.PRG, and SOLBKUP.PRG.

You are now ready to begin testing the system.

☐   **STEP 2: Load dBASE.**

Exit from the word processor and return to the DOS prompt. Use the DIR command to verify the presence of the five files created in Step 1, then place the first dBASE program disk in drive A (or enter a path command to the

```
Soleil America, Inc.
Personnel Information System
Release 1.0




            1) File Maintenance

            2) Report Menu

            3) Utility Programs

            4) Backup and Exit From System




            Please Choose An Option:
```

FIGURE 8.7 The main menu as displayed on the monitor

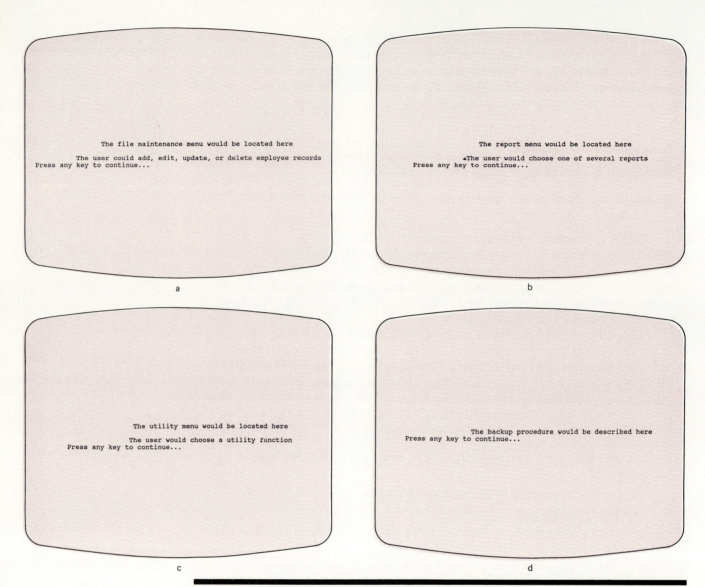

```
                    The file maintenance menu would be located here

                The user could add, edit, update, or delete employee records
Press any key to continue...
```

```
                           The report menu would be located here

                    ▲The user would choose one of several reports
Press any key to continue...
```

a

b

```
                    The utility menu would be located here

                 The user would choose a utility function
Press any key to continue...
```

```
                      The backup procedure would be described here
Press any key to continue...
```

c

d

FIGURE 8.8 Output of programs stubs: (a) output of file maintenance program stub (produced by the program of Figure 8.6a); (b) output of report menu program stub (produced by the program of Figure 8.6b); (c) output of utility menu program stub (produced by the program of Figure 8.6c); (d) output of backup program stub (produced by the program of Figure 8.6d)

subdirectory containing the dBASE program files on the hard drive, for example, `PATH \SAMPLER`). Load dBASE.

Make sure the printer is turned on, then enter the dBASE command, `SET PRINT ON`, to echo all output from the screen to the printer. In this way you will have a permanent (hard copy) record of the testing session.

☐ STEP 3: Test the system.

Enter the dBASE command, `DO SOLMAIN`, to invoke the main menu program and bring up the menu shown earlier in Figure 8.7. Observe how the menu displayed on the screen corresponds to the `@...SAY` statements in the program of Figure 8.5.

Supply a value other than 1, 2, 3, or 4 to verify that the system rejects invalid entries. Enter responses of 1, 2, and 3 (in several different sequences and/or combinations) to invoke the appropriate lower level programs, obtaining screen displays as shown in Figures 8.8a, b, and c. Note that after each lower level module is executed control returns to the main menu. Eventually, supply a response of 4 to invoke the backup-and-exit module (Figure 8.8d) thus leaving the Soleil Employee System and returning to DOS.

It is also more than likely that you will have made several errors (misspelling a word, omitting a closing quote, and so on) when you created the programs, causing dBASE to display the message "Cancel, Suspend, or Ignore" every time it encounters an error. We suggest you make a note of errors but otherwise ignore them as long as testing makes sense. Eventually, however, you will have to cancel and return to the dot prompt at which point you can use `MODIFY COMMAND` to fix your program, and repeat the cycle. In a short time, your programs will be fully debugged and testing should progress smoothly.

Additional Testing

Completing the hands-on exercise successfully demonstrates that the system passes control from one program to another as well as rejects invalid user responses. However, the exercise

```
***SOLFILE.PRG
***This program maps the file maintenance menu
***
STORE 'T' TO filemenu
DO WHILE filemenu = 'T'
   CLEAR
   @ 3,2 SAY 'File Maintenance Menu'
   @ 08,27 SAY '1) Add New Employee'
   @ 10,27 SAY '2) Edit Existing Employee'
   @ 12,27 SAY '3) Update Employee Salary'
   @ 14,27 SAY '4) Delete Existing Employee'
   @ 16,27 SAY '5) Exit to Main Menu'
   @ 21,27 SAY 'Please Choose An Option: '
   STORE 'T' TO menuloop
   DO WHILE menuloop = 'T'
      STORE ' ' TO fileopt
      @ 21,52 GET fileopt PICTURE '9'
      READ
      @ 22,2 SAY SPACE(77)
      DO CASE
         CASE fileopt='1'
            DO SOLADD.PRG
            STORE 'F' TO menuloop
         CASE fileopt='2'
            DO SOLEDIT.PRG
            STORE 'F' TO menuloop
         CASE fileopt='3'
            DO SOLUPD.PRG
            STORE 'F' TO menuloop
         CASE fileopt='4'
            DO SOLDEL.PRG
            STORE 'F' TO menuloop
         CASE fileopt = '5'
            STORE 'F' TO filemenu
            STORE 'F' TO menuloop
      OTHERWISE
         ? CHR(7)
         @ 23,17 SAY '*** Please Choose One of the Options Listed! ***'
      ENDCASE
   ENDDO
ENDDO
RETURN
```

FIGURE 8.9 Expanded file maintenance program (requires additional program stubs for testing)

encompassed only five of the 18 required programs, and three of these exist as program stubs. Clearly, additional work is necessary before the system is finally operational.

The next step would be to expand the four program stubs to accept user input, while you simultaneously develop additional program stubs for the next lowest level in the hierarchy chart. The testing would then expand to include every program within the hierarchy chart. Completing it successfully would verify that all 18 programs interact properly with one another.

Consider, for example, Figure 8.9 which expands the program stub for the file maintenance menu (shown earlier as Figure 8.6a). The logic is straightforward and closely parallels that of the DISPLAY-MAIN-MENU program which was explained earlier. Note, also, the requirement for four additional program stubs (SOLADD.PRG, SOLEDIT.PRG, SOLUPD.PRG, and SOLDEL.PRG) in order to fully test the file maintenance program.

Similarly, it is necessary to expand the other program stubs for the report generation menu, the utilities menu, and the backup option, creating additional program stubs for these as well. A second round of testing could begin as indicated in Hands-on Exercise 8–2. To facilitate testing we have created all of the necessary program stubs for you, and have placed them in a separate subdirectory on the convenience disk.

Hands-on Exercise 8–2:   Top-Down Testing/2

Objective: To continue testing through expansion of first level programs and development of additional program stubs for the next lowest level.

☐   STEP 1: Log onto the SOLSTUB subdirectory.

Boot DOS, then change to the SOLSTUB directory with the appropriate command:

```
CD B:\SOLSTUB ──────── With a floppy disk system
```

```
B> DIR

Volume in drive B is DATAMGT
Directory of  B:\SOLSTUB

.              <DIR>      2-04-89   12:08p
..             <DIR>      2-04-89   12:08p
SOLMAIN   PRG   1280      2-06-89    8:40a

SOLFILE   PRG   1280      2-06-89    9:17a
SOLREP    PRG   1544      2-06-89    9:16a
SOLUTIL   PRG    914      2-06-89    9:25a
SOLBKUP   PRG    720      2-06-89    9:27a

SOLADD    PRG    128      2-06-89    9:22a
SOLEDIT   PRG    128      2-06-89    9:22a
SOLUPD    PRG    128      2-06-89    9:22a
SOLDEL    PRG    128      2-06-89    9:22a

REP1      PRG    128      2-06-89    8:49a
SOLPROF   PRG    128      2-06-89    8:49a
LOCREP    PRG    128      2-06-89    8:49a
DEPTREP   PRG    128      2-06-89    8:50a
MIDREP    PRG    128      2-06-89    8:50a
RAISEREP  PRG    128      2-06-89    8:51a
PERFREP   PRG    128      2-06-89    8:51a

SOLBUILD  PRG    128      2-06-89    9:23a
SOLCODES  PRG    128      2-06-89    9:24a
```

Expanded file maintenance program

File maintenance stub programs

Report menu stub programs

Utility menu stub programs

FIGURE 8.10 SOLSTUB subdirectory

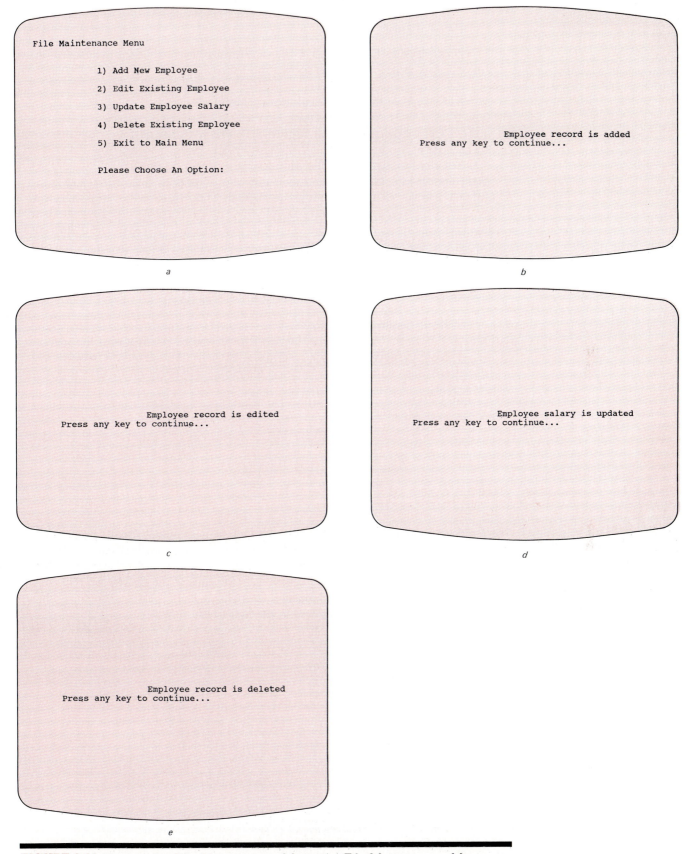

File Maintenance Menu

     1) Add New Employee

     2) Edit Existing Employee

     3) Update Employee Salary

     4) Delete Existing Employee

     5) Exit to Main Menu

     Please Choose An Option:

a

          Employee record is added
Press any key to continue...

b

          Employee record is edited
Press any key to continue...

c

          Employee salary is updated
Press any key to continue...

d

          Employee record is deleted
Press any key to continue...

e

FIGURE 8.11 Testing the File Maintenance Menu: (a) File Maintenance Menu (produced by Figure 8.9); (b) output of ADD program stub; (c) output of EDIT program stub; (d) output of UPDATE program stub; (e) output of DELETE program stub

```
CD C:\SAMPLER\SOLSTUB ──── With a hard disk drive
PATH \SAMPLER
```

Load dBASE. Enter the `DIR *.*` command to verify that the SOLSTUB subdirectory contains the files shown in Figure 8.10.

☐ **STEP 2: Test the File Maintenance Menu.**

Type `DO SOLMAIN` to begin testing. You will see the Soleil Employee System's main menu (shown earlier in Figure 8.7) which provides four options: file maintenance, report generation, utilities, and backup.

Enter a 1 to invoke the File Maintenance Menu. It, in turn, allows you to select one of four file maintenance functions. Respond 1, 2, 3, or 4 to add, edit, update, or delete an employee record. This, in turn, invokes a lower level program stub. (You might also try entering an invalid response to check the data validation capabilities built into the system.) Displays produced by testing the file maintenance program (and its associated program stubs) are shown in Figure 8.11.

When you are satisfied that the File Maintenance Menu program works, enter a 5 to return to the main menu of Figure 8.7.

☐ **STEP 3: Continue testing.**

Enter a 2 from the main menu (Figure 8.7) to invoke the Report Generation Menu. Experiment with various responses, both valid and invalid, eventually returning to the main menu. Continue testing by experimenting with the system's utility and/or backup portions.

When you are satisfied with the "complete" system, exit and return to the DOS prompt.

Advantages of Top-Down Implementation

The top-down approach to testing enables the highest (and most difficult) programs in a hierarchy chart to be tested earlier and more often than the lower level (and often trivial) programs. Thus any errors that do exist are found sooner in the development cycle and consequently are easier to correct. Of course, later versions of the system can still contain bugs, but these will be in lower level modules where fixing them is easier. The more difficult problems will already have been resolved in the initial tests.

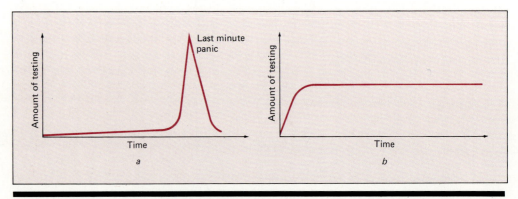

FIGURE 8.12 Top-down versus traditional testing: (a) traditional testing; (b) top-down testing

A second advantage of top-down testing is that testing and coding become parallel activities. This means that users (and project sponsors) continually see previews of the completed system. Thus, they are in an excellent position to correct any major flaws in the implementation of the system well before it is completed.

Figure 8.12 shows the differences between top-down and traditional testing. Figure 8.12a depicts the traditional way of testing in which no testing is done until the weekend before the system goes live (or your assignment is due). Last-minute panic sets in with abundant overtime and chaos. By contrast, Figure 8.12b indicates a more uniform pattern of testing, which begins almost immediately and continues throughout the project's duration.

Summary

The chapter returned to the Soleil America, Inc., case from Chapter 1 to focus on the relationships between programs within a system. Our intent, however, was not to spend an undue amount of time on programming per se, but to emphasize the system requirements and the way in which the solution would be developed. To that end we introduced the hierarchy chart as a design tool and showed how the development of the programs in the chart would be implemented in top-down fashion.

The chapter drew a distinction between structured programming and structured design, and between hierarchy charts and pseudocode. A hierarchy chart shows what has to be done but not when to do it, because it contains no decision-making logic. Pseudocode, on the other hand, specifies when and if a given program is executed. We say that a hierarchy chart is *functional* whereas pseudocode is *procedural*.

Last, but certainly not least, were the two hands-on exercises showing the practicality of the top-down approach to system testing. In addition, these exercises reviewed many of the dBASE programming commands from Chapter 7.

Key Words and Concepts

? CHR(7)	Nondocument file
@...GET	PRG extension
@...SAY	Program stubs
ASCII file	Pseudocode
CLEAR	QUIT
DO	RETURN
DO CASE	Structured design
DO WHILE	Structured programming
Hierarchy chart	Top-down testing
Information system	WAIT
Memory variable	

True/False

1. A system must be completely coded before any testing can begin.
2. A program in a hierarchy chart can be called from another program at the same level.
3. The highest level modules in a hierarchy chart should be tested first.
4. Pseudocode and hierarchy charts depict the same thing.
5. In a given system, the same program *cannot* be both a called and a calling program.

6. No program in a hierarchy chart should have more than one subordinate program.
7. Every program within a system should eventually return control to the program that called it initially.
8. No program in a hierarchy chart should have more than one managing program.
9. For efficiency, a hierarchy chart, should include programs that perform multiple functions.
10. An information system can be partially tested even if no data files are available.
11. Structured design is a procedurally oriented technique.
12. Structured programming is a functionally oriented technique.
13. A span of control of 1 or 2 is reasonable for most programs within a system.

Exercises

1. Distinguish between
   a. a called and a calling program
   b. a program stub and its completed version
   c. structured design and structured programming
   d. a system's hierarchy chart and a company's organizational chart
   e. the CLEAR and WAIT statements
   f. the DO CASE and DO WHILE statements
   g. the @...SAY and @...GET statements
   h. the RETURN and QUIT statements
   i. a functionally oriented technique and a procedurally oriented technique

2. Indicate precisely what the following dBASE statements do. (Use the Programmer's Notebook as appropriate.)
   a. QUIT
   b. CLEAR
   c. RETURN
   d. @2,70 SAY DATE()
   e. WAIT
   f. SET BELL OFF
   g. ?CHR(7)
   h. SET TALK OFF
   i. SET STATUS OFF

3. Obtain a sheet of ordinary graph paper and mark off an area that is 24 × 80. Use the dBASE program in Figure 8.5 to indicate precisely where the various messages will appear on a monitor. Using these figures as a guide, create a screen display that will display the Report Generation Menu.

4. Develop pseudocode for the File Maintenance, Report Generation, or Utility Menu programs (DISPLAY-MAINTENANCE-MENU, DISPLAY-REPORT-MENU, or DISPLAY-UTILITY-MENU) shown in the hierarchy chart in Figure 8.2. Use Figure 8.4 as a guide.

5. Given the completed programs and associated program stubs of Hands-on Exercise 8-2, indicate what messages will be produced if the following responses are entered in sequence: 5, 1, 4, 5, and 4. Can you begin to appreciate the results of top-down testing?

6. This problem specifically avoids a business context, and was selected because you are unfamiliar with it and consequently have no preexisting bias toward a solution.

   Develop a hierarchy chart (which is the eventual basis for a programming solution) to allow a person to play a series of tic-tac-toe games interactively against a computer. The following modules are used in our solution: PLAY-SERIES, PLAY-GAME, CLEAR-BOARD, GET-USER-MOVE, VALIDATE-USER-MOVE, CHECK-FOR-WINNER, UPDATE-BOARD, GET-COMPUTER-MOVE, DISPLAY-BOARD, and DISPLAY-MESSAGE. (The last module, DISPLAY MESSAGE, may be called from several places.)

Note that in developing the hierarchy chart you are concerned only with what the individual programs will do, not how they will do it. (The logic for the latter is developed in pseudocode when the programs are actually written.)

7. Again, we have chosen a nonbusiness problem to give you further practice with structured design. Develop a hierarchy chart for the game of black jack (also known as "21"). Indicate enough programs in your solution to accommodate:

   a. Doubling down—if the player's first two cards total 11, he or she may double the bet and receive one additional card.

   b. Purchasing insurance—if the dealer's "up" card is an ace, the player may place an additional side bet. If the dealer has "black jack," the player receives a payout of 2 to 1 on the side bet, but loses the initial bet. If the dealer does not have black jack, the side bet is lost and play continues.

   c. Splitting pairs—if the player has a pair he or she may double the bet and play two hands.

   The rules of black jack state that the dealer must draw with 16 or less, and stand with 17 or more. Your hierarchy chart should contain the necessary programs to keep a running total of the player's winnings (or losses).

After reading this chapter, you should be able to:

- Use the dBASE screen generator to create customized screens for application programs; describe how to toggle between the menu and blackboard within the screen generator.

- Use the screen generator to load fields from a DBF file; describe how to reposition these fields on the blackboard through dragging and how to insert additional text where appropriate.

- Use the screen generator to create picture templates and/or picture functions for selected fields.

- Describe the use of special effects such as color, reverse video, and delimiters.

- List at least three types of data validation checks; describe how these checks may be implemented within the context of the dBASE screen generator.

The dBASE Screen Generator

9

OUTLINE

Overview

dBASE includes several special capabilities to facilitate system development, among them report forms (Chapter 4), mailing labels (Chapter 5), and query files (Chapter 6). In this chapter we present the *screen generator*, another powerful feature that enables you to use the monitor as a *blackboard* and then have dBASE generate the necessary `@...GET` and `@...SAY` statements for use within a program.

The screen generator is presented within the context of an entirely new case study. The two hands-on exercises associated with the case fully describe how to use the screen generator. Implicit within this discussion is the concept of *data validation* and how various types of edit checks can be included within the screen generation process. The chapter also indicates how to incorporate special effects such as the use of color and reverse highlighting.

Case Preview

The case you are about to read deals with a stock broker interested in attracting additional clients. As you read the discussion, visualize the fields necessary for the broker to accomplish his or her goals and the form these fields should take within the file structure. Recall also the many decisions made in creating a file structure, namely:

1. the fields within the file structure
2. the size of each field
3. the data type of each field
4. the order of the fields within a record
5. the keys on which records can be retrieved

As you wrestle with your own solution, your major decisions will concern the fields to be included in the file structure. Some of the fields will be obvious, for example name and address, common to virtually every application. Others will be less obvious, for example, a prospect's telephone number (omitted by many of our students when we initially assigned this case as a homework assignment). The most important part of the design, however, deals with fields unique to the application.

Information on precisely which fields to include requires a true understanding of the physical system. This is gained only from discussions with the personnel involved. Since our broker is unavailable, you may want to contact your own to determine what he or she would want in the way of a system similar to the one we describe. Incorporate your findings into a file structure, then compare your solution to ours.

Michael Essman, Stock Broker

As the 747 taxied to the end of the runway, Michael Essman turned to his wife, smiled, then settled back into his seat for the long ride home. The two weeks in Australia had been fabulous, and the fact that his brokerage house had picked up the tab for the truly deluxe accommodations made it even better. Indeed, he was one of only 180 brokers out of the firm's 11,000 to have achieved sufficient sales production to merit the trip. The realization that he had accomplished this in less than five years made it all the more gratifying.

Last year's success was in the past however, and as the plane took off, Mike's thoughts turned to increasing his sales level in the coming year. He was motivated now more by ego than by money, although the money certainly helped, especially as his income had grown from almost nothing to well into six figures. Moreover, the client assets he had under management virtually guaranteed a very comfortable income as long as he maintained his existing accounts. Yes, he had what he wanted materially, but he still craved recognition within the industry as being among the very best. His problem was that of any salesman, namely how to increase sales production.

Mike thought of the approximately 10,000 cold calls he had made over the last year (40 calls a day, five days a week, 50 weeks a year), and of the 9500 rejections those calls had produced. Still, all and all they had yielded some 500 new accounts which is how he got to Australia in the first place. He thought fondly of his first manager, Norm MacGregor, who effectively reduced selling to a "numbers game." If the number of contacts were sufficiently large, the accounts would follow. Norm's advice to him was simply that "Selling is like shaving, do it every day or you're a bum." Mike knew that he couldn't rest on last year's laurels, no matter how great a year it had been.

The problem was that there were only so many hours in a day, and that it simply wasn't possible to increase the amount of time on the phone. He had gotten to the point where he could tell within the first minute of a conversation whether the contact was worth pursuing. It took him only another two minutes to determine the prospect's investment objective (growth or income) and the amount of money he or she had to invest. He realized for the first time that the system he maintained on 3 by 5 index cards, was not efficient for following up on those contacts who expressed an interest in additional information. Clearly, he needed a better way to manage repeat phone calls and/or followup mailings, especially when a prospect said, "Call me in two weeks," or "Send me the next annual report." Perhaps a computer might help, but how?

The major brokerage house he worked for provided adequate computer support for existing clients, but did nothing in the way of data management for prospective clients. Then it hit him, his goal for the coming year would be to use the PC sitting on his desk to solicit new accounts.

Case Solution

The solution to this or any other case begins with the design of the file structure, the importance of which we cannot overemphasize. Our file structure is shown in Figure 9.1 which may or may not correspond to what you envisioned as you read the case study. Indeed, whether or not our solutions are the same is not really important; there are many satisfactory answers. What is essential, however, is that the structure chosen contain all necessary data so that the system can perform as intended.

The need to include the prospect's name, address, and telephone number is apparent from the case preview and discussion. You should remember from the discussion in Chapter 5, however, why the prospect's name is separated into three fields (last name, first name, and prefix), and why his or her address is similarly divided. Recall also the discussion in Chapter 5 on field type, and the reason for designating both zip code and telephone number as character, rather than numeric fields.

The length of the telephone field is not as apparent. Given the necessity for including the area code, you might designate the minimum field size as 13 or even 14 characters rather than ten. In other words, we are accustomed to seeing telephone numbers of the form (305)284-6595 or even (305) 284-6595 (note the space between the area code and

Field	Field Name	Type	Width
1	LASTNAME	Character	16
2	FIRSTNAME	Character	12
3	PREFIX	Character	3
4	STREET	Character	24
5	CITY	Character	18
6	STATE	Character	2
7	ZIPCODE	Character	5
8	TELEPHONE	Character	10
9	OBJECTIVE	Character	1
10	AMOUNT	Numeric	7
11	INTEREST	Character	1
12	LASTCALL	Date	8

FIGURE 9.1 Suggested file structure

number), as opposed to 3052846595 which is much more difficult to read. Why then do we use only ten characters?

The answer is that only ten characters are required to store a telephone number (within a DBF or other data file), whereas the additional positions are necessary when generating printed reports and/or data entry screens. It is possible therefore to save space within the storage medium by designating the smaller length and subsequently converting to the more readable form for display by using dBASE commands.

A different design decision is introduced in the field for investment objective and illustrates the use of a one-position code to designate the prospect's investment goals. Here we enter a G or I, for growth or income respectively, as opposed to spelling out the investment objective. As well as saving space, using codes facilitates data entry, reduces the chance of error, and simplifies data validation.

The design of the file structure must also be broad enough to include all data necessary to fulfill the system's overall objectives, regardless of whether these objectives are stated implicitly or explicitly. It is logical, for example, to assume that the people contacted will express different degrees of interest (for example, high, moderate, or low) and provision must be made to capture this all important data. An alternative way of measuring client interest is to look at the date a client was last contacted, perhaps to do a special mailing to all people contacted within the last month, drop all contacts over a year old, and so on. Realize also that Michael will be more interested in clients with large amounts of money to invest (it takes no more time to buy 1000 shares of stock than 100) and so this field should be included as well.

The result of these deliberations has produced the file structure shown earlier in Figure 9.1. As you can infer from the discussion, there are no hard and fast rules for designing a file structure. The decisions made as to the fields to be included, their sizes and types, reflect the system's current (and future) needs and are subjective by nature.

Screen Design

The APPEND command enables new records to be added to a file. It positions the record pointer at the end of the currently selected DBF file and allows the new record to be added as depicted in Figure 9.2a. Although adding records in this way may not pose problems for the knowledgeable dBASE programmer, it can be intimidating for the less sophisticated end user. The Cursor Menu at the top of Figure 9.2a is less than obvious, the telephone number must be entered without parentheses to clarify the area code, and the LASTCALL field does not even appear on the screen (the field will appear via scrolling when the other fields have been entered).

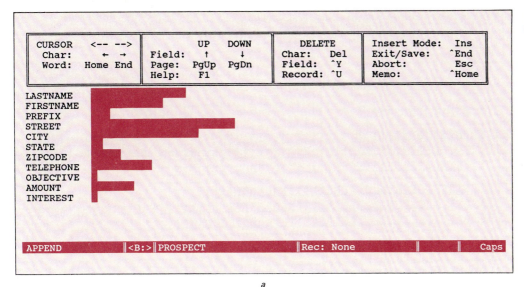

a

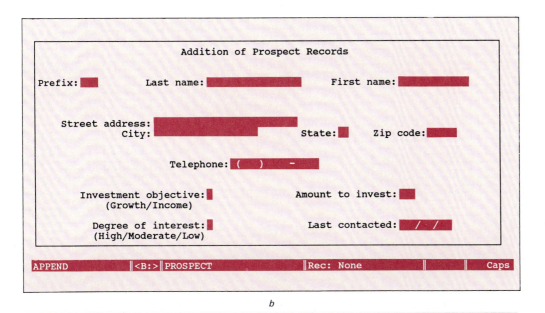

b

FIGURE 9.2 (a) Data entry via standard screen; (b) data entry via formatted screen

A better approach would be the customized screen of Figure 9.2b. Here the fields slated for data entry are spaced attractively on the monitor with appropriate formatting, for example, the parentheses within the telephone number and the slashes within the date field. The fields are also labeled more descriptively in that we are no longer restricted by the ten-character dBASE limitation on field names; for example, Degree of Interest appears in lieu of INTEREST. Note, too, that subtle help messages appear where appropriate in Figure 9.2b; for example, (High/Moderate/Low) is printed under the space where the degree of interest is to be entered.

As you would expect, additional work is required to generate customized screens of the type shown in Figure 9.2b, yet it is far less work than you might expect. It is certainly true that multiple @...SAY and @...GET statements are necessary to indicate the precise screen locations of the various fields, yet the dBASE screen generator is available to create these statements for you. In essence, this facility presents you with an empty screen called the *blackboard*, allows you to enter text anywhere you like using the cursor keys, then automatically generates the corresponding @...SAY and @...GET statements.

Hands-on Exercise 9–1:   The dBASE Screen Generator

Objective: To use the dBASE screen generator to create a customized screen for data entry; describe the use of the blackboard and how to toggle between the blackboard and the menu functions.

☐ **STEP 1: Create the PROSPECT file structure.**

Boot DOS, then place the convenience disk in drive B and change to the STOCK subdirectory with the appropriate command:

```
CD B:\STOCK ──────────── With a floppy disk system

CD C:\SAMPLER\STOCK ─────── With a hard disk drive
PATH C:\SAMPLER
```

Load dBASE, then create a file structure for PROSPECT.DBF, corresponding to the case study solution shown earlier in Figure 9.1.

☐ **STEP 2: Enter the screen generator.**

The CREATE SCREEN command initiates the screen generator in similar fashion to the process for report forms and mailing labels (as demonstrated in Chapters 4 and 5). Enter the CREATE SCREEN command as shown below, whereupon you will be asked for the name of the screen file:

```
. USE PROSPECT
. CREATE SCREEN
Enter screen file name:PROSPECT
```

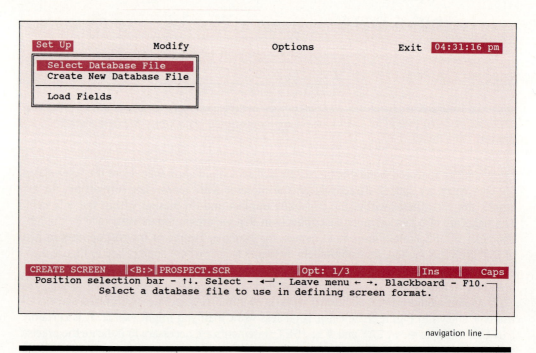

FIGURE 9.3 The Screen Generation Menu

Note that we have chosen to use the same name, PROSPECT, for the screen file as well as for the DBF file. You will then be presented with Figure 9.3, containing the Screen Generation Menu.

☐ **STEP 3: Toggle between the blackboard and menu.**
The last entry in the navigation line of Figure 9.3 shows that the F10 function key accesses the *blackboard*. Press this key and a blank screen appears; press the key a second time and the menu returns. In other words, the F10 key acts as a *toggle* switch between the menu and the blackboard.

Toggle to the blackboard, then experiment with the four arrow keys (up, down, right, and left) to position the cursor. Enter text as indicated in Figure 9.4. (The screen generator recognizes many WordStar commands that facilitate the process, for example, Ctrl F and Ctrl A will move the cursor one word right and left respectively.) You can also use the Ins key to toggle between the insert and replacement modes for entering text, and the Del key to delete individual characters.

End this step with the cursor positioned under the last line of text you entered, that is, in row 6 as indicated in the status bar at the bottom of Figure 9.4. Press the F10 key to return to the menu.

☐ **STEP 4: Load the LASTNAME, FIRSTNAME, and PREFIX fields.**
You should again see the Screen Generation Menu of Figure 9.3. Use the right and left arrow keys to highlight the Set Up option, then use the up and down arrow keys to highlight the Load Fields option, and press the Return key. A second box will appear on the screen which contains all the fields within the file structure of the PROSPECT.DBF.

Use the up and down arrow keys to highlight the first three fields (LAST-NAME, FIRSTNAME, and PREFIX), pressing the Return key as each field is highlighted. An arrow will appear in front of each selected field as shown in Figure 9.5.

Now press the F10 key to return to the blackboard with the fields you selected (LASTNAME, FIRSTNAME, and PREFIX) automatically entered for

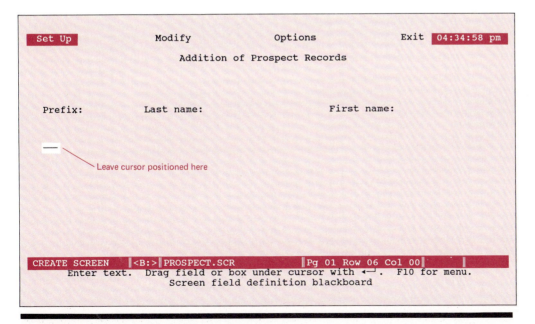

FIGURE 9.4 The blackboard

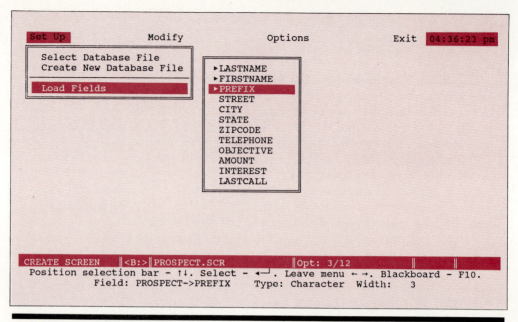

FIGURE 9.5 Loading fields

you at the position of the cursor (that is, at the beginning of row 6). You will see the two lines of text created earlier in Step 3, as well as the three selected fields as shown in Figure 9.6.

☐   **STEP 5: Dragging fields for data entry.**

Each of the fields in Figure 9.6 is followed by a number of Xs (16, 12, and 3, respectively) corresponding to the length of each field in the file structure (the LASTNAME, FIRSTNAME, and PREFIX fields were designated in the file structure as 16-, 12-, and 3-position character fields, respectively). The location of the Xs indicates the position on the screen where dBASE expects to receive

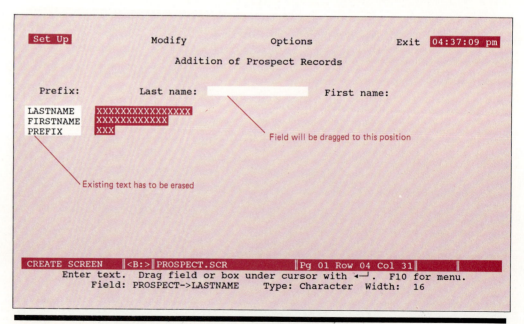

FIGURE 9.6 Dragging fields

values for those fields. It is necessary to move the Xs so that they are adjacent to the corresponding text description, a procedure known as *dragging* a field.

Move the cursor to the first X in the field for last name, then press the Return key. Now move the cursor to the desired position for data entry (that is, one space to the right of the text entry "Last name:"), and press the Return key. The 16 Xs corresponding to the data entry template for last name should move from row 6 to row 4. Repeat the procedure for the fields for first name and prefix.

Observe too that the field names LASTNAME, FIRSTNAME, and PREFIX (as extracted from the file structure) remain on the screen after the dragging operation has been completed. Accordingly, move the cursor to the appropriate location and use the Del key as required to erase the field names from the screen. (You can also use the WordStar commands Ctrl T and Ctrl Y to delete a word and a line, respectively.)

☐ **STEP 6: Enter the address fields.**

Remain in the blackboard and enter text for the address fields (street, city, state, and zip code). Remember to leave the cursor positioned under the last line where text was entered, then toggle back to the main menu and select the STREET, CITY, STATE, and ZIPCODE fields. Toggle again to the blackboard and you will see a screen corresponding to Figure 9.7.

Drag the various address fields to their appropriate positions as indicated in Step 5, then erase the field names.

☐ **STEP 7: Complete the screen.**

Complete the screen by selecting, then dragging, the remaining fields (TELE-PHONE, OBJECTIVE, AMOUNT, INTEREST, and LASTCALL) as shown in Figure 9.8. The latter is almost complete, except that the telephone field has not yet been *edited*, that is, parentheses are not shown for the area code, nor is there a hyphen within the number itself. The editing procedure for the telephone field is described later in Hands-on Exercise 9–2.

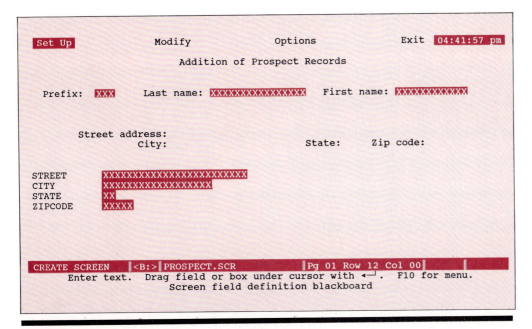

FIGURE 9.7 Entering the fields for address

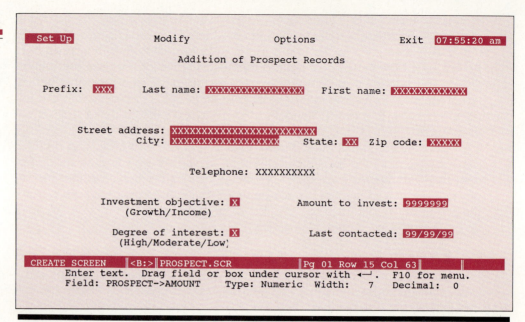

FIGURE 9.8 The "completed" screen

☐ **STEP 8: Save the completed screen.**

Exit the blackboard and return to the main menu using the F10 toggle switch. Use the right and left arrow keys to highlight the Exit option, then the up and down arrow keys to select the Save operation, whereupon you are returned to the dot prompt.

☐ **STEP 9: Append records to the file.**

Enter the **APPEND** command from the dot prompt and a data entry screen similar to Figure 9.2b will come into view. (There is a slight difference between the current screen and the one in Figure 9.2b as the latter included a *formatted* telephone field that will be developed in a subsequent hands-on exercise.)

Enter data for one or more records using prospect data of your own choosing. We suggest, however, that you try using deliberately invalid values in one or more fields (for example a letter in the amount field, a month of 13 in the date field, and so on) to observe what, if anything, dBASE will do.

Recall that dBASE takes you automatically from one field to the next if you completely fill the previous field, for example entering a three-character prefix such as Ms. automatically positions the cursor at the first position in the field for last name. You must, however, press the Return key to jump to the next field when you do not fill the current field. Thus, entering a six-character last name such as Barber requires you to press the Return key to move to the template for first name.

Press Esc when you are finished entering data in order to return to the dot prompt.

☐ **STEP 10: Disable the bell.**

The **SET BELL OFF** command suppresses the continual "beeping" at the end of a field, or when entering invalid data. If the bell is suppressed and you attempt to enter invalid data (for example, a letter in the numeric amount to invest field), the system simply refuses to accept the invalid entry.

☐ **STEP 11: The** `SET FORMAT TO` **command.**

The `SET FORMAT TO` command retrieves the format file (for example, PROSPECT.FMT) created by the screen generator and is issued prior to the `APPEND` command. (The command was not needed in this exercise since the screen was created and saved in Step 8, and thus was active when we appended records in Step 9. That is not the general case, however, and the command is normally issued prior to appending records to a file.)

Consider the following command sequence:

```
. SET BELL OFF
. USE PROSPECT
. APPEND
```
Add a record(s) via the standard screen of Figure 9.2a
Exit with Esc to save the new record
```
. SET FORMAT TO PROSPECT
```
——— *Retrieves the PROSPECT.FMT format file*
```
. APPEND
```
Add a record(s) via the customized screen of Figure 9.2b
Exit with Esc to save the new record
```
. DISPLAY ALL
```

The first APPEND is not preceded by a `SET FORMAT` command and hence records are added via the standard dBASE screen. By contrast, a `SET FORMAT` command is issued prior to the second `APPEND` command, and so the customized screen is retrieved.

☐ **STEP 12: View the directory.**

Exit dBASE, then enter a DIR *.* command and note the presence of the three files created in this exercise. The files all have a common file name PROSPECT, but different extensions: DBF, SCR, and FMT. The DBF file contains the file structure and was created in Step 1. SCR and FMT denote the presence of a *screen* and *format* file respectively, and were created in the screen generation process.

The format file, PROSPECT.FMT, is used in the data entry procedure as was shown in Step 11. The screen file, on the other hand, contains the various settings established in the exercise and is the file which can be subsequently modified, as we do in Hands-on Exercise 9–2.

Data Validation

As you should already know, dBASE incorporates some *data validation* capability within its *data entry* function. It is not possible, for example, to enter a month other than 1 through 12 within a date field. There are, however, many other types of data validation procedures of which you should be aware.

A *numeric* check ensures that a numeric field, such as the amount to invest, contains only numeric data whereas an *alphabetic* check will accept only alphabetic characters. A *range* (or limit) check ensures that a given entry is within normal bounds, for example, amount to invest must be at least $10,000.

Realize, too, that while many of these procedures are built directly into dBASE, and consequently are done automatically, many other types of data validation can only be done via programming. A *completeness* check, for example, requires that data for all necessary fields be entered before the new record can be appended to the file. A check for a *duplicate addition* ensures that the particular record has not already been added to the file. A *consistency* check verifies that values in two or more fields are consistent with one another, for example, the degree of interest expressed by a prospect should not be considered high if the date on which he or she was last contacted is over a year old.

Checking for a *valid code*, for example, checking that the investment objective is entered as either G or I (for growth or investment), also requires dBASE programming. Remember, too, that lowercase letters are treated differently from uppercase, and provision can be made to convert the data in some fields to uppercase upon data entry. (See Step 4 in Hands-on Exercise 9–2.)

Hands-on Exercise 9–2:   Data Validation

Objective: To modify the existing screen and format files to include data validation capabilities within the screen generation process.

☐   **STEP 1: Modify the PROSPECT data entry screen.**
Load dBASE as you did in Hands-on Exercise 9–1. Enter the `MODIFY SCREEN` command as shown below; you will then be asked for the name of the screen file to modify.

```
. MODIFY SCREEN
Enter screen file name: PROSPECT
```

Toggle to the blackboard using the F10 function key to once again view the screen of Figure 9.8.

☐   **STEP 2: Establish a picture function.**
Position the cursor on the first X of the telephone field (the field to which we will add editing characters). Now toggle back to the menu (with the F10 key), use the right and left arrow keys to highlight the Modify option, and press the Return key. Figure 9.9 will come into view.

Use the up and down arrow keys to highlight the picture function, then press the Return key. Enter a function value R as shown in the figure, and again press Return. Additional editing characters (such as the parentheses around the area code) can now be made to appear on the screen, without the need for additional space within the DBF file.

☐   **STEP 3: Establish a picture template.**
A fully edited telephone number requires a total of 14 positions, that is, (999) 999-9999. Thus, in addition to the ten digits required for the area code and number, we have allocated a left and right parenthesis around the area code, a space between the area code and phone number, and a hyphen within the phone number itself. The left and right parentheses, space, and hyphen are *editing* characters that appear on the data entry screen, but do not appear within the file structure itself. The editing characteristics of the telephone number are indicated by establishing a *picture template*.

Use the up and down arrow keys to highlight the picture template, then press the Return key. Enter the template as shown in Figure 9.10, press the Return key, then press F10 to toggle back to the blackboard. [Although the picture associated with telephone has effectively been expanded to (999) 999-9999, it will not appear that way until you save the screen, exit to the dot prompt, and return.]

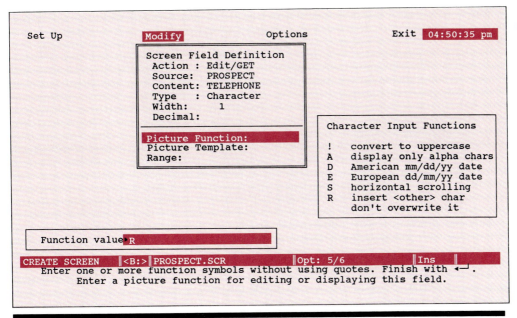

FIGURE 9.9 Establishing a picture function

☐ **STEP 4: Conversion to uppercase.**
The investment objective and degree of interest fields both require you to enter a single character, namely G or I for the former and H, M, or L for the latter. Recall also the different internal representation for upper- and lowercase letters, and that it is often convenient to convert lowercase codes to their uppercase equivalents so that the user may respond with either an upper- or lowercase letter.

Return now to the functions listed in Figure 9.9, observing the presence of a ! to convert to uppercase. In other words, you can establish a picture

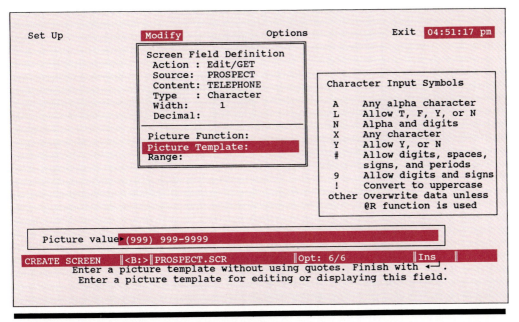

FIGURE 9.10 Establishing a picture template

function, for both the investment objective and degree of interest fields, that will automatically convert the input values to their uppercase equivalents.

Toggle to the blackboard and position the cursor on the X where investment objective is to be supplied. Toggle to the menu, select Modify, select the picture function, enter a !, and press the Return key. Repeat the process for the degree of interest field.

☐ STEP 5: Establish a range.

The screen generator includes the capability to implement a range check on numeric fields, for example, we will reject as invalid any amount less than $10,000. Toggle to the blackboard, position the cursor on the first character within the amount to invest field, then toggle back to the menu.

Select the Modify option, highlight the Range option, and press the Return key. Enter a lower limit of 10000 as shown in Figure 9.11 (do not type a comma), but no upper limit. In other words, the stock broker is not interested in clients below a minimum threshold, but he has no limit on the upper end. Establishing a range value will cause an error message during data entry if you try to enter a value less than $10,000 for this field.

You might also choose to enter a picture function of **z** for zero suppression, and a picture value of **9,999,999**. The former eliminates the appearance of high order (insignificant zeros) on the screen, while the latter improves the appearance of the input field.

☐ STEP 6: Exit dBASE.

Return to the menu and save the modified screen. Enter an **APPEND** command and view the modified screen. Enter data for one or more records, again deliberately using invalid values in order to observe what will happen. Press Esc when you are finished entering data in order to return to the dot prompt. Type **QUIT** to exit dBASE.

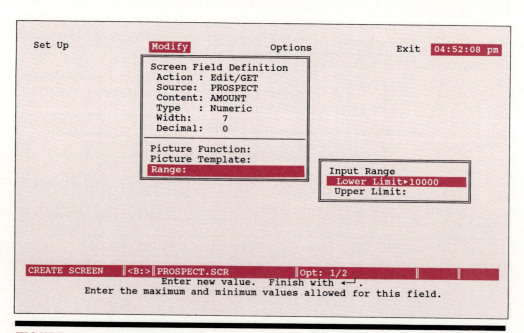

FIGURE 9.11 Establishing a range

The Generated Format File

As we have already indicated, the screen generator produces both a screen and format file, saved as PROSPECT.SCR and PROSPECT.FMT, respectively. The screen file contains the various settings established during the creation process and is used to subsequently modify a generated screen (as in Hands-on Exercise 9–2). The format file contains dBASE code which can be either called from, or incorporated into, a dBASE program, and which will be discussed further in Chapter 10.

In the interim, Figure 9.12 recapitulates what has been accomplished in the two hands-on exercises. Figure 9.12a contains the generated screen as it would appear from within the blackboard while Figure 9.12b contains the associated format file.

A useful exercise is to reconcile the two figures, for example, show how the `@...GET` and `@...SAY` statements correspond to the positions of the various fields as they appear on the screen. Note also the presence of the different picture functions and templates within the format file, and their corresponding appearance on the screen. Finally, note the use of the exclamation point within two fields to convert the input data to its uppercase equivalent.

Special Effects

Several additional features can be used to further enhance the appearance of the screens you create. It is very easy, for example, to develop menus in color (where a color monitor is available), surround portions of a screen with lines and/or boxes (recall the initial screen which appears every time dBASE is loaded), and so on. In this section, we briefly describe some of these special effects, and leave the rest to your imagination (and the Programmer's Notebook). We suggest that you continue to experiment with the existing screen and format files as they were established in the hands-on exercises.

The insertion of lines and/or boxes requires you to modify the existing PROSPECT.SCR file. Return to the dot prompt, enter the `MODIFY SCREEN` command, then supply PROSPECT as the name of the screen file. You will be returned to the menu associated with the screen generator, where three of the four choices (Set Up, Modify, and Exit) have already been discussed. Use the left and right arrow keys to highlight Options, press the Return key, and you will be presented with Figure 9.13.

Use the up and down arrow keys to highlight either single or double bar, then press the F10 key to toggle to the blackboard. You can draw a box around any portion of the screen merely by indicating the location of the upper left and lower right corners. Use the arrow keys to move the cursor to the upper left corner and press enter; move the cursor to where you want the lower right corner to be and press enter again. That's all there is to it.

Press the F10 key to toggle back to the menu, select the Exit option (with the left and right arrow keys), highlight Save (with the up and down arrow keys), and press the Return key. A modified version of the screen and format files with the box included is saved.

The appropriate `SET` command, issued from the dot prompt, introduces additional effects. Recall that you have already been exposed to the `SET` command to specify certain parameters, for example, `SET DEFAULT TO B` or `SET BELL OFF`. You can also use the command to establish color screens (where a color monitor is available), specify a reverse video effect (`SET INTENSITY`), and/or establish delimiters around a data field (`SET DELIMITER`).

Eight colors are available as indicated in Table 9.1. The screen itself is divided into three areas, each of which can have its color(s) changed. The command `SET COLOR TO B/W, R/GR, N` will result in a standard display of blue letters on a white background (B/W), a reverse video display of red letters on a brown background (R/GR), and a screen

```
  Set Up              Modify              Options              Exit  04:56:57 pm
                            Addition of Prospect Records

    Prefix:  XXX       Last name: XXXXXXXXXXXXXX      First name: XXXXXXXXXXX


           Street address: XXXXXXXXXXXXXXXXXXXXXXXX
                     City: XXXXXXXXXXXXXXXXX       State: XX  Zip code: XXXXX


                      Telephone: (999) 999-9999


         Investment objective: X          Amount to invest: 9,999,999
                (Growth/Income)


           Degree of interest: X             Last contacted: 99/99/99
              (High/Moderate/Low)

  CREATE SCREEN    ||<B:>||PROSPECT.SCR          ||Pg 01 Row 00 Col 00||         | Caps
         Enter text.  Drag field or box under cursor with ←┘.  F10 for menu.
                      Screen field definition blackboard
```

a

```
@  1, 25  SAY "Addition of Prospect Records"
@  4,  1  SAY "Prefix:"
@  4,  8  GET  PROSPECT->PREFIX
@  4, 18  SAY "Last name:"
@  4, 29  GET  PROSPECT->LASTNAME
@  4, 49  SAY "First name:"
@  4, 61  GET  PROSPECT->FIRSTNAME
@  8,  5  SAY "Street address:"
@  8, 21  GET  PROSPECT->STREET
@  9, 15  SAY "City:"
@  9, 21  GET  PROSPECT->CITY
@  9, 45  SAY "State:"
@  9, 52  GET  PROSPECT->STATE
@  9, 57  SAY "Zip code:"
@  9, 67  GET  PROSPECT->ZIPCODE
@ 12, 23  SAY "Telephone:"
@ 12, 34  GET  PROSPECT->TELEPHONE FUNCTION "r" PICTURE "(999) 999-9999"
@ 15,  8  SAY "Investment objective:"
@ 15, 30  GET  PROSPECT->OBJECTIVE FUNCTION "!" PICTURE "X"
@ 15, 44  SAY "Amount to invest:"
@ 15, 62  GET  PROSPECT->AMOUNT FUNCTION "z" PICTURE "9,999,999" RANGE 10000,
@ 16, 12  SAY "(Growth/Income)"
@ 18, 10  SAY "Degree of interest:"
@ 18, 30  GET  PROSPECT->INTEREST  FUNCTION "!"
@ 18, 46  SAY "Last contacted:"
@ 18, 62  GET  PROSPECT->LASTCALL
@ 19, 10  SAY "(High/Moderate/Low)"
```

b

FIGURE 9.12 Generated screen with corresponding format file: (a) generated screen at the end of Hands-on Exercise 9–2; (b) generated format file

border area outside the 80 × 25 display of black (N). If you are fortunate enough to have a color monitor, then by all means experiment with the color command (SET COLOR TO resets all screen parameters to default values; SET COLOR ON/OFF toggles between color and monochrome monitors on systems equipped with both).

The effects of the SET INTENSITY and SET DELIMITER commands can best be appreciated by experimentation. SET INTENSITY ON/OFF determines whether *reverse*

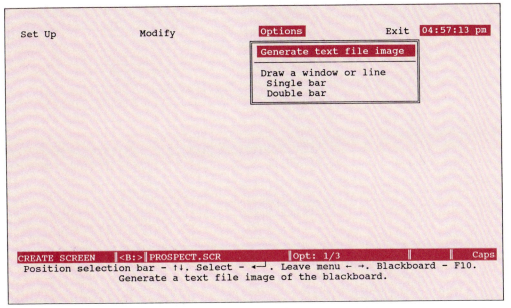

FIGURE 9.13 Adding lines to a generated screen

video is on or off during full-screen operations (it is on initially). SET DELIMITER ON/ OFF indicates whether the delimiting characters will offset the fields (it is off initially). The colon is used as the default delimiter, however, the SET DELIMITER TO command can change the delimiting character. Figure 9.14 illustrates various combinations of these parameters.

■ **TABLE 9.1**
dBASE Color Codes

Color	Code
Black	N
Blue	B
Green	G
Cyan	BG
Red	R
Magenta	BR
Brown	GR
White	W

Summary

The chapter introduced an entirely new case study that was subsequently used to present the dBASE *screen generator*. The case solution also reviewed various design considerations with respect to a file structure, namely which fields to include and the size and type of each field chosen. We touched on *data validation* concepts, and error-checking procedures which should be included within the data entry process. The chapter's emphasis, however, was on the screen generator and the procedures for using this powerful capability.

In essence, the screen generator enables you to use the monitor as a *blackboard* on which you enter text and/or move fields slated for data entry from one position to another.

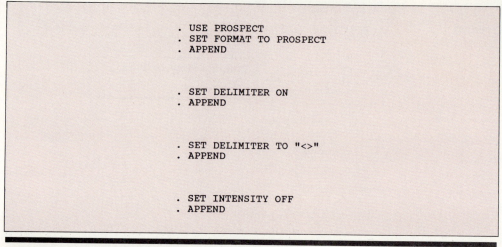

```
.  USE PROSPECT
.  SET FORMAT TO PROSPECT
.  APPEND


.  SET DELIMITER ON
.  APPEND


.  SET DELIMITER TO "<>"
.  APPEND


.  SET INTENSITY OFF
.  APPEND
```

FIGURE 9.14 The INTENSITY and DELIMITER parameters

The key to using the facility is the *F10* function key which serves as a *toggle* between the blackboard and menu, that is, you select a choice from the menu, toggle to the blackboard to implement that choice, then toggle back to the menu, and so on. Then, when you are satisfied with the appearance of the screen on the blackboard, you save the screen and the corresponding @...SAY and @...GET statements are generated for you. The tangible result of the process is a *format* file that can be used in conjunction with an APPEND command for data entry.

Key Words and Concepts

!	FMT extension
@...GET	Format file
@...SAY	Navigation line
Alphabetic check	Numeric check
APPEND	Picture function
Blackboard	Picture template
Code check	Range check
Completeness check	Reverse video
Consistency check	SCR extension
Ctrl A	Screen file
Ctrl F	SET BELL
Ctrl T	SET COLOR
Ctrl Y	SET DELIMITER
Data validation	SET FORMAT
Date check	SET INTENSITY
Dragging text	Screen generator
Duplication check	Toggle switch
F10 key	Valid code check

True/False

1. A screen generator capability is included with the dBASE III PLUS student version.
2. Creating a screen file automatically establishes a format file.

3. Using a SET FORMAT TO command negates the need for an APPEND command.
4. The SET FORMAT TO command cannot be used in conjunction with the EDIT command.
5. dBASE will not accept numeric values in a character field.
6. dBASE will not accept alphabetic values in a numeric field.
7. dBASE will under certain circumstances convert lowercase letters entered in a character field to uppercase.
8. A given field cannot have both a picture function and a picture template.
9. The screen generator restricts range checks to numeric fields only.
10. dBASE provides for formatting a screen in color (where a color monitor is available).
11. The screen generator uses the same menu conventions as do the facilities for mailing labels and report forms.
12. Specifying the command SET DELIMITER TO "<>" will, in and of itself, display the new delimiters around input fields.
13. dBASE will not append a new record to a file unless a value has been entered for every field within that record.
14. dBASE will not append a new record to a file if an existing record has the same social security number as the record to be added.
15. When designing a file structure, a person's first and last name should be designated as a single field for efficiency.

Exercises

1. Distinguish between
   a. a consistency check and a completeness check
   b. the @...GET and @...SAY statements
   c. a picture clause of 999 versus one of XXX
   d. a format file and a screen file
   e. the dBASE interactive and program modes
   f. Ctrl F and Ctrl A (when entering text)
   g. Ctrl G and Ctrl Y (when entering text)
   h. an APPEND command preceded by a SET FORMAT TO command as opposed to an APPEND command given in isolation
   i. appending data with and without SET BELL OFF in effect
   j. a numeric field specified with and without a range function
   k. the commands SET DELIMITER TO and SET DELIMITER ON
   l. the commands SET INTENSITY ON and SET INTENSITY OFF
   m. USE PROSPECT and SET FORMAT TO PROSPECT

2. Explain how it is possible for a ten-position field such as telephone (as defined in Figure 9.1) to require 14 positions in a data entry screen (such as Figure 9.2b). What is gained by this technique? Why is a similar approach *not* followed for a date field (that is, the date on which the prospect was last contacted requires eight positions in both the file structure and data entry screen).

3. Describe what is meant by each one of the following data validation checks. In each case, indicate whether the procedure can be accomplished within the screen generator or whether it requires additional programming.
   a. completeness check
   b. range (limit) check
   c. date check
   d. consistency check
   e. checking that a code exists
   f. alphabetic check

g. numeric check

h. checking for duplicate additions

i. checking for upper case

4. Introducing screen and format files brings the number of dBASE file types to eight, all of which are listed below. For each extension listed, describe the file's specific nature; how the file is created initially; and how the file's contents may be subsequently edited.

   a. DBF

   b. FMT

   c. FRM

   d. LBL

   e. NDX

   f. PRG

   g. SCR

   h. QRY

5. With respect to the file structure of Figure 9.1, indicate the commands needed to produce the following reports. Assume that the PROSPECT.DBF file has been created and that the commands are entered one at a time from the dot prompt. Be sure to indicate whatever commands are necessary to create and/or open the required indexes.

   a. An alphabetic list of all prospects.

   b. An alphabetic list of only those prospects with a high interest in investing.

   c. A list, in descending order by the amount of money to invest, of those prospects with a high interest and at least $10,000.

   d. A count of the number of prospects who meet the criteria for part c, above.

   e. A set of mailing labels, produced alphabetically within zip code, for prospects who meet the criteria for part c above (assume that the label form PROSPECT.LBL has already been created).

After reading this chapter, you should be able to:

- List the three basic file maintenance operations.

- List at least five types of data validation checks.

- Differentiate between a program and a procedure; explain what is meant by a dBASE procedure file.

- Describe the general function of SET commands; list at least five such commands and the specific purpose of each.

- Explain the role of memory variables in dBASE programming.

10

File Maintenance

Overview

The subject of file maintenance has already been broached in several places, beginning with the Soleil Employee System in Chapter 1. The initial example presented a completed, menu-driven system that enabled you to choose from various file maintenance operations; namely the *addition, modification,* or *deletion* of records within the context of the Soleil Employee System. Later chapters presented the necessary commands (APPEND, EDIT, BROWSE, DELETE, PACK, LOCATE, and FIND) to accomplish these operations.

Our discussion has, for the most part, taken place at the dot prompt (interactive mode) as opposed to the programming mode (command level). In this chapter, however, we change direction and approach the subject in considerably more detail, with development of the necessary program(s) for file maintenance as the eventual objective. As you shall discover, the subject is rather complex.

The stock broker system in Chapter 9 is used as the vehicle for program development. We develop the logic in pseudocode, introduce additional dBASE programming concepts [the SEEK statement for random retrieval, memory variables (public and private), and procedures], then present the completed program. The chapter also contains two hands-on exercises to demonstrate these capabilities.

Data Validation Revisited

The all-important subject of data validation was introduced in Chapter 9 in conjunction with screen generation. We saw that the preparation of the format screen and the subsequent addition of records via the APPEND command automatically invoked various dBASE validation procedures. It was not possible, for example, to place alphabetic data in a numeric field; in addition a range check could be imposed on the numeric fields.

Impressive as these capabilities are, they stop far short of what is necessary in a practical application. They do not, for example, preclude the addition of *duplicate* records or the inclusion of records with *incomplete* or *invalid* data. Indeed, we cannot overstate the case for data entry procedures which ensure, to the greatest extent possible, that initial data entry is done correctly; for once errors are introduced into a system they have a disturbing tendency to remain.

Although limited data validation can be accomplished from the dot prompt, more sophisticated procedures require custom dBASE programs. Accordingly, to demonstrate the difference between what can and cannot be accomplished from the dot prompt, we present two parallel hands-on exercises. The first is based entirely on the format screen of Chapter 9 and uses standard dBASE editing facilities. By contrast, the second exercise employs a custom program contained on the convenience disk.

Hands-on Exercise 10–1: Adding Records at the Dot Prompt

Objective: To add (APPEND) records from the dot prompt using the format file developed in Chapter 9; to show the inability of this technique to reject duplicate additions, incomplete records, and invalid codes.

☐   **STEP 1: Log onto the STOCK subdirectory.**
Place the convenience disk in drive B and log onto the STOCK subdirectory with the appropriate command from the DOS prompt:

```
CD B:\STOCK            ———————— With a floppy disk system

CD C:\SAMPLER\STOCK ——— With a hard disk drive
PATH C:\SAMPLER
```

☐   **STEP 2: Retrieve the PROSPECT.DBF file.**
Load dBASE, then enter the commands USE PROSPECT and DISPLAY STRUCTURE as shown in Figure 10.1. If there are any records in the file, enter the commands DELETE ALL and PACK to delete all the records.

☐   **STEP 3: Retrieve the format file.**
Enter the command SET FORMAT TO PROSPECT to activate the existing PROSPECT.FMT file. (You may also wish to enter the command SET BELL OFF to suppress the "beep" during data entry.) Enter the APPEND command and a screen resembling Figure 10.2 will appear.

☐   **STEP 4: Add the first record.**
Enter a complete and accurate record for Ms. Gail Smith, residing at 42–15

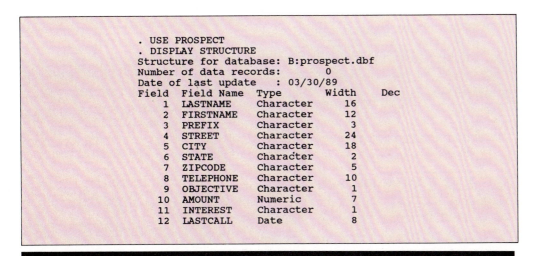

```
. USE PROSPECT
. DISPLAY STRUCTURE
Structure for database: B:prospect.dbf
Number of data records:        0
Date of last update    : 03/30/89
Field  Field Name   Type        Width   Dec
    1  LASTNAME     Character      16
    2  FIRSTNAME    Character      12
    3  PREFIX       Character       3
    4  STREET       Character      24
    5  CITY         Character      18
    6  STATE        Character       2
    7  ZIPCODE      Character       5
    8  TELEPHONE    Character      10
    9  OBJECTIVE    Character       1
   10  AMOUNT       Numeric         7
   11  INTEREST     Character       1
   12  LASTCALL     Date            8
```

FIGURE 10.1 File structure for PROSPECT.DBF

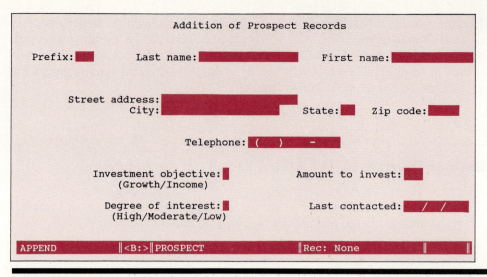

```
                           Addition of Prospect Records

     Prefix:▮▮        Last name:▮▮▮▮▮▮▮▮▮         First name:▮▮▮▮▮▮▮▮▮

            Street address:▮▮▮▮▮▮▮▮▮▮▮
                      City:▮▮▮▮▮▮▮▮▮▮      State:▮▮     Zip code:▮▮▮

                         Telephone: (▮▮▮) ▮▮-▮▮▮▮▮

          Investment objective:▮          Amount to invest:▮▮
             (Growth/Income)

            Degree of interest:▮            Last contacted:▮/▮/▮
          (High/Moderate/Low)


   APPEND           ‖<B:>‖PROSPECT                 ‖Rec: None       ‖         ‖
```

FIGURE 10.2 Format screen to add records

81st Street, Elmhurst, NY 11373, and whose telephone number is (718) 458–5000. Ms. Smith has $20,000 to invest, and is looking for growth rather than income. She is moderately interested and was last contacted on May 5, 1988. Note that when you have completed the last field, that is, the date on which Gail was last contacted, the system will automatically present you with a format screen for the next record.

☐   **STEP 5: Add an incomplete record.**
Repeat the procedure from Step 4, except this time you will deliberately enter an *incomplete* record. Enter data for Mr. Neil Goodman who also resides at 42–15 81st Street, Elmhurst, NY 11373. Move the cursor through the remaining fields without entering any additional data; that is, continue to press the Return key until you are presented with a new screen to add a third record.

☐   **STEP 6: Add a duplicate record.**
Reenter the *same* data for Gail Smith as you did in Step 4; you are deliberately (and erroneously) entering a duplicate record into the system.

☐   **STEP 7: Add a record with invalid data.**
Enter data for our fourth (and last) prospective client, Ms. Judith Friedberg who resides at 82–01 Britton Avenue, Elmhurst, NY 11373, and who may be reached at (718) 898–1611. Judith has $150,000 to invest and was last contacted on May 6, 1988. This time, however, you will enter *invalid* codes of X and Y for the investment objective and degree of interest fields respectively.
     Press Esc to save your additions and return to the dot prompt.

☐   **STEP 8: Verify the results of data entry.**
Enter the DISPLAY command as shown in Figure 10.3, in which only a limited number of fields are displayed for each record.
     Your results should be the same as ours, in that Gail Smith appears twice, Neil Goodman is missing data on the investment objective and degree of interest, and Judith Friedberg has invalid codes present in these fields.

```
. DISPLAY ALL LASTNAME,FIRSTNAME,OBJECTIVE,INTEREST OFF

LASTNAME        FIRSTNAME      OBJECTIVE  INTEREST
Smith           Gail           G          M
Goodman         Neil
Smith           Gail           G          M
Judith          Friedberg      X          Y
```

FIGURE 10.3 Verification of data entry

Limitations of the Dot Prompt

dBASE has two modes of operation. Commands may be executed one at a time, that is, *interactively*, from the dot prompt (as was done in the preceding exercise). Commands may also be stored in a file and executed collectively in the *command* mode (as in the next exercise). The quick response of the former is wonderful for the beginner, yet it is the latter which gives dBASE its real power. The difference can best be appreciated by comparing the two hands-on exercises.

The first exercise demonstrated the limitations of adding records from the dot prompt because it did not go far enough in terms of data validation. Accordingly, a program is developed for data entry and that program is the object of the second exercise. We construct examples parallel to the first exercise, except this time the data are entered through the data validation program rather than from the dot prompt. The program will automatically check data as it is entered, and reject duplicate additions, as well as records with missing fields and/or incorrect codes.

The program will also enable many records to be added in a single session by continually asking whether or not another record should be added or should the program be ended. (By extension, the program will not add blank records to the end of a DBF file as often happens when you append records from the dot prompt.)

The actual data validation is done in two phases. The record to be added is first checked against existing records to prevent a duplicate from being added, then the fields within the new record are checked for completeness and accuracy. The main question is how to search the existing file to determine whether or not the new record is present. Do we look for the entire record, or just a particular field(s) within the record, and if the latter, which field? Given the impracticality of checking for every field in every record, the search is normally restricted to a single field, known as a *key*. Social security number is chosen over last name because it (social security number) is *unique*, that is, no two individuals can have the same social security number, whereas several individuals can have the same last name.

In other words, the presence of a duplicate social security number indicates an error, whereas the existence of a duplicate last name does not necessarily imply an error. The occurrence of a second "Smith" in the file does not mean that Gail Smith was previously entered, only that an individual named Smith (of which there may be several) is already in the file. Conversely, the existence of a record with social security number 111-11-1111, means that the record about to be added is already in the file, in which case the error must be made known to the user.

The program in the second exercise will also prevent incomplete records from being added, as well as records with invalid codes. It must, therefore, check at some point for the presence of a value in every field and further that the values of certain fields are within specified ranges. (The investment objective must be G or I; the degree of interest must be H, M, or L; and the amount to invest must be at least $10,000.)

Hands-on Exercise 10–2:   Adding Records Through Programming

Objective: To add (APPEND) records through a program, and in so doing, demonstrate data validation capabilities not available from the dot prompt.

☐   **STEP 1: Delete all previously entered records.**

You must first restore the DBF file to its original state (that is, delete all records added in the first exercise). Accordingly, enter the commands:

```
.DELETE ALL
.PACK
.DISPLAY STRUCTURE
```

Once again, the **DELETE** command marks all records for deletion, the **PACK** command physically (permanently) removes the records, and the **DISPLAY STRUCTURE** command verifies that the file is empty.

☐   **STEP 2: Modify the structure of the PROSPECT.DBF file.**

The file structure does not currently contain a field for social security number and must be modified accordingly. Enter the command **MODIFY STRUCTURE** and Figure 10.4 comes into view. Leave the cursor positioned in the LASTNAME field, and press Ctrl N to insert a field. Enter **SSN** for the field name, **Character** for the field type, and **9** for the field width.

Press Ctrl End to save the modifications. A message will appear on the bottom of the screen requesting you to press the Return key to confirm the changes. Respond accordingly and you will be returned to the dot prompt.

☐   **STEP 3: Create a social security index.**

Enter the command **INDEX ON SSN TO SSN** to create a social security number index. Do not be concerned when the system returns the message "zero records indexed." This happens because the PROSPECT.DBF file is currently empty. (All records were deleted in Step 1.) A social security index must exist for the program to be successful.

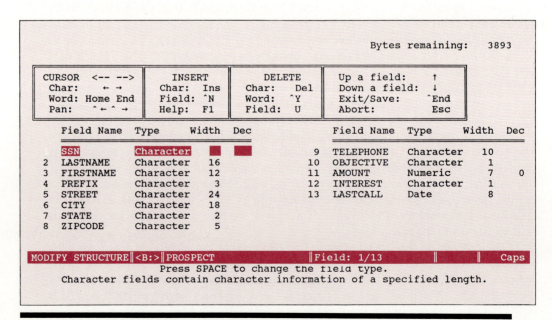

FIGURE 10.4 The MODIFY STRUCTURE command

☐ **STEP 4: Invoke the file maintenance program.**
The program to add records to the PROSPECT.DBF has been written for you and exists on the convenience disk. Enter the command **DO ADDRECD** to execute the program and begin adding records.

☐ **STEP 5: Enter data for the first record.**
The first essential difference between this program and adding records directly from the dot prompt is that you are asked for a social security number (to prevent the addition of duplicate records) before entering the remaining data. Enter the number 111–11–1111 for Gail Smith, then complete the rest of her record.

Figure 10.5 contains the two data entry screens. Figure 10.5a asks you

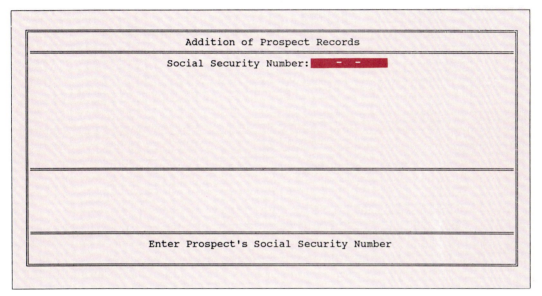

a

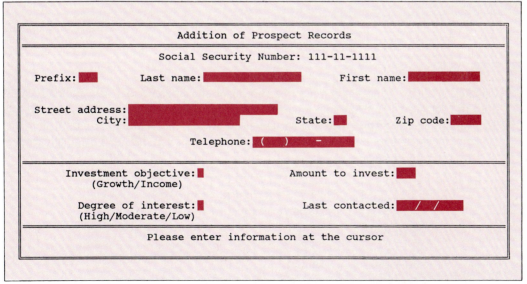

b

FIGURE 10.5 Data entry screens: (a) screen requesting social security number; (b) screen for data entry

to enter the social security number. The program then checks the file for the presence of the potential new record. Then, after a short pause, the data entry screen of Figure 10.5b appears. (Note that the social security number remains on the screen.)

When all of the data has been entered, you are asked whether you want to add another record; respond affirmatively and continue with the exercise.

☐   **STEP 6: Enter data for the remaining records.**
Enter the data for Neil Goodman (use 222–22–2222 as the social security number) but again *omit* the telephone number, investment objective, degree of interest, amount to invest, and date fields. The program will *not* let you proceed to the third record until these fields are completed (enter any values you choose).

Now repeat Step 6 from Hands-on Exercise 10–1 and attempt to enter a duplicate record for Gail Smith (with social security number 111–11–1111). Note, however, the system indicates that this social security number is already in the file, effectively preventing a duplicate record from being added.

Finally, repeat Step 7 from Hands-on Exercise 10–1 in which you enter data for Judith Friedberg (use 333–33–3333 as the social security number). Use X and Y respectively as the codes for investment objective and degree of interest, then observe how these invalid codes are rejected. (The program requires an input value for *every* field within the record before performing any data validation, that is, all fields must be entered before any are checked.)

Correct the errors in the record for Judith Friedberg, then exit the data entry function by typing **Q** to quit. You will be returned to the dot prompt.

☐   **STEP 7: Verify the results of data entry.**
Enter the **USE** and **DISPLAY** commands shown in Figure 10.6. This time you will see data for only three records (the duplicate addition of Gail Smith was prevented). Observe also that Neil Goodman's record is complete and that the record for Judith Friedberg contains valid codes in lieu of the X and Y which appeared before.

Type **QUIT** to exit dBASE and return to DOS.

The ADDRECD Program

Completing the two hands-on exercises has shown you the difference between adding records from the dot prompt and through a custom program. It has also acquainted you with the data validation capabilities that can be contained within the addition program, and the sequence in which these functions are executed. Hence, while you may have originally viewed

```
. USE PROSPECT
. DISPLAY ALL LASTNAME,FIRSTNAME,OBJECTIVE,INTEREST OFF

LASTNAME          FIRSTNAME       OBJECTIVE INTEREST
Smith             Gail            G         H
Goodman           Neil            G         H
Friedberg         Judith          I         L
```

FIGURE 10.6 Verification of data entry

the process of adding records to a file as a single task, it is, in reality, made up of several subservient functions.

It is necessary, for example, to map the screen so that values for the input variables can be entered. It is also necessary to check for the completeness of the input data, to check for the validity of the input data, and so on. Although a single program could have been written to encompass the entire addition process, the length of that program would make its development extremely difficult. Accordingly, the original program is divided into functional modules based on structured design principles, with each subservient function developed as a separate dBASE program.

Recall from our discussion of structured design in Chapter 8 that a *hierarchy chart* depicts the relationship of programs within a system to one another. It shows what has to be done but not when, and contains no indication of sequence or decision-making logic. The latter information is contained within the *pseudocode,* which is developed according to the elementary building blocks of structured programming as described in Chapter 7.

Thus, complete explanation of the ADDRECD program from the second exercise requires us to develop a hierarchy chart and its associated pseudocode. In addition, we need to present additional dBASE concepts and programming statements that will be included in the eventual program(s).

The Hierarchy Chart

The hierarchy chart in Figure 10.7 depicts the relationship of the individual programs to one another within the overall addition process. The program names are restricted to a maximum of eight characters, yet the function of the subservient programs should still be apparent.

The GETINPUT program obtains input values from the user for the fields within the prospect record. Similarly, you can expect the COMPLCHK program to perform a completeness check and the RANGECHK program to verify that the input data is within specified ranges. The role (or even need) of the two remaining programs is less obvious and stems from dBASE requirements. The INITVAR program initializes all *memory variables,* while the APPNDREC program replaces the fields in the DBF file with the values of the corresponding memory variables.

To understand the purpose of a memory variable, recall that the APPNDREC program began with the user first inputting a social security number. The program checked the existing file to ensure that the record about to be added did not already exist in the file. Only after an appropriate, that is, nonduplicate, social security number was input, would the program display the screen for data entry, requesting values for every single field within the prospect record.

The program then checked for completeness (every field required a value) and for valid codes and/or ranges in selected fields. The record was added only *after* all data were entered correctly, that is, the program would continually prompt for a missing field and/or for a

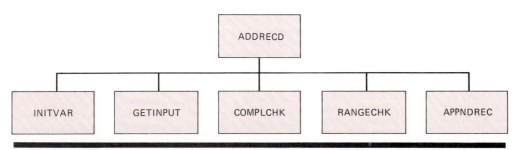

FIGURE 10.7 The hierarchy chart

correct value for the objective, degree of interest, and/or amount to invest. The point we are making is that the data you entered *was not added directly to the DBF file, but was stored temporarily in memory* until verified as correct.

A *memory variable* is a location within memory that temporarily stores data needed by a dBASE program. Data entered by the user is initially placed into memory variables, checked for accuracy, and only when proven correct, moved into fields within a DBF file.

The INITVAR program uses repeated STORE commands to initialize all memory variables, then the GETINPUT program obtains user inputs for these variables. The COMPLCHK program verifies that a value was, in fact, input for each memory variable, while the RANGECHK program further checks that the values (for some variables) are proper. Finally, the APPNDREC program appends a new record to the PROSPECT.DBF file and replaces fields in the new record with their memory variable counterparts.

Explanation of the hierarchy chart of Figure 10.7 is now complete in the sense that we know the *function* of each of its programs. It remains to link the programs to one another, and to indicate when (and how often) they are called. That, in turn, is the purpose of pseudocode.

Pseudocode

The pseudocode of Figure 10.8 is driven by an outer loop which adds records continually until you indicate a desire to quit. The loop is controlled by a switch (add-more-records-switch) initially set outside the loop, and eventually reset within the loop when you choose to exit.

```
Set add-more-records-switch on
DO WHILE add-more-records-switch is on          Inner loop prevents
    Set duplicate switch on                      the addition of
    DO WHILE duplicate switch is on              duplicate records
        Display message to enter social security number
        Get social security number of record to be entered
        IF social security number is in file
            Display message indicating duplicate number
        ELSE
            Set duplicate switch off
        ENDIF
    ENDDO

    Display screen requesting user to enter data
    Get user inputs for all fields
    Check user inputs for completeness
    Check user inputs for valid ranges
    Add validated record to file
                                                 Guarantees a valid user response
    Set answer-switch on
    DO WHILE answer-switch is on
        Display message to add more records or exit program
        DO CASE
            CASE A: (Add more records)
                Set answer-switch off
            CASE B: (Exit program)                Terminates outer loop
                Set answer-switch off
                Set add-more-records-switch off
            OTHERWISE:
                Display message requesting valid response
        ENDCASE
    ENDDO
ENDDO
RETURN
```

FIGURE 10.8 Pseudocode for add prospect record program

Within the loop itself there are many distinct operations, all of which have to occur in order to add a record. You enter the social security number of the record to be added, and the program checks that this number is not already in the file. This logic is contained within an inner loop, allowing you as many chances as necessary to enter a nonduplicate social security number.

Once a valid (that is, nonduplicate) social security number is obtained, the program displays a screen requesting values for the remaining fields (prefix, last name, first name, and so on). It checks for completeness and for proper entries in designated fields. The validated record is then added to the file, a process in which the temporary values in the memory variables are moved to the corresponding fields in the record structure.

At this point, addition of the current record is finished, whereupon the program displays a message asking whether additional records are to be added or the program terminated. The latter choice turns off the switch controlling the outer loop (add-more-records-switch) and the program ends.

In reviewing Figure 10.8 recall the structured programming discussion from Chapter 7, remembering that pseudocode is restricted to the basic building blocks of sequence, selection, iteration, and case. Observe, too, the use of vertical lines (our convention) to indicate the extent of the basic structures, and that the logic flows easily from the top down.

The dBASE Listing

The dBASE listing for the ADDRECD program is shown in Figure 10.9. The logic in the program parallels that of the pseudocode just developed, with its several DO statements transferring control to subordinate programs within the hierarchy chart.

Documentation for the program is shown in Figure 10.10. It contains a program narrative, a list of the called programs and procedures (a concept we will explain shortly), a copy of the associated file structure, and a brief description of the memory variables contained in the program.

Programs versus Procedures

The ADDRECD program contains a DO statement for each subordinate program in the hierarchy chart. For example, there is a DO statement to transfer control to the initialize variable program (DO initvar), a DO statement for the program to obtain user inputs (DO getinput), and so on. You will also see three *additional* DO statements for modules *not* found in the original hierarchy chart. These new entries (DO scrnclr, DO printmsg, and DO msgclear) are known as *procedures,* and their relationship to the ADDRECD program is shown in Figure 10.11.

A *procedure* is a group of dBASE commands, identified by a procedure name, and stored in a common procedure file. In other words, each of the *programs* in the hierarchy chart is stored in a separate program file, whereas the *procedures* are stored together in a common procedure file. The latter is read into memory and remains there while the ADDRECD program executes.

Consider Figure 10.12 containing the directory of program files present within the stock subdirectory. There are separate entries for the program files (INITVAR.PRG, GETIN-PUT.PRG, and so on), but no entries for the individual procedure files. There is, however, a single directory entry for the common procedure file, PROCLIB.PRG, the contents of which are shown in Figure 10.13.

Each procedure in Figure 10.13 begins with a PROCEDURE header naming the procedure, and ends with a RETURN statement sending control back to the calling program. The SCRNCLR procedure uses CLEAR statements to erase various portions of the screen, for example, lines 4 through 13, 15 through 19, and 21 through 22. It does not, however,

```
***ADDRECD.PRG
SET TALK OFF
SET BELL OFF
SET STATUS OFF
SET SAFETY OFF
SET PROCEDURE TO proclib.prg
USE prospect
SET INDEX TO ssn
@  1,  0  TO 23, 79      DOUBLE
@  3,  1  TO  3, 78      DOUBLE
@ 14,  1  TO 14, 78      DOUBLE
@ 20,  1  TO 20, 78      DOUBLE
@  2, 26  SAY "Addition of Prospect Records"
STORE .T. TO addrecs
DO WHILE addrecs
    STORE .T. to duplicate
    DO WHILE duplicate
        DO scrnclr
        STORE SPACE(9) TO mssn
        @ 4,23 SAY 'Social Security Number:'
        @ 4,47 GET mssn FUNCTION "r" PICTURE '999-99-9999'
        STORE "Enter Prospect's Social Security Number " TO message
        DO printmsg WITH message
        READ
        SEEK mssn
        IF .NOT. EOF()
            DO scrnclr
            @ 8,22 SAY 'Social Security Number: '
            @ 8,46 SAY mssn PICTURE '@R 999-99-9999'
            STORE 'SSN already in file - Press any key to continue' TO message
            DO printmsg WITH message
            SET CONSOLE OFF
            WAIT
            SET CONSOLE ON
            DO scrnclr
        ELSE
            STORE .F. to duplicate
        ENDIF
    ENDDO
    DO initvar
    DO getinput
    STORE '*** Checking data ... Please Wait ***' TO message
    DO printmsg WITH message
    DO complchk
    DO rangechk
    STORE '*** Record being added ***' TO message
    DO printmsg with message
    DO appndrec
    STORE 'Enter A to Add another record or Q to quit' TO message
    DO printmsg WITH message
    STORE .T. TO needanswer
    DO WHILE needanswer
        STORE ' ' TO moreadd
        @ 21,66 GET moreadd
        READ
        STORE UPPER(moreadd) TO moreadd
        DO msgclear
        DO CASE
            CASE moreadd = 'A'
                STORE .F. TO needanswer
            CASE moreadd = 'Q'
                STORE .F. TO needanswer
                STORE .F. TO addrecs
            OTHERWISE
                DO msgclear
                STORE '*** Please enter either A or Q! ***' TO message
                DO printmsg WITH message
        ENDCASE
    ENDDO
ENDDO
RELEASE ALL
CLOSE DATABASES
RETURN
```

FIGURE 10.9 The add record (ADDRECD) program

Program Narrative: ADDRECD.PRG

The ADDRECD program adds records to the PROSPECT.DBF file until the user inputs a response to quit the system. Each addition is preceded by a prompt to the user to input the social security number for the record to be added. The existing file is then checked for the presence of that number, and if the record is not already in the file, the program displays an additional screen to collect the input data. Incoming records are checked for completeness, valid codes, and appropriate ranges, and only when a record passes all validity checks is it added to the system. The actual routines to display the input screen, validate the incoming data, and add the record to the DBF file are performed within various called programs.

Called program(s):

INITVAR - Initializes all memory variables used to hold the input values for the various DBF fields (see Figure 10.14)

GETINPUT - Maps the screen in which the user inputs values for the various DBF fields; (see Figure 10.15)

COMPLCHK - Checks for the presence of data in every field of a record (see Figure 10.16)

RANGECHK - Checks for valid codes in the INTEREST and OBJECTIVE fields; checks for an appropriate range in the AMOUNT field (see Figure 10.17)

APPNDREC - Performs the actual addition to the DBF file via a series of REPLACE statements in which the values of the input memory variables are entered into the corresponding DBF fields (see Figure 10.18)

Procedures:

SCRNCLR - Clears out the inside of the box

MSGCLEAR - Clears out the message portion (line 21) of the box

PRINTMSG - Displays a message in line 21 of the screen; uses the current value of the message parameter from the ADDRECD program

Database file(s): PROSPECT.DBF

1 SSN	Character	9	8 ZIPCODE	Character	5
2 LASTNAME	Character	16	9 TELEPHONE	Character	10
3 FIRSTNAME	Character	12	10 OBJECTIVE	Character	1
4 PREFIX	Character	3	11 AMOUNT	Numeric	7
5 STREET	Character	24	12 INTEREST	Character	1
6 CITY	Character	18	13 LASTCALL	Date	8
7 STATE	Character	2			

Index file(s):

SSN.NDX - key: SSN of PROSPECT.DBF

Memory variables:

addrecs - Switch which controls major loop of entire program; set to True initially; set to False when user inputs "Q" to quit system

duplicate - Switch which prevents the addition of duplicate records; set to True prior to requesting social security number of new record; set to False when social security number is not found in the file

mssn - Contains the actual social security number of the record to be added

message - Contains any one of several messages which is passed to the PRINTMSG procedure

needanswer - Switch which controls the routine to obtain a user's response for adding additional records or quitting the system

moreadd - Contains the user's response to add more records or to quit system

FIGURE 10.10 Program documentation

erase lines 3, 14, or 20 (the horizontal lines created within the box), nor does it erase the box itself.

The MSGCLEAR procedure performs a similar function except it clears only line 21 near the bottom of the screen. Recall that the ADDRECD program was designed so that all of its messages appeared on the same line. Accordingly, the contents of that line need to be cleared as the program moves from one screen to the next and the message is no longer appropriate.

The PRINTMSG procedure displays a message on the screen. It contains a PARAM-ETERS statement, which accepts a value (parameter) from the calling program and enables that value to be used in the procedure. (A *parameter* is a variable available to two or more

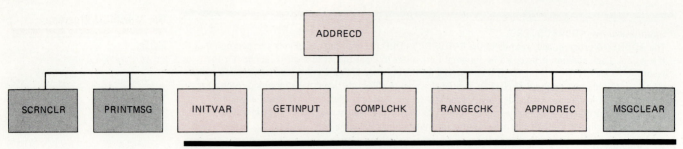

FIGURE 10.11 Revised hierarchy chart

programs or procedures and whose value may be set in any of those programs or procedures.) The PRINTMSG procedure is called from several places in the ADDRECD program, with each of the calling statements preceded by a STORE statement which establishes the value of the message.

The logic within the ADDRECD program determines which message is appropriate in the situation ("Enter Prospect's Social Security Number," "SSN already in file—Press any key to continue," and so on) and then sends this information to the PRINTMSG procedure. Thus, by using the message parameter's appropriate value, a single procedure is able to display all the messages mandated by the ADDRECD program regardless of where the messages originate. (The message itself is *centered* on line 21 using the LEN function (see the Programmer's Notebook for additional information.)

There is no logical difference with respect to the design principles of a hierarchy chart between transferring control to a program (a separate file with a PRG extension such as RANGECHK.PRG), or to a procedure contained within a procedure file. Nor can you tell by looking at a DO statement whether it refers to a procedure or another program, for example, the DO scrnclr statement in Figure 10.9 refers to a procedure within Figure 10.13, whereas the DO rangechk statement references a separate PRG file.

Thus, deciding whether to designate a particular function as a program or procedure is somewhat arbitrary. Conceptually every called program could have been created as a procedure within the common procedure file. Similarly, procedures could have been eliminated entirely by creating additional program files. We do, however, follow one rule of thumb. Frequently used routines are created as procedures rather than programs *because procedures execute more quickly than programs*. Observe, therefore, that each procedure (SCRNCLR, MSGCLEAR, and PRINTMSG) is called from several places within the ADDRECD program, whereas each program is called only once.

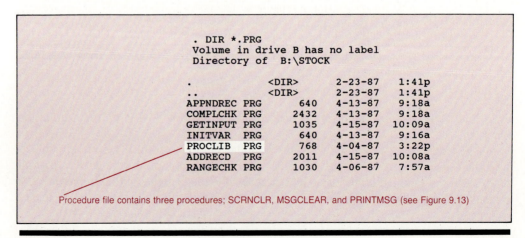

FIGURE 10.12 Program files in the STOCK subdirectory

210

```
***PROCLIB.PRG
***Procedure library for the Prospect Information System
***

PROCEDURE SCRNCLR
***This procedure clears out the inside of the box
@  4,2 CLEAR TO 13,77
@ 15,2 CLEAR TO 19,77
@ 21,2 CLEAR TO 22,77
RETURN
***

PROCEDURE MSGCLEAR
***This procedure clears out message portion of the box
@ 21,2 SAY SPACE(76)
RETURN
***

PROCEDURE PRINTMSG
***This procedure prints a message on line 21 of the screen
PARAMETERS message
DO msgclear
@ 21,(80 - LEN(message))/2 SAY message
RETURN
```

FIGURE 10.13 The procedure file

Procedures execute quickly because the common procedure file in which they reside is read into memory at the beginning of the program and remains in memory for the duration of the execution. (A SET PROCEDURE TO statement executed at the start of the ADDRECD program accomplishes this.) By contrast, individual program files must be read and loaded each time they are executed. Thus, when dBASE encounters a DO command within a program, it first checks the procedures in memory. If the entry in the DO statement is identified as a procedure, execution is immediate because the procedure is already in RAM. If, on the other hand, the entry is not found, execution is slower because the program file must first be read into RAM from disk.

Additional Program Listings

The remaining program listings are presented in the order in which they are called from the ADDRECD program. The name of each program, the figure in which it appears, and a brief description appears in Table 10.1. We suggest that you concentrate initially on the function of the individual programs and on how control is passed back and forth among the various programs in the overall system. Additional information on specific statements is presented after the program listings.

Additional dBASE Statements

The ADDRECD program and its associated subprograms contain several dBASE programming statements requiring additional explanation. These include SET statements, statements to draw boxes on the screen, public and private variables, the STORE and RELEASE statements, and the SEEK statement. Each of these is explained below with additional information contained in the Programmer's Notebook.

■ **TABLE 10.1**
Lower Level Programs

Program Name	Figure Number	Narrative Description
INITVAR	Figure 10.14	The INITVAR (initialize variable) program initializes 12 memory variables corresponding to the 12 field names in the PROSPECT.DBF structure. Subsequent programs will input values into these memory variables validate these values, and eventually replace the fields within the DBF file with the contents of their corresponding memory variable.
GETINPUT	Figure 10.15	The GETINPUT (get input) program consists mainly of @ ... GET and @ ... SAY statements used to map the screen and obtain user-supplied values for the memory variables. The statements themselves were created with the aid of the dBASE screen generator facility (as described in Chapter 9) which produced a format (FMT) file that was eventually incorporated into this program.
COMPLCHK	Figure 10.16	The COMPLCHK (completeness check) program ensures that data has been entered into each of the 12 memory variables. It consists of 12 loops (one for each memory variable), each of which executes repeatedly, until a nonblank value is received. The effects of including (omitting) this program are examined in Exercise 3 at the end of the chapter.
RANGECHK	Figure 10.17	The RANGECHK (range check) program ensures that the value of the investment objective field is entered as either G or I, that the degree of interest field is either H, M, or L, and that the amount of money to invest is at least $10,000. The effects of including (omitting) this program are examined in Exercise 3 at the end of the chapter.
APPNDREC	Figure 10.18	The APPNDREC (add record) program accomplishes the actual addition of a record to the existing PROSPECT.DBF file. It begins with an APPEND BLANK statement to add a blank record to the end of the file, then replaces the 12 fields within the record with the value of the corresponding memory variable.

SET Statements

The first several instructions of the ADDRECD program alter the default values of the indicated dBASE parameters. Consider Figure 10.19a, which contains 23 of these "on/off" switches, with the default value of each indicated in capital letters.

```
***INITVAR.PRG
***This program initializes the memory variables
***
PUBLIC mlastname,mfirstname,mprefix,mstreet,mcity,mstate,mzipcode
PUBLIC mtelephone,mobjective,mamount,minterest,mlastcall
STORE SPACE(16) TO mlastname
STORE SPACE(12) TO mfirstname
STORE '  ' TO mprefix
STORE SPACE(24) TO mstreet
STORE SPACE(18) TO mcity
STORE '  ' TO mstate
STORE '     ' TO mzipcode
STORE SPACE(10) TO mtelephone
STORE ' ' TO mobjective
STORE 0 TO mamount
STORE ' ' TO minterest
STORE CTOD('  /  /  ') TO mlastcall
RETURN
```

FIGURE 10.14 The initialization program

```
***GETINPUT.prg
***This program maps the screen for prospect information
***
@  6,  3   SAY "Prefix:"
@  6, 11   GET   mprefix
@  6, 20   SAY "Last name:"
@  6, 31   GET   mlastname
@  6, 52   SAY "First name:"
@  6, 64   GET   mfirstname
@  9,  3   SAY "Street address:"
@  9, 19   GET   mstreet
@ 10, 13   SAY "City:"
@ 10, 19   GET   mcity
@ 10, 45   SAY "State:"
@ 10, 52   GET   mstate PICTURE '!!'
@ 10, 61   SAY "Zip code:"
@ 10, 71   GET   mzipcode
@ 12, 28   SAY "Telephone:"
@ 12, 39   GET   mtelephone FUNCTION "r" PICTURE "(999) 999-9999"
@ 15,  8   SAY "Investment objective:"
@ 15, 30   GET   mobjective FUNCTION "!" PICTURE "X"
@ 15, 44   SAY "Amount to invest:"
@ 15, 62   GET   mamount FUNCTION "z" PICTURE "9,999,999"
@ 16, 12   SAY "(Growth/Income)"
@ 18, 10   SAY "Degree of interest:"
@ 18, 30   GET   minterest FUNCTION "!"
@ 18, 46   SAY "Last contacted:"
@ 18, 62   GET   mlastcall
@ 19, 10   SAY "(High/Moderate/Low)"
STORE 'Please enter information at the cursor' TO message
DO printmsg WITH message
READ
RETURN
```

FIGURE 10.15 The get input program

SET TALK (default ON) controls whether responses from dBASE commands are displayed on the screen. This information is useful in the interactive mode, but confusing in the program mode where it interferes with the screen design and other messages displayed by the program. Consequently, the parameter should be turned off.

SET BELL (default ON) determines whether a "beep" is heard during certain operations, such as data entry when the end of an input field is reached. Although this warning may seem appropriate initially, you can quickly tire of the noise and hence the parameter is turned off.

SET STATUS (default ON) determines whether the status bar appears or not. The status line, however, is of little value given the presence of custom menus within a program, and hence the parameter is set to off.

SET SAFETY (default ON) controls whether a confirmation message [for example, "index file already exists, overwrite (yes or no)"] will be provided before certain files are overwritten. Again, this information is useful from the dot prompt, but confusing to a user within the programming mode, and the parameter is turned off.

SET CONSOLE (default ON) controls output to the screen. The statement is used in the ADDRECD program immediately before and after a WAIT command to suppress the "Press any key to continue" prompt produced by the WAIT statement. This enables the programmer to insert a more specific message and also to place that message anywhere on the screen.

Figure 10.19b contains additional SET parameters, except these variables are set to values other than on or off. Recall, for example, the SET DEFAULT TO B command introduced in earlier chapters to change the default drive for dBASE files. Similarly, the SET INDEX TO command changes the active index (for example, SET INDEX TO ssn, as was done in the ADDRECD program).

```
***COMPLCHK.PRG
***This program checks to see if data has been entered
***
DO WHILE mprefix = '  '
    DO msgclear
    STORE '*** Please Enter a Prefix ***' TO message
    DO printmsg WITH message
    @ 6,11 GET mprefix
    READ
ENDDO
DO WHILE mlastname = '                      '
    DO msgclear
    STORE '*** Please Enter a Last Name ***' TO message
    DO printmsg WITH message
    @ 6,31 GET mlastname
    READ
ENDDO
DO WHILE mfirstname = '              '
    DO msgclear
    STORE '*** Please Enter a First Name ***' TO message
    DO printmsg WITH message
    @ 6,64 GET mfirstname
    READ
ENDDO
DO WHILE mstreet = '                '
    DO msgclear
    STORE '*** Please Enter a Street Address ***' TO message
    DO printmsg WITH message
    @ 9,19 GET mstreet
    READ
ENDDO
DO WHILE mcity = '            '
    DO msgclear
    STORE '*** Please Enter a City ***' TO message
    DO printmsg WITH message
    @ 10,19 GET mcity
    READ
ENDDO
DO WHILE mstate = '  '
    DO msgclear
    STORE '*** Please Enter a State ***' TO message
    DO printmsg WITH message
    @ 10,52 GET mstate PICTURE '!!'
    READ
ENDDO
DO WHILE mzipcode = '      '
    DO msgclear
    STORE '*** Please Enter a Zipcode ***' TO message
    DO printmsg WITH message
    @ 10,71 GET mzipcode
    READ
ENDDO
DO WHILE mtelephone = '                '
    DO msgclear
    STORE '*** Please Enter a Telephone Number ***' TO message
    DO printmsg WITH message
    @ 12,39 GET mtelephone PICTURE '@R (999) 999-9999'
    READ
ENDDO
DO WHILE mobjective = ' '
    DO msgclear
    STORE '*** Please Enter an Objective ***' TO message
    DO printmsg WITH message
    @ 15,30 GET mobjective PICTURE '!'
    READ
ENDDO
DO WHILE mamount = 0
    DO msgclear
    STORE '*** Please Enter an Amount to Invest ***' TO message
    DO printmsg WITH message
    @ 15,62 GET mamount PICTURE '@Z 9,999,999'
    READ
ENDDO
DO WHILE minterest = ' '
    DO msgclear
    STORE '*** Please Enter an Interest Level ***' TO message
    DO printmsg WITH message
    @ 18,30 GET minterest PICTURE '!'
    READ
ENDDO
DO WHILE DTOC(mlastcall) = '  /  /  '
    DO msgclear
    STORE '*** Please Enter the Date of the Last Call ***' TO message
    DO printmsg WITH message
    @ 18,62 GET mlastcall
    READ
ENDDO
RETURN
```

FIGURE 10.16 The completeness check program

```
***RANGECHK.PRG
***This program validates data input for proper values
***
STORE .F. TO validsw
DO WHILE .NOT. validsw
   DO msgclear
   IF mobjective = 'G' .OR. mobjective = 'I'
      STORE .T. TO validsw
   ELSE
      STORE 'Enter G or I for investment objective' TO message
      DO printmsg WITH message
      @ 15,30 GET mobjective PICTURE '!'
      READ
   ENDIF
ENDDO
STORE .F. TO validsw
DO WHILE .NOT. validsw
   DO msgclear
   IF minterest = 'H' .OR. minterest = 'M' .OR. minterest = 'L'
      STORE .T. TO validsw
   ELSE
      STORE 'Enter H, M, or L for degree of interest' TO message
      DO printmsg WITH message
      @ 18,30 GET minterest PICTURE '!'
      READ
   ENDIF
ENDDO
STORE .F. TO validsw
DO WHILE .NOT. validsw
   DO msgclear
   IF mamount >= 10000
      STORE .T. TO validsw
   ELSE
      STORE 'Amount to invest must be at least 10,000' TO message
      DO printmsg WITH message
      @ 15,62 GET mamount PICTURE '@Z 9,999,999'
      READ
   ENDIF
ENDDO
RETURN
```

FIGURE 10.17 The range and code validation program

```
***APPNDREC.PRG
***This program accomplishes the actual addition of a new record,
***by replacing fieldnames within a DBF record with the contents
***of the respective memory variables
***
APPEND BLANK
REPLACE ssn WITH mssn
REPLACE lastname WITH mlastname
REPLACE firstname WITH mfirstname
REPLACE prefix WITH mprefix
REPLACE street WITH mstreet
REPLACE city WITH mcity
REPLACE state WITH mstate
REPLACE zipcode WITH mzipcode
REPLACE telephone WITH mtelephone
REPLACE objective WITH mobjective
REPLACE amount WITH mamount
REPLACE interest WITH minterest
REPLACE lastcall WITH mlastcall
RETURN
```

FIGURE 10.18 The append record program

```
SET BELL ON/off          SET ECHO on/OFF          SET SAFETY ON/off
SET CARRY on/OFF         SET ESCAPE ON/off        SET SCOREBOARD ON/off
SET CENTURY on/OFF       SET EXACT on/OFF         SET STATUS ON/off
SET CONFIRM on/OFF       SET FIXED on/OFF         SET STEP on/OFF
SET CONSOLE ON/off       SET HEADINGS ON/off      SET TALK ON/off
SET DEBUG on/OFF         SET HELP ON/off          SET TITLE ON/off
SET DELETED on/OFF       SET INTENSITY ON/off     SET UNIQUE on/OFF
SET DOHISTORY on/OFF     SET MENUS ON/off
```

a

```
 1 - SET ALTERNATE     9 - SET FIELDS       17 - SET MESSAGE
 2 - SET CATALOG      10 - SET FILTER       18 - SET ORDER
 3 - SET COLOR        11 - SET FUNCTION     19 - SET PATH
 4 - SET DATE         12 - SET FORMAT       20 - SET PRINT
 5 - SET DECIMALS     13 - SET HISTORY      21 - SET PROCEDURE
 6 - SET DEFAULT      14 - SET INDEX        22 - SET RELATION
 7 - SET DELIMITERS   15 - SET MARGIN       23 - SET TYPEAHEAD
 8 - SET DEVICE       16 - SET MEMOWIDTH    24 - SET VIEW
```

b

FIGURE 10.19 SET commands: (a) SET ON/OFF commands; (b) SET TO commands

The SET PROCEDURE TO statement specifies the name of the procedure file, PRO-CLIB.PRG in our program, containing the called procedures. The statement causes the designated procedure file to be read into memory to enable subsequent execution of the individual procedures. (You can establish as many procedure files as necessary, except each procedure file is limited to a maximum of 32 procedures, and only one procedure file can be in memory at one time.)

Drawing Boxes

The various menus produced during the addition process were always enclosed within a box, with horizontal lines used to separate portions of the screen from one another. The lines of the box were produced by the four @ ... DOUBLE statements near the beginning of the program which draw double lines where indicated.

The first of these draws a box around the entire screen by indicating the coordinates of the upper left and lower right corners (row 1, column 0 and row 23, column 79, respectively). The next three statements draw horizontal lines in rows 3, 14, and 20, respectively.

STORE and RELEASE

STORE and RELEASE are used with memory variables. The STORE command allocates space for a variable in memory, and/or assigns a value to the memory variable, erasing what was previously there. (dBASE requires that space for a memory variable be allocated before obtaining a value with a GET statement.) Consider:

Syntax:
STORE expression TO variable name

Examples:
```
STORE ' ' TO moreadd
STORE SPACE(9) TO mssn
STORE .T. TO addrecs
STORE '*** Please enter either A or Q ***' TO message
```

All the statements are taken from the ADDRECD program. The first example allocates a single position to the memory variable `moreadd`, whereas the second uses the dBASE `SPACE` function to assign nine positions to the variable `mssn`. The third example assigns a value of true to the indicated variable, whereas the final illustration stores a character string to `message`.

The `RELEASE` command removes the indicated memory variables from memory and is normally among a program's concluding statements. dBASE limits the number of memory variables that can be active at any one time and thus it is (sometimes) necessary to release variables no longer needed. Consider:

Syntax:
```
RELEASE variable-list [ALL]
```

Examples:
```
RELEASE mfirstname, mlastname
RELEASE ALL
```

The first example frees only the indicated variables. Specifying `ALL` in the second example frees every variable in memory.

SEEK

The `SEEK` command finds a record in an indexed file. The format of the command is `SEEK expression`, where the expression can be a number, character string (surrounded in single or double quotes), or a memory variable. Note that the expression must be a value of the index key.

Consider Figure 10.20 (reproduced from the ADDRECD program) which uses the `SEEK` statement to check for the presence of a duplicate social security number. In essence, the user is asked to input the social security number of the record to be added; the program then checks for the existence of a record with that social security number.

The `@...GET` statement (in conjunction with the `READ` statement) obtains the social security number and stores it in the memory variable `mssn`. The `SEEK` statement then searches the active DBF file for that value. If the number is found, that is, if the end-of-file is *not* reached, the duplication message is displayed and the user is asked for another social security number. If, on the other hand, the number is not found, that is, the end-of-file is reached, the loop ends and the program continues.

Public and Private Variables

The `PUBLIC` and `PRIVATE` commands classify memory variables and determine how individual programs (or procedures) within a large system access these variables. *All memory variables created from a program file are considered private unless declared public.* A private variable is available only to the program in which it is created and to all programs called by that program.

```
USE prospect                        ← Active index is required
SET INDEX TO ssn
        .
          .
            .
STORE .T. to duplicate
┌─ DO WHILE duplicate
│      DO scrnclr
│      STORE SPACE(9) TO mssn                    ← user enters social security number
│      @ 4,23 SAY 'Social Security Number:'
│      @ 4,47 GET mssn FUNCTION "r" PICTURE '999-99-9999'
│      STORE "Enter Prospect's Social Security Number " TO message
│      DO printmsg WITH message
│      READ              ← SEEK statement searches for social security number
│      SEEK mssn
│   ┌─ IF .NOT. EOF()
│   │      DO scrnclr
│   │      @ 8,22 SAY 'Social Security Number: '
│   │      @ 8,46 SAY mssn PICTURE '@R 999-99-9999'
│   │      STORE 'SSN already in file - Press any key to continue' TO message
│   │      DO printmsg WITH message
│   │      SET CONSOLE OFF
│   │      WAIT
│   │      SET CONSOLE ON
│   │      DO scrnclr              ← EOF condition indicates record not found
│   │   ELSE
│   │      STORE .F. to duplicate
│   └─ ENDIF
└─ ENDDO
```

FIGURE 10.20 The SEEK command

With respect to our system, all variables created by the ADDRECD program are automatically available to every other program, because the ADDRECD program calls every other program, that is, it resides at the top of the hierarchy chart. However, variables created in the subordinate programs (that is, the modules on the hierarchy chart's second level) are not available to other programs on the same or higher level unless they are declared public.

Consider, for example, the INITVAR program of Figure 10.14 which initializes (and simultaneously creates) the memory variables used to store the user input for mlastname, mfirstname, mprefix, and so on. Since these variables must be accessed by every other program, they have to be made available to the other programs, and hence are declared PUBLIC at the beginning of the program.

Summary

This chapter discussed concepts of file maintenance with emphasis on the program(s) for the addition of records to a file. The need for data validation was stressed throughout, as were the benefits of performing file maintenance through programming as opposed to doing it interactively (that is, from the dot prompt). The bulk of the chapter was devoted to developing the ADDRECD program and the associated *pseudocode* and *hierarchy chart*.

Understanding the resultant program required the introduction of additional dBASE concepts and programming statements. These included SEEK, procedure files, public and private variables, memory variables, STORE, RELEASE, and various SET statements.

Key Words and Concepts

APPEND BLANK
BROWSE
Command mode
Completeness check
Data validation
DELETE
Dot prompt
Duplication check
EDIT
Format file
Hierarchy chart
Initializing variables
Interactive mode
Logical deletion
Memory variable
MODIFY COMMAND
MODIFY STRUCTURE
PACK
PARAMETERS

Physical deletion
Private variable
Procedures
Pseudocode
Public variable
Range check
RELEASE
SEEK
SET BELL
SET FORMAT
SET SAFETY
SET STATUS
SET TALK
SPACE ( )
STORE
Structured design
Structured programming
Unique key

True/False

1. There are three basic types of file maintenance operations.
2. Certain types of data validation can be accomplished without programming.
3. Use of procedures in lieu of individual program files will speed up program execution.
4. A single procedure file, such as PROCLIB.PRG, may contain several procedures.
5. A memory variable's value can be established with either a @ GET or a STORE statement.
6. There is no limit on the number of memory variables that can be active at one time.
7. There is no limit on the number of procedures that can be contained in a single procedure file.
8. The same procedure can be called from more than one program.
9. A procedure may be written with or without the PARAMETERS statement.
10. The SEEK statement is associated with a memory variable.
11. A DO statement is used to call either a program or a procedure.
12. The RETURN statement is normally the last statement in either a called program or a procedure.
13. The READ statement may be used in lieu of a @ ... GET statement to obtain the values of input variables.

Exercises

1. Distinguish between:
   a. a procedure file and a procedure name
   b. @ 1,0 TO 23,70 DOUBLE and @ 1,0 TO 1,70 DOUBLE
   c. @ 1,0 TO 23,70 DOUBLE and @ 1,0 TO 23,70

d. a program and a procedure

e. a DO statement and a RETURN statement

f. a called and a calling program

g. a completion check and a range check

h. SPACE(2) and ' '

2. The following dBASE code segments were extracted from various programs in the chapter. Explain the precise function of each group of statements (you can execute the individual statements from the dot prompt to see what they do).

a.
```
SET CONSOLE OFF
WAIT
SET CONSOLE ON
```

b.
```
@  4,2 CLEAR TO 13,77
@ 15,2 CLEAR TO 19,77
@ 21,2 CLEAR TO 22,77
```

c.
```
@  1,0 TO 23,79 DOUBLE
@  3,1 TO  3,78 DOUBLE
@ 14,1 TO 14,78 DOUBLE
@ 20,1 TO 20,78 DOUBLE
```

d.
```
@ 21,(80-LEN(message))/2 SAY message
```

e.
```
SEEK mssn
```

3. Important as data validation is, it nevertheless extracts a price in terms of increased execution time. The ADDRECD program, for example, invokes two lower level programs, COMPLCHK and RANGECHK, to ensure that all fields have been completed and that valid codes have been entered. Modify the ADDRECD program so that these checks are no longer implemented, then repeat Step 5 of Hands-on Exercise 10–2.

a. Do you notice an appreciable change in the program's execution time?

b. Would this increase significantly as large numbers of records are entered into the file?

c. Would it make sense to modify the COMPLCHK program to check for only a few fields, rather than every field?

■ OBJECTIVES

After reading this chapter, you should be able to:

- Describe how a database differs from a conventional file; explain the advantages of database organization.

- Describe what is meant by the currently selected DBF file; discuss how multiple files can be open at the same time and how relationships are established among files.

- Describe fully the use of the SELECT and SET RELATION commands.

- Discuss the purpose of a dBASE view file; describe how to create and modify these files.

- Discuss the purpose of the DISPLAY STATUS command and describe its output.

11

Relational Databases

OUTLINE

OVERVIEW

The term *database* is perhaps the most misused term associated with the study of computers. Strictly speaking, a database implies *two or more related files* and should not be used in conjunction with systems built around a single file. In other words, the examples presented thus far (Soleil, the menu-driven system for the United States, the Dade County Zoo, and the stock broker examples) were all based on a single file, and hence would not classify as true database systems. Nevertheless, they provided realistic dBASE applications, and went far to illustrate the power of the language.

In this chapter, however, we move to a true database application. We introduce a new case study and present the idea of a *relational database*. We then move quickly into a hands-on exercise to show how these theoretical concepts are implemented in dBASE.

The chapter continues by presenting several new dBASE statements associated with the relational model. We cover the use of multiple work areas and the SELECT statement, introduce the SET RELATION command, and discuss the creation of *view* files. We develop a second hands-on exercise to show how these statements can be used from the dot prompt, then incorporate them into a complete program.

CASE PREVIEW

The case you are about to read is set within the context of the Coral Springs Soccer Association (CSSA), a youth-oriented athletic league in South Florida. The Association is seeking to automate its registration procedure and to facilitate monitoring of its *teams, players, coaches,* and *sponsors*. These elements have a definite relationship to one another (a team consists of up to 15 players and is assigned a coach and a sponsor). The essence of the case is how to best structure the data.

One approach is to develop a single team file, with each team record containing data about the players, coach, and sponsor assigned to that team. As we shall see, that design leads to problems of *redundancy* because a given individual may coach (or sponsor) more than one team. This, in turn, creates problems in file maintenance. A better approach is to develop separate files for each of the entities in question.

Coral Springs, Florida, is a residential community of approximately 70,000 people located in the northwest corner of Broward County. The city takes great pride in its excellent park and recreational facilities which have enabled the growth of a number of independently run sports leagues. Foremost among these is the Coral Springs Soccer Association which registered approximately 3000 players for the 1988–1989 season.

Notification for soccer signups appears several times in local newspapers; parents then enroll their youngsters in the program. At registration, the Association gathers data about players and also about coaches and sponsors. The Board of Directors subsequently meets to decide how many teams it will have in each age group, and manually assigns players, coaches, and sponsors to the individual teams.

The soccer program is open to all children aged 6 to 16 living in the city. Age group classifications are maintained at two-year intervals, beginning with the "Under 8s," and continuing to the "Under 16s." Boys and girls play in separate divisions. Rules of the game are modified to accommodate the younger players and to further the Association's instructional philosophy. The "Under 8s," for example, play with smaller goals, employ only seven players to a side, use a size 3 ball, and play 20-minute halves. The "Under 10s" move up to a size 4 ball, a regulation field, and 25-minute halves, and so on.

The Association collects a $25 annual registration fee from each participant. Additional money is raised by soliciting support from the local business community. Sponsors contribute $175 per team, and range from branch offices of national corporations (for example, Wendy's), to local businesses (Poogie's Pools), to individuals (Dr. Getz's Decay Fighters). The money enables the Association to supply every player with a T-shirt and matching soccer socks, as well as provide paid referees for each game. The money is further used to buy soccer balls, goalie uniforms, and other equipment, and to send selected teams to national tournaments.

Every child who registers is guaranteed a place on a recreational team. The Association maintains a balance among teams by rating players according to their ability before making team assignments. A player's rating ranges from one to five (one being the best). The ratings are kept confidential and used only to balance the teams.

The Association also maintains a competitive (traveling) division for players in the "Under 10" and older classifications. Interested players are asked to try out for the competitive teams before the season starts and, if selected, are removed from the recreational league. Any boy or girl not selected for a competitive team is automatically assigned to a recreational team.

The success of the Coral Springs Soccer Association is due to the community's phenomenal support. In addition to the nearly 200 sponsors, parents give freely of their time to serve as voluntary coaches. (The Association expects its coaches to be licensed by the Florida Youth Soccer Association, which requires attendance at various coaching clinics.)

The soccer program's growth has prompted the Association to seek its own computer processing. The Board of Directors would like a system that would facilitate player registration and track both coaches and sponsors.

CASE SOLUTION

The initial concern in this, or any other system, is how best to structure the data so that the eventual solution is capable of meeting the client's information needs. Since the objective of this case is to illustrate the advantages of database processing over a single file representation, we present both ways of structuring the data and then draw comparisons. Accordingly, the first solution is based on a single team file and will be shown to have several limitations. The second solution is a true *database* and consists of four files (for the players, teams, coaches, and sponsors).

Single File Representation

The single file solution is shown in Figure 11.1. Each record within the file contains data about a particular team; for example, whether it is competitive or recreational. In addition, each record contains data about the coach, sponsor, and players assigned to that team.

There are five teams in our example, each with a *unique* six-character team number. The first character indicates whether the team is for boys or girls (B or G). The next three characters indicate the age group (U10 denotes 10 and under), and the last two, the team number within the particular age and sex division. Thus, team GU1001 is the first team in the girls' 10-and-under division.

Figure 11.1 at first glance appears to satisfy the case requirements. There are, however, three specific types of problems associated with this solution. These are:

1. difficulties in *modifying* existing data due to data *duplication*
2. difficulties in *adding* a new player, coach, or sponsor, because these entities must first be associated with a particular team
3. difficulties in *deleting* a team because the players, coach, and/or sponsor associated with that team may be inadvertently dropped from the Association

The first problem, modifying data about a coach or sponsor, arises only when a particular entity is associated with multiple teams, and occurs because data about that entity is *duplicated* in the file. Assume, for example, that data about a duplicated coach, for example, Coach Grauer, changes. We would then have to search through the entire file of Figure 11.1 to find *all* instances of the data and then make the *identical* modification (for example, a change in his address and phone) in each of these places. A similar procedure would have to be followed should data about a duplicated sponsor (for example, Wendy's) change. This is, to say the least, a time-consuming and error-prone procedure.

Adding a new player, coach, or sponsor may not seem to pose a problem, yet it presents potentially far greater difficulty than that of redundant data. As Figure 11.1 is currently constructed, adding any one of these entities requires that a team record already exists, which is the exact opposite of the physical system. The Association conducts its registration to sign up players, coaches, and sponsors, and then creates teams based on the number of individuals who sign up, rather than the other way around.

Deleting a record in Figure 11.1 poses different problems. What happens, for example, if the Association subsequently decides not to field a specific team in the Girls 10 and Under division, because too few players come out? Consider the consequences if team GU1001 were deleted. The team would disappear as expected, but so would the data for the coach (Osberger), sponsor (J.C. Penny), and players (Aiken and Anderson) which is not intended. The Association would want to assign these individuals to other teams, but that is not easily done given the structure of Figure 11.1.

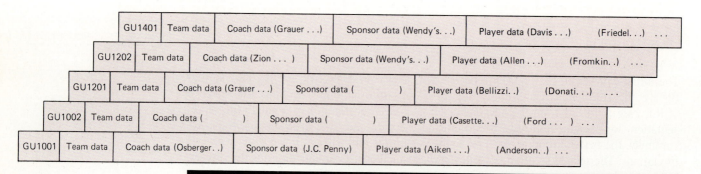

FIGURE 11.1 Single file solution

Database Representation

A better solution appears in Figure 11.2, which uses independent files for the teams, players, coaches, and sponsors. The files are linked to one another via a series of pointers and collectively constitute a *database*. Although this arrangement may appear more complicated than the single file solution, it enables the changes just described to be implemented with considerably less effort.

Consider first how the files in Figure 11.2 are related to one another. Every team record in Figure 11.2b contains a *unique* team identification (GU1001, GU1002, and so on). Similarly, every coach record in Figure 11.2c contains a *unique* coach identification (C0001, C0002, and so on), and every sponsor record in Figure 11.2d contains a *unique* sponsor identification. These fields can then be used to derive complete information about any given team.

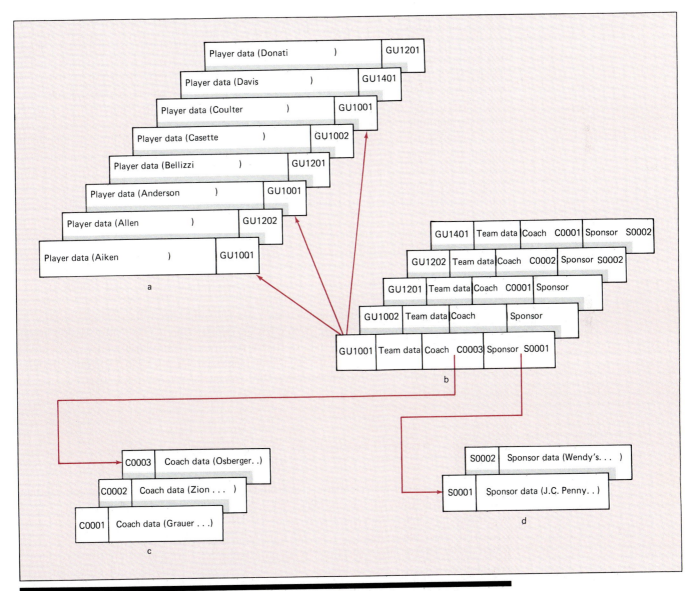

FIGURE 11.2 Multiple file solution: (a) player file; (b) team file; (c) coach file; (d) sponsor file

Assume, for example, that you want to know all about the coach, sponsor, and players assigned to team GU1001. You would retrieve the team record from Figure 11.2b, which in turn contains a coach and sponsor identification of C0003 and S0001, respectively. You would then search through the coach file for the record whose coach identification is C0003, and through the sponsor file for the record with a sponsor identification of S0001. Finally, you would go through the player file and retrieve every player record whose team identification is GU10001. The process is depicted graphically in Figure 11.2.

The task of establishing pointers in the various files and linking them to one another is far less cumbersome than you might imagine, as dBASE does much of the process automatically. For the time being, however, accept that a database has several advantages over single file organization, and that the problems associated with data duplication and adding and deleting individual records are greatly reduced.

Consider the necessity of changing data for a coach assigned to two teams, for example, Coach Grauer. All that would be required is to go into the coach file, find the appropriate record (Record 1) and make the necessary changes. The modification in coaching data will then be automatically reflected for the teams that Grauer coaches.

The records for the two teams with this coach (teams GU1201 and GU1401 in Figure 11.2b) do not actually contain the coach's data, but rather *pointers* to the corresponding coach record in Figure 11.2c. These pointers (that is, the coach's identification number) do *not* change, only the coach's data in Figure 11.2c. In other words, a data change for a particular coach is made in only one place (the coach file), yet that change will be reflected whenever pointers are used to retrieve the coach's data.

Adding a new record for a player, coach, or sponsor can be done immediately in the appropriate file *without* affecting data in any other file. In other words, the Association can add a player, coach, or sponsor when these individuals appear at registration, without waiting for an empty team record to be created. This is far easier than the approach of Figure 11.1 which required the team to be available in order to add one of the other entities to the system.

Deleting a team (or any other record) is also easier in Figure 11.2 than with the single file organization. You could delete the record for team GU1001 from Figure 11.2b without affecting the corresponding player, coach, or team records. Realize, however, that while the coach and sponsor records for Osberger and J.C. Penny still exist in their respective files, they would not be tied to any particular team.

Accordingly, the pointers in other team records would have to be changed in order to provide new assignments. Thus, you would assign Coach Osberger to team GU1002 by entering a coach identification of C0003 in that team's record. Similarly, you would enter a sponsor identification of S0001 in the record for team GU1201 to assign J.C. Penny. Finally, the players formerly associated with team GU1001 (Aiken, Anderson, and Coulter) would also have to have their pointers changed to a new team, for example to GU1002.

Implementation in dBASE

Each of the four files (player, team, coach, and sponsor) in the database solution requires its own file structure as shown in Figure 11.3. Each file structure has its own set of fields which were developed from the case description.

The player file in Figure 11.3a contains the player's birth date, sex, and rating, fields which are needed by the Association to assign the player to an appropriate team. A player's record also contains a phone number and an address, as well as a team identification field. The latter will hold the number of the team to which the player is assigned, thereby linking the player and team file to one another.

The team file in Figure 11.3b contains a *unique* team identification field for each team, in addition to fields for the coach and sponsor identification, which provide links to the

```
. USE PLAYER
. DISPLAY STRUCTURE
Structure for database: B:PLAYER.dbf
Number of data records:        21
Date of last update   : 05/02/87
Field  Field Name  Type      Width
    1  LAST_NAME   Character     12
    2  FIRST_NAME  Character     10
    3  BIRTH_DATE  Date           8
    4  SEX         Character      1
    5  RATING      Character      1
    6  TEAM_ID     Character      6
    7  PHONE       Character      7
    8  STREET      Character     24
    9  CITY        Character     16
   10  STATE       Character      2
   11  ZIP_CODE    Character      5
** Total **                     93
```
a

```
. USE TEAM
. DISPLAY STRUCTURE
Structure for database: B:TEAM.dbf
Number of data records:        5
Date of last update   : 05/02/87
Field  Field Name  Type      Width
    1  TEAM_ID     Character     6
    2  DIVISION    Character     1
    3  COACH_ID    Character     5
    4  SPONSOR_ID  Character     5
** Total **                    18
```
b

```
. USE COACH
. DISPLAY STRUCTURE
Structure for database: B:COACH.dbf
Number of data records:        3
Date of last update   : 05/02/87
Field  Field Name  Type      Width
    1  COACH_ID    Character      5
    2  LAST_NAME   Character     16
    3  FIRST_NAME  Character     12
    4  LICENSE     Character      1
    5  NUM_TEAMS   Numeric        1
    6  PHONE       Character      7
    7  STREET      Character     24
    8  CITY        Character     16
    9  STATE       Character      2
   10  ZIP_CODE    Character      5
** Total **                     90
```
c

```
. USE SPONSOR
. DISPLAY STRUCTURE
Structure for database: B:SPONSOR.dbf
Number of data records:        2
Date of last update   : 05/02/87
Field  Field Name  Type      Width
    1  SPONSOR_ID  Character      5
    2  NAME        Character     20
    3  CONTACT     Character     16
    4  NUM_TEAMS   Numeric        1
    5  AMOUNT_PD   Numeric        4
    6  PHONE       Character      7
    7  STREET      Character     24
    8  CITY        Character     16
    9  STATE       Character      2
   10  ZIP_CODE    Character      5
** Total **                    101
```
d

FIGURE 11.3 dBASE file structures: (a) PLAYER.DBF; (b) TEAM.DBF; (c) COACH.DBF; (d) SPONSOR.DBF

coach and sponsor files, respectively. Several teams may have the same values entered for either of these fields, which would indicate that the same individual is coaching (or sponsoring) multiple teams. The team file also contains a field for division indicating whether a team is in the competitive or recreation division. (It would also have been possible to extend the file structure to include other fields such as a team nickname, team colors, and so on, but this was not done.)

The file structures for the coach and sponsor records are shown in Figures 11.3c and 11.3d. Each coach (sponsor) is assigned a *unique* identification that links records in these files to their respective teams. In addition, each file contains a number-of-teams field indicating the number of teams with which an individual (coach or sponsor) is currently working (unassigned coaches and/or sponsors have a value of zero in this field). The nature of the remaining fields in each record should be apparent from the field name and case description.

Hands-on Exercise 11–1 will demonstrate how these concepts are implemented in dBASE. The exercise begins by generating team rosters based on existing DBF files contained on the convenience disk. It then directs you to make various changes to the individual files, and ends with a revised set of rosters reflecting the changes that have been made. Some things to look for in the exercise:

- *The address of an individual coaching two teams, Bob Grauer, will be changed:* The change will be made in only one place (the COACH.DBF file), but will be properly reflected in all the rosters of teams coached by this person.

- *A team, GU1001, will be deleted:* A team record will be removed from the TEAM.DBF file, but the coach, sponsor, and player records associated with this team will remain in their respective files. These individuals must, however, be assigned to new teams by altering the appropriate pointers in the team and player files.

- *A new sponsor, Poogie's Pools, will be added:* The sponsor record will be added in the SPONSOR.DBF file, but will be assigned to a team by changing a pointer in the TEAM.DBF file.

Hands-on Exercise 11–1: Generating Team Rosters

Objective: To demonstrate the file maintenance operations within a database.

☐   STEP 1: Log onto the soccer subdirectory.

Place the convenience disk in drive B, log onto the soccer subdirectory with the proper command according to your configuration, then load dBASE as prescribed for your system:

```
CD B:\SOCCER ──────────── On a floppy disk system

CD C:\SAMPLER\SOCCER ──── On a hard disk drive
PATH C:\SAMPLER
```

☐   STEP 2: Examine the directory.

Enter the DIR command (with no parameters) from the dot prompt to list all of the DBF files (four in this case) on the current subdirectory. The following should appear on your monitor:

```
. DIR
Database Files      # Records      Last Update
TEAM.DBF                    5      05/09/87
PLAYER.DBF                 21      05/09/87
COACH.DBF                   3      05/09/87
SPONSOR.DBF                 2      05/09/87
```

As expected from the case solution, there are four DBF files, one each for the teams, players, coaches, and sponsors. The system currently has five teams, 21 players, three coaches, and two sponsors as can be determined from the number of records in each of the respective files. (Although the number of players may strike you as unrealistically small, recall that all our systems were developed to run on the *student* version of dBASE, which is limited to 31 records. This is, in effect, the only limitation of the student version and consequently should pose no problem in explaining the relational capabilities inherent in the program.)

☐   STEP 3: Print the team rosters.

Enter the command DO ROSTER from the dot prompt to execute the program to print the team rosters. The rosters of Figure 11.4 will appear on your monitor, one team at a time. Note, too, that if your computer is connected to a printer, you may find it useful to enter the SET PRINT ON command before executing the roster program.

☐   STEP 4: Change data for an existing coach.

The easiest way to find the particular record slated for change is through the FIND command which positions the record pointer at the record in question. The FIND command requires that the file be open in conjunction with an index. Accordingly, enter the commands:

```
. USE COACH INDEX COACHID
. FIND C0001
. EDIT
```
— *Opens coach file and coach index*
— *Searches for the appropriate record*

The index file in this example, COACHID.NDX, already exists on the convenience disk and is based on the COACH_ID field within the COACH.DBF file. Hence, to retreive Grauer's record you have to know the corresponding value of the COACH_ID field, in this case C0001. (It would also be possible to create a second index, based on the coach's last name, and retrieve records on it, for example, FIND Grauer.)

Once Grauer's record has been found, change the address field from 2133 NW 102 Terrace to 1845 Merion Lane, then press Ctrl End to save the changes. The address change will subsequently be reflected in all team rosters associated with this coach.

☐ STEP 5: Delete a team

Removing a team record (for example, TEAM_ID GU1001) from within the TEAM.DBF file is easy, and is accomplished this way:

```
. USE TEAM INDEX TEAMID
. FIND GU1001
. DISPLAY
. DELETE
. PACK
```
— *Confirms that the proper record will be deleted*

Once again, FIND is used to locate the record slated for deletion, whereas the DISPLAY command is executed to confirm that you have, in fact, found the proper record. Note, too, that the coach, sponsor, and players formerly associated with this team must be reassigned as described in Step 6 below.

☐ STEP 6: Reassign the coach, sponsor, and players.

Removing the team record does not affect the corresponding player, coach, and sponsor records within their respective files. You must, however, *reassign* these individuals to different teams now that their original team (GU1001) no longer exists. Accordingly:

a. Assign Coach Osberger to the other team in the Girls' 10 and Under division (GU1002) which is currently without a coach. Enter the commands:

```
. FIND GU1002
. DISPLAY
. EDIT
```
— *Confirms that the proper record will be edited*
— *Enter C0003 as the Coach Id for this team*

b. Assign the sponsor, J.C. Penny, to the Girls 12 and Under Competitive team (GU1201) which is currently without a sponsor. (Alternatively, J.C. Penny could have been assigned to team GU1002.) Enter the commands:

```
. FIND GU1201
. DISPLAY
. EDIT
. Press Ctrl End
```
— *Confirms that the proper record will be edited*
— *Enter S0001 as the Sponsor_Id for this team*
— *Saves all changes made in the TEAM.DBF file*

c. Reassign the players which requires us to leave the team file and open the player file. Enter the commands:

```
. USE PLAYER INDEX PLAYERID
. FIND GU1001
. EDIT
```
— *Opens the player file and its index*

You should be positioned at the first player (Aiken) on team GU1001. Change the team assignment to GU1002, then use the PgUp key to get to the next player (Anderson), make the appropriate change, and so on. Press Ctrl End to save the changes when you are finished.

☐ **STEP 7: Add a new sponsor.**

The Association has recruited a new sponsor for the one team currently without one (TEAM_ID GU1002). Accordingly, you will enter data for the new sponsor in the SPONSOR.DBF file, then make the appropriate assignment within the TEAM.DBF file. The new sponsor is Poogie's Pools, located on 10000 Sample Road, Coral Springs, Florida 33065. The contact person is Mary Smith who can be reached at 753–2000; no money has yet been paid to the Association.

```
                    CORAL SPRINGS SOCCER ASSOCIATION
     Team Number: GU1001                 Girls, Under 10, Competitive

     Coach: John Osberger           Sponsor: J.C. Penny
            20010 NW 9th Court                Ralph Cordell
            Coral Springs  FL 33065           3300 University Drive
            Telephone: 753-8248               Coral Springs  FL 33065
            Class E License                   Telephone: 755-6570

                   Player            Birthdate        Rating
                   ------            ---------        ------
             Allison Aiken           07/28/78           1
             Nancy Anderson          10/31/78           1
             Sara Coulter            03/29/78           2


                      PRESS ANY KEY TO CONTINUE
```
a

```
                    CORAL SPRINGS SOCCER ASSOCIATION
     Team Number: GU1002                 Girls, Under 10, Recreational

     Coach:                         Sponsor:


         Telephone:      -
         Class   License                       Telephone:      -

                   Player            Birthdate        Rating
                   ------            ---------        ------
             Aliana Casette          03/19/79           3
             Julianne Ford           02/01/78           3
             Leah Martineau          03/23/79           4
             Laura Wellbery          10/03/78           3
             Gina Wilson             03/31/78           4


                      PRESS ANY KEY TO CONTINUE
```
b

FIGURE 11.4 Team rosters before any modification: (a) GU1001; (b) GU1002; (c) GU1201; (d) GU1202; (e) GU1401

```
                 CORAL SPRINGS SOCCER ASSOCIATION

Team Number: GU1201              Girls, Under 12, Competitive

Coach: Robert Grauer             Sponsor:
       2133 NW 102 Terrace
       Coral Springs  FL 33065
       Telephone: 753-0345
       Class E License                    Telephone:      -
       _____
             Player        Birthdate     Rating
             ------        ---------     ------
           Maria Bellizzi    04/15/77       2
           Tanya Donati      09/20/77       1
           Danielle Ferraro  03/09/77       1
           Mary Kate Fetters 03/16/77       3
           Jessica Grauer    03/16/77       1
           Jessica Martineau 07/28/77       1
           Norma Pagan       10/10/77       2

                 PRESS ANY KEY TO CONTINUE
```

c

```
                 CORAL SPRINGS SOCCER ASSOCIATION

Team Number: GU1202              Girls, Under 12, Recreational

Coach: Steve Zion                Sponsor: Wendy's
       10020 NW 6th Court                 Jill Simmons
       Coral Springs  FL 33065            1234 Sample Road
       Telephone: 752-2475                Coral Springs  FL 33065
       Class E License                    Telephone: 755-1000
       _____
             Player        Birthdate     Rating
             ------        ---------     ------
           Meredith Allen    04/16/77       2
           Lori Fromkin      03/06/77       4
           Heather Holton    05/26/77       3
           Cara O'Brien      07/06/77       2



                 PRESS ANY KEY TO CONTINUE
```

d

```
                 CORAL SPRINGS SOCCER ASSOCIATION

Team Number: GU1401              Girls, Under 14, Competitive

Coach: Robert Grauer             Sponsor: Wendy's
       2133 NW 102 Terrace                Jill Simmons
       Coral Springs  FL 33065            1234 Sample Road
       Telephone: 753-0345                Coral Springs  FL 33065
       Class E License                    Telephone: 755-1000
       _____
             Player        Birthdate     Rating
             ------        ---------     ------
           Melissa Davis     01/05/76       1
           Laurie Friedel    07/04/76       1




                 PRESS ANY KEY TO CONTINUE
```

e

Assign the next consecutive sponsor identification, S0003, to this sponsor. Enter the commands:

```
USE SPONSOR INDEX SPONSRID ——— The sponsor index will be updated
APPEND ——————————————————— Add the new sponsor
Press Ctrl End ——————————— Saves the new record in the
                                     SPONSOR.DBF file
```

☐ **STEP 8: Assign the new sponsor.**

The addition of a record to the sponsor file does not assign the new sponsor to a team; that is, the latter operation can only be done within the team file. Accordingly, do the following:

```
USE TEAM INDEX TEAMID
FIND GU1002 ———————————— Finds the appropriate team
EDIT ——————————————————— Enter S0003 as the Sponsor_Id for this team
Press Ctrl End ————————— Saves the change in the TEAM.DBF file
```

☐ **STEP 9: Rerun the player rosters.**

Rerun the roster program from the dot prompt (DO ROSTER) whereupon a new set of rosters will be produced. Verify that the changes made in the individual DBF files are reflected in the new team rosters. Accordingly, you should see:

a. Only four teams instead of five, as team GU1001 has been deleted.
b. Three new players (Aiken, Anderson, and Coulter) on team GU1002 who were formerly assigned to GU1001. Note, too, that this team is now coached by John Osberger and sponsored by Poogie's Pools.
c. A new address for Coach Bob Grauer who appears on two rosters (GU1201 and GU1401).
d. A new sponsor, J.C. Penny, for team GU1201.

☐ **STEP 10: Exit dBASE.**

Type QUIT to exit dBASE and return to the DOS prompt.

dBASE Commands and Concepts

The exercise just completed demonstrated the database capabilities of dBASE within the context of a completed program. The exercise did not, however, discuss the program per se, and consequently made no mention of the specific commands needed to accomplish these tasks. Accordingly, the individual commands are presented in this section, then incorporated into a second hands-on exercise.

SELECT

Use of a database requires that several files be open simultaneously, a situation made possible by the availability of multiple *work areas*. dBASE provides for ten such work areas (numbered from 1 to 10), each of which can contain one *open* DBF file and its associated indexes. The USE command *opens* the file (that is, retrieves the file from disk) while the SELECT command chooses in which of the ten work areas the file will be opened. Consider an abbreviated syntax for both commands:

Syntax:
```
SELECT [n] ——— n goes from 1 to 10
USE filename [INDEX file-list]
```

Example:
```
SELECT 1
USE TEAM ———— Opens the TEAM.DBF file in area 1
SELECT 2 ———— The COACH.DBF file is the current file
USE COACH
```

The combination of SELECT and USE commands opens the TEAM.DBF and COACH.DBF files in areas 1 and 2, respectively. (It is also possible to omit the SELECT statement for area 1 and default to the first work area, the situation in the text to date.) Note too, that although both files (TEAM and COACH) are *open,* only one is *current,* the current file being the one in the work area which was last selected (COACH.DBF in work area 2 in the example).

SET RELATION

The SET RELATION command is the basis by which dBASE links the active DBF file to a DBF file in another area. Once a relationship is established, the record pointers move in concert with one another; that is, whenever the record pointer in the first file is moved, the record pointer in the related file is moved as well. SET RELATION requires a *common field* (a field with the same field name, type, width, and contents) to be present in both files, and further that one file be indexed on this field. An abbreviated syntax, together with an example linking the team and coach files, is shown below:

Syntax:
```
SET RELATION TO key-expression INTO file-name
```

Example:
```
SELECT 1
USE TEAM ———————————————— Team file is opened in area 1
SELECT 2
USE COACH INDEX COACHID ——— Coach file is opened along with its index in area 2
SELECT 1 ———————————————— Team file is made the currently selected DBF file
SET RELATION TO COACH_ID INTO COACH
```

The SET RELATION command is best described with the aid of Figure 11.5, which uses COACH_ID as the common field. The SET RELATION command will automatically position the record pointer associated with the COACH.DBF file to the third record so that information for Coach Osberger is available in conjunction with team GU1001.

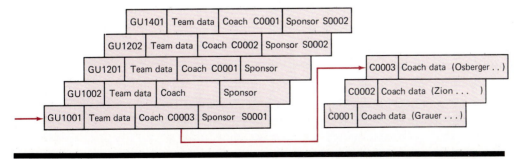

FIGURE 11.5 The SET RELATION command

View Files

A *view file* (extension VUE) is a convenient way of storing the relationships between files so that relationships may be reestablished at a later date. In addition, a view file contains information on which database and/or index files are open, and the work area(s) to which these files have been assigned.

View files are created in one of two ways. The CREATE VIEW command initiates a menu-driven procedure (analogous to CREATE REPORT, CREATE LABEL, and/or CREATE SCREEN), which eventually produces the view file. We find it easier, however, to enter individual commands (SELECT, SET RELATION, SET FIELDS, and so on) directly from the dot prompt, and then issue the command CREATE VIEW FROM ENVIRONMENT. The latter will store all open database and index files, the relations between these files, as well as any limitation on which fields are to be displayed.

Regardless of how it was created initially, an existing view file can be changed with the MODIFY VIEW command, just as existing report forms, label forms, and format files are similarly modified. The SET VIEW command retrieves an existing view file and all its settings.

DISPLAY STATUS

The DISPLAY STATUS command shows all currently open files and their associated work areas. It also displays the keys used to create the open index files, any current relationships, the function key settings, and the SET command settings. The command is by no means restricted to systems with relational databases.

CLEAR ALL

The CLEAR ALL command closes all open database, index, and format files, erases all memory variables, and sets the current work area to 1. The format of the statement is simply CLEAR ALL.

Hands-on Exercise 11–2:   Relational Databases

Objective: To demonstrate dBASE commands which link two DBF files to one another; to create and modify a view file.

☐   **STEP 1: Log onto the SOCCER subdirectory.**
Log onto the SOCCER subdirectory, then load dBASE as prescribed for your system.

```
CD B:\SOCCER ─────────────── On a floppy disk system

CD C:\SAMPLER\SOCCER ──── On a hard disk drive
PATH C:\SAMPLER
```

☐   **STEP 2: Open the team and coach files.**
Enter the SELECT and USE commands as shown below to open the team and coach files in work areas 1 and 2, respectively. List the records in each file as indicated. (Note that only a few of the fields in the coach file are displayed so that the output for each record fits conveniently on one line.)

```
. SELECT 1
. USE TEAM
. LIST TEAM_ID,DIVISION,COACH_ID,SPONSOR_ID
Record#     TEAM_ID    DIVISION    COACH_ID    SPONSOR_ID
      1     GU1002     R           C0003       S0003
      2     GU1201     C           C0001       S0001
      3     GU1202     R           C0002       S0002
      4     GU1401     C           C0001       S0002
```

──COACH.DBF file is opened with an index

```
. SELECT 2
. USE COACH INDEX COACHID
. LIST COACH_ID,LAST_NAME,FIRST_NAME,LICENSE,PHONE
Record# COACH_ID LAST_NAME FIRST_NAME LICENSE PHONE
      1 C0001    Grauer    Robert     E       7530345
      2 C0002    Zion      Steve      E       7522475
      3 C0003    Osberger  John       E       7538248
```

☐ **STEP 3: Relate the team and coach files.**

Relate the team file to the coach file by selecting the first work area, and entering the appropriate SET RELATION command as shown below. Note that for this command to work, both files must contain a COACH_ID field, and further, the coach file must have been opened (in Step 2) with this field as the key of the active index.

```
. SELECT 1
. SET RELATION TO COACH_ID INTO COACH
```

To determine the effects of the SET RELATION command, position the record pointer at a specific record within the *team* file, then observe the effect on the *coach* file. Consider:

```
. GO TOP
. DISPLAY
Record#     TEAM_ID    DIVISION    COACH_ID    SPONSOR_ID
      1     GU10012    R           C0003       S0003
. SELECT 2
. DISPLAY COACH_ID,LAST_NAME,FIRST_NAME,LICENSE,PHONE
Record# COACH_ID LAST_NAME FIRST_NAME LICENSE PHONE
      3 C0003    Osberger  John       E       7538248
```

The GO TOP command positions the record pointer at the first record in the team file, which has a value of C0003 for the COACH_ID field. The SELECT 2 command makes the coach file the active file, and the subsequent DISPLAY command displays the data from the related record in the coach file. In other words, the SET RELATION command links the team and coach files so that whenever the pointer to a team record is moved, the pointer in COACH.DBF is also moved to the corresponding coach record.

☐ **STEP 4: Display (list) fields from both files.**

You can display fields from an open DBF file in other than the currently selected work area by qualifying the field name with the file name. For example, the entry COACH->LAST_NAME refers to the field LAST_NAME from the COACH.DBF file (The arrow consists of a hyphen followed by a greater-than sign.) Consider:

```
. SELECT 1                 — Command entered on 1 line
. DISPLAY TEAM_ID,DIVISION,COACH->LAST_NAME,
COACH->LICENSE,COACH->PHONE
Record#  TEAM_ID  DIVISION  LAST_NAME  LICENSE  PHONE
      1  GU10012  R         Osberger   E        7538248
```

The SELECT statement makes the file in the first work area (TEAM.DBF) the active file. The subsequent DISPLAY statement shows the current TEAM_ID (as determined by the position of the record pointer in the TEAM.DBF file) together with the corresponding coach information as extracted from the COACH.DBF file.

You can also use a SET FIELDS command to limit the fields shown in a DISPLAY (or LIST) command. Consider:

```
. SET FIELDS TO TEAM_ID,DIVISION,COACH->LAST_NAME,
COACH->LICENSE,COACH->PHONE
. DISPLAY                             — Command entered on 1 line

Record#  TEAM_ID  DIVISION  LAST_NAME  LICENSE  PHONE
      1  GU1001   C         Osberger   E        7532848

. LIST

Record#  TEAM_ID  DIVISION  LAST_NAME  LICENSE  PHONE
      1  GU1002   R         Osberger   E        7538248
      2  GU1201   C         Grauer     E        7530345
      3  GU1202   R         Zion       E        7522475
      4  GU1401   C         Grauer     E        7530345
```

☐ **STEP 5: Create a view file.**

All the current information (the files in use, their associated work areas, the relation in effect, and the fields to be displayed) can be saved in a *view file*, which in turn may be created from the current settings:

```
. CREATE VIEW FROM ENVIRONMENT
Enter view file name: COACH

. CLEAR ALL ——————————— Closes all open files
. LIST
                      — Error message appears; press the Esc key to return to the dot prompt
No database is in USE. Enter file name:

. SET VIEW TO COACH
. LIST

Record#  TEAM_ID  DIVISION  LAST_NAME  LICENSE  PHONE
      1  GU1002   R         Osberger   E        7538248
      2  GU1201   C         Grauer     E        7530345
      3  GU1202   R         Zion       E        7522475
      4  GU1401   C         Grauer     E        7530345
```

The CREATE VIEW FROM ENVIRONMENT command creates a view file (COACH.VUE) which is subsequently saved on the default drive. The CLEAR ALL command is issued only to show that all existing files have been closed; the SET VIEW command then retrieves the view file. Finally, the LIST command demonstrates that the settings established in Steps 3 and 4 have indeed been preserved.

☐ **STEP 6: Modify the view file.**

A view file can be modified in much the same way as other specialized dBASE files (report forms, label forms, and so on). Assume, for example, that we wish to modify the COACH.VUE file to print the coach's first name in addition to the other information. Enter the command MODIFY VIEW COACH at the dot prompt, after which Figure 11.6a will appear on the screen.

Figure 11.6a contains the opening (set up) menu indicating the presence of four DBF files in the current subdirectory, two of which appear in the current

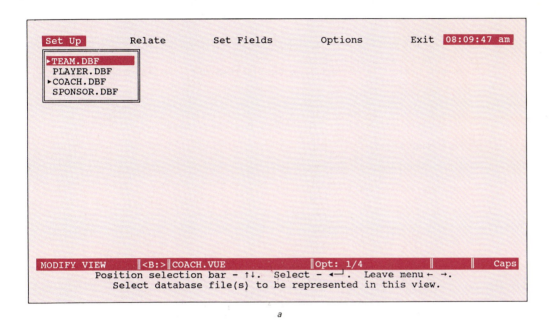

a

b

FIGURE 11.6 Modifying a view file: (a) screen 1; (b) screen 2

view. Use the right (and left) arrow keys to highlight the Set Fields option, the down (and up) arrow keys to highlight COACH.DBF, and press the Return key. You are now in a position to add (remove) fields from within the COACH.DBF file that will appear in subsequent LIST and/or DISPLAY commands. Use the up and down arrow keys to highlight the FIRST_NAME field and press the Return key to toggle the FIRST_NAME field on. Then use the right (and left) arrow keys to select the Exit option, and save the modified view file. You should be back at the dot prompt.

Enter the SET VIEW and LIST commands as shown on the next page to verify that the modification to the view file has been done successfully, as indicated by the appearance of the FIRST_NAME field. Consider:

```
Currently Selected Database:
Select area:  1, Database in Use: B:TEAM.dbf   Alias: TEAM
      Related into: COACH
      Relation: COACH_ID

Select area:  2, Database in Use: B:COACH.dbf   Alias: COACH
      Master index file:  B:COACHID.NDX  Key: coach_id

File search path:
Default disk drive: B:
Print destination:  PRN:
Margin =       0
Current work area =     1
```

a

```
ALTERNATE - OFF   DELETED   - OFF   FIXED     - OFF   SAFETY     - ON
BELL      - ON    DELIMITERS - OFF   HEADING   - ON    SCOREBOARD - ON
CARRY     - OFF   DEVICE    - SCRN   HELP      - ON    STATUS     - ON
CATALOG   - OFF   DOHISTORY - OFF   HISTORY   - ON    STEP       - OFF
CENTURY   - OFF   ECHO      - OFF   INTENSITY - ON    TALK       - ON
CONFIRM   - OFF   ESCAPE    - ON    MENU      - ON    TITLE      - ON
CONSOLE   - ON    EXACT     - OFF   PRINT     - OFF   UNIQUE     - OFF
DEBUG     - OFF   FIELDS    - ON
```

b

```
Programmable function keys:
F2  - assist;
F3  - list;
F4  - dir;
F5  - display structure;
F6  - display status;
F7  - display memory;
F8  - display;
F9  - append;
F10 - edit;
```

c

FIGURE 11.7 The DISPLAY STATUS command: (a) files in use; (b) dBASE switch settings; (c) function key settings

```
. SET VIEW TO COACH
. LIST
Record# TEAM_ID DIVISION LAST_NAME FIRST_NAME LICENSE PHONE
      1 GU1002  R        Osberger  John       E       7538248
      2 GU1201  C        Grauer    Robert     E       7530345
      3 GU1202  R        Zion      Steve      E       7522475
      4 GU1401  C        Grauer    Robert     E       7530345
```

☐ **STEP 7: The DISPLAY STATUS command.**

Enter the DISPLAY STATUS command at the dot prompt, producing Figure 11.7. (dBASE will display the information in Figure 11.7 over several screens, with the intervening message, "Press any key to continue," appearing between screens.)

Figure 11.7a shows all information for each selected work area and also indicates the current work area. Figure 11.7b displays the current settings for various dBASE switches (see the Programmer's Notebook for the precise meaning of the various switches). Finally, Figure 11.7c displays the current settings of the function keys.

☐ **STEP 8: Exit dBASE.**

Type QUIT at the dot prompt to leave dBASE and return to DOS.

The Roster Program

Completion of the second hands-on exercise should have familiarized you with two important commands, SELECT and SET RELATION, which are used in conjunction with the multiple DBF files. The exercise was restricted, however, in the sense that these commands were entered from the dot prompt as opposed to being included in a program, and further because only the team and coach files were open. Accordingly, we move now to a program that uses these commands in conjunction with all four files.

The program we develop is the one from the first hands-on exercise to generate team rosters. The pseudocode is shown in Figure 11.8 and the completed program in Figure 11.9.

```
Open the team, coach, sponsor, and player files
Select the TEAM.DBF file as the active file
DO WHILE team records remain
   Display the appropriate team heading information
   Set relation into the coach file
   Display the associated coach information
   Set relation into the sponsor file
   Display the associated sponsor information
   Set relation into the player file
   Select the PLAYER.DBF file as the active file
   DO WHILE players are on this team
      Display player data
      Get next player record
   ENDDO
   Select the TEAM.DBF file as the active file
   Get next team record
ENDDO
RETURN
```

FIGURE 11.8 Pseudocode for the roster program

```
***ROSTER.PRG
***CALLS: CLASSIFY.PRG
***This program maps the screen with the team rosters
SET TALK OFF
SET SCOREBOARD OFF
SET STATUS OFF
CLEAR
@ 1,1 TO 23,79  DOUBLE
@ 11,2 TO 11,78 DOUBLE
SELECT 1
USE TEAM INDEX TEAMID
SELECT 2
USE COACH INDEX COACHID                              Multiple DBF files are open at one time
SELECT 3
USE SPONSOR INDEX SPONSRID
SELECT 4
USE PLAYER INDEX PLAYERID
SELECT 1                             The TEAM .DBF file is made the active file
DO WHILE .NOT. EOF()
    STORE 'CORAL SPRINGS SOCCER ASSOCIATION' TO mtitle
    SET COLOR TO W+/N
    @ 2,(80 - LEN(mtitle))/2 SAY mtitle
    SET COLOR TO
    @ 4,3  SAY "Team Number:"
    @ 4,16 SAY  TEAM->TEAM_ID
    DO CLASSIFY
    SET RELATION TO coach_id INTO coach              Finds the appropriate coach record
    @ 6,3  SAY "Coach:"
    @ 6,10  SAY  TRIM(COACH->FIRST_NAME) + ' ' +TRIM(COACH->LAST_NAME)
    @ 7,10  SAY  COACH->STREET
    @ 8,10  SAY  TRIM(COACH->CITY)+' '+TRIM(COACH->STATE)+' '+COACH->ZIP_CODE
    @ 9,10  SAY "Telephone:"
    @ 9,21  SAY  COACH->PHONE  FUNCTION "R"  PICTURE "999-9999"
    @ 10,10  SAY "Class"
    @ 10,16  SAY  COACH->LICENSE
    @ 10,18  SAY "License"
    SET RELATION TO sponsor_id INTO sponsor          Finds the appropriate sponsor record
    @ 6,43  SAY "Sponsor:"
    @ 6,52  SAY  SPONSOR->NAME
    @ 7,52  SAY  SPONSOR->CONTACT
    @ 8,52  SAY  SPONSOR->STREET
    @ 9,52  SAY  TRIM(SPONSOR->CITY)+'  '+TRIM(SPONSOR->STATE)+' '+SPONSOR->ZIP_CODE
    @ 10,52 SAY "Telephone:"
    @ 10,63  SAY  SPONSOR->PHONE  FUNCTION "R"  PICTURE "999-9999"
    @ 12,16  SAY "     Player              Birthdate          Rating"
    @ 13,16  SAY "     ------              ---------          ------"
    SET RELATION TO team_id INTO player
    STORE 14 TO mline                                Finds the first player on this team
    SELECT 4
    DO WHILE team_id = team->team_id
        @ mline,18  SAY  TRIM(PLAYER->FIRST_NAME) + ' ' + PLAYER->LAST_NAME
        @ mline,41  SAY  PLAYER->BIRTH_DATE
        @ mline,59  SAY  PLAYER->RATING
        STORE mline + 1 TO mline
        SKIP                                         Moves the record pointer within the player file
    ENDDO
    STORE 'PRESS ANY KEY TO CONTINUE' TO message
    @ 22,(80 - LEN(message))/2 SAY message
    SET CONSOLE OFF
    WAIT
    SET CONSOLE ON
    SELECT 1
    SKIP                                             Moves the record pointer within the team file
    @ 2,2 CLEAR TO 10,78
    @ 12,2 CLEAR TO 22,78
ENDDO
CLEAR
SET STATUS ON
SET SCOREBOARD ON
SET TALK ON
RETURN
```

FIGURE 11.9 The roster program

In the pseudocode, the team file is selected as the active file, and a DO WHILE loop is executed as long as records remain in that file. The team data from the current record is displayed, a relation into the coach file is established, and the corresponding coach information is shown. Similar steps are followed for the sponsor file.

The player file requires a different procedure because several players are associated with a given team. Accordingly, an inner loop is entered which displays data for all players on that team. (The precise way in which this is done has to do with how the player file is indexed, and is further explained in conjunction with the completed program.) The team file is again made the active file, a new team record is read, and the process begins anew.

Figure 11.9 shows the completed program and should present little difficulty. (It may be helpful, however, to review the output produced by this program from the first hands-on exercise.) The program begins with the usual housekeeping commands to disable the TALK, SCOREBOARD, and STATUS features. The screen is cleared and a double-line border is drawn.

Four successive pairs of SELECT and USE commands open the team, coach, sponsor, and player files in work areas 1, 2, 3, and 4, respectively. Observe, however, that the latter three are opened with an index as required by the subsequent SET RELATION commands. Note, too, that a concatenated index was created for the player file which results in the players being listed alphabetically within each roster. Work area 1 (containing the team file) is selected as the active area and the main loop is entered.

Information for the current team record is displayed by a series of @ ... SAY statements and by a called program contained on the convenience disk. (The contents of CLASSIFY.PRG, however, are not central to the discussion, and thus are not mentioned further.) A relation is set into the coach file and after which the associated coach data is displayed. A second relation is set into the sponsor file, and the sponsor data is shown as well.

A relation is next set into the player file positioning the record pointer on the first player record for the current team. The player file is made active and a second loop is entered to display player data. One line is printed for each player until all players on the current team have been listed; in other words, until the value in TEAM_ID field in the player record no longer matches the TEAM_ID from the team record.

It is important also to point out the presence of *two* distinct SKIP commands within the program. The SKIP command within the inner loop moves to the next player record, whereas the SKIP in the outer loop moves to the next team record. Both commands are required, otherwise, the program will not work as intended.

Summary

The chapter presented an entirely new case study designed specifically to show the advantages of a database approach over single file representation. We began with a conceptual discussion of database organization, then moved directly into a hands-on exercise that demonstrated file maintenance operations in a database environment.

The chapter also covered specific dBASE commands used in conjunction with multiple files constituting a database. These included SELECT to designate a particular work area, SET RELATION to link one file to another, and DISPLAY STATUS to show the settings currently in effect. We described how to create and modify a view file, then demonstrated all of these commands in a second hands-on exercise.

CLEAR ALL	Relation
CREATE VIEW	SELECT
Current file	SET FIELDS
DISPLAY STATUS	SET RELATION
Function keys	SET VIEW
MODIFY VIEW	View files
Open file	Work area
	->

True/False

1. The identical field name can appear in multiple DBF files.
2. A SET RELATION command can link more than two DBF files at one time.
3. dBASE allows multiple DBF files to be *open* simultaneously.
4. dBASE allows multiple DBF files to be *current* simultaneously.
5. All the files within a database must each contain the same number of records.
6. dBASE provides a total of ten work areas.
7. Pressing the F6 function key is equivalent to entering the DISPLAY STATUS command.
8. CREATE VIEW and CREATE VIEW FROM ENVIRONMENT are equivalent commands.
9. A single DISPLAY (or LIST) command can reference fields from more than one DBF file.
10. The SET FIELDS command *cannot* be used in conjunction with a view file.

Exercises

1. Distinguish between:
   a. A file and a database
   b. CREATE VIEW and CREATE VIEW FROM ENVIRONMENT
   c. An open file and an active file
   d. USE and SELECT
   e. Including (omitting) a SELECT command before a USE command
   f. DISPLAY STATUS and DISPLAY STRUCTURE
   g. Pressing the F5 and F6 function keys
   h. The field names, COACH_ID and COACH->COACH_ID
2. Use the existing files in the SOCCER subdirectory to create the following reports, all of which are to be produced from the dot prompt. Do this problem only *after completing the first hands-on exercise* so that everyone in the class will be working with the identical data and can expect the same answers.
   a. A list of coaches who have not been assigned to teams, listing the coach's name, phone number, and license
   b. A list of teams without coaches
   c. An alphabetic list of players who have not been assigned to teams, listing the player's name, birthdate, sex, rating, and phone number
   d. A list of all teams with both a coach and a sponsor
   e. A list of sponsors who haven't paid any money, listing the sponsor's name, contact person, and phone number
   f. A series of mailing labels for sponsors, produced in alphabetic order
   g. A list of all coaches, listing the coach's name and phone number
   h. A list of all coaches without a license

3. Use the existing DBF files in the SOCCER subdirectory to make the following roster changes, then rerun the roster program after all changes have been made. As in the previous exercise, be sure you have completed the first hands-on exercise in the chapter, so that everyone in the class is working with identical data.

   a. Change the team assignment for Meredith Allen from team (GU1202) to team (GU1201).

   b. Drop Coach Grauer from the girls 14-and-under competitive team; Coach Osberger will take his place.

   c. Add the following players:

   Nicole Casette, 6/6/77, Rating 2, to team GU1202
   Ivy Cordell, 8/11/76, Rating 1, to team GU1401
   Sara Osberger, 11/24/76, Rating 2, to team GU1401
   Jessica Syltie, 3/23/75, Rating 1, to team GU1401

   d. Change the contact person for Wendy's from Jill Simmons to Cory Kruell.

   e. Change Lori Fromkin's player rating from 4 to 2.

   f. Delete player Nancy Anderson from the system as her family has moved out of Coral Springs.

4. Examining the SOCCER subdirectory on the convenience disk reveals the presence of a screen and format file, with SCR and FMT extensions.

   a. How were these files created?

   b. Which of the files is directly dependent on the other? That is, explain the files' relationship to one another.

   c. Which file can be input directly into a word processor for incorporation into a dBASE command file?

   d. Explain how the authors used these file(s) in creating the ROSTER.PRG program file. Do you use the same technique in writing your programs?

5. List the *current* and *open* file(s) for each of the command sequences shown below:

Set 1:

```
. SELECT 1
. USE PLAYER
. SELECT 2
. USE COACH
```

Set 2:

```
. SELECT 1
. USE PLAYER
. USE COACH
```

Set 3:

```
. SELECT 1
. USE PLAYER
. SELECT 2
. USE COACH
. SELECT 1
```

OVERVIEW

The *Programmer's Notebook* is a convenient reference for the individual learning dBASE, as well as for the experienced programmer. The Notebook lists commands and functions in *alphabetic* order, with the material on each divided into four sections: Syntax, Discussion, Tips, and Related Topics. The Notebook is not intended to replace the Ashton-Tate reference manual, and hence does not include every command and function available in dBASE.

The Notebook does, however, cover most commands and functions, and certainly those used most frequently. It also presents significant material not found in the Ashton-Tate publication (or elsewhere); hence we are confident that you will find it to be a useful reference.

Table NB.1 on page 249 lists the commands and functions appearing in the Programmer's Notebook.

The Programmer's Notebook

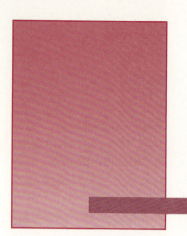

APPEND

Syntax: `APPEND [BLANK]`

Discussion: The `APPEND` command places you in a full-screen data entry mode from which new records can be added to the end of the currently selected database file. The command produces an *input template* on the screen for the next successive record in the file; for example, if there are currently 120 records in the active file, an input template is produced for record 121. The template shows every field in the file structure, providing an input area for each field equal to its respective width. The cursor is positioned initially in field 1, column 1, from where data can be entered in the desired fields.

If the number of characters entered in a given field does not fill the space allocated for that field, the Return key must be pressed to move to the next successive field. If, however, the allocated space is filled completely, the cursor moves automatically to the next field (or to field 1 of the next record, if you are in the last field of the current record). If no data is to be entered for a particular field, press the Return key to move the cursor to the next field.

Any attempt to enter an illegal character (for example, a letter in a numeric field) will produce a beep, and the entry will be ignored. The cursor will remain in position, waiting for a valid entry.

You can move between fields within a given record by using the up and down arrow keys. The contents of any existing entry can be edited by merely typing over what was previously entered or by inserting or deleting characters. Table NB.2 summarizes the keystroke combinations used in the `APPEND` mode.

As we alluded earlier, entering data in the last field of a record automatically brings up the input template for the next record. You may add as many records as desired, or you may terminate the `APPEND` process, and return to the dot prompt—saving all of the records previously appended—by pressing the Return key *immediately* when the new record's input template appears.

Ctrl End and Ctrl W also terminate the `APPEND` process, saving all the records previously added. However, these keys must be pressed as soon as data for the last record is entered and should be used only if the last key pressed was not one that brought up the input template for the next record. In other words, pressing either Ctrl End or Ctrl W after moving to a new input template causes a blank (superfluous) record to be added at the end of the file. Ctrl Q and/or the Esc key also terminate the `APPEND` process and return to the dot prompt, but this time, saving all previously appended records *except* the one whose input template is currently displayed on the screen.

■ **TABLE NB.1**
Commands and Functions in the Programmer's Notebook

APPEND	LIST HISTORY	SET DEVICE
APPEND FROM	LIST MEMORY	SET DOHISTORY
ASSIST	LIST STATUS	SET ECHO
AVERAGE	LIST STRUCTURE	SET ESCAPE
BOF()	LOCATE	SET EXACT
BROWSE	LOWER()	SET FIELDS
CDOW()	LTRIM()	SET FILTER
CHR()	MAX()	SET FORMAT
CLEAR	MIN()	SET FUNCTION
CLOSE	MODIFY COMMAND	SET HEADING
CMONTH()	MODIFY LABEL	SET HELP
CONFIG.DB	MODIFY QUERY	SET HISTORY
CONTINUE	MODIFY REPORT	SET INDEX
COPY	MODIFY SCREEN	SET INTENSITY
COUNT	MODIFY STRUCTURE	SET MEMOWIDTH
CREATE	MODIFY VIEW	SET MENU
CREATE LABEL	MONTH()	SET ORDER
CREATE QUERY	PACK	SET PATH
CREATE REPORT	PRIVATE	SET PRINT
CREATE SCREEN	PUBLIC	SET PROCEDURE
CREATE VIEW	QUIT	SET RELATION
CTOD()	READ	SET SAFETY
DATE()	RECALL	SET SCOREBOARD
DAY()	RECNO()	SET STATUS
DELETE	REINDEX	SET STEP
DELETED()	RELEASE	SET TALK
DIR	REPLACE	SET TYPEAHEAD
DISPLAY	REPORT FORM	SET UNIQUE
DISPLAY HISTORY	RESTORE	SET VIEW
DISPLAY MEMORY	RESUME	SKIP
DISPLAY STATUS	RETURN	SORT
DISPLAY STRUCTURE	RTRIM()	SPACE()
DO	RUN	STORE
DO CASE	SAVE	STR()
DO WHILE	@...SAY...GET	SUBSTR()
DTOC()	SEEK	SUM
EDIT	SELECT	TIME()
EJECT	SET	@...TO
EOF()	SET ALTERNATE	TRIM()
FIND	SET BELL	UPPER()
GO	SET CATALOG	USE
HELP	SET CENTURY	VAL()
IF	SET COLOR	WAIT
IIF()	SET CONFIRM	YEAR()
INDEX ON	SET CONSOLE	ZAP
INSERT	SET DATE	?
JOIN	SET DEBUG	*
LABEL FORM	SET DEFAULT	&
LEN()	SET DELETED	&&
LIST	SET DELIMITERS	

All *open associated indexes* are updated as new records are appended. Conversely, indexes not open are not updated and so no longer match the database. If these indexes are subsequently opened, they must be reindexed before they can be used reliably.

The APPEND BLANK option adds one blank record to the end of the currently selected database and returns to the dot prompt. It does not invoke the full-screen input mode and is primarily used in command programs. After an APPEND BLANK command is issued, the record pointer is moved to that blank record.

■ **TABLE NB.2**
Keystroke Combinations for APPEND **Command**

Keystroke	Function
→ or ←	Moves cursor one character to the right or left
↑ or ↓	Moves cursor to the previous or next field within the current record
PgUp, PgDn	Moves cursor to the previous or next record in the database file (in physical order of entry, even when an index is active)
Ins	Toggles between the insert and replacement modes
Del	Deletes character the cursor is on
Ctrl-Y	Deletes all characters in the entry template of the current field beginning at the cursor position
Ctrl-U	Marks/unmarks the current record for deletion (toggle switch)
Ctrl-W, Ctrl-End	Saves all appended records, including the current record and retruns to the dot prompt
Ctrl-Q, Esc	Saves all appended records except for the current record and returns to the dot prompt

Tips:

1. You may design a custom screen for data entry either by creating a format file or a program file with the appropriate @...SAY...GET commands. This enables you to supply more meaningful prompts for each field's entry template, include necessary messages to guide data entry, and even restrict access to certain fields for security reasons. This is especially useful if the data entry operator has little or no dBASE experience.

2. To enter data into a memo field, press the Ctrl PgDn keys when the cursor is positioned in the memo field's entry template. This will bring up the memo text editor for memo text entry. When you issue the editor's save command, you will be returned to the next successive field's entry template to continue data entry.

3. Use of the PgUp and PgDn keys in the APPEND mode moves you between records in the database according to the database's physical order and not according to any active index's logical order.

4. Existing records can be edited in the APPEND mode by paging to the appropriate record and editing the field contents.

5. If a field entry is longer than the field width, and you continue to type past the last position in the field, the extra characters will be typed in the next field. SET CONFIRM ON prevents this from happening as it requires the Return key to be pressed at the end of every field (whether the field is filled or not) in order to move to the next field. However, since SET CONFIRM ON requires an extra keystroke, many users prefer that SET CONFIRM be OFF (the default setting). If SET CONFIRM is OFF, it is wise to SET BELL ON (also the default setting) so that a warning beep is sounded when the entry being typed in reaches the end of the field.

6. The display of control key functions at the top of the screen can be turned on or off from the dot prompt by the SET MENU ON/OFF command (the default is ON). It can also be toggled on or off from within the APPEND mode with the F1 function key.

7. The appearance of the template can be changed with the SET DELIMITERS, SET INTENSITY, and SET COLOR commands.

8. Appended records may not be saved to disk or reflected in the directory until the file is closed with a CLOSE or QUIT command.

Related Topics: Append From
                     @...SAY...GET
                     CLOSE
                     CREATE SCREEN
                     SET BELL
                     SET CARRY
                     SET CONFIRM
                     SET FORMAT
                     SET INDEX
                     SET MENU

APPEND FROM

Syntax: APPEND FROM <filename> [FOR <condition>]
                          [TYPE <file type>]

Discussion: The APPEND FROM command copies records from an existing file to the end of the currently selected database. The file from which the records are copied is assumed to be a database (DBF) file unless otherwise specified, five additional file types (DELIMITED, SDF, DIF, SYLK, and WKS) being possible and which are discussed with the COPY command.

Specifying a database file as the source file will copy data only for fields common to both files, that is, fields in the target file that have no matching field name in the source file are left blank. Fields in the source file larger than their counterparts in the target file are truncated if they contain character data, or are replaced by asterisks if they are numeric.

Specifying a DELIMITED file as the source file assumes that commas separate the fields, that double quotes surround the character fields, and that each record ends with a carriage return and a line feed. The data are copied field by field, beginning with the leftmost character in each field. If the source file has more fields than the target database, the data in the extra fields are lost; if, however, the source file has fewer fields, the remaining fields in the target database are left blank.

Specifying an SDF file as the source file assumes that the records are fixed length, that a carriage return and line feed are at the end of each record, and that the fields are exactly the same length as those in the target database. Extra data in the source file will be lost, whereas too little data causes blank fields in the target database.

Specifying a SYLK, WKS, or DIF file as the source file causes each row in the spreadsheet to be treated as a record and each column as a field. The layout of the spreadsheet columns should match the structure of the target database for the data to be appended properly. In addition, column headings in the spreadsheet should be deleted before executing the APPEND command (that is, row 1 should contain the first record).

Tips:

1. Records marked for deletion in the source DBF file will be appended to the target database, but will *not* be similarly marked after the APPEND operation is completed. Specification of SET DELETED ON, however, prior to the APPEND command, will prevent the marked records from being appended in the first place.

2. When appending from another database file, fields common to both files do not have to be in the same order in the file structure, nor do they have to be the same type (although

the data does have to be consistent with the new type). The fields do, however, have to be identically named.

3. A DELIMITED WITH BLANK clause assumes that one blank space separates the fields in the source file.

4. Any open indexes in the currently selected work area are automatically updated when the data are appended.

Related Topics: APPEND
COPY
MODIFY STRUCTURE
SET DELETED

ASSIST

Syntax: ASSIST

Discussion: The ASSIST command invokes a full-screen, menu-driven help program through which many common operations can be accomplished. The operations include:

1. Creating new database (DBF) and/or ancillary files (NDX, FMT, LBL, QRY, FRM, VUE)
2. Opening existing database and ancillary files
3. Modifying existing database and ancillary files
4. Appending/editing/deleting records in a DBF file
5. Displaying data from a DBF file
6. Moving the file pointer and searching for specific data
7. Sorting/indexing a DBF file
8. Generating reports/labels
9. Performing simple summary calculations
10. Performing simple operating system tasks (copying/erasing/renaming files)

Instructions on the navigation line provide information for moving between the various options in the Assist Menu. As a general rule, the right and left arrow keys move you between the options on the menu bar with the corresponding submenu options being displayed in a box beneath the highlighted main menu option. The up and down arrow keys highlight options within a submenu and the Return key selects the highlighted option. Depending on the operation being performed, this process may be repeated through several levels of submenu options. As selections are made from the menus, the actual command is continually built on the action line (as though it were being entered from the dot prompt).

If an error is made in the selection process, the Esc key can be used to undo the selection. Each time the Esc key is pressed, you are returned one level to the previous submenu (unless you are at the main menu, whereupon you are returned to the dot prompt).

Tips:

1. The first letter of the option name may be pressed to highlight the option immediately, rather than using the right and left arrow keys; for example, pressing the letter C will immediately display the submenu for the CREATE option.
2. The initial Assist Menu (which appears when dBASE is first loaded) can be made to

disappear by pressing the Esc key. You can also prevent the menu from appearing at all by deleting the COMMAND = ASSIST line in the CONFIG.DB file.

3. The F1 key (HELP) may be pressed while in the ASSIST mode to obtain more information on the main menu option currently selected.
4. Submenu options are available only in the context of the operations currently in effect, that is, some submenu choices may *not* be possible at any given time. For example, you cannot select the APPEND command unless a DBF file has already been opened.
5. It is generally more efficient to enter commands directly from the dot prompt rather than build the commands via the ASSIST mode. Accordingly, the facility is best used by beginners to learn the command syntax, and is generally avoided by more experienced programmers.

Related Topics: CONFIG.DB
                     HELP

AVERAGE

Syntax: AVERAGE [<expression list>][<scope>][WHILE <condition>] [FOR < condition>][TO <memvar list>]

Discussion: The AVERAGE command computes the arithmetic mean of numeric fields and/or arithmetic expressions involving numeric fields. The command computes an average for *every* numeric field in the currently selected database, unless an expression list is included in the command, that is, including the expression list will restrict the computation to only those numeric fields specified in the list.

Every record in the database will be included in the computation unless the command contains a scope, FOR, or WHILE parameter. Thus, the command

    AVERAGE salary

includes every record in the DBF file in computing the average salary, whereas the command

    AVERAGE salary NEXT 10

includes only the next 10 records. (The records included begin with the one at the current position of the record pointer.) Similarly, the command

    AVERAGE salary FOR location = '40'

computes the average salary for only those employees at location 40.

The results of the AVERAGE command (the field names and their respective averages) are displayed on the screen immediately after the command is issued (as long as SET TALK is ON), but are not otherwise saved. To preserve the results for future use, the TO clause must be specified with a valid memory variable included for each field expression averaged.

Tips:

1. In the absence of an expression list, an average is computed for every numeric field in the current database, whether it makes sense to do so or not. Thus, if a zip code was defined as a numeric field, an average of the zip codes will be computed, even though it will be a meaningless number.

2. When using a TO clause to save multiple averages to memory variables, the averages are computed in the order that the fields are listed in the expression list, and are then assigned to the memory variables in the order of the memvar list. Thus, in the command

```
AVERAGE field1,field2 TO memvar1,memvar2
```

the average of field1 is assigned to memvar1 and the average of field2 to memvar2.

Related Topics: SUM
                     COUNT

BOF FUNCTION

Syntax: BOF()

Discussion: The BOF(), *Beginning of F*ile, function indicates whether or not an attempt has been made to move the record pointer above the first record in the file, returning a logical value of true (.T.) or false (.F.). The function is typically used in programs which process a file in reverse order, that is, from the last record to the first. A simple example of such a program, to print the name and salary for every record, is shown below:

```
USE solemp
GO BOTTOM
DO WHILE .NOT. BOF()
    ? name,salary
    SKIP -1
ENDDO
```

The BOF() condition is considered true only when an attempt has actually been made to move above the first record; that is, it is *not* true when the record pointer is on the first record. Consider:

```
USE solemp
GO TOP
? BOF()
.F.  ——————— dBASE response
SKIP -1
? BOF()
.T.  ——————— dBASE response
```

The BOF() function will not be reset to false until the record pointer is repositioned to record 2 or beyond.

Tips:

1. The first *logical* record (according to the master index) will be considered the beginning-of-file, unless no index is open, in which case it is the first *physical* record.
2. Any attempt to move the record pointer above the beginning of the file causes the record pointer to remain positioned on record 1. This differs from the end-of-file situation where an attempt to move beyond the last record actually does so, moving it to an end-of-file marker with a record number one greater than the last record.
3. A separate value of the BOF() function is maintained for each of the 10 available work

areas. However, when testing for the condition in a particular file, that file must be the one in the currently selected work area.

Related Topics: EOF()
RECNO()
SKIP

BROWSE

Syntax: BROWSE[FIELDS<fieldlist>][FREEZE<field>][LOCK<n>]
[NOFOLLOW][NOMENU][WIDTH <n>][NOAPPEND]

Discussion: BROWSE is a full-screen command that permits file maintenance operations to the currently selected database, including appending, editing, and deleting records. Up to 17 records may be displayed on the screen at one time, with each record displayed on a single line. The fields are presented in columns, but only as many fields as will fit within the screen's 80-character width are displayed at one time. Left and right scrolling is permitted to access undisplayed fields. Table NB.3 summarizes the various keystroke combinations that may be used in the BROWSE mode.

The current position of the record pointer determines the first record shown in the screen display (that is, the highlighted record). The keystrokes in Table NB.3 may then be used to edit fields in the highlighted record and/or to move to another record.

To append new records, move the highlight beyond the last record in the database; you will then be asked if another record is to be added. A response of Y brings up an input template for the new record, whereas a response of N returns you to the BROWSE mode.

The FIELDS clause will include just the listed fields in the screen display, thereby making these fields the only ones available for modification. (The order in which the fields are listed is also the order in which they are displayed.)

The FREEZE clause restricts editing to the specified field while still displaying the other fields. For example, the command

BROWSE FIELDS lastname,location,salary FREEZE salary

displays the three fields listed for each record, but highlights only the SALARY field, that is, SALARY is the only field on which editing is possible.

The LOCK clause specifies the number of *contiguous* fields that will remain fixed on the left side of the screen display during a scrolling operation and is quite helpful when

---

■ **TABLE NB.3**
Keystrokes for the BROWSE Command

Keystroke	Function
→ or ←	Moves cursor one character to the right or left
Home, End	Moves cursor one field to the right or left
↑ or ↓	Moves highlight to the previous or next record
PgUp, PgDn	Scrolls one screen up or down
Ctrl →, Ctrl ←	Scrolls one field to right or left
Ctrl-Y	Deletes all characters in the entry template beginning at the current cursor position
Ctrl-U	Marks/unmarks current record for deletion (functions as toggle switch)
Ctrl-W, Ctrl-End	Saves all edited/appended records, including the current one, and exits
Ctrl-Q, Esc	Saves all edited/appended records except the current one, and exits

certain fields are needed on the screen at all times (for example, lastname or account number).

The NOFOLLOW clause has an effect only when an index is in use and further when the key field (accordinng to the active index) is being edited. Assume for example, that social security number is the active index, and that a social security number is changed from 111111111 to 666666666. Normally (that is, without the NOFOLLOW clause), the screen display would shift immediately to the next several records beginning with social security number 666666666. Specifying NOFOLLOW, however, will keep the display where it is (that is, on the records that followed 111111111), even though the edited record has been logically moved. This is a very important clause when you are performing a great many edits on a very large database, and you want to perform the edits in the order of the original logical sequence.

The NOMENU clause prevents access to the BROWSE menu bar. Normally, a simple menu (which allows quick access to specific records and has the ability to LOCK and FREEZE records) can be invoked by pressing the F10 key.

The NOAPPEND clause prevents records from being appended while in the BROWSE mode.

The WIDTH clause specifies the maximum width that any field can have in the screen display. A field's entire contents can still be accessed, even if not displayed, by using the right and left arrow keys to scroll through the field contents.

Tips:

1. The easiest way to view additional fields that do not fit on the screen is to limit the display width of the visible fields (with the WIDTH clause), and/or limit the number of fields that are displayed (with the FIELDS clause). Either of these techniques is generally preferable to scrolling.
2. Do not append records when the FIELDS clause has been specified, because data input will be restricted to these fields.
3. NOMENU and NOAPPEND are useful when the BROWSE mode is initiated from a program, because they limit the operations a data entry operator can perform. The FIELDS clause can also be helpful in this situation as it can be used to prevent access to certain fields for security purposes.
4. Memo fields cannot be displayed or accessed from the BROWSE mode.
5. The LOCK clause should not include so many fields that it prevents scrolling. The number of fields that can be locked will vary from file to file and will depend on the specific field widths involved.
6. Any records deleted with Ctrl U during the BROWSE mode have only been logically rather than physically deleted, that is, the file must still be packed to permanently delete these records.

Related Topics: EDIT
APPEND
SET INDEX TO

CDOW FUNCTION

Syntax: CDOW(<date expression>)

Discussion: The CDOW() function returns the day of week in character format (Sunday, Monday, and so on) corresponding to the specified date expression. The argument in the

CDOW() function may assume several different forms as shown in the following table:

Function	Nature of the Argument
CDOW(hiredate)	Date field
CDOW(memdate)	Date memory variable
CDOW(DATE())	DATE() function itself
CDOW(CTOD("12/25/88"))	CTOD() conversion function
CDOW(DATE() + 10)	Expression with date arithmetic

Tips:

1. The CDOW() function works only on date fields, that is, a character date may *not* be used as the argument unless it is first converted with the CTOD() conversion function.
2. The CDOW() function is often used in program files and/or report forms to display a date in a more attractive format. For example, given a system date of 08/03/89, the command

```
@ 20,20 SAY "Today is " +                            Command entered on 1 line
        CDOW(DATE()) + ', ' + DTOC(DATE())
```

returns the string "Today is Thursday, 08/03/89".

Related Topics: CMONTH()
CTOD()
DATE()
DTOC()

CHR FUNCTION

Syntax: CHR(<ASCII number>)

Discussion: The CHR() function returns the ASCII character corresponding to the number specified in the function. (The number itself must be a positive integer between zero and 255.) The function provides access to the complete ASCII character set, most importantly to those characters with no direct keyboard equivalent (for example, printer control codes, foreign language characters, graphics characters, and so on).

Tips:

1. The ASCII character 7 rings the bell and is useful in a program to signal that an invalid response has been entered. (The bell will be sounded whether SET BELL is ON or OFF.) Consider:

```
DO CASE
   CASE opt = '1'
      .
        .
          .
   OTHERWISE
      ? CHR(7)
      @ 22,25 SAY "Please enter 1,2, or 3"
ENDDO
```

2. ASCII characters can be sent to the printer to produce special effects, such as condensed or boldface type. The particular ASCII characters are hardware specific; for example, the ASCII character 15 indicates compressed print on many Epson and Okidata printers. (The printer must be toggled on with a `SET PRINT ON` command or Ctrl P before the ASCII character is sent.) Consider:

```
SET PRINT ON
? CHR(15)
REPORT FORM EMPLOYEE
? CHR(18)
SET PRINT OFF
```

The ASCII character 18 is used on these same printers to return to regular print, which should be done as a matter of course at the end of printing.

Related Topics: `SET PRINT`
   `SET BELL`

CLEAR

Syntax: `CLEAR`
   `CLEAR ALL`
   `CLEAR FIELDS`
   `CLEAR GETS`
   `CLEAR MEMORY`
   `CLEAR TYPEAHEAD`

Discussion: The `CLEAR` command functions very differently depending upon the modifier in use. Consider:

1. `CLEAR`, issued with no modifier, erases the entire screen and repositions the cursor either to the screen's upper left corner (command mode), or to the screen's lower left corner (interactive mode).
2. `CLEAR ALL` closes all open database (DBF) and related (NDX, FMT, FRM, DBT, and CAT) files, releases all memory variables, and selects work area 1. It does not close any open alternate or program (procedure) files.
3. `CLEAR FIELDS` cancels the field lists in all work areas, whether the field lists were established through a `SET FIELDS TO` command or by opening a view file.
4. `CLEAR GETS` releases all `@...GETs` issued since the last `CLEAR ALL`, `CLEAR GETS`, or `READ` command. Note that unless otherwise increased or decreased in the CONFIG.DB file, a total of 128 `@...GETs` are permitted before a `CLEAR GETS` command must be issued.
5. `CLEAR MEMORY` releases all public and private memory variables.
6. `CLEAR TYPEAHEAD` clears all characters from the keyboard buffer and is used to prevent fast typists from outrunning the keyboard. The existence of a buffer allows typists to enter data in anticipation of future prompts and before actual processing. This practice can, however, result in unintended or erroneous characters remaining in the buffer which would subsequently be read as data by the executing program. Accordingly, `CLEAR TYPEAHEAD` is most useful immediately before a `READ` or `WAIT` command, to ensure

that the buffer is empty, and that dBASE acts on intentionally typed characters, rather than on incorrectly typed ones remaining in the buffer.

Tips:

1. `CLEAR` can be used in conjunction with the `@...TO` command to erase a rectangular portion of the screen as specified by the two sets of row and column coordinates. Consider:

   `@ row,col CLEAR TO row,col`

   The first set of coordinates specifies the upperleft corner of the rectangle while the second set specifies the lower right corner. Given that dBASE recognizes a screen of 25 rows and 80 columns, the row value(s) may be any integer from zero through 24, whereas the column value(s) may be any integers from zero through 79.

2. `CLEAR GETS` cancels any `@...GET` commands that a `READ` command has not yet collected. Accordingly, any pending `GET` statements must be read before a `CLEAR GETS` command is executed.

3. All memory variables needed for future processing must be saved before executing a `CLEAR MEMORY` command.

Related Topics: `@...GET`
`@...TO`
`CLOSE`
`READ`
`RELEASE`
`SAVE`
`SET FIELDS ON/OFF`
`SET FIELDS TO`
`SET TYPEAHEAD TO`

CLOSE

Syntax: `CLOSE <filetype>/ALL`

Discussion: The `CLOSE` command closes all open files, or only open files of a specific file type. The command cannot be issued without a parameter, that is, `CLOSE` by itself is not a valid command and will cause an error message.

The effects of the command depends on the indicated file type as follows:

CLOSE ALL: Closes all open files of all types without affecting memory.

CLOSE ALTERNATE: Closes the current alternate file, as was previously opened with the `SET ALTERNATE` command.

CLOSE DATABASES: Closes all database files and their associated indexes and format files, in all 10 work areas.

CLOSE FORMAT: Closes the open format file in the currently selected work area, as was previously opened with a `SET FORMAT` command.

CLOSE INDEXES: Closes all open indexes in the currently selected work area.

CLOSE PROCEDURE: Closes the current procedure file, as was previously opened with a `SET PROCEDURE` command.

_____

1. A USE command issued with no other parameters will close the DBF file and its associated indexes in the currently selected work area. This is often preferable to issuing a CLOSE DATABASES command which closes the DBF files in all 10 areas.

Related Topics: QUIT
  SET ALTERNATE
  SET INDEX
  SET FORMAT
  SET PROCEDURE
  USE

CMONTH FUNCTION

Syntax: CMONTH(<date expression>)

Discussion: The CMONTH() function returns a character name (January, February, and so on) corresponding to the month in the specified date expression. The argument in the CMONTH() function may assume several different forms as shown in the following table:

Function	Nature of the Argument
CMONTH(hiredate)	Date field
CMONTH(memdate)	Date memory variable
CMONTH(DATE())	DATE() function itself
CMONTH(CTOD("12/25/88"))	CTOD() conversion function
CMONTH(DATE() + 10)	Expression with date arithmetic

Tips: _____

1. The CMONTH() function works only on date fields, that is, a character date may *not* be used as the argument unless it is first converted with the CTOD() conversion function.
2. The CMONTH() function is often used in program files and/or report forms to display a date in a more attractive format. For example, given a system date of 01/08/89, the command

Command is entered on one line

```
@ 20,20 SAY "Today is " + CMONTH(DATE()) + " "
   + STR(DAY(DATE()),2) + ", " + STR(YEAR(DATE()),4)
```

returns the string "Today is January 08, 1989". (Note that the day and year must be converted to strings in order to be concatenated with the other character type data.)

Related Topics: CTOD()
  DATE()
  CDOW()
  STR()
  DAY()
  YEAR()

CONFIG.DB

Discussion: The CONFIG.DB file enables you to customize the standard dBASE program. The file can be created with the nondocument mode of a word processor, or with dBASE's own `MODIFY COMMAND` editor. The commands included in CONFIG.DB are entered one command per line, in no particular order, and in any combination of upper- and lowercase letters. Their purpose can be to:

1. Automatically execute a dBASE command when dBASE is loaded.
2. Reprogram the function keys.
3. Change the default status of the `SET...ON/OFF` commands and selected other `SET` commands, such as the one establishing the default drive.
4. Establish external word processors as the text editors for `MODIFY COMMAND` and for creating memo fields.
5. Change the size of the HISTORY and TYPEAHEAD buffers.

The bulk of the commands apply, however, to changing the status of the many `SET...ON/OFF` and `SET...TO` commands. The syntax of commands used in the CONFIG.DB file is simply

        <keyword> = <value>

and as such, is *different from that of the equivalent command when issued at the dot prompt.* (A further difference is that quotation marks are not used in CONFIG.DB commands even when they would appear in their counterpart command at the dot prompt.) Consider:

Dot Prompt Command	CONFIG.DB Command
`SET BELL OFF`	`BELL = OFF`
`SET DEFAULT TO B`	`DEFAULT = B`
`SET HISTORY TO 30`	`HISTORY = 30`
`SET FUNCTION 6 TO "USE FILE1"`	`F6 = USE FILE1`

The CONFIG.DB file is read when dBASE is loaded, and so must be stored in the same subdirectory as the DBASE.EXE file, or in a subdirectory that has been specified in the DOS `PATH` command. (A CONFIG.DB file is not required as dBASE will establish default settings in its absence.)

Tips: _____

1. The CONFIG.DB file can be made to automatically execute a particular dBASE program file whenever dBASE is loaded by including a `COMMAND =` statement, for example,

        COMMAND = DO MAINMENU

   This is especially useful in setting up a custom system for users who never work from the dot prompt and who are interested only in a specific application program.
2. Examining the CONFIG.DB file provided with dBASE reveals a `COMMAND=ASSIST` statement that automatically brings up the dBASE ASSIST mode. Hence, to bypass the ASSIST mode just delete this line from the CONFIG.DB file.
3. The `PROMPT =` command will change the dBASE dot prompt to a new prompting character, for example,

        PROMPT = COMMAND>

   will replace the dot prompt with COMMAND>

4. The CONFIG.DB file is not to be confused with the CONFIG.SYS file, which DOS uses to establish various system parameters, such as the maximum number of files and buffers that can be open at one time. The CONFIG.SYS file must be located in the root directory of the disk from which the system is booted, and requires the following two commands to properly load dBASE:

```
files = 20
buffers = 15
```

Note, however, that for systems with only 256K bytes, the number of buffers allocated should be four, rather than 15.

CONTINUE

Syntax: CONTINUE

Discussion: The CONTINUE command searches the currently selected database, beginning with the current record, for the next record meeting the search condition specified in the most recently issued LOCATE command. The command operates within the scope of the LOCATE command, if one was specified; if not it searches until the end-of-file is reached or a record is found.

The record number of the found record is displayed on the screen (as long as SET TALK is ON), and the record pointer is moved to that record. If, however, a record meeting the designated condition is not found, an "End of Locate Scope" message is displayed instead and the record pointer is moved to the end-of-file, or to the last record included in the scope of the associated LOCATE command.

As many CONTINUE commands as necessary can be issued until the end-of-file (or scope) is reached, to find all the records meeting the search condition.

Tips:

1. The CONTINUE command repositions the record pointer but does *not* display the found record. Accordingly, a subsequent DISPLAY command is necessary to view the found record.
2. The CONTINUE command begins its search at the current position of the record pointer as determined by the previously executed LOCATE (or CONTINUE) command. Hence, commands moving the record pointer should not be issued between a LOCATE and its subsequent CONTINUE commands, or the search will be compromised.
3. If a filter condition is active, the CONTINUE command ignores records not meeting the filter condition. Similarly, records marked for deletion are also ignored when SET DELETED is ON.

Related Topics: LOCATE
SET DELETED
SET FILTER

COPY

Syntax:
```
COPY TO <newfilename> [<scope>] [FIELDS <fieldlist>]
[WHILE <condition>] [FOR <condition>] [TYPE <filetype>]
```

Discussion: The COPY command creates a new database file with a file structure identical to that of the currently selected database. All the records in the currently selected database are copied to the new file (including those marked for deletion), unless a scope parameter, or a FOR or WHILE clause, is included. Specification of these clauses copies only a subset of the records to the new file, as specified by the scope or as determined by the condition. For example, the command,

```
COPY TO newfile NEXT 20
```

will copy the next 20 records in the database (including the one on which the record pointer is set) to the file named NEWFILE.DBF, whereas the command

```
COPY TO newfile2 FOR location = '40'
```

will copy only those records having a location code of 40.

All the fields in the original file structure will be copied to the new file unless a FIELDS clause is included to indicate the subset of fields to be copied to the new file. The command

```
COPY TO newfile FIELDS lastname,initials
```

creates a new database file named NEWFILE.DBF, consisting of only two fields (with identical types and widths to those in the source file) in its file structure.

Omission of the TYPE clause produces a new file with the standard default extension of DBF, whereas its inclusion produces a file in one of five alternate file formats for use in other application programs such as Lotus or Multiplan.

Each of the five TYPE specifications is discussed below:

1. DELIMITED [WITH <delimiter>/BLANK], for example:

```
COPY TO newfile TYPE DELIMITED
COPY TO newfile TYPE DELIMITED WITH *
COPY TO newfile TYPE DELIMITED WITH BLANK
```

The DELIMITED option creates an ASCII text file normally used with applications, such as a mail-merge, that read records sequentially from the beginning of a file to the end. Each record in the copied file ends with a carriage return and line feed. A comma separates fields within a record, double quotes surround character data (although a different delimiter can be specified by using DELIMITED WITH <delimiter>), and trailing blanks are not included. Dates are converted to eight-digit numbers in which the first four digits indicate the year and the second four, the month and day. The copied file is assigned a default extension of TXT.

2. DIF, for example:

```
COPY TO newfile TYPE DIF
```

The DIF option creates a file suitable for input to VisiCalc. Fields are converted to columns and records are converted to rows. The copied file is assigned a default extension of DIF.

3. SDF (System Data Format), for example:

```
COPY TO newfile TYPE SDF
```

The SDF option creates an ASCII text file consisting of fixed-length records. The length of every record in the copied file is identical because the field widths in the original database file are maintained, with blanks used to pad the field if necessary (character fields are copied left justified and numeric fields are copied right justified). Each record ends with a carriage return and a line feed. No delimiters are used between fields, which are identified by their starting position in the file. The copied file is assigned a default extension of .TXT

4. SYLK, for example:

```
COPY TO newfile TYPE SYLK
```

The SYLK option creates a file suitable for input to Multiplan (a spreadsheet program). Fields are converted to columns and records are converted to rows. The copied file is not assigned a default extension.

5. WKS, for example:

```
COPY TO newfile TYPE WKS
```

The WKS option creates a file suitable for input to Lotus 1-2-3. Fields are converted to columns and records are converted to rows. The copied file is assigned a default extension of WKS.

Tips:

1. Records marked for deletion are copied to the new file unless SET DELETED is ON.
2. The existence of a filter condition causes only those records meeting the filter condition to be included in the COPY process. If a filter has been set, and a FOR or WHILE clause is included, only those records meeting the filter condition will be tested in the FOR or WHILE condition.
3. The existence of a field list causes only those fields to be copied to the new file. If a field list is active and a FIELDS clause is included in the COPY command, the clause may include only the active fields.
4. The COPY command copies record by record, and consequently can be time consuming with a large file. Use of the DOS COPY command is usually faster and more efficient.
5. The COPY command can be used to make a temporary backup copy of a database file, a wise decision before making major changes in the data.
6. The directory date for the new database file will be the same as the directory date for the source file, not the date on which it was copied.
7. Whether an index is active or not determines the order in which the records are copied to the new file. If no index is active, the records are copied in physical order; if an index is active, the records are copied to the new file in the logical order of the active index.
8. Including a period (.) as the last character of the file name will override the default extension, resulting in no extension at all.
9. The COPY command overwrites an existing file of the same name with no warning unless SET SAFETY is ON.

Related Topics: APPEND FROM
SET DELIMITED
SET SAFETY
RUN

COUNT

Syntax: `COUNT [<scope>][WHILE <condition>][FOR <condition>]`
            `[TO <memvar>]`

Discussion: The `COUNT` command counts (tallies) the number of records in the currently selected database. Every record will be counted unless the command contains a scope parameter, or a FOR or WHILE clause. In other words, `COUNT` with no parameters returns a count of all the records in the database.

Including either a FOR or WHILE parameter causes only those records matching the specified condition to be counted. For example, the command

    `COUNT FOR location = 'Texas'`

returns the number of records with a location of Texas. Specification of a scope parameter, for example,

    `COUNT REST FOR location = 'Texas'`

causes the command to begin counting from the current position of the record pointer (as opposed to the beginning of the file, as is done with a default scope of ALL).

The tally determined by the `COUNT` command is displayed on the screen immediately after the command is issued (as long as SET TALK is ON), but is not otherwise saved. The TO clause must be specified, as in

    `COUNT FOR location = 'Texas' TO locnumbr`

to save the tally to a valid numeric memory variable. The print command (?), that is, `? locnumbr`, may then be used to view the `COUNT` command's results.

Related Topics: `SUM`
                    `AVERAGE`

CREATE

Syntax: `CREATE <filename>`

Discussion: The `CREATE` command defines the file structure of a new database (DBF) file, adds the new file to the disk directory, and, if requested, opens the newly created file for data entry. (The discussion associated with this command is longer than for most other commands because it includes related material on the various field types permitted within the file structure.) The command may be specified with or without a file name, for example, `CREATE SOLEMP`, or simply `CREATE`, in which case dBASE prompts for the file name. (The file name itself is limited to eight characters.)

After a `CREATE` command has been issued, dBASE presents a field definition screen in which the fields within the file structure are defined one at a time (from one to 128 fields are permitted). Three pieces of information are required for each field—name, type, and width.

The *field name* is from one to 10 characters long, must begin with a letter, and may be composed of letters, digits, and an embedded underscore character. No blanks are permitted.

There are five permissible *field types*, character being the default. A *character* field stores any printable ASCII character, including letters, numbers, special characters, and blanks. The maximum width of a character field is 254 characters.

A *numeric* field contains numbers which are positive or negative, integer or decimal. The only characters permitted within a numeric field are the digits zero through nine, a decimal point, and a plus (+) or minus (−) sign. No commas, parentheses, or dollar signs are allowed. The maximum width of a numeric field is 19 characters, with the decimal point and negative sign each requiring one position. Up to 15 decimal places can be specified, but the number of decimal places must be at least two less than the total field width (to account for a leading zero and a decimal place).

A *date* field uses one of several formats, as determined by the SET DATE command. The default is mm/dd/yy (the width is eight characters) and the slashes appear automatically in the input template. Arithmetic calculations may be performed on date fields, for example, subtracting (or adding) one date from (to) another to determine the number of days between the two dates. (A date field may not, however, be used in comparisons unless it is first converted to a character string with the DTOC function.)

A *logical* field accepts only a single character (its default width is one character) representing either a value of true or false. An entry of T, t, or Y, y represents a true value whereas F, f, N, or n represent a false value.

A *memo* field stores large blocks of text and has a default width of 10 characters. When a memo field is defined in a file structure, dBASE automatically creates a database memo file with the same name, but with a .DBT extension, to store the text. The memo field in the .DBF file actually contains only a pointer to the beginning position of the text in the .DBT file.

The *field type* (character, numeric, date, logical, or memo) is chosen in one of three ways by:

1. Pressing the enter key if the default type (character) is desired.
2. Pressing the first letter of the desired field type, for example, N for numeric.
3. Pressing the space bar to toggle through the different field types, and pressing the enter key after the desired type appears.

The specification of the *field width* (and the cursor's subsequent position) depends on the field type. For example, pressing the Return key after entering the width of a character field moves the cursor to the next field, whereas pressing the Return key after entering the width of a numeric field moves the cursor to the entry space for the number of decimal places. (Accordingly, you must enter the number of decimal places, 0–15, and then press the Return key to move to the beginning of the entry template for the next field.) Default widths are entered automatically for date, logical, and memo fields, causing the cursor to be automatically positioned at the entry template for the next field.

Informational messages are displayed continually at the bottom of the screen to remind you of dBASE rules and limitations. In addition, the status line will show the file name, the drive on which the file will be saved, and the field where the cursor is currently located. The number of bytes remaining (from the maximum record size of 4000) is also indicated in the upper right-hand corner of the screen.

Should you violate any dBASE restrictions, a beep will sound and an error message will appear at the bottom of the screen. dBASE requires you to correct the entry before proceeding further. Table NB.4 contains the various keystroke combinations associated with the CREATE command.

The newly defined file structure is saved by pressing the Ctrl and End keys simultaneously, the Ctrl and W keys simultaneously, or the Return key when you are on the blank field definition template following the last defined field. In any event, the message: "Press Enter to confirm. Any other key to resume", appears at the bottom of the monitor. Pressing Enter at this point saves the file structure as is, whereas pressing any other key returns you to the field definition templates for further editing. (If, for some reason, you decide not to

■ **TABLE NB.4**
Keystroke Combinations for CREATE **Command**

Keystroke	Function
→ or ←	Moves cursor one character to the right or left
↑ or ↓ arrows	Moves cursor to the previous or next field
PgUp, PgDn	Scrolls through field definitions when more than one screen is required
Ins	Toggles between the insert and replacement modes
Del	Deletes character cursor is on
Ctrl-Y	Deletes all characters in entry template, beginning at the current cursor position
Ctrl-U	Deletes entire field definition at current cursor position
Ctrl-N	Inserts a field definition template at current cursor position
Ctrl-W, Ctrl-End	Saves structure and exits to dot prompt
Ctrl-Q, Esc	Aborts operation and exits to dot prompt

save the file structure, press either the Ctrl and Q keys simultaneously or the Esc key to abandon the operation.)

After the file structure has been saved, dBASE will ask whether you want to begin entering data with the message, "Input data records now? (Y/N)". A response of Y takes you to the full-screen APPEND mode, whereas an N returns you to the dot prompt.

Tips:

1. Choose field names that describe the field contents or purpose, because they are easier to remember and use.
2. Do not use a dBASE reserved word (command or function) as a field name.
3. Use the numeric field type only for fields that will be involved in calculations. Fields that are "numeric," but which are not used in calculations (for example, zip codes and social security numbers) should be defined as character fields. Specifying the character rather than the numeric field type increases processing efficiency and also displays leading zeros (which do not appear for numeric fields).
4. Logical fields should be named in such a way as to reflect the true condition, for example, LTR_SENT to indicate whether or not a letter was sent. Using the true (rather than false) condition makes programming statements easier to follow as in the following example:

```
IF ltr_sent
    statements if letter sent
ELSE
    statements if letter not sent
ENDIF
```

5. Logical fields are automatically initialized to false and you need only press the enter key (during data entry) to accept the default value.
6. The display of control key functions at the top of the screen can be turned on/off from the dot prompt by the SET MENU ON/OFF command (the default is ON). It can also be toggled on/off from within the APPEND mode with the F1 function key.

Related Topics: CREATE LABEL
CREATE QUERY
CREATE REPORT
CREATE SCREEN
CREATE VIEW
SET MENU

CREATE LABEL

Syntax: `CREATE LABEL <filename>`

Discussion: The `CREATE LABEL` command invokes a full-screen, menu-driven procedure that steps you through the design of a mailing label. The result is a *label form* file (with extension LBL unless otherwise specified) which is used to generate mailing labels via the `LABEL FORM` command.

The `CREATE LABEL` Menu has three choices, *Options*, *Contents*, and *Exit*, each with a submenu. To enter a submenu, highlight the selection with the right or left arrow key and press the Return key, or press the selection name's initial letter (O, C, or E). Within the submenus themselves, menu items offering predefined values, such as label size, are chosen by highlighting the selection and pressing Return until the desired value is displayed. For those menu items where a user-supplied value is necessary (for example, the contents of a mailing label), the Return key must be pressed to choose the item and then pressed a second time to complete the entry.

The Options menu is used to establish the physical dimensions of the label form, providing a choice between several predefined forms or enabling a custom form to be created if existing ones are not suitable. The choice of a predefined form causes dBASE to enter the appropriate dimensions automatically, whereas a custom form allows the user to specify any or all of the following:

LABEL WIDTH: a value between one and 120
LABEL HEIGHT: a value between one and 16
LEFT MARGIN: a value between zero and 250
LINES BETWEEN LABELS: a value between zero and 16
SPACES BETWEEN LABELS: a value between zero and 120
LABELS ACROSS PAGE: a value between one and 15

The Contents menu presents an empty label form of the same height (number of lines) as specified in the Options menu. It is here that you enter the contents for each line in the mailing label using fields in the associated database file (for example, first name, initial, and last name for line 1; street address for line 2, and so on). The contents are specified using any valid dBASE expression (up to 60 characters long), and may consist of field names, constants, and/or functions. (An entry does not have to be made for every line in the label form.)

The Exit menu enables the label form to be saved or abandoned. If abandoned, the results of the current session are lost. In either event, control returns to the dot prompt from where normal dBASE processing can continue.

Tips:

1. `CREATE` and `MODIFY` can be used interchangeably to create and/or modify label forms. The determining factor in whether a new form is created or an existing form modified is whether or not the label form already exists.
2. A database (DBF) file must be open for a label form to be created. Should this not be the case, a prompt requesting the name of the database file is presented.
3. The field names entered in the label contents must match the field names in the currently selected database. Mistakes can be avoided by pressing the F10 key to retrieve the associated file structure, and selecting the field names with the cursor keys, rather than retyping them. (Only fields from the currently selected database are made available unless a field list containing fields from an unselected database has been made active through a previously issued `SET FIELDS` command.)

4. The use of commas to separate field names on the same line, for example,

```
prefix,TRIM(firstname),lastname
```

causes a blank space to be inserted between adjacent fields when the labels are printed, for example, "Ms. Jessica Kinzer". Concatenated character strings can be used to control the use of blank spaces. Hence, the entry

```
TRIM(city) + ", " + state + "     " + zip
```

would produce "Elmhurst, NY   11373", leaving no blank space between the last character in the city field and the following comma, and placing three blank spaces between the state and the zip code.

5. An IIF() function can be used in the label contents to conditionally print a field, for example,

```
IIF(initial=" ",TRIM(fname),TRIM(fname)+" "+initial),lname
```

Using the IIF function keeps an extra blank from appearing between the first and last names if there is no middle initial. (Note, however, that because the label entry is limited to 60 characters, spaces between operators must often be eliminated to complete the entry.)

6. A label form can also be used for continuous-form Rolodex cards, index cards, or even a noncolumnar report that is 16 lines long or less.

7. The presence of the Cursor Movement Menu can be toggled on and off with the F1 function key.

Related Topics:
```
CREATE REPORT
IIF()
LABEL FORM
SET FIELDS
```

CREATE QUERY

Syntax: `CREATE QUERY <filename>`

Discussion: The `CREATE QUERY` command invokes a full-screen, menu-driven procedure that builds a filter condition for use with the currently selected database. The result is a query file (with extension QRY unless otherwise specified), through which the filter condition can be later activated with a `SET FILTER` command. Storing a filter condition within a query file is most useful when the same condition is needed from session to session, as it is easier to build the condition once, save it, and reuse it as necessary.

The `CREATE QUERY` Menu has four selections, *Set Filter*, *Nest*, *Display*, and *Exit*, each with a submenu. To enter the submenu, highlight the selection with the right or left arrow key and press the Return key, or press the selection name's initial letter (S, N, D, or E). Within the menus themselves, menu items offering predefined values are chosen by highlighting the selection and pressing the Return key until the desired value is displayed. For those menu items where a user-supplied value is necessary, the Return key must be pressed to choose the item and then pressed a second time to complete the entry.

The Set Filter menu allows you to build the condition one element at a time by selecting a field and relational operator and then entering an ending constant or expression. The expression supplied must be appropriate to field type and may be a character string, numeric constant, arithmetic expression, or date expression. A logical connector (for example, .AND. or .OR.) can then be selected from a connector menu to build a *compound con-*

dition, in which case the entire process is repeated. Up to seven individual conditions can be connected.

The Nest menu changes the way in which a compound condition is evaluated by inserting parentheses to alter the normal sequence of operations. In the absence of parentheses, NOT is evaluated first, then AND, and then OR. Adding parentheses, however, changes the order because any condition within parentheses is evaluated first. Choose Add from the Nest menu selection to enter a set of parentheses or Remove to delete an existing set. (Note, too, that to change the location of existing parentheses, you must first remove them, then add them in the new location.)

The Display menu effectively tests the filter condition just developed by displaying the first record meeting the condition. The PgUp and PgDn keys can then be used to page through the database, stopping on only those records satisfying the condition. Should an error in the filter condition be discovered, it can be corrected by returning to the Set Filter and/or Nest menu and repeating the earlier procedure.

The Exit menu enables the query file to be saved (simultaneously activating the condition) or abandoned (in which case, the results of the current session are lost). In either event, control returns to the dot prompt from where normal dBASE processing can continue.

Tips:

1. `CREATE` and `MODIFY` can be used interchangeably to create and/or modify query files. The determining factor in whether a new file is created or an existing file modified is whether or not the file already exists.
2. A database (DBF) file must be open for a query file to be created. Should this not be the case, a prompt requesting the name of the database file is presented.
3. A query file, even though menu driven, requires a knowledge of dBASE syntax and an understanding of relational and logical operators. Avoid the use of .NOT. by stating conditions in the positive form whenever possible. This is because .NOT. may lead to confusing and erroneous results, for example, the condition .NOT. A .OR. .NOT. B is *always* true.
4. Conditions within a compound condition may be added or deleted as necessary. To delete an existing condition, select its line number, then press Ctrl U. To insert a new condition, select the line number where you wish it to go, press Ctrl N and add the condition (the condition will be inserted above the line selected).
5. The `DISPLAY STATUS` command shows the filter condition in effect.

Related Topics: `SET FILTER`

CREATE REPORT

Syntax: `CREATE REPORT <filename>`

Discussion: The `CREATE REPORT` command invokes a full-screen, menu-driven procedure that steps you through the design of a column-oriented report. The result is a *report form* (with extension FRM unless otherwise specified) that can be subsequently used to generate printed reports via the `REPORT FORM` command which merges records from the currently selected database with the report form.

The `CREATE REPORT` Menu has five selections, *Options, Groups, Columns, Locate,* and *Exit,* each with a submenu. To enter a submenu, highlight a selection with the right or left arrow key and press the Return key, or press the selection name's initial letter (O,

G, C, L, or E). Within the submenu themselves, menu items offering predefined values (for example, double spacing) are chosen by highlighting the selection and pressing the Return key until the desired value is displayed. For those menu items where a user-supplied value is necessary (for example, the contents of a particular column), the Return key must be pressed to choose the item and then pressed a second time to complete the entry.

The Options menu establishes the overall appearance and physical characteristics for each page in the report by providing the:

PAGE TITLE: A four-line title (with up 60 characters per line) can be specified. Each line of the title should be entered beginning in column 1 (the title is automatically centered) and further should be entered *without* quotation marks.

PAGE WIDTH: The maximum number of characters permitted on one line (a value between one and 500).

LEFT MARGIN: The number of spaces between the left edge of the paper and the first printing column.

RIGHT MARGIN: The number of spaces between the right edge of the paper and the last printing column.

LINER PER PAGE: The number of printed lines per page (a value between one and 500).

DOUBLE SPACE REPORT: Toggle yes or no.

PAGE EJECT BEFORE PRINTING: Toggle yes or no.

PAGE EJECT AFTER PRINTING: Toggle yes or no.

PLAIN PAGE: A page heading consisting of a page number, the system date, and an optional report heading are printed on the top left corner of every page (unless a plain page is specified).

The Groups menu is used only when the report is subdivided into groups according to like values of a key expression. Using this option requires the associated database file to be indexed on the key expression because all records with like values must appear together for the Groups selection to work properly. The selections in this menu include:

GROUP ON EXPRESSION: The key field or expression upon which the report is grouped.

GROUP HEADING: The heading used to introduce each new group is displayed on its own line (the heading should *not* be enclosed in quotes).

SUMMARY REPORT ONLY: Suppresses detail lines, showing only group subtotals for all the numeric fields, as well as totals for the entire report.

PAGE EJECT AFTER GROUP: Determines whether the information for each group begins on a new page.

SUBGROUP EXPRESSION: A secondary grouping level within the first level. There must be a secondary key in the master index of the database opened with the report form.

SUBGROUP HEADING: The heading for the subgroup which follows the same limitations as the Group heading.

The Columns menu is used to specify the contents, heading, and width for every column in the report, one column at a time. In addition, when a numeric field is specified for the column contents, the number of decimal places (if different than in the file structure) should be entered as should whether or not to total the field (the default is to provide a total). The column contents can be any valid dBASE expression. The heading is left justified in the column and can consist of up to four lines (of 50 characters each). The width of the column defaults to the width of the field expression or to the width of the heading, whichever is greater.

After data for the first column have been entered, press the PgDn key to begin entering information for the next column. After that, use the PgDn and PgUp keys to move from column to column to make modifications as the report format is built. (To add a column to the report between two existing columns, press Ctrl N. The column will be added to the left of the current column. To delete an existing column, press Ctrl U when the data for that column is in the Column display area.)

The report layout is shown at the bottom of the screen to help assess what changes need to be made and how much room is left on the page. Different symbols are used to indicate the type and width of data for each column. X denotes character data, # represents numeric data that will be totaled, 9 indicates numeric data that will not be totaled, and .L. implies a logical field.

The Locate menu provides a quick and easy way to access individual columns for revision. Choose a field name and it is displayed in the Column area for editing.

The Exit menu enables the report form to be saved or abandoned. (If abandoned, the results of the current session are lost.) In either event, control returns to the dot prompt from where normal dBASE processing can continue.

Tips:

1. CREATE and MODIFY can be used interchangeably to create and/or modify report forms. The determining factor in whether a new form is created or an existing form modified, is whether or not the report form already exists.
2. A database (DBF) file must be open for a report form to be created and, should this not be the case, a prompt requesting the name of the database file is presented.
3. The field names entered in the report form must match the field names in the currently selected database. Mistakes can be avoided by pressing the F10 key to retrieve the associated file structure, then selecting the field names with the cursor keys, rather than retyping them. (Only fields from the currently selected database are made available unless a field list containing fields from an unselected database is made active through a previously issued SET FIELDS command.)
4. The NOEJECT and PLAIN clauses in the REPORT FORM command *override* contradictory values for these parameters within the report form file.
5. The page title cannot contain any field names or memory variables (even with the macro notation); that is, it must be a character string not enclosed in quotes.
6. In situations where the report form capability is inadequate, a custom report can be generated through a program containing @...SAY commands (with the DEVICE set to PRINT).
7. A character field is always left justified in its column, but can be moved to the right by concatenating it with the appropriate number of blank spaces, for example,

    ```
    "     " + location
    ```

    Note, too, that increasing the column width allocated to any character field automatically moves the next column in the report farther toward the right.
8. A numeric field is always right justified, but can be moved left by converting it to a character string and concatenating it with the appropriate number of blanks, for example,

    ```
    "     " + STR(salary,6)
    ```

9. A field may be deliberately *wrapped to two lines* by decreasing the column width, perhaps to print an address with the street on one line and the city, state, and zip code on the next. The address would be entered in one column as

    ```
    street + TRIM(city) + ", " + state + " " + zip
    ```

    with the column width set to the width of the street field only. Note, too, that any field wrapped in this way should be entered in the *rightmost* column on the page so that there will be no problem when a line feed is generated.
10. Multiple substrings can be concatenated in the same column to produce a more pleasing result, for example,

```
SUBSTR(ssn,1,3) + "-" + SUBSTR(ssn,4,2) + "-" + SUBSTR(ssn,6)
```

11. An IIF function can be used in a column entry to enhance the unappealing .T. or .F. normally displayed for logical variables. Consider:

```
IIF(fee_paid, "Fee is paid", "Fee is still owed")
```

The display is much clearer and more attractive than one showing just a .T. or an .F.

12. The presence of the Cursor Movement Menu can be toggled on and off with the F1 function key.

Related Topics:
```
CREATE LABEL
IIF()
REPORT FORM
@...SAY
SET DEVICE
SET FIELDS
STR()
SUBSTR()
```

CREATE SCREEN

Syntax: `CREATE SCREEN <filename>`

Discussion: The `CREATE SCREEN` command invokes a full-screen, menu-driven procedure to design a custom screen for use with the currently selected database. The result is the creation of two files, a format file and a screen file (with extensions of FMT and SCR, respectively). The format file (consisting entirely of `@...SAY`, `@...GET`, and `@...TO` commands) can be activated at any time with a `SET FORMAT TO` command that displays the custom screen in response to a subsequently issued `APPEND`, `EDIT`, or `INSERT` command. The screen file is created only so that the format file can be later modified through the blackboard of the `CREATE` and/or `MODIFY SCREEN` commands.

The `CREATE SCREEN` Menu has four selections, *Set Up, Modify, Options,* and *Exit,* each with a submenu. To enter a submenu, highlight a selection with the right or left arrow key and press the Return key or press the selection name's initial letter (for example, S, M, O, or E). Within the submenus themselves, menu items offering predefined values are made by highlighting the selections and pressing the Return key until the desired value is displayed. For those menu items where a user-supplied value is necessary, the Return key must be pressed to choose the item and then pressed a second time to complete the entry.

The Set Up menu allows an existing database to be selected (from a menu of databases on the default drive) or a new database to be created. The latter is a tedious process, however, and it is far easier to create a database in the usual manner (with the `CREATE` command). Once a database file has been selected, the Load Fields option is used to place some or all of the fields on the blackboard. The F10 function key is used to toggle back and forth between the blackboard and the main menu.

The Modify menu provides the means for defining the file structure of a new database, for modifying the file structure of an existing database, and for defining picture *templates, functions,* and *ranges* for the loaded fields. The options in this menu include:

ACTION: Determines whether an `@...SAY` or an `@...GET` is generated for the current field.

SOURCE: Indicates the name of the currently selected database.

CONTENT: Supplies the name of the current field.

TYPE, WIDTH, AND DECIMALS: Displays these parameters as they are defined in the file structure. Changing any of these values will also modify the file structure.

FUNCTIONS AND TEMPLATES: Enables picture clauses to be built for the current field.

RANGE: Enables a range to be entered for subsequent data validation during data entry.

The Options menu allows a text file to be generated (an ASCII representation of the SCR file), a single bar line or box to be drawn, or a double bar line or box to be drawn. (The latter two choices produce an `@...TO` command in the format file.)

The Exit menu enables the file to be saved or abandoned. (If it is abandoned the current session's results are lost.) In either event, control returns to the dot prompt from where normal dBASE processing can continue.

Tips:

1. `CREATE` and `MODIFY` can be used interchangeably to create and modify screen files. The determining factor in whether a new file is created or an existing one modified is whether or not the file already exists.
2. The screen file exists only to enable the format file to be modified through the screen generator. Hence, once changes have been made directly to the format file (for example, with a text editor), the screen file loses its utility because it no longer matches the format file.
3. No more than three or four fields should be moved onto the blackboard at one time because it is difficult to reposition fields if too many are loaded together.
4. Existing lines and boxes can be deleted by placing the cursor anywhere on the line and pressing Ctrl U.
5. The format file produced by the `CREATE SCREEN` command can be used as the basis for a program (PRG) file that appends or edits data, that is, the program would be developed around the `@...SAY` commands in the format file.
6. A screen display contains 24 lines, whereas only 20 lines are shown on the blackboard at any given time; hence the row and column of the current cursor position are displayed on the status bar. Note, too, that should the screen display go beyond 24 lines, dBASE automatically generates `READ` commands within the format file to separate the screen pages. This is a very different use of the `READ` command and applies to format files only.
7. Clear, well-laid-out screens are critical to the ease with which an application can be used. Consistency from screen to screen within a system is also very important.

Related Topics: `APPEND`
`EDIT`
`INSERT`
`MODIFY COMMAND`
`READ`
`@...SAY...GET`
`SET FORMAT TO`
`@...TO`

CREATE VIEW

Syntax: `CREATE VIEW <filename>`

Discussion: The `CREATE VIEW` command invokes a full-screen, menu-driven procedure that enables you to relate database (DBF) files to one another. The result is a view file (with extension VUE unless otherwise specified) that can be activated at any time with a SET VIEW command to establish the same system of relationships. The view file contains pertinent information regarding the environment, including the databases belonging to the view, their associated memo files and indexes, the work areas in which they were opened, the relationship between the databases, and any active field list, filter condition, or format file.

Although the CREATE VIEW command contains the necessary options to do all of the above, *we strongly suggest you establish the environment through individual commands at the dot prompt, then issue the single command* CREATE VIEW FROM ENVIRONMENT *to save the results to a view file*. This is far easier than using the various menus in the CREATE VIEW command, and also enables the view to be tested and debugged before it is saved.

The CREATE VIEW menu has five options, *Set Up, Relate, Set Fields, Options*, and *Exit*, each with a submenu. To enter a submenu, highlight the selection with the right or left arrow key and press the Return key or press the selection name's initial letter (for example, S, R, S, O, or E). Within the submenus themselves, menu items offering predefined values are chosen by highlighting the selection and pressing the Return key until the desired value is displayed. For those menu items where a user-supplied value is necessary, the Return key must be pressed to choose the item and then pressed a second time to complete the entry.

The Set Up menu opens the desired database files and their associated indexes from a list of files on the default drive (or catalog, if one is in use). The first file is opened in work area 1 (after which, its indexes are chosen as well), the second in work area 2, and so on until all the files are placed in their respective areas. Note, too, that as each file is selected, it is marked with a > in the menu to distinguish it from those files that haven't been opened.

The Relate menu designates an initial database file (as the foundation for the relationship), then indicates a second (related) file together with the field on which the relationship is to be established. (The field must be common to both files, with a master index based on that field opened for the related file.) Other relationships are established in much the same way, but are restricted because they must always begin with the last *related* file and cannot include a file already in a relationship.

The Set Fields menu builds a field list (if one is desired) by listing all the open database files regardless of whether or not they were included in a relationship. The process for building a field list is the *reverse* of what is normally done. Every field in every open database is included unless it is explicitly excluded. Thus, as you select a file, a menu of field names is displayed, and only the fields to be excluded must be toggled off.

The Options menu designates a filter condition and/or a format file, although neither is required. The format file can be chosen from the menu of format files on the default drive, whereas the filter condition must be explicitly specified; that is, it cannot be chosen by opening an existing query file.

The Exit menu enables the view file to be saved (and activated as well) or abandoned. (If it is abandoned, the current session's results are lost.) In either event, control returns to the dot prompt from where normal dBASE processing can continue.

Tips:

1. CREATE and MODIFY can be used interchangeably to create and modify view files. The determining factor in whether a new file is created or an existing one modified is whether or not the file already exists.
2. dBASE "remembers" which file and associated index files were open when the CREATE VIEW command was invoked, so that if the view file is abandoned the original working environment is restored.
3. Within the CREATE VIEW process, reselecting a previously selected file actually unselects it, implicitly canceling any relationships in which it was involved.

4. No more than 15 dBASE files of all types may be open at any one time, a requirement often forgotten when working within the `CREATE VIEW` environment.
5. Two databases can be related on the basis of their record numbers instead of on the basis of a common field. In this situation, the related file should not be indexed and RECNO() should be entered rather than a linking field name.
6. The `DISPLAY STATUS` command will show the established environment.

Related Topics:
```
SELECT
SET FIELDS
SET FILTER
SET FORMAT
SET INDEX
SET RELATION
SET VIEW
USE
```

CTOD FUNCTION

Syntax: `CTOD(<character expression>)`

Discussion: The `CTOD()`, *C*haracter *TO D*ate, function converts a date entered as a character string to its equivalent date type value. The mm/dd/yy default format can be changed with the `SET DATE` and/or `SET CENTURY` commands.

The `CTOD()` function is *required* when creating date type memory variables, replacing date fields with character dates, or when creating conditions that compare date fields to character dates, for example,

```
STORE CTOD("01/01/88") TO mhiredate
REPLACE birthdate WITH CTOD (mbirthdate)
REPORT FORM employee FOR hiredate = CTOD("06/01/87")
```

Not using the `CTOD()` function would, in the first case, result in a character variable being created, and in the other two instances, a "Data Type Mismatch" error.

Tips:

1. The `CTOD()` function enables date arithmetic to be performed with character dates. For example, the command

```
? DATE()-CTOD("05/31/88")
```

will return the number of days between today's date and May 31, 1988. (If today's date is the earlier date, a negative number will be returned.)
2. An error message will *not* be produced if an invalid date is entered; instead the invalid date will be converted to its equivalent calendar date. For example, the command

```
STORE CTOD("10/45/88") TO mdate
```

results in 11/14/88 being stored in the memory variable mdate.
3. If the `SET DATE` command is in effect to establish a different format, the new format must be used with the `CTOD()` function or erroneous dates will be generated. For example, if the date has been set to ANSI (yy.mm.dd) in lieu of the default American format (mm/dd/yy), the command

```
STORE CTOD("01/05/88") TO mdate
```

will place 02.05.29 (that is not a typographical error) into mdate, without any indication of an error.

4. Regardless of whether SET CENTURY is ON or OFF, any date entered with a two-digit year is assumed to be a 20th century date; to enter a date from another century, you must specify a four-digit year such as

```
STORE CTOD("04/18/1775") TO olddate
```

Related Topics: DATE()
DTOC()
SET DATE
SET CENTURY

DATE FUNCTION

Syntax: DATE()

Discussion: The DATE() function returns the system date as obtained from DOS, in the mm/dd/yy default format. (A different format, for example, dd/mm/yy, can be established with the SET DATE command.) The value that the DATE() function returns is a *date* (as opposed to character) field, and can be used in date arithmetic with no conversion required. However, displaying the function in a character string requires it first be converted to character data with the DTOC() conversion function, for example,

```
? "Today is " + DTOC(DATE())
```

Tips:

1. Be sure to enter the date correctly when booting the system, because that is the date the DATE() function returns. (It is also the date stamped on all files created.)
2. The dBASE DATE() function *cannot* be used to set the system date. (The DOS DATE command can, however, be accessed from within dBASE to set the system date using a RUN command as in RUN DATE.)
3. The DATE() function may itself be the argument for other dBASE date functions, for example, CMONTH(DATE()) or CDOW(DATE()).
4. The DATE() function can be used to store the system date to a memory variable such as

```
STORE DATE() TO mtoday
```

Related Topics: CDOW()
CMONTH()
DAY()
DTOC()
MONTH()
RUN
SET DATE
YEAR()

DAY FUNCTION

Syntax: `DAY(<date expression>)`

Discussion: The DAY function returns a numeric value from one to 31, corresponding to the day of the month in the specified date expression. The argument in the `DAY()` function may assume several different forms as shown in the following table:

Function	Nature of the Argument
`DAY(hiredate)`	Date field
`DAY(memdate)`	Date memory variable
`DAY(DATE())`	DATE() function itself
`DAY(CTOD("12/25/88"))`	CTOD() conversion function
`DAY(DATE() + 10)`	Expression with date arithmetic

Tips:

1. The `DAY()` function works only on date fields; a character date may *not* be used as the argument unless it is converted with the `CTOD()` conversion function.
2. The `DAY()` function is often used in program files and/or report forms to display a date in a more attractive format. For example, given a date of 01/08/89, the command

Command is entered on one line

```
@ 20,20 SAY "Today is " + CMONTH(DATE()) + " " +
      STR(DAY(DATE()),2) + ", " + STR(YEAR(DATE()),4)
```

returns the string "Today is January 08, 1989". (The day and year must be converted to strings to be concatenated with the other character type data.)

Related Topics:
`CMONTH()`
`CTOD()`
`DATE()`
`MONTH()`
`STR()`
`YEAR()`

DELETE

Syntax: `DELETE [<scope>][WHILE <condition>][FOR <condition>]`

Discussion: The DELETE command marks a record(s) in the currently selected database for deletion. Only a single record will be deleted unless a scope parameter, or a FOR or WHILE condition, is specified to indicate that more than one record is to be marked at a time, for example, `DELETE NEXT 10` or `DELETE FOR location = '40'`.

The position of the record pointer is unaffected if DELETE is specified with no additional parameters. DELETE ALL or DELETE REST, however, moves the record pointer to the end of the file, whereas any other scope parameter will reposition the record pointer at the last record marked for deletion. Including a WHILE condition moves the record pointer to the record *after* the last record meeting the condition, while specifying a FOR clause moves the record pointer to the end of the file.

Records marked for deletion are still accessible and are processed by subsequent dBASE commands. However, when these records are displayed or listed, they are indentified by an asterisk next to the record number. Similarly, a delete message appears on the status line when "deleted" records are browsed or edited.

Tips:

1. A SET DELETED ON command causes subsequent dBASE commands to ignore records marked for deletion, treating them as if they were not physically present; that is, the logically deleted records are "hidden" from dBASE commands. SET DELETED OFF returns to the normal processing mode in which all records are processed regardless of their deleted status.
2. Commands that access records by record number, for example, GOTO 3, or EDIT RECORD 3, will operate even if SET DELETED is ON. The INDEX and SORT commands also operate on all records when SET DELETED is ON.
3. The DELETED() function returns a value of .T. (true) if a record has been marked for deletion and a value of .F. (false) if it has not. This function can be used to display or count the records marked for deletion, as shown:

```
LIST FOR DELETED()
COUNT FOR DELETED()
```

or to archive deleted records, as in

```
COPY TO archive FOR DELETED()
```

Remember, however, that SET DELETED must be OFF for these commands to execute properly.
4. A record other than the current record can be deleted with the command DELETE RECORD <n>, where n is a valid record number.

Related Topics: RECALL
PACK
ZAP
SET DELETED
DELETED()

DELETED FUNCTION

Syntax: DELETED()

Discussion: The DELETED() function returns a logical value of true (.T.) or false (.F.), depending on whether the current record is marked for deletion (true), or not (false). The function is used most often to process all the deleted records in a file with a single command, for example,

```
LIST FOR DELETED()
COPY TO archive FOR DELETED()
COUNT FOR DELETED()
```

Tips:

1. Whenever SET DELETED is ON, records marked for deletion are hidden, and the DELETED() condition will *not* indicate any records. In other words, SET DELETED must be OFF for commands using the DELETED() function to work properly.
2. The current record's status (that is, whether or not it is marked for deletion) can be viewed with the command ? DELETED(), which will display either .T. or .F. for marked and unmarked records, respectively.

Related Topics: DELETE
SET DELETED

DIR

Syntax: DIR [<drive:>][<path>][<skeleton>][TO PRINT]

Discussion: The dBASE DIR command displays information about files stored on disk. It is parallel in function to the DOS command except that it is executed from within dBASE, and is therefore more convenient.

If the command is issued with no parameters (for example, DIR), it displays the names of all DBF files on the default disk together with the number of records, the date of the last update, and the file size in bytes. It also indicates the total number of bytes used by .DBF files, the total number of .DBF files, and the number of bytes remaining on the disk. If a drive or path is included in the command (for example, DIR A: or DIR C: \DBASE\SOLEIL), it will display the above information for all .DBF files on the designated drive or subdirectory.

The skeleton parameter enables the DOS wild card characters, ? and *, to be used within the DIR command. The question mark represents any *single* character in its position in the file name, whereas the asterisk denotes any number of characters in the file name. For example:

DIR ?.DBF: Lists all files with one-character file names that have a DBF extension.
DIR *.PRG: Lists all file names that have a .PRG extension, regardless of the length of the filename.
DIR S?.NDX: Lists all two-character file names that have a .NDX extension and begin with the letter S.
DIR S*.NDX: Lists all file names that have a .NDX extension and begin with the letter S, regardless of the length of the filename.

Whenever the skeleton parameter is used, the file names are listed in columns across the screen (for a maximum of four columns). The only information given is the file name, the total number of bytes used by the files listed, the total number of files listed, and the number of bytes remaining on the disk.

Tips:

1. The directory listing will not always reflect changes made to the database (for example, the correct number of records) until after the file is closed with a CLOSE DATABASES or USE command.
2. Regardless of whether or not a SET PATH TO command has been issued, only files

from the current (logged) subdirectory are listed. In other words, a path parameter is required within the DIR command to list files in other subdirectories.

Related Topics: SET PATH TO

DISPLAY

Syntax: `DISPLAY [<scope>][<expN list>][WHILE <condition>]`
`[FOR < condition>][OFF][TO PRINT]`

Discussion: The DISPLAY command exhibits all fields for one or more records from the currently selected database. The default scope is one, so that issuing the command with no parameters causes only the current record to be shown. A scope, FOR, or WHILE parameter may be used to output multiple records, for example:

```
DISPLAY ALL
DISPLAY NEXT 10
DISPLAY FOR location = '42'
```

If the output the command produces requires more than 20 lines, the data is exhibited one screen at a time with a pause between screens, that is, a key has to be pressed for the display to continue. The DISPLAY command with no parameters does *not* reposition the record pointer, whereas including a scope parameter, or a FOR or WHILE clause, alters its position. Specification of a scope of ALL or REST moves the record pointer to the end-of-file, as does a FOR condition. Specification of NEXT as the scope parameter repositions the pointer to the last record in the scope, whereas including a WHILE condition moves it to the record beyond the last record meeting the condition.

An expression list can be included to show only selected fields and/or to display complex expressions such as

```
DISPLAY ssn,initials,lname
DISPLAY ALL ssn,TRIM(initials) + ' ' + lname
DISPLAY ssn,(salary2-salary1)/salary1*100
```

A heading line always precedes the screen display and includes the names of the individual fields or the expressions used. The display width of each expression is determined by either the field width, as established by the file structure, or the width of the heading, whichever is greater.

The contents of a memo field are not displayed, unless the field name is specified in an expression list. The default display width for a memo field is 50 columns, but the SET MEMOWIDTH command can modify that. If no expression list is specified, a memo field has the word "memo" displayed as the field contents.

The OFF parameter suppresses the record number. The TO PRINT parameter echoes the results of the command to the printer.

Tips:

1. If the data to be displayed is too long to fit on one line, both the heading and the data wrap to successive lines, making the output difficult to read. The SET FIELDS command or an expression list can be used to limit the display to essential fields and avoid the wrap to the next line.

2. The heading line shows the field names and expressions exactly as they were entered in the command line; if the command was typed in uppercase letters, the heading line will also be uppercase.

3. The SET HEADING OFF command suppresses the heading line. This is a useful procedure when using a long or complex expression.

4. No record is displayed if the record pointer is at the end-of-file. In this instance, only the heading line will appear, then control returns to the dot prompt.

5. Deleted records will not be displayed if SET DELETED is ON, unless the record pointer is specifically moved to the specific record, for example,

```
DISPLAY RECORD 5
```

or

```
GOTO 5
DISPLAY
```

The same principle holds for records not matching the condition set by a SET FILTER command; that is, records not matching the filter condition are ignored unless the record pointer is specifically moved to the record.

6. Fields from database files in other than the currently selected work area can be displayed by including the file alias with the field name in the command, for example,

```
DISPLAY ssn,lname,location->loccode
```

This is usually done only when a SET RELATION command is in effect.

7. The LIST command operates in similar fashion, except that its default scope is ALL. In addition, LIST does not pause between screenfuls of data as does the DISPLAY command.

Related Topics:
```
LIST
SET DELETED
SET FILTER
SET FIELDS
SET MEMOWIDTH
SET RELATION
?
@...SAY...GET
```

DISPLAY HISTORY

Syntax: DISPLAY HISTORY [LAST <n>] [TO PRINT]

Discussion: The DISPLAY HISTORY command displays the list of commands currently stored in history memory which, by default, is the 20 most recently executed commands. (The number can be increased or decreased with the SET HISTORY command.)

Specifying the LAST <n> clause, where <n> is a number less than history's capacity, will list only the most recently executed <n> commands.

Including the TO PRINT clause echoes the results to the printer.

Tips:

1. The screen display pauses every 16 lines until a key is pressed to continue the listing.
2. Any of the commands stored in the history memory can be recalled to the dot prompt,

from where it may be edited and/or reissued. Repeatedly pressing the up arrow key redisplays the previous commands beginning with the one most recently executed. Once the desired command is at the dot prompt, the right and left arrow keys are used to edit the command (in either the insert or replacement modes), and the Return key will reexecute the command. Note too, that while the up arrow key progressively moves toward the commands issued longest ago, the down arrow key moves toward the most recently issued commands.

3. Newly executed commands will *not* be stored in the history memory when SET HISTORY is OFF, although previously stored commands can still be recalled, edited, and reissued. SET HISTORY must be turned back ON to resume storing commands.

4. SET DOHISTORY ON is an excellent debugging tool because it stores commands executed from a program file together with commands executed from the dot prompt.

Related Topics: SET DOHISTORY
SET HISTORY

DISPLAY MEMORY

Syntax: DISPLAY MEMORY [TO PRINT]

Discussion: The DISPLAY MEMORY command provides information about the current memory variables including:

1. The name, status (public or private), type, stored value, and size of every active memory variable.
2. The number of active memory variables.
3. The number of additional memory variables remaining.
4. The amount of memory used by existing memory variables.
5. The amount of memory remaining for use by additional memory variables.

A maximum of 256 memory variables may be active at any one time. In addition, the memory variables may use a maximum of 6000 bytes (unless otherwise established by the MVARSIZ command in the CONFIG.DB file). However, even if the amount of memory is increased beyond 6000 bytes, the maximum number of memory variables remains fixed at 256.

If the memory variable display exceeds what will fit on one screen, the display pauses after each screen, waiting for the user to press any key to continue. The TO PRINT clause echoes the screen display to the printer. If the printer is not ready, an error message will be displayed.

Tips:

1. The DISPLAY MEMORY command is a very useful debugging tool when programming problems occur.
2. The display of a numeric memory variable shows the variable as it appears in displays and as it is stored in memory (the two can be very different, especially with regard to the number of decimal places). Note, too, that the default width for numeric memory variables is 10 bytes.
3. Private memory variables (those created in programs or procedures and not explicitly declared as public) are released from memory as soon as the program or procedure that created them is terminated. These variables will not, therefore, be included in DISPLAY MEMORY output obtained from the dot prompt. Hence, in order to view the contents of

private memory variables, you must either temporarily include DISPLAY MEMORY and WAIT commands at strategic points in the program, or temporarily declare the memory variables PUBLIC (either in the program itself or from the dot prompt before running the program).

4. Memory variables saved to .MEM files for use in future dBASE sessions with the SAVE command can only be viewed after they have been loaded into memory with the RE-STORE command.

5. LIST MEMORY displays the same information as DISPLAY MEMORY, except that it does not pause between screenfuls of information.

Related Topics: LIST MEMORY
                       RELEASE
                       RESTORE
                       SAVE

DISPLAY STATUS

Syntax: DISPLAY STATUS [TO PRINT]

Discussion: The DISPLAY STATUS command provides information about the current dBASE III PLUS session including:

1. The current search path
2. The default drive
3. The destination printer port
4. The left margin setting for reports and labels
5. The current work area
6. The status of most SET...ON/OFF commands
7. The function key settings

In addition, the command will display the names of all open database files and, for each file, the number of its work area and its alias. As applicable, it will also supply (for each work area) the name of an active format file, information regarding an active relationship or any active filter condition, the names of all open indexes and their respective keys, and an open memo (.DBT) file name.

Specifying TO PRINT will direct the output display to the printer as well as to the screen.

Tips:

1. DISPLAY STATUS is a helpful debugging tool when problems occur during a session and/or when your memory fails you.
2. LIST STATUS provides the same information and differs only in that it does not pause between screens as the DISPLAY STATUS command does.

Related Topics: DISPLAY MEMORY
                       LIST STATUS

DISPLAY STRUCTURE

Syntax: `DISPLAY STRUCTURE [TO PRINT]`

Discussion: The `DISPLAY STRUCTURE` command displays the following information about the currently selected database file:

1. The file name (including the drive and pathname)
2. The number of records in the file
3. The date of the last update to the file
4. The name, type, and width (including decimals for numeric fields) of every field in the file structure
5. The total number of bytes per record

If the structure is large enough to require more than one screen (that is, it contains more than 16 fields), the display pauses after each screen, prompting you to press any key to continue.

Tips:

1. The total number of bytes per record is one more than the sum of all of the field widths. The extra byte is for the deleted record marker (∗).
2. This command is used to verify the spelling of a field name, its width, and/or field type.

Related Topics: `LIST STRUCTURE`

DO

Syntax: `DO <filename> [WITH <parameter list>]`

Discussion: The `DO` command executes an individually stored program file or a procedure in an open procedure file. The command may be issued either from the dot prompt or from within a program file.

When a `DO` command is issued, dBASE searches any open procedure file for a procedure with the specified name. If none is found, dBASE continues by searching the default disk for a PRG file with the specified file name. dBASE will search other than the default disk if the drive (and path, if applicable) is specified with the file name, and will search for other than a PRG file if the extension is explicitly specified with the file name.

The program containing the `DO` command is known as the *calling* program; the program named in the `DO` command is termed the *called* program. When the called program terminates, control is passed back to the calling program, to the statement immediately following the `DO` command.

The `WITH` clause passes *parameters* to the called program, which in turn stores the values in private memory variables it initializes with a `PARAMETERS` command. (The `PARAMETERS` command must be the first executable command in the called program.) The values of the parameters in the `WITH` clause are assigned sequentially to the memory variables in the `PARAMETERS` command, requiring the number of parameters in the `WITH` clause to equal the number of memory variables in the `PARAMETERS` command. The names of the parameters do *not*, however, have to be the same as those of the memory variables in the `PARAMETERS` command.

Tips:

1. If a procedure in an open procedure file has the same name as a PRG file, the procedure will always be the one executed.
2. Each DO that specifies a program file counts as an open file towards the 15-file limit until the program terminates and control returns to the calling program. Individual procedures are considered part of a procedure file and do not count toward the limit; that is, only the procedure file itself is counted.
3. Memory variables created within the calling program are available to the called program and any program it calls. Changes made in the value of any of these variables are passed back to the calling program. On the other hand, memory variables created within a called program are not available to the calling program.
4. A program ends when the last command in the file has been executed and control is returned to the calling program (or the dot prompt). A RETURN command should be entered as the last line of every program, although this is not required.
5. A DO command may not call an open program file.
6. The use of parameters permits programs having generalized coding to perform a specific task, determined by the values passed to the called program. For example, the program MESG1.PRG

```
**MESG1.PRG
PARAMETERS message,mrow,mcol
@ mrow,mcol SAY message
RETURN
```

will display a message at a given screen location, depending on the values it receives from the program that called it. For example, in the following program,

```
STORE 20 TO mr
STORE 10 TO mc
STORE 'Please enter a Y or N' TO msg
DO mesg1.prg WITH msg,mr,mc
```

the message will be displayed at line 20, column 10, whereas another program whose coding is

```
STORE 12 TO mr
STORE 15 TO mc
STORE 'Please enter option' TO msg
DO mesg1.prg WITH msg,mr,mc
```

will display a different message at line 12, column 15.

Related Topics: SET PROCEDURE
RETURN

DO CASE

Syntax: DO CASE
```
CASE <condition>
    <commands>
[CASE <condition>
    <commands>]
[OTHERWISE
    <commands>]
ENDCASE
```

Discussion: DO CASE is a structured programming command that selects one of several alternative courses of action. Execution begins by evaluating the first condition and, if necessary, continuing with each subsequent condition until a true condition is found. Upon reaching a true condition, every command between that CASE statement and the next condition is executed. The remaining lines are then skipped and control passes to the first command after the ENDCASE statement.

The CASE structure begins and ends with DO CASE and ENDCASE, respectively, each of which must be coded on its own line. Every CASE statement is also coded on its own line, as is the optional OTHERWISE statement. The latter follows the last CASE and specifies commands to be executed if none of the preceding conditions are true. If the OTHERWISE statement is omitted and none of the preceding conditions are true, control passes directly to the first command after the ENDCASE statement. The commands following either a CASE or OTHERWISE statement may be any valid dBASE command.

Indentation within a CASE statement is used only to improve readability and is not required by dBASE. However, as with the IF...ELSE...ENDIF and DO WHILE structures, indentation is highly recommended because it helps tremendously in making program logic more understandable.

Tips:

1. A DO CASE structure is preferable to using nested IFs with more than three levels. DO CASE runs slightly faster and is also easier to follow.

2. DO CASE is an ideal structure to use when one course of action must be chosen from several alternatives, and consequently is recommended for creating menu-driven programs. Consider:

```
DO CASE
   CASE input = 1
      DO program_1
   CASE input = 2
      DO program_2
   CASE input = 3
      DO program_3
   OTHERWISE
      DISPLAY 'error message'
ENDCASE
```

3. Nested CASE structures are permitted. In addition, IF and DO WHILE structures may be used within the CASE structure as one of the commands to be executed. Be careful, however, to ensure that the nested structures are complete (that is, every IF has an ENDIF, every DO WHILE an ENDDO, and every DO CASE an ENDCASE).

4. Consistent indentation (typically, three spaces) within the structure is strongly recommended.

Related Topics: IF...ELSE...ENDIF
                      DO WHILE

DO WHILE

Syntax: DO WHILE <condition>
                 <commands>
              ENDDO

Discussion: DO WHILE is a structured programming command that executes the included commands repeatedly as long as the specified condition is true. The condition is tested *before* any of the included commands are executed. Hence, if the initial test of the condition is false, control passes immediately to the first command after the DO WHILE statement. If, however, the condition is true, the included commands are executed in order until the ENDDO is reached. Control then returns to the DO WHILE statement and the condition is tested once again. The process is repeated until the condition becomes false, whereupon control passes to the statement after the ENDDO, terminating the loop.

As indicated, the condition is tested at the beginning of the loop, meaning that if the condition becomes false midway through the command list, the rest of the commands are still executed. Only when the ENDDO is reached, and control is transferred back to the DO WHILE, will the condition be evaluated as false and the loop terminated.

Provision must be made to ensure that the condition in the DO WHILE statement eventually becomes false, or else the loop will be repeated endlessly. Should this occur, the only way to terminate processing is to press the Esc key.

Nested DO WHILE loops (one DO WHILE performed within another DO WHILE loop) are permitted provided that an ENDDO terminates each DO WHILE. Since dBASE ignores any additional text appearing on the same line as an ENDDO statement, it is helpful to label the ENDDO portion of the command as shown:

```
DO WHILE city = 'Miami'
   .
   .
   .
   DO WHILE zip = '33176'
      .
      .
      .
   ENDDO (zip)
ENDDO (city)
```

Indentation within a DO WHILE statement is used only to improve readability and is not required by dBASE rules. However, as with the IF...ELSE...ENDIF and DO CASE structures, indentation is highly recommended as it helps tremendously in making program logic more understandable.

Tips: _____

1. DO WHILE .NOT. EOF() performs the same set of steps for all records in a database file, for example,

```
USE solemp
DO WHILE .NOT. EOF()
   ? lastname, firstname
   SKIP
ENDDO
```

The SKIP command is necessary within the loop to move the file pointer to the next record in the file until the end-of-file is reached and the loop is terminated. Indeed, if SKIP were erroneously omitted, the condition controlling the loop would never be false and the program would loop indefinitely.

2. Consistent indentation (typically, three spaces) within the structure is strongly recommended.

3. Compound conditions may be included using the logical operators .AND. and .OR. You

must, however, repeat the field name or memory variable in each part of a complex clause, even if the field name or variable name is the same, for example,

```
DO WHILE city = 'Miami' .OR. city = 'New York'
```

4. A LOOP command may be included within the DO WHILE structure to bypass remaining commands and go directly to the ENDDO statement, in effect returning to the top of the DO WHILE structure to reevaluate the condition. Consider:

```
DO WHILE condition 1
    Statement 1
    IF condition 2
        LOOP
    ENDIF
    Statement 2
ENDDO
```

We recommend, however, that LOOP statements be avoided (by reworking logic) because they violate basic precepts of structured programming.

5. An EXIT command may be included within the DO WHILE structure to make an abnormal (premature) exit from the loop by passing control directly to the first command after the ENDDO. We also recommend against using EXIT because it, too, violates basic precepts of structured programming.

Related Topics: IF...ELSE...ENDIF
DO CASE

DTOC FUNCTION

Syntax: DTOC(<date expression>)

Discussion: The DTOC(), *Date TO Character*, function converts a date expression to an equivalent character string. The argument of the function can be a date field, a date memory variable, the result of the DATE() function, the result of a CTOD() conversion function, or the result of an expression involving date arithmetic. The default format of the argument is mm/dd/yy, but can be changed with the SET DATE and SET CENTURY commands.

The DTOC() function is required when storing a date (such as the system date or a date field) to a character type memory variable, when replacing character fields with dates, or when concatenating a date with a character string, for example,

```
STORE DTOC(DATE()) TO mdate
REPLACE cdate WITH DTOC(DATE()
? " Today is " + DTOC(DATE())
```

Not using the DTOC() function would, in the first case, result in a date variable being created rather than a character variable and would, in the next two cases, result in a "Data Type Mismatch" error.

Tips:

1. If the display format of a date has been changed with the SET DATE command, the format of the character date returned by the DTOC() function will reflect the change.

2. SET CENTURY must be ON for the DTOC() function to display a four-digit year. This is especially important if the century is other than the 20th century.

3. In an index whose key expression consists of a character and a date field, the date *cannot* simply be converted to character data with a DTOC() function. This is because character data are sequenced by comparing the characters one by one beginning with the leftmost character, implying that all dates beginning with 01 come before dates beginning with 02, regardless of the year; for example, 01/01/88 would come before 02/15/87. Correcting this problem requires either a SET DATE ANSI command to rearrange the date into yy/mm/dd format, for example,

```
SET DATE ANSI
INDEX ON location + DTOC(hiredate) TO locdate
```

or an INDEX ON command with the following key:

Command is entered on one line

```
INDEX ON location + SUBSTR(hiredate,7,2) +
   SUBSTR(hiredate,1,2) + SUBSTR(hiredate,4,2) TO
   locdate
```

The latter command sequences by location, and within the same location, by characters 7 and 8 of hire date (the year), then within year by characters 1 and 2 of hire date (the month), then within month by characters 4 and 5 of hire date (the day).

Related Topics: CTOD()
DATE()
INDEX ON
SET CENTURY
SET DATE
SUBSTR()

EDIT

Syntax: EDIT[<scope>][FIELDS<fieldlist>][WHILE<condition>]
[FOR <condition>]

Discussion: EDIT is a full-screen command used to modify the field contents of a record or group of records in the currently selected database. Issuing the command with no parameters, that is, EDIT, displays the contents of every field in the record at the current position of the record pointer. The contents of any field can be modified by moving the cursor to the desired field and entering the necessary changes (using either the insertion or replacement modes, and/or by deleting characters). After editing the current record, the next (or previous) record may be retrieved for editing using the PgDn (or PgUp) keys.

The keystroke combinations used with the APPEND command pertain to EDIT as well (see Table NB.2 on page 250), as do many of the principles for data entry. There is an obvious difference between the commands, however, namely that empty input templates are displayed in the append mode, whereas existing field contents are shown in the edit mode. A more subtle difference is that any attempt to move beyond the last record in the edit mode causes dBASE to return to the dot prompt, whereas moving beyond the last record in the append mode continues to add records. In other words, records may *not* be appended in the edit mode, although records can be edited in the append mode.

The edit mode can be exited at any time by pressing Ctrl W (Ctrl End) to save the changes made to all records, or by pressing the Esc key (Ctrl Q) to save all changes *except* those made to the current record.

The FIELDS clause limits editing to those fields specified in the field list because they are the only ones for which input templates are displayed on the screen. The fields will be listed in the order in which they appear in the field list, rather than according to their position in the record structure.

Including a FOR or WHILE condition will limit access to those records meeting the specified condition. For example,

```
EDIT FOR location = '40'
```

allows only those records with a location code of 40 to be edited. Note, too, that regardless of where the record pointer is positioned (for example, on record 10), the first record meeting the condition is the record displayed, even if that record is above the current record (for example, record 1). Pressing the PgDn key will then display the next record meeting the condition, rather than the next physical record (or logical record, in the case of an open index).

Tips:

1. The contents of a memo field can be edited by pressing Ctrl PgDn when the cursor is positioned in the input template of the memo field. The memo text editor is activated, and when the editor's save command is issued, the cursor is repositioned in the template of the next field to continue editing the record.
2. The EDIT command can indicate a specific record number, EDIT RECORD 5, for example, in which case the specified record rather than the current record is displayed.
3. A custom screen for editing data may be displayed by opening a format file or executing a program file containing the appropriate @...SAY...GET commands. Custom screens enable you to supply more meaningful prompts for input templates, include necessary messages to guide data entry, and even restrict access to certain fields for security reasons.
4. The PgUp and PgDn keys move between records according to the physical order of the database if no index is open, or according to the logical order of the open master index.
5. If data are entered beyond the last position in an input template, the extra characters are made part of the next field. This can be prevented if SET CONFIRM is ON, which requires the Return key to be pressed at the end of every field (whether or not the field is filled) to move to the next field.
6. The display of control key functions at the top of the screen can be toggled on and off, using either the SET MENU command at the dot prompt, or the F1 function key in the EDIT mode.
7. The appearance of the template can be changed with the SET DELIMITERS, SET INTENSITY, and SET COLOR commands.
8. Editing is limited to the field list established by a previously issued SET FIELDS command. A FIELDS clause may also be included in the EDIT command to further limit the subset of available fields. Note, however, that the FIELDS clause can only specify active fields, or else a "Variable not found" error message will result.
9. The EDIT command will not access deleted records when SET DELETED is ON, unless the record pointer is specifically moved to the deleted record with a GOTO command or an EDIT RECORD<n> command. The same holds true for records not meeting an active filter condition.

Related Topics: APPEND
BROWSE
SET COLOR
SET CONFIRM
SET DELETED
SET DELIMITERS
SET FIELDS
SET FILTER
SET FORMAT
SET INTENSITY
SET MENU

EJECT

Syntax: EJECT

Discussion: The EJECT command issues a form feed to the printer. The paper has to be aligned initially and the printer set to top-of-form for the command to work properly. In addition, the form length setting in the printer should be consistent with the length of paper being used. Refer to the printer's manual for specific instructions.

Tips:

1. The SET PRINT status does not affect the EJECT command; the command can be issued whether SET PRINT is ON or OFF.
2. If the printer is not on line when the command is issued, an error message will appear on the screen. In some cases, the computer may even lock and require rebooting, a situation which can result in data loss.
3. When DEVICE is set to print, an EJECT command is not needed if the row number in the current @...SAY command is lower than the row number in the previous @...SAY command, as the form feed will be done automatically.
4. In some instances, the last line to be printed is held in the print buffer and will not appear until the next printing operation begins. Issuing an EJECT command will force the line from the buffer as it advances the page, completing the report or listing.
5. The REPORT FORM command automatically issues a form feed before printing, unless a NOEJECT clause is specified.

Related Topics: REPORT FORM
SET DEVICE
SET PRINT

EOF FUNCTION

Syntax: EOF()

Discussion: The EOF(), *E*nd *O*f *F*ile, function indicates whether or not the record pointer has moved beyond the last record in the file, returning a logical value of true (.T.)

or false (.F.). The function is typically used in programs which process a file sequentially, from the first record to the last. A simple example of such a program, to print the name and salary for every record, is shown below:

```
USE solemp
DO WHILE .NOT. EOF()
    ? name,salary
    SKIP
ENDDO
```

The EOF() condition is considered true only when the record pointer has moved *beyond* the last record, that is, it is *not* true when the record pointer is on the last record. Consider:

```
USE solemp
GO BOTTOM
? EOF()
.F. ——————————— dBASE response
SKIP 1
? EOF()
.T. ——————————— dBASE response
```

The EOF() function will not be reset to false, until the record pointer is moved back into the file, for example, by a GO TOP or SKIP-5 command.

Tips:

1. The last *logical* record (according to the master index) will be considered the end-of-file, unless no index is open, in which case it is the last *physical* record.
2. Any attempt to move the record pointer beyond the last record in the file actually moves it to an end-of-file marker, with a record number one greater than that of the last record. This differs from the BOF() situation where an attempt to move the record pointer above the first record leaves it set at the first record.
3. A separate value of the EOF() function is maintained for each of the 10 available work areas. However, when testing for the condition in a particular file, that file must be the one in the currently selected work area.
4. In general, commands processing all the records in a database file (for example, LIST, REPORT FORM, COPY FOR, DISPLAY FOR) set the EOF() function to true. In addition, unsuccessful LOCATE, FIND, and SEEK commands will also set the function to true.
5. Issuing a DISPLAY command when the record pointer is positioned at the end-of-file displays the heading line only.

Related Topics: BOF()
                       RECNO()
                       SKIP

FIND

Syntax: FIND <character string/numeric value>

Discussion: The FIND command searches the key field of the master index for the first record matching the specified string or numeric value. If a record is found, it moves the record pointer to that record and returns a dot prompt. (FIND will merely reposition the record pointer and will *not* display the found record; a subsequent DISPLAY command is needed to view the record.) If, however, the search is unsuccessful, a "No Find" message is displayed (as long as SET TALK is ON) and the record pointer is repositioned to the end-of-file.

The character string in a FIND command need not be enclosed in quotes unless leading blanks are an essential portion of the string. For example, the commands

        FIND Jones

and

        FIND "Jones"

are equivalent and *different from* the command

        FIND "   Jones"

Nor is it necessary to specify the complete character string being sought, so long as SET EXACT is OFF. In other words, the command

        FIND B

will position the record pointer at the first record whose key value begins with a "B", whereas the command

        FIND Bor

will position the record pointer at the first record whose key value begins with "Bor".

The requirement of the FIND command that an active index be used implies that records with like search keys will be grouped together; that is, if there is another record with the same key value, it will be sequenced immediately beneath the values of the first. Hence, once the first record is found, the second can be accessed with a SKIP command (to move the record pointer) and viewed with a DISPLAY command (to verify that the key does, in fact, match). Indeed, all records with the same key value can be retrieved by repeatedly issuing SKIP and DISPLAY commands until the value of the key field no longer matches the character string or numeric value specified in the FIND command.

Tips:

1. A numeric value used in a FIND command must be a numeric constant, for example, FIND 11122. Moreover, the FIND command will *not* search for a partial numeric value as it would for a partial character string; that is, FIND 111 will *not* retrieve a record whose key is 11122.
2. Upper- and lowercase letters are treated as different characters, whether SET EXACT is ON or OFF. For example, the command

        FIND MILLER

   will not find a key value of "Miller" or "miller".
3. FIND conducts a much more rapid search than does the corresponding LOCATE command. FIND, however, requires an index and limits the search to a value *equal* to the character string or numeric value. LOCATE, on the other hand, can search for values "greater than," "less than," or "not equal to."
4. The FIND command can search for a character string stored in a memory variable, but only if the macro symbol (&) is used with the memory variable name. For example, the commands

        STORE 'Borow' TO mname

and

```
FIND &mname
```

instruct dBASE to search for the *value stored in mname* rather than for the character string "mname". (A parallel SEEK command does not require the macro notation and is easier to use with memory variables. It is therefore more likely to appear in program files.)

5. The FIND command *cannot* search for a numeric value that has been stored in a memory variable, even if the macro symbol (&) is used with the memory variable name. Nor can numeric expressions such as (newsalary − oldsalary)/oldsalary ∗ 100 be used in the FIND command. (A SEEK command is required in both instances.)

6. The FIND command ignores records not meeting an active filter condition. Similarly, records marked for deletion are also ignored when SET DELETED is ON.

Related Topics: LOCATE
SEEK
SET DELETED
SET FILTER
SET EXACT
SKIP

GO/GOTO

Syntax: [GO/GOTO] <expN>
GO/GOTO TOP/BOTTOM

Discussion: The GO/GOTO command positions the record pointer of the currently selected database file to a specified record. It must provide either the record number or an expression from which the record number may be calculated.

Specifying GO/GOTO TOP will position the record pointer at record 1 if no index is active or, if an index is active, at the first record according to the logical order of the index. GO/GOTO BOTTOM functions similarly, positioning the record pointer to the last physical record in the database if no index is active or, if an index is active, to the last record in the logical sequence of the index.

The record pointer may also be repositioned by simply entering the desired record number at the dot prompt. For example, entering the number 5 in response to the dot prompt will position the record pointer at record 5.

The GO/GOTO command also functions for records marked for deletion, even if SET DELETED is ON.

Tips:

1. A numeric expression may be used in the GO/GOTO command. For example, GO 6/2 will position the record pointer to record 3.

2. When a GO/GOTO command is issued, dBASE merely responds with another dot prompt. To verify that the record pointer has been positioned correctly, issue a DISPLAY command or a ? RECNO() command.

3. For clarity in a program file, use the GO/GOTO form of the command, rather than just the record number, to move the record pointer.

4. The SKIP, FIND, and LOCATE commands all reposition the record pointer in the file.

Related Topics: `FIND`
`LOCATE`
`SET DELETED`
`SKIP`
`SEEK`

HELP

Syntax: `HELP [keyword]`

Discussion: The `HELP` command brings up the dBASE online help facility. If the command is entered with a keyword, for example, `HELP DISPLAY`, the help screen specific to the keyword is brought up immediately. If, however, it is entered without a keyword, that is, `HELP`, a menu system is initiated with six initial choices:

1. GETTING STARTED: Explains how to use the help facility.
2. WHAT IS A: Defines common dBASE terms (file, expression, memory variable).
3. HOW DO I: Explains basic dBASE housekeeping tasks (saving, deleting, copying files).
4. CREATING A DBF: Explains the rules for creating a database file.
5. USING AN EXISTING DBF: Explains basic tasks involving a database file (add, delete, sort, index).
6. COMMANDS AND FUNCTIONS: Provides information on beginning and advanced commands.

Selections are made from the opening menu by highlighting the desired option and pressing the Return key, or by simply pressing the option number. If there is a submenu, additional selections are made in the same way.

If a specific topic contains more than one information screen, the PgDn key will bring up the subsequent screen(s) with a beep sounding when there are no further screens on the topic. The PgUp key is used to return to previous screens and eventually to the previous menus.

When information screens are displayed, the cursor is located in an input template on the screen's last line. Any command or function name can be entered and the help program will immediately display the corresponding information screen.

The Esc key terminates the help facility and returns the dot prompt.

Tips:

1. The F1 function key always brings up the help facility, that is, the F1 key cannot be reprogrammed with the `SET FUNCTION` command, or with the `F1 =` command in the CONFIG.DB file.
2. If the HELP.DBS file is erased from the dBASE disk or subdirectory, the help facility will not be available. (On a two floppy disk system, the HELP.DBS file should be on the second disk.)
3. `HELP` and `ASSIST` are not equivalent commands. `ASSIST` aids in building and executing actual dBASE commands; `HELP` merely describes those commands.
4. If an invalid command is entered (that is, the syntax is improper), dBASE will automatically offer help unless `SET HELP` is OFF. A negative response to this prompt returns to the dot prompt, whereas a positive response brings up the online help facility. (If the HELP.DBS file has been erased, help will still be offered, although none will be forthcoming and the dot prompt will reappear.)
5. Even if `SET HELP` is OFF, the help facility can still be accessed by typing in `HELP` at the dot prompt, or by pressing F1. In other words, the `SET HELP OFF` command controls the offer of help when command syntax is incorrect, but does not affect its availability.

Related Topics: `SET HELP`
`ASSIST`
`SET FUNCTION`

IF

Syntax:

```
IF <condition>
   <command>
[ELSE
   <command>]
ENDIF
```

Discussion: `IF...ELSE...ENDIF` is a structured programming command that evaluates a condition and selects a course of action depending on whether the condition is true or false. Indenting commands under both `IF` and `ELSE` is not required by dBASE, but is highly recommended to make the program easier to read and debug.

The `IF` command may be written with or without a corresponding `ELSE`. In its simplest form,

```
IF <condition>
   <command>
ENDIF
```

every command between `IF` and `ENDIF` is executed if the condition is true. If, however, the condition is false, control passes immediately to the command after `ENDIF`.

In its more complex form,

```
IF <condition>
   <command>
ELSE
   <command>
ENDIF
```

the command tests the condition and executes the commands between `IF` and `ELSE` if the condition is true. If, however, the condition is false it executes the commands between `ELSE` and `ENDIF`. In either case, after the appropriate set of commands has been executed, control passes to the first command after `ENDIF`.

The condition in an `IF` statement may be any dBASE expression that can assume either a true or false value. For example:

- A *comparison* using relational operators:

```
IF age < 40
```

- A *compound condition* using .AND., .OR., or .NOT.:

```
If age < 40 .AND. city = 'Chicago'
```

- A *logical variable*:

```
IF bill_pd
```

- A *function* that results in a value of true or false:

```
IF DELETED()
```

or

```
IF EOF()
```

The ELSE clause is optional, but when present, must be coded on a line by itself. ENDIF, however, is always required to mark the end of the decision structure and also must be coded on a line by itself.

The commands within the IF...ELSE...ENDIF structure may be any valid dBASE command, including another IF structure. Including one IF command within another is called *nesting*, an example of which is shown below:

```
IF condition1
   <commands if condition1 is true>
ELSE
   IF condition2
      <commands if condition2 is true>
   ELSE
      <commands if condition2 is false>
   ENDIF   (condition2)
ENDIF   (condition1)
```

In this example, condition 2 is evaluated only if condition 1 is false. Note that each IF has its own ENDIF, and that the entire second IF command (the IF and its associated ELSE and ENDIF) is located completely within the first IF structure.

We recommend that you not go beyond three levels of nested IFs. Decision structures more complex than that should be coded with a DO CASE command.

Tips:

1. There may only be one ELSE statement for each IF...ENDIF.
2. ELSE and/or ENDIF refer to the closest unpaired IF. Be sure that all ELSE clauses are properly paired with the appropriate IF and that there is an ENDIF for every IF.
3. Any text coded on the same line as ENDIF is ignored (that is, treated as a comment). Accordingly, parenthetical information can be included to indicate a reference to the associated IF, and is especially helpful with multiple and/or nested IFs. For example:

```
IF EOF()
   STORE .F. TO MVAR
ELSE
   IF bill_pd
      ? 'The bill is paid'
   ELSE
      ? 'The bill is not paid'
   ENDIF (bill_pd)
ENDIF (eof)
```

4. Compound conditions may be evaluated by using the logical operators .AND. and .OR. However, the field name or memory variable must be repeated in each portion of a complex clause, even if the field or variable name is the same, for example,

```
IF choice = 0 .OR. choice = 9
```

5. The proper syntax for a logical field or variable is IF <logical name> or IF .NOT. <logical name>. In other words, you may *not* use IF <logical name> = .T. or IF <logical name> = .F.
6. Consistent indentation (typically, three spaces) within the structure is strongly recommended.

IIF FUNCTION

Syntax: IIF(<logical expression>,<expression1>,<expression2>)

Discussion: The IIF() function provides conditional processing in situations where IF...ELSE...ENDIF cannot be used, such as at the dot prompt, in report forms, or in mailing label forms. The function evaluates the logical expression and returns either expression 1 if it is true or expression 2, if it is false.

The logical expression can be anything that evaluates to true or false. Expressions 1 and 2 can be expressions, constants, fields, or memory variables of any type, so long as they are both *the same type*; that is, expression 1 cannot be a numeric field if expression 2 is a character field.

Tips:

1. The IF command is more powerful and more conducive to structured programming. It should be used exclusively in program files in lieu of a comparable IIF() function. IIF() should be used only in instances where the other is not possible.
2. The IIF() function is useful as a *content entry* in report forms and/or mailing label forms. Consider, for example, the situation in which a middle initial is not always present and where it is desirable to eliminate the extra spaces that would appear if no initial were supplied. An IFF() function could be used as a content entry to as follows:

Command is entered on one line
```
IIF(initial = " ",TRIM(firstname) + " " + lastname,
     TRIM(firstname) + " " + initial + " " + lastname)
```

3. The IIF() function can prevent calculations that do not make sense, as well as calculations whose execution would produce erroneous results. The LIST command shown below lists the last name, salary, and percent salary increase (where appropriate) for all employees in the currently selected database file.

Command is entered on one line
```
LIST lastname,salary,
     (IIF(oldsalary=0,0,(salary-oldsalary/oldsalary*100)
```

The percent salary increase is computed only for employees who have a nonzero value for old salary (that is, new employees would not have an old salary and hence no increase would be determined). Note, too, that in the absence of the IIF() function, any attempt to compute a percent salary increase where old salary does not exist would result in division by zero.

4. The IIF() function can be used to enhance the unappealing .T. or .F. normally displayed for logical variables. Consider:

Command is entered on one line
```
LIST lastname,
     IIF(fee_paid,"Fee is paid","Fee is still owed")
```

The LIST command would display the last name of every person in the file, together with an indication of whether or not the fee has been paid. The results of such a command are much clearer and more attractive than a display showing just a .T. or a .F.

5. Nested (embedded) IIF() functions are also possible, though in general are not recommended. Consider:

```
IIF(size = "S", 25,IIF(size = "M",50,100))
```

The function will return a value of 25 if size equals "S", 50 if size = "M", and 100 otherwise.

Related Topics: IF...ELSE...ENDIF
                     CREATE REPORT
                     CREATE LABEL

INDEX ON

Syntax: INDEX ON <key expression> TO <filename> [UNIQUE]

Discussion: The INDEX ON command creates (and opens) an index file for the currently selected database, allowing it to be processed in a logical sequence different from the physical order in which the records were appended. The index contains only the record number and the corresponding value of the key expression for *every* record in the database file. The newly created index is assigned a default extension of NDX, unless another extension is explicitly specified.

The key expression can be a single field (character, numeric, or date), or it can be an expression involving several fields, up to 100 characters long. However, a key expression consisting of multiple fields must be a character expression, requiring that numeric and date fields be converted to character data through string and date conversion functions respectively. Multiple keys are listed in the expression according to their importance, with the most important (primary) key listed first, the next most important (secondary) key listed next, on down to the least important key.

Four examples of the INDEX command are shown:

```
INDEX ON saldate TO index1
INDEX ON lastname TO index2
INDEX ON location + lastname TO index3
INDEX ON location + STR(salary,6) TO index4
```

These commands create indexes sequenced in chronological order according to saldate (INDEX1.NDX), alphabetic order by last name (INDEX2.NDX), alphabetic order by location and within each location in alphabetic order by last name (INDEX3.NDX), and alphabetic order by location and within each location by increasing salary (INDEX4.NDX).

The UNIQUE option results in an index file that has only one entry for each value of the key field. Thus, if two or more records in a file have the same key value, only the first record encountered will be included in the index. Specifying the UNIQUE clause produces the same results as indexing the file when SET UNIQUE is ON.

Tips:

1. Logical and memo fields cannot be used in the key expression of an INDEX command, either as a single field or as part of a complex expression.

2. An index does not physically reorder the database file. It merely specifies a logical order in which the file is to be processed.

3. In an index whose key expression consists of both a character and a date field, the date *cannot* simply be converted to character data with a DTOC function. This is because character data are sequenced by comparing the characters one by one, beginning with the leftmost character, implying that all dates beginning with 01 come before dates beginning with 02, regardless of the year; for example, 01/01/88 would come before 02/15/87. Correcting this problem requires either a SET DATE ANSI command to rearrange the date into yy.mm.dd format, for example,

```
SET DATE ANSI
INDEX ON location + DTOC(hiredate) TO locdate
```

or an INDEX ON command with the following key:

Command is entered on one line

```
INDEX ON location + SUBSTR(hiredate,7,2) +
   SUBSTR(hiredate,1,2) + SUBSTR(hiredate,4,2) TO
   locdate
```

The latter command sequences by location, and within the same location, by characters 7 and 8 of hire date (the year), then within each year by characters 1 and 2 of hire date (the month), then within each month by characters 4 and 5 of hire date (the day).

4. An index can be created in *descending* numeric order by specifying a key expression that converts each key field value to its negative equivalent, as in

```
INDEX ON -salary TO dsalary
```

or

```
INDEX ON -1 * salary TO dsalary
```

5. An index can be created according to the results of a calculation, for example,

```
INDEX ON (new-old)/old * 100 TO increase
```

However, although the index is based on the results of the calculation, the database file has not been modified to include the result. Hence, to display the result, the calculation itself would have to be included in a DISPLAY or LIST command or as the column contents in a report form file.

6. Updating a database file will automatically update all active indexes (those opened in the most recent USE...INDEX or SET INDEX TO command). If, however, there are more than seven indexes for a database file (the maximum allowed open at one time), or if some or all the indexes were not open at the time of the update, the nonopen indexes must be subsequently opened and reindexed. This is extremely important because opening an out-of-date index does not produce an error message, just unreliable information.

7. The INDEX ON command always operates on the *entire* database; that is, indexing a subset of records is not possible. Records marked for deletion are included in the index (even if SET DELETED is ON), as are records not matching any active filter condition.

8. An index can be created on any character, numeric, or date field in the file structure, even if that field is not included in an active field list.

9. The INDEX ON command implicitly closes any active indexes in the currently selected work area and opens only the index it creates.

10. The SORT command need not be used to create a file whose physical and logical order are the same, as sorting a large database file is quite time consuming. Index the file instead, then with the index open, copy the file to a new file. The original database file can then be deleted and the new file renamed with the name of the original file. The same procedure should be used periodically with frequently updated index files because processing slows remarkably as the logical and physical order grow more disparate.

11. If the target file of an INDEX ON command has the same name as an existing file and SET SAFETY is ON, dBASE will ask before overwriting the file. If, however, SET SAFETY is OFF, the file will be overwritten with no warning.
12. Every dBASE application should have a utility program (using INDEX ON rather than REINDEX) that, as part of its file recovery procedure, rebuilds every index.

Related Topics: REINDEX
SORT
SET INDEX
SET ORDER
SET UNIQUE
USE

INSERT

Syntax: INSERT [BLANK][BEFORE]

Discussion: The INSERT command displays an input template enabling a single record to be added to the active database *immediately below the current record*. Hence, if the command is issued when the record pointer is on record 6, an input template for record 7 will be displayed, and all the remaining records will be renumbered after the insertion. Only one record at a time may be inserted, so that after data for the new record have been entered, control is returned to the dot prompt.

Data is entered in much the same way as in the APPEND mode, except that paging to previous or subsequent records is not allowed. (See Table NB.2 in the discussion on the APPEND command.) Pressing Ctrl W or Ctrl End saves the inserted record, whereas the Esc key cancels the insertion.

Including the BLANK clause causes a blank (empty) record to be inserted immediately below the current record *without* displaying the input template. The record pointer is re-positioned at the blank record, at which point an EDIT, BROWSE, or REPLACE command can be used to enter data.

Specifying the BEFORE clause inserts the new record immediately *above* the current record rather than below. BEFORE and BLANK may appear together in the same command, for example, INSERT BLANK BEFORE inserts a blank record above the current record.

Tips:

1. Multiple records can be appended if the INSERT command is issued when the record pointer is on the last record. In other words, INSERT will function the same way as APPEND when the record pointer is on the last record.
2. If an index is active when the INSERT command is issued, the new record will be appended to the end of the database regardless of where the record pointer is positioned.
3. If a field list has been established with the SET FIELDS command, the input template will contain only the active fields. The exception is when the INSERT command is issued with the record pointer on the last record, in which case the template contains all fields, whether or not they are active.

Related Topics: APPEND
SET FIELDS

JOIN

Syntax: `JOIN WITH <alias> TO <filename> FOR <condition>`
`        [FIELDS <field list>]`

Discussion: The `JOIN` command creates a new database (DBF) file by merging records from the currently selected database with records from a second open database, as identified in the WITH clause. The new file structure contains all the fields in the current database, together with all the fields in the second database, unless a field list is included. In that case, the new file contains only the listed fields. (Duplicate field names are not permitted so that if the same field name is present in both files, only the field from the currently selected file is copied.)

The joining process begins by setting the record pointer to the first record in the currently selected database. Every record in the second file is checked against this record and, whenever the specified condition is satisfied, data from the two records is combined to form a single record in the new (joined) file. After all the records in the second file have been evaluated, the record pointer is positioned to the next record in the current database. The second file is again searched record by record for true conditions, and again, whenever one is found, data from the two records is combined to form a new record in the joined file. This process is repeated for every record in the currently selected database.

Consider, for example, a banking application that maintains two distinct files, for accounts and for customers. (One customer can have several accounts, but each account can be associated with only one customer.) The commands

```
SELECT 2
USE customer                    Command is entered on one line
SELECT 1
USE account
JOIN WITH customer TO custacct
    FOR cust_id = customer-<cust_id
```

will copy data from the existing customer and account files to a new file, CUSTACCT.DBF, which has as many records as the original account file. However, each record in the new file will have the corresponding customer data along with the account data.

Tips: _____

1. The joining process is expensive in terms of time and space requirements, especially when large databases are involved. The `SET RELATION` command provides a faster and more efficient way to relate two databases.
2. The maximum number of fields in the joined file cannot exceed 128, and any fields beyond this number are lost from the second file. For example, if the currently selected and the second database files contain 100 and 50 fields, respectively, only the first 28 fields from the WITH file are included. The rest are discarded.

Related Topics: `SET RELATION`

LABEL FORM

Syntax: `LABEL FORM <label filename> [<scope>] [SAMPLE]`
`            [WHILE <condition>] [FOR <condition>]`
`            [TO PRINT] [TO FILE <filename>]`

Discussion: The LABEL FORM command merges data from the currently selected database with the specified label format file, printing the generated labels to the screen. The default scope is ALL so that one label will be created for every record from the database, unless a scope, FOR, or WHILE clause is included in the command. The labels will be printed according to the logical sequence of the master index or, if no index is open, according to the physical order of the currently selected database.

After the labels are generated, the record pointer is repositioned to the end-of-file, unless NEXT is indicated as the scope parameter or a WHILE condition is included. Specifying NEXT as the scope parameter repositions the record pointer to the last record listed (unless NEXT goes beyond the end-of-file, in which case, the record pointer is set to the end-of-file). Including a WHILE condition moves the record pointer one record beyond the last record meeting the specified condition.

The TO PRINT clause produces the labels on the printer as well as on the screen. (If the printer is not on line, an error message will be displayed.) The SAMPLE clause provides the opportunity to align labels in the printer before the actual labels are generated, by printing a dummy label with asterisks to indicate positioning. The program then pauses and asks if another dummy label should be printed.

The TO FILE clause prints the labels to an ASCII text file.

Tips:

1. The LABEL FORM command is not restricted to mailing labels per se, but can also be used in other applications where a "mailing label" format is appropriate; for example, Rolodex cards.
2. All necessary database files and their associated indexes must be opened before the LABEL FORM command is issued. Additionally, if the label form references fields from files in unselected work areas, the proper relationships must have been previously set.
3. Mailing labels are generated only for those records meeting the filter condition. Similarly, labels are not generated for any records marked for deletion when SET DELETED is ON.
4. A syntax error results if the label form includes fields not specified in the active field list, that is, all fields in the label form must have been activated with a SET FIELDS command.
5. The SET CONSOLE OFF command will suppress the screen display during printing. Remember also to set the console back on when printing is complete so that processing can proceed normally, for example,

```
SET CONSOLE OFF
LABEL FORM employee TO PRINT
SET CONSOLE ON
```

6. ASCII characters may be sent to the printer before actual printing, perhaps to specify compressed print or some other option such as

```
SET PRINT ON
? CHR(15)
LABEL FORM employee TO PRINT
? CHR(18)
SET PRINT OFF
```

Although the ASCII character 15 is shown in the example, it is by no means universally used by all printers. (Consult your own printer's manual for specifics.) Remember, too, to restore the printer to normal printing as soon as the labels are completed.

Related Topics: CHR()
                 CREATE/MODIFY LABEL
                 REPORT FORM
                 SET CONSOLE
                 SET DELETED
                 SET FILTER
                 SET FIELDS

LEN FUNCTION

Syntax: LEN(<character expression>)

Discussion: The LEN() function returns the number of characters in the specified character string. The character expression in the function can be a character field, memory variable, character expression enclosed in quotes, concatenated character expression, or the result of a function that returns a string. The LEN() function is illustrated in the table below, in which "Chris" and "Anderson" have been stored to the memory variables, mfirst and mlast, respectively.

Function	Value
LEN(mfirst)	5
LEN(mlast)	8
LEN(mfirst + mlast)	13
LEN("Chris Anderson")	14

Tips:

1. Specifying a *character field* as the argument returns the field length as defined in the file structure, not the length of the data entered in the field. Specifying a *memory variable*, however, returns the length of the data entered into the variable.
2. The TRIM() function physically deletes trailing blanks so that the LEN() function no longer counts them. For example, if Milgrom is stored in the character field lastname (defined as a 12-position field in the file structure), the functions LEN(lastname) and LEN(TRIM(lastname)) return lengths of 12 and 7, respectively.
3. The LEN() function can be used to center messages, for example,

        STORE "Please enter another option" TO message
        @ 20,(80 - LEN(message))/2 SAY message

The length of the message is first subtracted from 80 (the number of characters that can fit across the screen) to determine the number of blank spaces remaining on the line. This value is then divided by two to obtain the starting column, effectively centering the message.

Related Topics: TRIM()
                 @...SAY

LIST

Syntax: LIST [OFF] [<scope>] <expression list>]
             [WHILE <condition>][FOR <condition>] [TO PRINT]

Discussion: The LIST command displays the data in the currently selected database. The default scope is ALL, and the expression list defaults to every field in the file, so that LIST with no additional parameters displays every field for every record. A FOR and/or WHILE condition can be included to limit the number of records displayed to just those meeting the condition. Similarly, specifying an expression list will restrict the display to the fields listed. Records are listed in the physical order of the database file unless there is an active index, in which case they are listed according to the logical sequence of the index.

After listing, the *record pointer is repositioned to the end-of-file,* unless NEXT is indicated as the scope parameter or a WHILE condition is included. Specifying NEXT as the scope parameter repositions the record pointer to the last record listed (unless NEXT goes beyond the end-of-file, in which case the record pointer is set to the end-of-file). Including a WHILE condition moves the record pointer one record beyond the last record meeting the specified condition.

The screen display is always preceded by a heading line which includes the individual field names (or expressions). The display width of each expression is determined by either the field width, as established by the file structure, or the width of the heading, whichever is greater.

The contents of a memo field are not displayed unless the field name is specified in an expression list. The default display width for a memo field is 50 columns, but can be modified with the SET MEMOWIDTH command. If no expression list is specified, a memo field has the word "memo" displayed as the field contents.

The OFF parameter suppresses the display of the record number. The TO PRINT clause echoes the results of the command to the printer.

Tips:

1. The LIST command always begins with the first record in the file (or the first record according to the active index) unless NEXT is specified as the scope parameter. Including NEXT causes the command to begin with the record at the current position of the record pointer.
2. When a record is too long to be displayed on one line, the output is wrapped to the next line(s), making it difficult to determine which data belongs to which field, especially when multiple records are displayed. The SET FIELDS command or an expression list can be used to limit the display to the essential fields and avoid the wrap to the next line(s).
3. The heading line shows the field names and expressions exactly as they were entered in the command line. If the command was typed in uppercase letters, the heading line will also be uppercase.
4. The SET HEADING OFF command can suppress the heading line, a useful procedure when using a long or complex expression.
5. Deleted records will not be listed if SET DELETED is ON. The same principle holds for records not matching the condition set by a SET FILTER command; that is, records not matching the filter condition are treated as if they were not in the file.
6. Fields from database files in other than the currently selected work area can be displayed by including the file alias with the field name in the command, as in

```
LIST ssn,lname,location->loccode
```

This is usually only done when a SET RELATION command is in effect.
7. The LIST command does not pause between screens when the display requires more than a single screen; that is, the display continues to scroll until the last record is listed. (This is the major difference between LIST and DISPLAY ALL, which pauses every 20 lines.) You can, however, press Ctrl S or Ctrl NumLock to interrupt the listing, then press any key to continue. You can also press the Esc key to cancel the command entirely.

Related Topics: DISPLAY
SET DELETED
SET FIELDS
SET FILTER
SET HEADING
SET MEMOWIDTH
SET RELATION

LIST HISTORY

Syntax: LIST HISTORY [TO PRINT]

Discussion: The LIST HISTORY command displays the same information as the DISPLAY HISTORY command, but without pausing between screens. (See the DISPLAY HISTORY command for additional information.)

LIST MEMORY

Syntax: LIST MEMORY [TO PRINT]

Discussion: The LIST MEMORY command displays the same information as the DISPLAY MEMORY command, but without pausing between screens. (See the DISPLAY MEMORY command for additional information.)

LIST STATUS

Syntax: LIST STATUS [TO PRINT]

Discussion: The LIST STATUS command displays the same information as the DISPLAY STATUS command, but without pausing between screens. (See the DISPLAY STATUS command for additional information.)

LIST STRUCTURE

Syntax: LIST STRUCTURE [TO PRINT]

Discussion: The LIST STRUCTURE command displays the same information as the DISPLAY STRUCTURE command, but without pausing between screens. (See the DISPLAY STRUCTURE command for additional information.)

LOCATE

Syntax: `LOCATE [<scope>][WHILE <condition>][FOR <condition>]`

Discussion: The `LOCATE` command searches the currently selected database for the first record meeting the specified FOR condition. A successful search displays the record number (as long as `SET TALK` is ON) and repositions the record pointer to that record. If, however, the search is unsuccessful (that is, no record is found), the message "End of Locate Scope" is displayed and the record pointer is repositioned at the end-of-file (or end-of-scope, if one was specified).

The `LOCATE` command begins its search with the first record in the file and continues until a record is found or the end-of-file is reached, whichever occurs first. Including a scope parameter and/or a WHILE condition will, however, alter the way in which the search is performed. A scope of NEXT begins at the current (rather than first) record and continues only through the specified number of records. A scope of REST also begins at the current record, but continues through the rest of the file (or until a record is found). Finally, a WHILE condition also begins at the current record, but continues only until the condition is no longer true.

Additional records meeting the search condition are found with the `CONTINUE` command, that is, `CONTINUE` causes dBASE to search for the next record meeting the same condition as in the most recently executed `LOCATE` command. A successful search moves the record pointer to that record, from where another `CONTINUE` command may be issued, and so on, until eventually all the records meeting the condition have been located.

Tips:

1. Any field, except a memo field, can be included in the search condition. Moreover, `LOCATE` can be used to search for values equal to, greater than, or less than the specified criteria and does *not* require a master index. `FIND`, on the other hand, can only search the key field of the master index and for equal values.
2. The `LOCATE` command does not display the found record, but merely repositions the record pointer to that record. A subsequent `DISPLAY` command is necessary to view the record.
3. Only one search condition can be in effect at any one time in any one work area, although a different condition can be in effect for each of the 10 available work areas. If a particular work area is left and then later reselected, the last search condition in that area is "remembered." Be sure, however, that the record pointer has not been repositioned since the last record was found, or the results of the search may be unreliable when subsequent `CONTINUE` commands are issued.
4. When `SET EXACT` is OFF a search will be successful if the characters in the search string match the characters in the same positions in the field value, even if the strings are of different lengths, for example,

   `LOCATE FOR lastname = 'B'`

   will find the first record in which the last name begins with the letter "B". Note, however, that case is always considered, and that "B" does not match "b", even when `SET EXACT` is OFF.
5. The `LOCATE` operation ignores records not meeting the filter condition. Similarly, records marked for deletion are also ignored when `SET DELETED` is ON.
6. The search condition can include a field *not* specified in the field list established by a `SET FIELDS` command.

CONTINUE
FIND
SEEK
SET DELETED
SET EXACT
SET FILTER
SET FIELDS

LOWER FUNCTION

Syntax: LOWER(<character string>)

Discussion: The LOWER() function converts all the uppercase letters in the specified character string to their lowercase equivalents. The argument may be a character string, character field or memory variable, or a concatenated string expression, as shown in the following table:

Function	Nature of the Argument
LOWER("THIS IS A STRING")	Character string
LOWER(lastname)	Character field
LOWER(memname)	Memory variable
LOWER("TODAY IS" + DTOC(DATE()))	Concatenated string

Tips:

1. The LOWER(), UPPER(), and SUBSTR() functions can be combined to convert the initial character in a field to uppercase, and the remaining characters to lowercase, for example,

Command is entered on one line

```
REPLACE lname WITH UPPER(SUBSTR(lname,1,1)) +
    LOWER(SUBSTR(lname,2))
```

A single REPLACE command can be used to make the substitution for every record in the currently selected database by specifying a scope of ALL.

2. Most systems allow the user to respond with upper or lowercase letters, complicating the data validation process. The problem is solved by converting the response to a uniform standard (either all upper- or all lowercase), and then testing for only one set of permitted responses. For example, in a system in which A, B, C, or D or a, b, c, or d are valid, the following code would suffice:

```
@10,20 GET response PICTURE 'A'
STORE LOWER(response) to response
IF response < 'a' .OR. response > 'd'
    @12,2 SAY 'Please respond with a, b, c, or d'
ENDIF
```

Related Topics: UPPER()
SUBSTR()

LTRIM FUNCTION

Syntax: `LTRIM(<character expression>)`

Discussion: The `LTRIM()` function strips leading blanks from a character expression. The expression may be a character field or memory variable, character string enclosed in quotes, or a concatenated string. The `LTRIM()` function is especially useful when working with a string produced as a result of the `STR()` conversion function, because the latter often contains leading blanks. Consider for example, the difference in two concatenated strings, with and without the LTRIM function.

Without the LTRIM function:

```
? "Your raise is " + STR(raise,7) + " dollars"
Your raise is   750 dollars"
```

With the LTRIM function:

```
? "Your raise is " + LTRIM(STR(raise,7)) + " dollars"
Your raise is 750 dollars
```

Tips:

1. The `LTRIM()` function can improve the appearance of report forms and/or mailing labels by using the function in a content entry to concatenate character data.

Related Topics:
```
CREATE LABEL
CREATE REPORT
RTRIM()
STR()
TRIM()
```

MAX FUNCTION

Syntax: `MAX(<numeric expression-1>,<numeric expression-2>)`

Discussion: The `MAX()` function returns the larger of two expressions, each of which may be a numeric field, memory variable, constant, or complex expression. The function `MAX(1000,salary * .05)`, for example, multiplies the salary value in the current record by .05, compares it to 1000, and returns the larger of the two values.

The `MAX()` function can be used for conditional processing or display purposes at the dot prompt, within a report or label form (as a content entry), or in any other situation where an `IF` command cannot be used. For example, records can be updated from the dot prompt to reflect a 5 percent across-the-board salary increase, with a minimum raise of $1000, using the command

```
REPLACE ALL salary WITH MAX(salary+1000,salary*1.05)
```

Similarly, a report form can be constructed to reflect the proposed salaries by entering the same `MAX()` function for column contents.

Tips: _____

1. The MAX() function in and of itself *cannot* be used to find the record having the maximum value in a particular field. However, a program using the function can be written to do so as follows:

```
USE solemp
STORE salary TO maxsal
DO WHILE .NOT. EOF()
    STORE MAX(maxsal,salary) TO maxsal
    SKIP
ENDDO
```

Related Topics: IIF()
                       MIN()
                       IF

MIN FUNCTION

Syntax: MIN(<numeric expression 1>,<numeric expression 2>)

Discussion: The MIN() function returns the smaller of two expressions, each of which may be a numeric field, memory variable, constant, or complex expression. The function MIN(1000,salary * .05), for example, multiplies the salary value in the current record by .05, compares it to 1000, and returns the smaller of the two values.

The MIN() function can be used for conditional processing or display purposes at the dot prompt, within a report or label form (as a content entry), or in any other situation where an IF command cannot be used. For example, records can be updated from the dot prompt to reflect a 5 percent across-the-board salary increase, with a maximum raise of $1000, using the command

```
REPLACE ALL salary WITH MIN(salary+1000,salary*1.05)
```

Similarly, a report form can be constructed to reflect the new salary level by entering the same MIN() function for column contents.

Tips: _____

1. The MIN() function in and of itself *cannot* be used to find the record having the minimum value in a particular field. However, a program using the function can be written to do so, as follows:

```
USE solemp
STORE salary TO minsal
DO WHILE .NOT. EOF()
    STORE MIN(minsal,salary) TO minsal
    SKIP
ENDDO
```

Related Topics: IIF()
MAX()
IF

MODIFY COMMAND

Syntax: MODIFY COMMAND <filename>

Discussion: The command, MODIFY COMMAND, activates the dBASE word processor. As such, it is unlike any of the other MODIFY commands (MODIFY LABEL, MODIFY REPORT, MODIFY STRUCTURE, and so on) because its primary function is to create and/ or edit program (.PRG) and format (.FMT) files. MODIFY COMMAND can also be used to create or edit any standard ASCII text file.

MODIFY COMMAND may be invoked with or without specifying the desired file name, that is, if no file name is specified, dBASE will prompt for one. dBASE will then search for the named file and, if it exists, load it into memory and place it on the screen for editing. If, however, no file with that name exists, a new file is created and the screen cleared for text entry. The words "Edit: ⟨filename⟩" appear on the top line of the screen to let you know that you are in the editor.

Text is entered as it is with any word processor (Table NB.5 summarizes the basic editing functions). MODIFY COMMAND is adequate for entering and editing short program files, but lacks many of the advanced features needed for creating longer, more complex programs (such as a search and replace capability, and the ability to perform block operations).

Tips: _____

1. The drive and directory designators may be specified with the file name to create and/ or edit files in other than the default directory.

■ **TABLE NB.5**
Keystroke Combinations for MODIFY COMMAND

Keystroke	Task
→ or ←	Moves cursor one character to the right or left
↑ or ↓	Moves cursor to the previous or next line
F1	Toggles cursor menu on/off
Ctrl-Z	Moves cursor to beginning of line
Ctrl-B	Moves cursor to end of line
PgDn	Scrolls screen forward 18 lines
PgUp	Scrolls screen backward 18 lines
Ctrl-6, Del	Deletes character cursor is on
Ctrl-KB	Reformats paragraph
Ctrl-KF	Finds first occurrence of a specified string
Ctrl-KL	Finds next occurrence of string found with Ctrl-KF
Ctrl-KR	Reads in an external file at cursor
Ctrl-KW	Writes entire file to an external file
Ctrl-N	Inserts a blank line at cursor
Ctrl-Y	Deletes line cursor is on
Ctrl-V	Toggles between insert and replacement modes
Ctrl-Q, Esc	Exits to dot prompt without saving changes
Ctrl-W, Ctrl-End	Exits to dot prompt and saves changes

2. Any time an existing file is edited, and the edited version is saved, the previous version is saved as a backup file with a .BAK extension.

3. MODIFY COMMAND supplies a default extension of .PRG when a file is created. If a different extension (for example, FMT) is desired, it must be explicitly specified when assigning the file name. Note also that in searching for the file named in the MODIFY COMMAND instruction, dBASE will look only for files with a .PRG extension unless a different extension is explicitly specified, such as MODIFY COMMAND STOCK.FMT.

4. The dBASE word processor can process files only to a maximum length of 5000 bytes. Accordingly, larger files require the nondocument (unformatted) mode of a word processor. Should you attempt to work with a file larger than 5000 bytes in the dBASE word processor, a warning message will be issued, and sections of the text may be unreliable or, worse yet, lost when the file is saved.

5. An external word processor may be accessed from within dBASE (assuming sufficient memory is available) by issuing a RUN command, or through a TEDIT command in the CONFIG.DB file. (The latter specifies that an external word processor is to be loaded rather than the dBASE word processor whenever a MODIFY COMMAND is issued.) It is usually more convenient to use the RUN command to access the external word processor, rather than affect the more permanent change accomplished by the TEDIT command. In this way, MODIFY COMMAND can be used with the dBASE editor for short programs and simple editing and the RUN command with an external word processor (which takes considerably more time to load) for larger files or advanced features. Another option is to use a RAM-resident utility program, such as Sidekick, as the text editor. RAM-resident programs are always present in memory, and consequently access is extremely fast and convenient.

6. Every dBASE command must begin on a new line and be terminated with a hard carriage return. The latter is produced by pressing the enter key and is indicated on the monitor by a < symbol in the rightmost column. Lengthy commands, however (a dBASE command may contain up to 254 characters), may extend over several lines. As commands are entered, they are automatically word-wrapped to the next line when column 66 is reached. In this instance, the rightmost column is left blank (to indicate a soft carriage return) and the < symbol will not appear until the enter key is pressed at the end of the logical command line.

    A command line may also be manually divided at any point by typing a semicolon (;), pressing the enter key, and continuing the command on the next line. The semicolon prevents a hard carriage return from being inserted. Remember that the command continues with the next line's first character and hence you must be careful not to omit any necessary spaces.

    A correct and incorrect example of a manually divided command line are shown below.

    Correct:

    ```
    REPORT FORM location FOR loc = '20';
     .AND. title = '301'
    ```

    Incorrect (no space between 20 and .AND.):

    ```
    REPORT FORM location for loc = '20';
    .AND. title = '301'
    ```

7. Although a line exceeding 65 characters cannot be entered, additional characters (beyond the 65-character limit) may be inserted into existing text up to a maximum of 79 characters per line. You may also read in files with 79 characters per line.

8. Hard copy of a .PRG or .FMT file can be obtained with the command:

    ```
    TYPE <filename> TO PRINT
    ```

9. Memo fields cannot be edited with `MODIFY COMMAND`.
10. `MODIFY FILE` is an alternative syntax for this command. In this form, there is no default extension and so any extension must be explicitly specified.

Related Topics: `CONFIG.DB`
`RUN`
`TYPE`

MODIFY LABEL

Syntax: `MODIFY LABEL`

Discussion: The `MODIFY LABEL` and `CREATE LABEL` commands can be used interchangeably. See `CREATE LABEL`.

MODIFY QUERY

Syntax: `MODIFY QUERY`

Discussion: The `MODIFY QUERY` and `CREATE QUERY` commands can be used interchangeably. See `CREATE QUERY`.

MODIFY REPORT

Syntax: `MODIFY REPORT`

Discussion: The `MODIFY REPORT` and `CREATE REPORT` commands can be used interchangeably. See `CREATE REPORT`.

MODIFY SCREEN

Syntax: `MODIFY SCREEN`

Discussion: The `MODIFY SCREEN` and `CREATE SCREEN` commands can be used interchangeably. See `CREATE SCREEN`.

MODIFY STRUCTURE

Syntax: `MODIFY STRUCTURE`

Discussion: The `MODIFY STRUCTURE` command displays the file structure of the currently selected database allowing new fields to be added and/or existing fields to be edited or deleted. The screen display is the same as for the CREATE command, except that CREATE displays blank input templates whereas MODIFY STRUCTURE shows existing information in the templates. The keystroke combinations for the CREATE command are applicable (see Table NB.4 on page 267), as are the general discussion and the tips.

The MODIFY STRUCTURE command automatically creates a backup copy of the original DBF file and, after the changes have been made, copies the data in the original file to the modified version. The original file is also retained on disk with the same file name and a BAK extension. The rules for copying data back to the modified file are quite precise and depend on whether fields were added or deleted, field names were changed, field widths increased or decreased, and field types altered.

As you might expect, a newly created field will be left blank in the copied file, whereas data for a deleted field will be irretrievably lost. Changing the name of an existing field will produce a prompt asking if the original data should be copied to the renamed field. A response of "Yes" will copy the data, whereas a response of "No" will result in its loss.

Increasing an existing field's width causes no problems. Decreasing the width of an existing field will truncate *character* data too long to fit in the shortened field and will fill *numeric* fields with asterisks if the data no longer fits. Changing the field type does not result in data loss as long as the original data is consistent with the new type (for example, both date fields and numeric fields can be changed to character fields without losing data. However, a character field containing alphabetic data cannot be changed to a numeric field without corresponding data loss.)

Tips:

1. Field names and widths should *not* be changed in the same session because data will be lost for the field(s) whose names are changed, even if the widths are not altered for these fields. If it is necessary to modify both names and widths, change the names with one MODIFY STRUCTURE command and the widths with another.
2. Existing indexes may no longer match the database file once the structure has been modified, especially if changes were made to the keys on which the indexes were based. Use the INDEX ON command as a precautionary measure to rebuild existing indexes.
3. Press Ctrl-Home to toggle a menu mode for the MODIFY STRUCTURE command ON and OFF. The menu is convenient when the database structure is very large because it allows direct access to the desired field rather than having to page through every field.

Related Topics: CREATE

MODIFY VIEW

Syntax: MODIFY VIEW

Discussion: The MODIFY VIEW and CREATE VIEW commands can be used interchangeably. See CREATE VIEW.

MONTH FUNCTION

Syntax: MONTH(<date expression>)

Discussion: The MONTH() function returns a numeric value from 1 to 12, corresponding to the month of the specified date expression. The argument in the `MONTH()` function may assume several different forms as shown in the following table:

Function	Nature of the Argument
`MONTH(hiredate)`	Date field
`MONTH(memdate)`	Date memory variable
`MONTH(DATE())`	DATE() function itself
`MONTH(CTOD("12/25/88"))`	CTOD() conversion function
`MONTH(DATE() + 10)`	Expression with date arithmetic

Tips:

The `MONTH()` function works only on date fields, that is, a character date may *not* be used as the argument unless it is first converted with the `CTOD()` conversion function.

Related Topics:

```
CMONTH()
CTOD()
DATE()
DAY()
STR()
YEAR()
```

PACK

Syntax: `PACK`

Discussion: The `PACK` command physically removes all records previously marked for deletion from the active database file. The records are permanently removed and can no longer be recalled (recovered). Note, too, that since there are no scope, FOR, or WHILE clauses associated with the command, *every* marked record is affected.

Tips:

1. Records marked for deletion should be checked before issuing a `PACK` command so that erroneously marked records can be recalled if necessary. You can obtain a listing of the records slated for deletion with either of the following commands:

```
DISPLAY ALL FOR DELETED()
LIST TO PRINT FOR DELETED()
```

2. It is recommended that the `PACK` command be issued with no open indexes, after which all existing indexes must be explicitly updated. You can accomplish the latter with a `SET INDEX` command (to open all of the indexes), followed by a `REINDEX` command to affect the necessary updates.

3. After a `PACK` command has been issued, the space previously taken by the deleted records is freed for use by the system. The space is not technically made available, however, until after the file has been closed.

4. `ZAP` is equivalent to combining a `DELETE ALL` and a `PACK` command. The `ZAP` command will irretrievably remove every record in the database, leaving only an empty file structure.

PRIVATE

Syntax: PRIVATE <memvar list>
                    or
            PRIVATE ALL [LIKE/EXCEPT <skeleton>]

Discussion: The PRIVATE command is used in program files to declare one or more memory variables as local to that program, thus making the memory variable(s) available only to that program or programs that it calls. All PRIVATE memory variables are automatically released from memory as soon as control is passed back to the calling program or the dot prompt, as the case may be.

Tips:

1. A memory variable declared as PRIVATE in one program may have the same name as a memory variable declared PUBLIC in a higher-level program, and changes made to that PRIVATE variable during program processing will not interfere with the original value of the like-named PUBLIC variable. The latter is in fact temporarily "hidden" until the PRIVATE variable is released from memory, at which time it is reinstated with its original values in tact.
2. The upper limit of 256 active memory variables applies to both the PUBLIC and PRIVATE memory variables.
3. The wild card characters used in the skeleton are the asterisk (*) and the question mark (?). The * matches one or more characters from its position to the end of the memory variable name. The ? matches any *single* character in that exact position in the memory variable name.
4. When a program terminates and passes control back to its calling program, all private memory variables are automatically released and no explicit RELEASE ALL command is required. Hence, to preserve the values of PRIVATE variables, a SAVE command should be issued or the variables declared PUBLIC before the program terminates. This is especially helpful in debugging situations.
5. If a RESTORE command is executed from within a program, the restored memory variables are declared PRIVATE. If, on the other hand, the command is executed from the dot prompt, the restored memory variables are declared PUBLIC.
6. ALL LIKE and ALL EXCEPT are mutually exclusive and *cannot* be used in the same command.

Related Topics: PUBLIC
                     RELEASE
                     RESTORE
                     SAVE

PUBLIC

Syntax: PUBLIC <memvar list>

Discussion: The PUBLIC command is used in program files to declare one or more memory variables as global, thereby making them accessible to all programs (including higher level programs) and causing them to be retained in memory even after the program in which they were created terminates. (A memory variable is normally released from memory when the program in which it was created returns control to its calling program or the dot prompt, whichever the case may be.)

Tips:

1. A memory variable declared as PRIVATE in one program may have the same name as a memory variable declared PUBLIC in a higher-level program, and changes made to that PRIVATE variable during program processing will not interfere with the original value of the like-named PUBLIC variable. The latter is in fact temporarily "hidden" until the PRIVATE variable is released from memory, at which time it is reinstated with its original values in tact.
2. The upper limit of 256 active memory variables applies to both the PUBLIC and PRIVATE memory variables.
3. When a program terminates and passes control back to its calling program, all private memory variables are automatically released and no explicit RELEASE ALL command is required. Hence, to preserve the values of PRIVATE variables, a SAVE command should be issued or the variables declared PUBLIC before the program terminates. This is especially helpful in debugging situations.
4. If a RESTORE command is executed from within a program, the restored memory variables are declared PRIVATE. If, on the other hand, the command is executed from the dot prompt, the restored memory variables are declared PUBLIC.
5. A memory variable must be declared PUBLIC before it is initialized (assigned its initial value).
6. All memory variables created at the dot prompt are PUBLIC by default.

Related Topics: PRIVATE
                    RELEASE
                    RESTORE
                    SAVE

QUIT

Syntax: QUIT

Discussion:
The QUIT command closes all open files and returns control to the operating system. The command may be issued at any time and need not be preceded by a CLOSE DATABASES (or similar command). The QUIT command automatically writes to disk all changes made since the files were last closed.

The QUIT command is the *only* safe way to exit from dBASE. Rebooting the system or removing a floppy disk without quitting can damage open files rendering the databases unusable.

Tips:

1. Use QUIT to exit from a custom system so that the user is taken to DOS rather than left stranded at the dot prompt.

READ

Syntax: READ [SAVE]

Discussion: The READ command is used in conjunction with the @...SAY...GET command to create custom screens for full-screen data entry and editing. The READ command initiates the actual data entry process, whereas the @...SAY...GET commands merely map the screen with prompts and input templates. Execution of the READ command positions the cursor at the first input template, from where it can be moved into any of the fields and/or memory variables displayed by the @...GET commands issued since the last READ or CLEAR command.

No data value is stored into its corresponding field or memory variable until the user exits from the full-screen mode by pressing the Esc key or by completing the last input template. Until then, the user may go back and forth between fields, editing data as desired. The program segment below illustrates this concept; it maps the screen, then allows the user to move among all six templates until data entry in the memory variable mcity is completed or the Esc key is pressed. At that time all GETs preceding the READ are cleared, and the cursor can no longer be moved back to those fields for further editing. Consider:

```
CLEAR
@ 2,5 SAY 'Enter last name:' GET mlname
@ 3,5 SAY 'Enter first name:' GET mfname
@ 4,5 SAY 'Enter age:' GET mage
@ 5,5 SAY 'Enter sex:' GET msex
@ 6,5 SAY 'Enter street address:' GET maddress
@ 7,5 SAY 'Enter city:' GET mcity
READ
   .
   .
   .
```

What if, however, the program specifications mandate that the value of msex be validated immediately after input, requiring a READ command (as well as a validation routine) to be inserted immediately below the GET msex command line. Execution of that READ would cause the cursor to be repositioned in the maddress input template (after msex was validated), with the first four input templates now *inaccessible* for further editing.

Specification of the SAVE clause, however, does not clear the GETs so that a subsequent READ activates not only the GETs immediately preceding it, but those preceding the READ SAVE also. Hence, in the same example, inserting a READ SAVE command immediately below the GET msex command line (in lieu of a simple READ) permits the value of msex to be validated without rendering the first four input templates inaccessible. The drawback to this approach is that after the READ SAVE command is executed, the cursor is repositioned in the input template for mlname, requiring the user to cursor through all the data already entered, to return to where data entry left off (with maddress).

A READ command is also used in multi-screen format files to indicate where one screen ends and another begins. The PgUp and PgDn keys can then be used when the format file is active to page back and forth between screens. (Using the READ command is appropriate for format files only and is *not* permitted in program files.)

Tips:

1. It is entirely possible to exceed the maximum number of GETs permitted in a program if the READ SAVE command appears often enough. Issuing a CLEAR GETS command before the maximum is exceeded will alleviate the problem. It is also possible to increase the allowed maximum, from 128 to 1023, with a GETS = command in the CONFIG.DB file.

2. Any dBASE commands physically above a READ SAVE command are not reexecuted, that is, a READ SAVE command makes the previous GETs accessible for data entry, but does not move execution backward in the program.

3. A single data validation procedure, executed after all the data have been entered for an entire record, is often preferable to validating each field immediately after it is entered.

Related Topics:
CLEAR GETS
CREATE SCREEN
@...SAY...GET
SET FORMAT TO

RECALL

Syntax: RECALL [<scope>][WHILE <condition>][FOR <condition>]

Discussion: The RECALL command removes the deletion marker from records slated for deletion, reinstating them as active records in the database. The default scope is one. Thus RECALL, with no parameters, recalls only the record at the current position of the record pointer (assuming that it has been previously marked for deletion; if not, the command has no effect). Including a scope parameter (RECALL NEXT 10), a FOR or WHILE clause (RECALL FOR location = '40'), or a combination of the two (RECALL NEXT 10 FOR location = '40') will recall all previously deleted records within the specified scope and/or that meet the indicated condition.

Tips:

1. The RECALL command has *no* effect once deleted records have been physically removed from the database with the PACK or ZAP command.

2. RECALL ALL has no effect when SET DELETED is ON.

3. If SET DELETED is ON, logically deleted records will not be found in a FIND or LOCATE command, nor will they appear when the file is edited or browsed. Hence, to recall a record when SET DELETED is ON, you must explicitly specify the record number (for example, record 4) in one of two ways:

        RECALL RECORD 4

   or

        GOTO 4
        RECALL

4. When in the EDIT or BROWSE modes, Ctrl U acts as a toggle switch that recalls/deletes records.

RECNO FUNCTION

Syntax: RECNO ()

Discussion: The RECNO() function returns the record number of the record at the current position of the record pointer in the currently selected database. The command ? RECNO() displays the record number on the screen.

Tips:

1. Any attempt to move the record pointer beyond the last record in the file repositions it to the end-of-file marker, with a record number one greater than that of the last record. By contrast, any attempt to move the record pointer above the first record leaves it positioned on the first record.
2. The RECNO() function returns a value of one for an empty database.

Related Topics: BOF()
EOF()

REINDEX

Syntax: REINDEX

Discussion: The REINDEX command rebuilds all open index files in the currently selected work area, using the original key expressions stored with the index. The command is used primarily to update indexes that were closed when records were added to or deleted from the associated database, or when existing records had their key fields edited. (Indexes open when a database file is updated are automatically updated themselves. Unopened indexes, however, become immediately obsolete when the database file is updated and must be rebuilt to reflect the changes.)

Tips:

1. All index files listed in the USE...INDEX command or the SET INDEX TO command are considered open, and hence will be automatically updated.
2. Opening an index that is not current will not necessarily produce an error message. However, using such an index may cause inconsistent and/or incorrect information and should be avoided.
3. Every dBASE custom application should, as part of its file recovery procedure, have a utility for rebuilding all its index files. Further, the indexes should be rebuilt from scratch with INDEX ON, rather than merely reindexed. (INDEX ON is recommended because

it is possible that damage to the index files would have rendered dBASE unable to read the index keys properly.)

4. The PACK command automatically reindexes all open index files.

5. An index file originally created with an INDEX ON command that included a UNIQUE clause (or one created when SET UNIQUE was ON) will retain its UNIQUE status when reindexed, whether SET UNIQUE is ON or OFF at the time of reindexing.

Related Topics: INDEX ON
PACK
SET INDEX
SET UNIQUE

RELEASE

Syntax: RELEASE <memvar list> [ALL [LIKE/EXCEPT <SKELETON>]]

Discussion: The RELEASE command removes currently active memory variables from memory, thereby freeing the associated space for future memory variables to use. One or more variables can be released with a single command, for example,

```
RELEASE mnumber
RELEASE mlname,mfname,mssn
```

Other forms of the command include:

RELEASE ALL: Releases all currently active memory variables.

RELEASE ALL LIKE: Uses wild card characters (* and ?) to release groups of similarly named memory variables.

RELEASE ALL EXCEPT: Uses wild card characters to release all memory variables except those that match the skeleton.

Once a memory variable is released from memory, it is permanently deleted and cannot be retrieved. A SAVE command can be issued before the RELEASE to save the memory variables to a memory file.

Tips:

1. The wild card characters used in the skeleton are the asterisk (*) and the question mark (?). The * matches one or more characters from its position to the end of the memory variable name. The ? matches any *single* character in that exact position in the memory variable name.

2. CLEAR MEMORY and RELEASE ALL are equivalent when issued from the dot prompt because both release *all* current memory variables. When issued from within a program, however, RELEASE ALL will release only the memory variables created within that specific program (PRIVATE) whereas CLEAR MEMORY still releases all memory variables (PUBLIC and PRIVATE).

3. When a program terminates and passes control back to its calling program, all PRIVATE memory variables are automatically released and no explicit RELEASE ALL command is required. Hence, to preserve the values of PRIVATE variables, a SAVE command should be issued, or the variables declared PUBLIC, before the program terminates.

Related Topics: `CLEAR MEMORY`
`SAVE`
`PUBLIC`
`PRIVATE`

REPLACE

323

REPLACE

Syntax: `REPLACE [<scope>] <field> WITH <exp> [,<field>`
`WITH <exp>,...] [WHILE <condition>][FOR`
`<condition>]`

Discussion: The `REPLACE` command stores new data in specified fields of one or more records in the currently selected database. This, in effect, overwrites the existing data. The default scope is one, so that issuing the command with no additional parameters affects only the record at the current position of the record pointer. Multiple `REPLACE` commands can be issued for the same record. For example, the commands

`REPLACE salary2 WITH salary1`

and

`REPLACE salary1 WITH msalary`

will store the value currently in salary1 in salary2, and then store the value in the memory variable msalary in salary1. Alternatively, the two commands could have been combined into a single command:

`REPLACE salary2 WITH salary1,salary1 WITH msalary`

The data type of the expression being stored must match the field type of the field into which it is stored, otherwise a "Data Type mismatch" error results. A numeric field, for example, cannot be replaced with character data, nor can a character field be replaced with numeric data. In addition, the width of the expression should not be larger than the width of the replaced fields. Should this occur, character data will be truncated, whereas numeric data will be lost and the field filled with asterisks.

A scope clause can be included to store the same expression in the same field for a group of records. For example,

`REPLACE ALL salary WITH salary * 1.10`

will reflect an across-the-board 10 percent increase in salary for every record, whereas the command

`REPLACE NEXT 5 salary WITH salary * 1.10`

gives a 10 percent increase to the next 5 employees (beginning with the record at the current position of the record pointer).

Including a FOR or WHILE condition will replace the field contents for only those records that meet the specified condition. For example,

`REPLACE salary WITH salary * 1.10 FOR location = '42'`

gives a 10 percent raise to only those employees at location 42.

Tips:

1. The REPLACE command is often used in programs that append new records to a database. Commands are issued to GET memory variables, validate them, append a blank record to the database, and then replace the blank fields with the contents of the memory variables.

2. A REPLACE command that includes a scope parameter or a FOR/WHILE condition, moves the record pointer to the last record replaced or to the end-of-file, depending on the parameter used. REPLACE ALL and REPLACE...FOR both move the record pointer to the end-of-file. REPLACE NEXT moves it to the last record in the scope and REPLACE...WHILE moves it one record beyond the last record meeting the specified condition. A REPLACE command issued with no scope or FOR/WHILE condition does not reposition the record pointer.

3. The REPLACE command should *not* be used to change the value of the key field when the associated index is open. Should it become necessary to change the value of a key field, the replacement is better done with the indexes closed, after which the file should be reindexed.

4. Any attempt to replace an inactive field (that is, a field not contained in the current field list) produces a "Variable not Found" error message.

5. The REPLACE command affects only those records meeting an active filter condition. In similar fashion, the REPLACE command does *not* affect records marked for deletion if SET DELETED is ON.

Related Topics: APPEND
                       SET DELETED
                       SET FIELDS
                       SET FILTER
                       STORE

REPORT FORM

Syntax: REPORT FORM <filename>] [WHILE <condition>]
               [FOR <condition>] [PLAIN]
               [HEADING <expression>]
               [NOEJECT] [TO PRINT]
               [TO FILE <filename>][SUMMARY]

Discussion: The REPORT FORM command merges data from the currently selected database with the specified report format file, printing the generated report to the screen. The default scope is ALL so that a report will include every record from the database, unless a scope, FOR, or WHILE parameter is specified. The records will be listed according to the logical sequence of the master index or, if no index is open, according to the physical order of the currently selected database.

After the report is generated, the *record pointer is repositioned to the end-of-file,* unless NEXT is indicated as the scope parameter or a FOR or WHILE condition is included. Specifying NEXT as the scope parameter repositions the record pointer to the last record listed (unless NEXT goes beyond the end-of-file, in which case the record pointer is set to the end-of-file). Including a WHILE condition moves the record pointer one record beyond the last record meeting the specified condition whereas including a FOR condition moves it to the last record meeting the condition.

By default, the page number and date are printed in the upper left-hand corner of every page in the report. The HEADING option will include a page heading (in addition to the report title) that will be centered on the same line as the page number. For example,

```
REPORT FORM salary HEADING '1988 Salary Report'
```

The PLAIN clause suppresses these three elements (page number, date, and heading line).

The TO PRINT clause produces a copy of the report on the printer as well as on the screen. An initial form feed is executed before the printing begins, although a NOEJECT clause can suppress this action. The printer must be on line or an error message will be displayed.

The TO FILE clause prints the report to an ASCII text file, which can be subsequently modified with a word processor.

The SUMMARY clause suppresses the display of all detail lines producing a report that shows only group subtotals and totals.

Tips:

1. All necessary database files and their associated indexes must be opened before the REPORT FORM command is issued. Additionally, if the report form references fields from unselected work areas, the proper relationships must have been previously set.
2. Detail lines are generated only for those records that meet the filter condition. Similarly, detail lines are not generated for any records marked for deletion when SET DELETED is ON.
3. A syntax error results if the report form includes fields not specified in the active field list, that is, all fields in the report form must appear in any current field list.
4. The SET CONSOLE OFF command will suppress the screen display during printing. It must be set back on when the printing is complete so that processing can proceed normally, for example,

```
SET CONSOLE OFF
REPORT FORM employee TO PRINT
SET CONSOLE ON
```

5. The PLAIN and the HEADING options are mutually exclusive and should not appear together in the same command.
6. Specifying the PLAIN, NOEJECT, and SUMMARY clauses at the dot prompt overrides corresponding parameters established when the report form was initially created.
7. ASCII characters may be sent to the printer before actual printing, perhaps to specify compressed print or some other option, for example,

```
SET PRINT ON
? CHR(15)
SET PRINT OFF
REPORT FORM employee TO PRINT
SET PRINT ON
? CHR(18)
SET PRINT OFF
```

The ASCII characters 15 and 18, for compressed and normal print, respectively, are by no means universally used by all printers. (Consult your own printer's manual for specifics.) Remember too, to restore the printer to normal printing as soon as the report is finished as shown above.

Related Topics: `CHR()`
`CREATE/MODIFY REPORT`
`LABEL FORM`
`SET FILTER`
`SET FIELDS`
`SET DELETED`
`SET CONSOLE`

RESTORE

Syntax: `RESTORE FROM <filename> [ADDITIVE]`

Discussion: The `RESTORE` command brings the values of memory variables stored in the specified file into memory, simultaneously releasing any variables already in memory when the command was executed. Specifying the ADDITIVE clause will, however, combine the memory variables in the file with those already in memory, keeping the latter variables from being released. Note, too, that when the ADDITIVE clause is included, any existing memory variables with the same name as a restored memory variable will be overwritten and the original value lost.

Tips:

1. If the `RESTORE` command is executed from within a program, the restored memory variables are declared `PRIVATE` (local to the program). If, on the other hand, the command is executed from the dot prompt, the restored memory variables are declared `PUBLIC`.
2. Up to 256 memory variables can be active at one time, collectively taking a maximum of 6000 bytes in memory. (The amount of available memory can be increased or decreased with a `MVARSIZ` command in the CONFIG.DB file, but the number of memory variables is fixed at 256.)
3. Once a memory variable has been restored, its value may be changed with subsequent `STORE` commands.

Related Topics: `RELEASE`
`SAVE`
`PUBLIC`
`PRIVATE`

RESUME

Syntax: `RESUME`

Discussion: The `RESUME` command continues execution of a suspended program at the point where it was originally interrupted. The command makes sense only within the context of a debugging session, which was initiated by the user's decision to suspend execution of a program in order to execute additional debugging statements (such as `DISPLAY MEMORY` and `DISPLAY STATUS`).

Related Topics: `SET STEP`

RETURN

Syntax: `RETURN [TO MASTER]`

Discussion: The `RETURN` command closes the program file in which it is located, then transfers control back to either the calling program or the dot prompt, depending on where the program was originally called. At that point, the program containing the `RETURN` command is no longer counted toward the maximum of 15 files which can be open at one time.

The TO MASTER clause bypasses any intermediate level programs, returning control immediately to the highest level program, typically the user's entry into the system.

Tips:

1. In the absence of a `RETURN` statement, a program terminates with the last physical command and control is then transferred back to the calling program (or dot prompt). Good coding standards suggest, however, that a `RETURN` command be included in every program and procedure.
2. The `RETURN TO MASTER` command should rarely, if ever, be used because it violates the one entry point/one exit point philosophy of structured methodology. Instead, control should be returned one step at a time until the highest level program is reached.
3. Execution of a `RETURN` command also releases all private memory variables (those created within the program). The `RETURN` command does not, however, affect database files, index files, format files, alternate files, and procedure files which remain open after the transfer of control has taken place.

Related Topics:
```
CLOSE
DO
QUIT
PUBLIC
PRIVATE
RELEASE
```

RTRIM FUNCTION

Syntax: `RTRIM(<character expression>)`

Discussion: The `RTRIM()` function strips trailing blanks from the specified character string and is identical in all respects to the `TRIM()` function.

Related Topics:
```
TRIM()
LTRIM()
```

RUN

Syntax: `RUN <command>`
         or
         `! <command>`

Discussion: The RUN command enables a DOS command to be executed from within a dBASE session. Issuing the command will temporarily suspend dBASE processing, execute the specified DOS command, and return to dBASE at the point where it was interrupted. Use of the RUN command requires enough additional memory (beyond the 256K needed by dBASE) so that COMMAND.COM can be loaded into memory along with dBASE. COMMAND.COM must also be available to dBASE when the RUN command is issued, meaning that on a two-drive system, a copy of COMMAND.COM must exist on the *second* dBASE program disk.

Tips: _____

1. It is easier to perform a COPY, ERASE, or RENAME operation on multiple files with the RUN command, rather than with their dBASE equivalents, because the dBASE syntax does not recognize wild card characters with these commands. In other words, the dBASE command ERASE *.BAK would result in a syntax error, whereas RUN ERASE *.BAK would execute successfully.
2. Increasing the amount of memory allocated to dBASE (with a MAXMEM command in the CONFIG.DB file) decreases the memory available for loading COMMAND.COM; posing a potential problem.
3. Memory resident programs, such as Sidekick, are invoked with the program's "hot keys," and thus *do not* depend on the dBASE RUN command. Indeed, using Sidekick's notebook function (or a similar capability in another program) is the easiest way of editing dBASE program files because it requires neither an external word processor nor use of the dBASE MODIFY COMMAND.
4. The RUN command also enables other program files (with extensions of COM, EXE, or BAT) to be executed from within dBASE.

Related Topics: CONFIG.DB

SAVE

Syntax: SAVE TO <filename> [ALL LIKE/EXCEPT <skeleton>]

Discussion: The SAVE command stores all currently active memory variables to the specified file. The latter is assigned a default extension of MEM unless another extension is explicitly specified in the file name.
    The ALL LIKE and ALL EXCEPT clauses may be used to save only a similarly named subset of the current memory variables, depending on whether they match (ALL LIKE) or do not match (ALL EXCEPT) the specified skeleton. The skeleton can use either or both of two wild card characters, the * and the ?. The * matches one or more characters from its position to the end of the file name, whereas the ? matches any *single* character in its exact position in the file name. For example,

    SAVE TO constant ALL LIKE mr*

will save all current memory variables that begin with "mr" to a file named CONSTANT.MEM, regardless of the length of the memory variable name. By contrast the command

    SAVE TO constant ALL EXCEPT ???3

will save all current memory variables to a file named CONSTANT.MEM *except* those having a 3 as the last character of a four-character name.

1. Program constants that need to be preserved from one dBASE session to the next can be saved in one session and restored in the next.
2. `PRIVATE` memory variables should be saved before the program in which they are contained is terminated, otherwise they will be automatically released when the program returns control to its calling program.
3. The skeleton need not use a wild card character, and thus can be used to save a particular memory variable. For example,

        SAVE TO memfile ALL LIKE mcount

will save only the memory variable mcount to the memory file.
4. ALL LIKE and ALL EXCEPT are mutually exclusive and *cannot* be used in the same command.
5. A `SAVE` command that specifies an existing file name overwrites the entire file, and consequently does not add the newly saved variables to those originally in the file. dBASE will ask if the file should be overwritten, provided `SET SAFETY` is ON. If `SET SAFETY` is OFF, however, the existing file will be overwritten with no warning and the values of the formerly saved variables will be irretrievably lost.

Related Topics: RESTORE
RELEASE
SET SAFETY

@...SAY...GET

Syntax: `@ <row,col> [SAY <exp> [PICTURE <template>]]`
`[GET <field/memvar> [PICTURE <template>]]`
`[RANGE <exp>,<exp>][CLEAR]`

Discussion: The `@...SAY...GET` command allows precise control of screen displays for both input and output, displaying text or input templates at the screen location specified by the row and column coordinates. The screen display consists of 25 rows (numbered 0 through 24 from top to bottom), and 80 columns (numbered 0 through 79 from left to right). The expression in the SAY clause can be any valid dBASE expression, other than a memo field. It can be a character string,

    @ 10,10 SAY 'Soleil America, Inc.'

the contents of a field or memory variable,

    @ 12,10 SAY lastname

or a syntactically correct complex expression,

    @ 14,10 SAY 'Employee's Last Name: ' + lastname

The GET clause displays an input template for an existing field or memory variable, and also displays the currently stored data for editing or replacement. Note, however, that `@...GET` only defines the input template and must be used in conjunction with a READ command in order to activate the full-screen data entry mode.

An `@...SAY...GET` can include a SAY clause by itself, a GET clause by itself, or

■ **TABLE NB.6**
Standard Function Symbols

@C	Displays CR after a positive number
@X	Displays DB after a negative number
@(	Displays negative number in parentheses
@B	Displays number left-justified in input template
@Z	Displays a blank space instead of a zero value
@D	Displays date in American format (mm/dd/yy)
@E	Displays date in European format (dd/mm/yy)
@A	Permits only alphabetic characters
@!	Permits any character, and converts all alphabetic characters to uppercase
@R	Permits nonstandard characters to appear in the template, but does not store the characters with the data
@S(n)	Limits the display to the first (n) characters of the field and scrolls the field contents through the display

both clauses in the same command. When both are included as in the command,

```
@ 10,10 SAY 'Enter last name: ' GET lastname
```

the input template associated with the GET clause is displayed one space to the right of the text displayed by the SAY clause.

The SAY and GET clauses may both contain an optional PICTURE clause, which defines the format of the information displayed or input and, when used with a GET, restricts the data that can be input. The PICTURE clause consists of an optional *function* and a required *template,* and must be delimited with quotes, for example, PICTURE '@F XXXXXXX'. The F represents 1 of 11 formatting *functions,* whereas the X's denote a combination of *template* symbols. The function (if it is used) must precede the template, and be separated from it by a space.

Tables NB.6 and NB.7 show the standard symbols for functions and templates. The difference between a function and a template is that a function applies to the field as a whole, whereas templates are created with a separate symbol for every character. The picture clause 'XX999', for example, establishes an input template five-characters wide, which will accept any character in the two leftmost positions, but only numeric digits in the remaining three positions.

Any character at all may appear in a template, but characters other than the standard symbols in Table NB.6 have no special meaning and will be entered, as is, into the input template. Consider:

```
@ 10,5 GET mphone1 PICTURE '(999)999-9999'
```

and

```
@ 10,5 GET mphone2 PICTURE '@R (999)999-9999'
```

The only difference between the two is the @R function in the second PICTURE clause. In both examples, the nonstandard template characters (the parentheses and the hyphen) are automatically displayed in the input template during data entry and the cursor skips over these positions. Including the @R function in the second example prevents the extra characters from being stored with the field, that is, mphone2 requires a field length of 10, whereas mphone1 requires 13 positions.

The RANGE clause is used with numeric and date variables to specify the minimum and maximum values that may be entered in response to an @...GET. Any entry that falls outside the specified range causes an error message and a prompt for another value. A single boundary (upper or lower) may be specified, provided a comma is placed in the appropriate

■ **TABLE NB.7**
Standard Template Symbols

9	Limits input to numeric digits and their sign (+ or −)
#	Limits input to numeric digits, their signs, and blanks
A	Limits input to alphabetic characters
L	Limits input to logical values
N	Limits input to alphabetic or numeric characters, and does not permit special characters
X	Accepts any character
!	Displays alphabetic character in uppercase
,	Displays the comma if there is a numeric digit on both sides of the comma
$	Displays $ in place of leading zeroes
*	Displays * instead of leading zeroes
.	Indicates decimal position

position to indicate which boundary was supplied. Specifying boundary dates also requires the CTOD conversion function, for example,

```
@ 10,10 GET hdate RANGE CTOD('01/01/82')
```

which specifies January 1, 1982, as the earliest date that can be entered but gives no upper limit.

Tips:

1. The status, navigation, and message lines normally use lines 22 through 24 on the screen, but these lines can be freed for custom screen displays with the SET STATUS OFF command. Note, however, that when SET STATUS is OFF, dBASE substitutes line 0 for some status messages. Hence, for complete screen control this line must be freed with SET SCOREBOARD OFF.

2. With an @...SAY command, all fields in the expression must be the same data type. Thus, if a character string is to be displayed with a date or numeric field, the date or number must be converted to a character string using a STR() or DTOC() conversion function, for example,

```
@ 10,10 SAY 'Date Hired: ' + DTOC(hdate)
@ 12,10 SAY 'Salary: ' + STR(salary,6)
```

Alternatively, a pair of statements could be used for each command:

```
@ 10,10 SAY 'Date Hired: '
@ 10,22 SAY hdate
```

and

```
@ 12,10 SAY 'Salary: '
@ 12,18 SAY salary
```

thus eliminating the need for conversion.

3. A memory variable must be explicitly created (initialized) before issuing a GET command, for example,

```
STORE '          ' TO mlastname
STORE 0 to msalary
STORE .T. TO mloop
STORE CTOD('  /  /  ') TO msaldate
```

Variables consisting of long strings of blanks are best initialized with the SPACE() function to avoid counting spaces, for example,

```
STORE SPACE(30) TO mname
```

The data type of the initial value assigned determines the data type of the memory variable. Numeric memory variables are given a field length of 10 digits with no decimal places (unless decimal places are present in the initial value). Character fields assume the length of the assigned character string, up to a maximum of 254 characters.

4. The functions @C, @D, and @(cannot be used with an @...GET clause; @A and @R have no meaning within an @...SAY clause.

5. The @R function is useful in fields such as a telephone or social security number to display the data in an easily understood format, without storing the special characters in the database. For example, the PICTURE clause, '@R 999-99-9999', displays a social security number as 123-45-6789, but requires only nine positions in the database, storing the digits 123456789.

6. Templates may be used to insert commas into numeric fields to produce a more readable number, such as

```
@10,10 SAY salary1 PICTURE '999,999,999'
```

Any comma not preceded by a significant digit will be suppressed. Hence, given the above template, the number 1200 would be displayed as 1,200 while the number 1200000 would appear as 1,200,000.

7. The output of an @...SAY command will be sent to the printer, provided a SET DEVICE TO PRINT command has been previously issued. However, successive @...SAY commands should map the page from top to bottom and from left to right in order to avoid unintentional page breaks. In other words, when confronted with a row number lower than the row number in a previous command, dBASE ejects the page and prints at the proper row and column coordinates on the next page.

Related Topics:
```
CLEAR
DTOC()
SET SCOREBOARD
SET DEVICE
SET STATUS
STR()
@...TO
?
```

SEEK

Syntax: SEEK <expression>

Discussion: The SEEK command contains *all* the capabilities inherent in the FIND command and, in addition, enables a search on an *expression involving one or more memory variables.* (The FIND command can only specify a character string or a numeric constant as its search condition.) Because the FIND command cannot search for an expression, and because it is cumbersome to use the macro notation in finding values stored in memory variables, SEEK is more likely to be used in program files. FIND, on the other hand, is more convenient to use from the dot prompt.

As with the FIND command, the requirement that an active index be used implies that records with like values of the search key will be grouped together; that is, if there is another record with the same key value it will be sequenced immediately beneath the first record. Hence, the second record can be accessed with a `SKIP` command (to move the record pointer) and viewed with a `DISPLAY` command (to verify that the key does, in fact, match). Indeed, all records with the same key value can be retrieved by repeatedly issuing `SKIP` and `DISPLAY` commands until the key field value no longer matches the character string or numeric value specified in the `SEEK` command.

Tips:

1. The `SEEK` command requires that the character string used as the search expression be enclosed in quotes to differentiate it from a memory variable. This differs from the `FIND` command where quotation marks are optional, that is,

   ```
   FIND Jones ───────── Valid for FIND; invalid with SEEK
   FIND "Jones" ─────── Valid for both FIND and SEEK
   ```

2. A *partial* character string may be stored in the memory variable used in the search expression as long as `SET EXACT` is OFF and the specified string consists of the initial characters in the key value. For example,

   ```
   STORE "Sm" to mname
   SEEK mname
   ```

   will position the record pointer to the first record having a key value that begins with "Sm".

3. The `SEEK` command will *not* search for a partial numeric value as it will for a partial character string, that is, `SEEK 111` will *not* retrieve a record whose key is 111222.

4. Upper- and lowercase letters are treated as different characters, whether `SET EXACT` is ON or OFF. The commands

   ```
   STORE 'MILLER' to mname
   SEEK mname
   ```

   will not find a key value of Miller or miller.

5. `SEEK` conducts a much more rapid search than does the corresponding `LOCATE` command. `SEEK`, however, requires an index and limits the search to a value *equal* to the character string or numeric value. `LOCATE`, on the other hand, can search for values "greater than," "less than," or "not equal to."

6. The `SEEK` command ignores records not meeting an active filter condition. Similarly, records marked for deletion are also ignored when `SET DELETED` is ON.

Related Topics: `FIND`
                       `LOCATE`
                       `SET DELETED`
                       `SET FILTER`

SELECT

Syntax: `SELECT <work area/alias>`

Discussion: The `SELECT` command designates one of 10 available work areas as the currently selected work area, causing subsequent dBASE commands to apply (in general) to the database file in the selected work area. Only one work area can be active (current) at any given time.

Multiple work areas are of no concern if database files are opened (and closed) one at a time. However, using more than one database file simultaneously requires that each database file be placed in its own work area by first selecting the area and then opening (using) the file. (Area 1 is automatically chosen in the absence of a `SELECT` command.) For example, the commands

```
USE solemp

SELECT 2
USE location

SELECT 3
USE title
```

will open the SOLEMP.DBF, LOCATION.DBF, and TITLE.DBF files in areas 1, 2, and 3, respectively. In addition to its database file, each work area keeps track of related memo files, up to seven active index files, an active format file, an active filter condition, and any established relationship. Data can be accessed in any open database file, whether or not that file is in the current work area.

A work area is selected (made current) in one of three ways by indicating:

1. the number of the work area (a value from one to 10), such as `SELECT 3`.
2. the default *alias* of the work area (a letter from A through J, corresponding to the numbers 1 through 10), such as SELECT C.
3. the name (alias) of the open file in the work area, such as `SELECT employee`.

dBASE maintains an independent record pointer in each of the work areas. Selecting a particular work area and repositioning the record pointer in that area does *not* affect the record pointers for files in other work areas. In other words, if the record pointer in area 1 is on record 15 and area 3 is selected, the record pointer in area 1 remains on record 15, despite the movements of the record pointer in area 3. In addition, when area 1 is reselected, its record pointer is still on record 15 and will not be moved to record 1, as happens when the file is opened.

Relationships can be established between open files, enabling more sophisticated systems to be developed than if just one database file was available. This is accomplished by the `SET RELATION` command, which links files together in such a way that the record pointers move in conjunction with one another. In other words, commands that move the record pointer in one file will automatically reposition the record pointer in a related file to the corresponding record.

Tips:

1. The first file opened does not have to be placed in area 1, that is, any of the other areas may be selected.
2. A field or fields from a database file in other than the current work area can be accessed by using the file alias with the field name, for example,

```
SELECT employee
DISPLAY lastname,location->loc_name
```

The last name field belongs to the EMPLOYEE.DBF file in the current work area and is displayed as usual. The loc_name field, however, belongs to the LOCATION.DBF file and is referenced with the appropriate file alias. (A relationship between these two files should have been previously established to make the display meaningful.)
3. A `SET FIELDS` command may include fields from database files in unselected work

areas by including the file's alias with the field name, as in

```
SET FIELDS TO lname,loc,location->loc_name
```

4. The USE command with no file name closes the database file in the currently selected work area, whereas CLOSE DATABASES closes the database files in all the work areas.
5. The same dBASE file may not be open in more than one work area at the same time.
6. Even though 10 work areas are available, (each being able to hold a maximum of one database file, seven index files, a format file, and related memo files), a maximum of 15 files of all types can be open at once. (Any open database, index, memo, format, procedure, alternate, program, report form, label form, or memory files count against the 15-file limit.) Any attempts to open more than this maximum will result in a "Too many files open" error message.

Related Topics: CLOSE
SET FIELDS
SET RELATION
USE
DISPLAY STATUS

SET

Syntax: SET

Discussion: The SET command invokes a full-screen menu for viewing and/or changing the status of other SET commands. The command produces a horizontal menu bar across the top of the screen, offering a choice of seven different options, each representing a subset of available SET commands. As each option is highlighted (by pressing either the right or left arrow keys or the key corresponding to the initial letter of the option name) the corresponding subset of commands appears in a box beneath the option. The seven menu items are:

1. OPTIONS: SET commands that have two values to choose from (ON/OFF, SCREEN/PRINT)
2. SCREEN: SET commands that affect the characteristics of the screen display
3. KEYS: SET commands that reprogram the function keys (F2—F10 only)
4. DISK: SET commands that establish the default drive and search path
5. FILES: SET commands that open Alternate, Format, and Index files
6. MARGINS: SET commands that establish a left print margin or the display width for memo fields
7. DECIMALS: SET commands that establish the maximum number of decimal places for displaying numeric data

The status of a particular SET command is changed by selecting the appropriate menu item, highlighting the submenu choice within that item (using the up/down arrow keys) and then, depending on the item chosen, either pressing the Return key until the desired setting appears or entering the appropriate information. For example, the status of SET DELETED can be changed by selecting Options, highlighting Deleted, and pressing the Return key until the status is OFF (or ON, as the case may be).

The SET command is exited by pressing the Esc key. All changes are retained and remain in effect until they are once again modified, or the dBASE session is terminated.

Tips:

1. The default setting of many SET commands can be changed by including them in the CONFIG.DB file, and specifying the desired status.
2. The status of individual SET commands can also be changed by issuing the appropriate SET command from the dot prompt or from within program files.
3. SET commands altered in a program file should be returned to the default setting before exiting the program (if returning to the dot prompt).

Related Topics: CONFIG.DB

SET ALTERNATE

Syntax: SET ALTERNATE TO <filename>
SET ALTERNATE ON/*OFF*

Discussion: The SET ALTERNATE commands enable screen output (commands typed in, information dBASE sends to the screen, error messages, and so on) to be echoed to a file, in addition to appearing on the screen. The output of full-screen commands such as EDIT, APPEND, and BROWSE is not included.

The SET ALTERNATE TO command creates and opens an ASCII text file (with a default extension of TXT) to hold the output. SET ALTERNATE ON initiates echoing, whereas SET ALTERNATE OFF stops the echoing, but does not close the file. Another SET ALTERNATE ON will resume sending the screen output to the file, appending it to the end of the existing data. Repeated SET ALTERNATE ON and OFF commands may be issued, with the output being appended to the end of the file each time SET ALTERNATE is turned ON.

The alternate file is permanently closed when either a CLOSE ALTERNATE or SET ALTERNATE TO command (with no file name specified) is issued. A subsequent SET ALTERNATE TO command specifying the same file name causes the existing file *to be overwritten,* even if a subsequent SET ALTERNATE ON command is never issued.

Tips:

1. Alternate files are widely used to record a sequence of commands from the dot prompt, together with the responses, to aid in problem solving.
2. The alternate file may be subsequently edited with a word processor to facilitate the development of system documentation and/or dBASE tutorials.
3. A SET ALTERNATE OFF and a CLOSE ALTERNATE command should both be issued before attempting to work with the alternate file to ensure that the file has been properly written to disk.
4. The TYPE command, (TYPE <filename>.TXT), can be used to view the contents of an alternate file from the dot prompt. Including the TO PRINT parameter produces hard copy as well.
5. If a file already exists on the disk with the same name as the one specified in the SET ALTERNATE TO command, it will be overwritten with no warning regardless of whether SET SAFETY is ON or OFF. *Be careful.*

Related Topics: CLOSE
                SET DEBUG
                SET ECHO
                SET SAFETY

SET BELL

Syntax: SET BELL *ON*/OFF

Discussion: The SET BELL command determines whether or not a bell will ring when a user attempts to enter invalid data (for example, character data in a numeric field) or when data completely fill an input template. The choice between ON (bell rings) and OFF (bell doesn't ring) is one of personal preference with valid arguments both pro and con. Leaving it on warns you if you make a mistake, but becomes annoying as well because the bell sounds every time a field is filled even though no error has been made. (The bell will sound, for example, at the end of a logical field because the input template consists of only one character and is always filled.)

Tips:

1. The ASCII character 7 rings the bell, regardless of the status of SET BELL. Consider:

```
DO CASE
    CASE opt = '1'
        .
        .
        .
    OTHERWISE
        ? CHR(7)
        @21,15 SAY 'Please re-enter'
ENDCASE
```

2. Many users choose to SET CONFIRM ON when SET BELL is OFF, so that pressing the Return key is necessary at the end of every input template. This prevents a user from overtyping one field into the next without warning.
3. Consistency throughout a system, regarding the status of SET BELL and SET CON-FIRM, is important so that the user always knows what is expected and does not have to guess during data entry.

Related Topics: CHR()
                   SET CONFIRM
                   ?

SET CATALOG

Syntax: SET CATALOG TO <filename>
             SET CATALOG ON/*OFF*

Discussion: The SET CATALOG TO command opens an existing catalog file or, if no such file name exists, creates and opens a new one. Then, as long as the catalog is open, information about each file created from the dot prompt is stored in the catalog. The information includes the file name, path, alias, and type, as well as an 80-character file description requested by dBASE when the file is created. In addition, each nondatabase file (an index file, format file, and so on) is linked in the catalog to its particular database file.

The utility of the catalog revolves around a query feature that helps select correct ancillary files. Any command that uses a file name as part of its syntax can include a query (?) in place of the file name. The USE ? command, for example, displays on the screen a list of all the database files in the open catalog. The PgUp and PgDn arrow keys can be used to highlight the various file names, together with the description entered at the time the file was created, and pressing the Return key will open the highlighted file.

A query can also be used to access other files contained in the catalog, as shown in the examples below:

```
SET FORMAT TO ?
SET INDEX TO ?
MODIFY REPORT ?
MODIFY SCREEN ?
SET VIEW TO ?
SET FILTER TO ?
REPORT FORM ?
```

However, rather than list all of the files of the particular file type, only those associated with the currently selected database are shown, making it easier to select the proper ancillary file.

To ensure that the catalog is kept current, a SET CATALOG TO command should be issued at the beginning of a session. Should it become necessary to create a file that is not to be stored in the catalog, such as a temporary database or index, the catalog should be turned off with a SET CATALOG OFF command. This keeps the catalog from being further updated. At the appropriate time, a SET CATALOG ON can be issued to resume catalog maintenance. Note, however, that even when SET CATALOG is OFF, the catalog is not closed and the query feature may still be used.

SET CATALOG TO, issued without a file name, closes the catalog file.

Tips: ───

1. A separate catalog should be maintained for each application and should be established before any files belonging to the system are created.
2. An open catalog file is automatically placed in work area 10, thereby reducing the number of available work areas to 9.
3. A catalog (CAT) file is analagous to a database file with one record appended to the catalog for every file created while the catalog is open. The file structure contains seven fields:

```
PATH
FILE_NAME
ALIAS
TYPE
TITLE
CODE
TAG
```

The .CAT file can be displayed and updated from the dot prompt as can any database file. You should not, however, modify the structure as that can render the catalog unusable.

SET CENTURY

Syntax: `SET CENTURY ON/`*`OFF`*

Discussion: The `SET CENTURY` command determines how the year portion of dates is input and displayed. The default format is two digits, with the 20th century assumed. `SET CENTURY ON` changes the display to four digits, making it possible to work with dates from other centuries.

Tips:

1. `SET CENTURY` does not affect how dates are stored internally, only how they are input or displayed. For example, if a date of 12/25/2010 is entered when `SET CENTURY` is ON, it will be displayed as 12/25/10 when `SET CENTURY` is OFF, and as 12/25/2010 when `SET CENTURY` is reset to ON.
2. Non-20th century dates cannot be entered when `SET CENTURY` is OFF, because the input template provides only two digits for year. Non-20th century *memory variables* can, however, be created by entering a four-digit year, for example,

        STORE CTOD('07/04/1776') TO memdate

   Note, however, that the date will be displayed as 07/04/76 until `SET CENTURY` is ON, at which time it will be shown as 07/04/1776.
3. The `YEAR()` function returns a four-digit year, regardless of whether `SET CENTURY` is ON or OFF. All other commands displaying a date will show either a two- or four-digit year, corresponding to the status of `SET CENTURY`.
4. If a date calculation results in a non-20th century date, the correct century will be retained even if `SET CENTURY` is OFF.

Related Topics: `CTOD()`
                      `DATE()`
                      `DTOC()`
                      `SET DATE`
                      `YEAR()`

SET COLOR

Syntax: `SET COLOR ON/OFF`
              `SET COLOR TO [<standard>, [<enhanced>], [<border>], [<background>]]`

Discussion: The `SET COLOR ON` command enables the user to switch back and forth between a color and a monochrome monitor in systems equipped with both. The default value is the monitor in use when dBASE is loaded.

The effects of SET COLOR TO differ, depending on what type of monitor is in use. In any event, the command provides for three distinct areas known as the *standard display area, enhanced display area,* and *border.* In addition, a color monitor requires *foreground* and *background* color for the standard and enhanced display areas. Available colors, and their respective codes, are shown in the table below:

Color	Code
Black	N
Blue	B
Brown	GR
Cyan	BG
Green	G
Magenta	RB
Red	R
White	W
Blank	X

The SET COLOR TO command separates the foreground and background colors for a given area with a slash and separates the different areas with a comma. Thus, the command

```
SET COLOR TO W/B,R/W,N
```

displays white text on a blue background in the standard display area, red text on a white background in the enhanced area, and a black border (borders can only be one color). A plus sign (+) may be included with either foreground color to create high intensity text, for example,

```
SET COLOR TO W+/B,R+/W,N
```

You need not change the colors in all three areas every time, although you must use initial comma(s) to indicate the omission of positional items. For example, to change the display in the enhanced area to red on white (leaving the other two areas alone), use the command

Comma indicates standard display parameter omission

```
SET COLOR TO ,R/W
```

Default values will be used (white on black in the standard display area, black on white in the enhanced area, and a black border) for any unspecified options.

The SET COLOR TO command can be used on a monochrome monitor to create inverse video, high intensity, underlined, or blinking text. Consider:

Code	Effect
+	High-intensity text
U	Underlined text
U+	Underlined high-intensity text
I	Inverse video
*	Blinking text

For example, the commands

```
SET COLOR TO W+/N
SET COLOR TO U
```

provide high intensity white text on a black background, and underlined text, respectively. The SET COLOR TO command, with no additional parameters, resets the screen to the default values in all the areas for either type of monitor.

1. The standard and enhanced display areas may each be assigned any pair of colors. Choose carefully, however, as a pleasing, easy-to-look-at screen is very important.
2. Specifying X as a foreground color within the SET COLOR TO command displays blank text (effectively hiding it from view), a feature that can be used to keep user-supplied passwords, security codes, and so on, from being displayed as they are entered.
3. Blinking and high intensity can be specified for color or monochrome monitors. Underlining and inverse video can only be used on monochrome monitors.
4. The default colors can be changed with a COLOR = command, in the CONFIG.DB file. In addition, including a COLOR = ON command will designate the color monitor as the active monitor (in systems with two monitors), regardless of which was in use when dBASE was loaded.
5. The SET COLOR TO command can be used immediately before an @...SAY command within a program to create a special effect. Remember, however, to reset the colors back to normal immediately afterwards, for example,

```
SET COLOR TO *
@ 20,20 SAY 'Please enter another option'
SET COLOR TO
```

6. Cyan, magenta, and brown are created by combining other colors. Similarly, other colors can be created with different code combinations.

Related Topics: SET DELIMITERS
                      SET INTENSITY

SET CONFIRM

Syntax: SET CONFIRM ON/*OFF*

Discussion: The SET CONFIRM command determines whether or not the cursor moves automatically to the next input template when data completely fill the current template. The choice between ON (having to confirm each entry with the Return key even when the template is filled) and OFF (automatic advancement to the next field) is one of personal preference with valid arguments both pro and con. SET CONFIRM ON lends consistency to data entry, but also slows it to some degree.

Tips: _____

1. Many users choose SET CONFIRM ON when SET BELL is OFF, so that pressing the Return key is necessary at the end of every input template. This prevents a user from overtyping one field into the next without any warning.
2. Consistency throughout a system, regarding the status of SET BELL and SET CONFIRM, is important so that the user always knows what is expected and does not have to guess during data entry.

Related Topics: SET BELL

SET CONSOLE

Syntax: `SET CONSOLE` *`ON`*`/OFF`

Discussion: The `SET CONSOLE` command is used from within program files to turn the screen display on and off. It affects sequential output such as listings, report forms, label forms, and output from the `?` and `DISPLAY` commands. It does not, however, affect screen displays resulting from full-screen commands such as `@...SAY`, `APPEND`, or `EDIT`, nor does it inhibit dBASE error messages.

Tips:

1. `SET CONSOLE OFF` has no effect when issued from the dot prompt, that is, `SET CONSOLE` is always ON in the interactive mode.
2. dBASE error messages and command responses such as "No Find" and "100% indexed" are suppressed with `SET TALK OFF` and are not affected by the `SET CONSOLE` command.
3. It is often convenient to suppress the screen display when report forms or mailing labels are printed; for example,

```
SET CONSOLE OFF
REPORT FORM...TO PRINT
LABEL FORM...TO PRINT
SET CONSOLE ON
```

It is important, however, to turn the console back on when the reports/labels are finished.
4. The `WAIT` command is often preceded with `@...SAY` commands to print custom messages, then bracketed with `SET CONSOLE ON` and `OFF` to suppress the standard message that the `WAIT` command produces, for example,

```
@...SAY          Commands to map the custom message
SET CONSOLE OFF
WAIT
SET CONSOLE ON
```

Related Topics:
```
LABEL FORM
REPORT FORM
SET DEVICE
SET TALK
WAIT
```

SET DATE

Syntax: `SET DATE` *`AMERICAN`*`/ANSI/BRITISH/FRENCH/GERMAN/ITALIAN`

Discussion: The `SET DATE` command determines which of six formats will be used for displaying and inputting all date fields. The choices are:

```
AMERICAN: mm/dd/yy
    ANSI: yy.mm.dd
 BRITISH: dd/mm/yy
  FRENCH: dd/mm/yy
  GERMAN: dd.mm.yy
 ITALIAN: dd-mm-yy
```

The default format is AMERICAN. Date arithmetic, indexing on a single date field, and date comparisons can all be done regardless of the format in effect.

1. The SET DATE command does *not* affect dates stored in character fields. Accordingly, be careful when converting character dates with the CTOD() conversion function. The character date must be in a format consistent with the SET DATE format, that is,

```
SET DATE ITALIAN
STORE CTOD ('25-12-89') TO memdate
```

   or

```
SET DATE FRENCH
STORE CTOD ('25/12/89') TO memdate
```

2. The input template for a date field reflects the format as established by the SET DATE command.
3. The ANSI format should be used when a date field is combined with a character field as the key expression for an index, to ensure that dates are sequenced by year, month, and day. For example,

```
SET DATE ANSI
INDEX ON DTOC (hiredate) + lastname TO date
```

   (See Tip 3 for the INDEX command for a further explanation.)
4. SET CENTURY ON is necessary to display and input four-digit years, and is essential when working with non-20th century dates.
5. The default date format can be changed with a DATE = command in the CONFIG.DB file.

Related Topics: CTOD()
                       DTOC()
                       INDEX
                       SET CENTURY

SET DEBUG

Syntax: SET DEBUG ON/*OFF*

Discussion: The SET DEBUG command determines whether output from the SET ECHO command is sent to the screen (SET DEBUG OFF), or to the printer (SET DEBUG ON). The SET DEBUG command is used as a debugging tool in conjunction with the SET ECHO command and has no effect unless SET ECHO is ON. SET DEBUG ON directs the output to the printer rather than to the screen, so that a program's formatted screen displays are not disrupted.

Tips:

1. Since SET ECHO and SET DEBUG can both be set ON from within a program, it is often more efficient to isolate the problem to a particular section of code and set the parameters ON immediately before that section, rather than before running the entire program. Remember to set both parameters OFF at the end of the problem code and to eventually delete the commands altogether when debugging is finished.

Related Topics: SET ECHO
                         SET DOHISTORY
                         SET STEP
                         SET TALK

SET DEFAULT TO

Syntax: SET DEFAULT TO <drive>

Discussion: The SET DEFAULT command designates a drive other than the logged drive as the default. In a two-floppy drive system, for example, you will want to load dBASE from drive A, and use drive B for your data disk. You do this by entering SET DEFAULT TO B from the dot prompt *after* dBASE has been loaded. In this way dBASE will still look to drive A as the logged drive (under DOS) for the overlay files, and to drive B for its DBF and other user-created files. The SET DEFAULT TO command does not change the logged drive.

Tips:

1. The SET DEFAULT TO command does not check to see if the disk drive specified actually exists, and no error message is given if it does not. If an invalid drive is designated, the logged drive remains as the default drive.
2. DISPLAY STATUS verifies the default drive.
3. A DEFAULT = command may be included in a CONFIG.DB file to establish a default drive. This is useful in a two-drive floppy disk system in that drive B can be automatically established as the default when dBASE is loaded.
4. Every dBASE application should be in its own subdirectory. In addition, the dBASE program files should be in yet another subdirectory (for example, DBASE). The following procedure may then be used to load dBASE and log onto the appropriate subdirectory:
   a. Remain in DOS and log onto the subdirectory containing the dBASE *application* files.
   b. Set a path to the dBASE program files, for example, by issuing the DOS command PATH\DBASE.
   c. Load dBASE from the application subdirectory by typing dBASE at the DOS prompt.

Related Topics: CONFIG.DB
                         SET PATH TO
                         DISPLAY STATUS

SET DELETED

Syntax: `SET DELETED ON/`*`OFF`*

Discussion: The `SET DELETED` command determines whether records marked for deletion are processed by other dBASE commands; that is, `SET DELETED ON` causes dBASE to ignore records marked for deletion, treating them as though they were not physically in the database. For example, assume that record 3 is marked for deletion, that `SET DELETED` is ON, that the record pointer is on record 1, and that the command `LIST NEXT 5` is issued. dBASE will list records 1, 2, 4, 5, and 6, bypassing record 3.

There are, however, two times when deleted records are processed, even when `SET DELETED` is ON—when the record pointer is on the deleted record or when a record number of a deleted record is explicitly specified in a command. If we were to continue with the above example and enter the `GOTO 3` command immediately before `LIST NEXT 5`, dBASE would return records 3, 4, 5, 6, and 7; that is, record 3 would be listed because the record pointer began at record 3. In similar fashion, the command `EDIT RECORD 3` will bring up record 3 for editing, whereas that record would not otherwise be accessible (with the PgUp and PgDn keys) during an `EDIT` session.

Tips: _____

1. The `INDEX ON` and `REINDEX` commands process *all* the records in a database file, including those marked for deletion, whether `SET DELETED` is ON or OFF.
2. The `RECALL ALL` command has no effect (that is, no records are recalled) when `SET DELETED` is ON. A specific record can, however, be recalled by including the record number in the command, for example, `RECALL RECORD 3`.
3. `SET DELETED ON` does not reposition the record pointer, even if the current record is marked for deletion.

Related Topics: `DELETE`
                       `DELETED()`
                       `INDEX`
                       `PACK`

SET DELIMITERS

Syntax: `SET DELIMITERS TO[<character expression/DEFAULT>]`
               `SET DELIMITERS ON/`*`OFF`*

Discussion: The `SET DELIMITERS` command determines whether a beginning and ending character (delimiters) will offset input templates. Delimiters are used in addition to, or instead of, reverse video.

Delimiters will only appear when `SET DELIMITERS` is ON (initially, it is OFF). The default delimiters, a pair of colons, can be changed with a `SET DELIMITERS TO` command, enclosing the new delimiters in quotation marks. For example,

```
SET DELIMITERS TO "<>"
SET DELIMITERS ON
```

will display input templates set off by the less-than and greater-than signs. The delimiters can be reset to the default value (colons) with a SET DELIMITERS TO DEFAULT command.

Tips:

1. If only one delimiter is specified in the SET DELIMITERS TO command, it will appear before and after the input template. If two different delimiters are specified, the first appears before the input template and the second one after.
2. Common delimiters used are [], {}, (), and <>.
3. The reverse video display of the input template is suppressed with SET INTENSITY OFF. Templates will then be differentiated only by the presence of delimiters. Accordingly, the SET INTENSITY and SET DELIMITERS parameters should *not* both be OFF at the same time.
4. New default delimiters can be set with a DELIMITERS = command in the CONFIG.DB file.
5. SET DELIMITERS ON, with no subsequent SET DELIMITERS TO command, displays the default delimiters for all input templates. A SET DELIMITERS TO command, on the other hand, is ineffective unless a SET DELIMITERS ON command accompanies it.

Related Topics: SET COLOR
                                    SET INTENSITY

SET DEVICE

Syntax: SET DEVICE TO PRINT/*SCREEN*

Discussion: The SET DEVICE command determines whether output of an @...SAY command is sent to the printer or screen, with the printer usually being designated for custom reports. It is important to reset the DEVICE to the screen when output to the printer is completed so that processing will resume normal operations. For example,

```
SET DEVICE TO PRINT
@ 5,10 SAY "Employee Last Name:" + lastname
@ 7,10 SAY "Employee Initials:" + initials
    .
    .          Additional @...SAY commands
    .
SET DEVICE TO SCREEN
```

Tips:

1. SET DEVICE TO PRINT affects only @...SAY commands; all other output (for example, dBASE error or informational messages) continues to go to the screen.
2. Printing may not begin immediately following execution of an @...SAY statement as data is held in the print buffer area. It is good practice, therefore, to follow the concluding @...SAY command with an EJECT command to force data from the buffer area.
3. A form feed is automatically issued when DEVICE is set to PRINT, and an @...SAY command specifies a row smaller than the row in the previous @...SAY command. This feature can be used to produce page breaks at the appropriate points in the report.

4. Two parallel sets of @...SAY commands (with the device set to SCREEN and PRINT respectively) are necessary if output is to be sent to both screen and printer. (Alternatively, the commands could be put into a loop or procedure and executed twice, once for each device.)

5. Any GET commands included with an @...SAY...GET command are ignored when SET DEVICE is TO PRINT.

Related Topics: EJECT
                      @...SAY
                      SET PRINT

SET DOHISTORY

Syntax: SET DOHISTORY ON/*OFF*

Discussion: The SET DOHISTORY command determines whether commands issued from program files are stored in history memory. SET DOHISTORY ON will cause program commands to be stored in history memory in the order in which they were executed, so that a subsequent DISPLAY HISTORY command may be used to display them. Commands in history memory may also be recalled to the dot prompt, from where they may be edited and reissued. Note, too, that when SET HISTORY is OFF, no dBASE commands, whether executed from a program or from the dot prompt, are recorded in history memory; that is, SET HISTORY must be ON for SET DOHISTORY to be effective.

Tips:

1. Commands executed from the dot prompt are stored in history memory (as long as SET HISTORY is ON) whether SET DOHISTORY is ON or OFF.
2. SET DOHISTORY ON should be used only for program debugging, because it slows execution.
3. A SET HISTORY TO command (to increase the number of commands stored in history memory) should be issued in conjunction with SET DOHISTORY ON. The size of the increase depends on the code and the extent of the problem, and will probably require some trial and error.
4. Since SET DOHISTORY can be set ON from within a program, it is often more efficient to isolate the problem to a particular section of code and set the parameter ON immediately before that section, rather than before running the entire program. Remember to SET DOHISTORY OFF at the end of the problem code and to eventually delete the command altogether when debugging is finished.

Related Topics: DISPLAY HISTORY
                      SET HISTORY
                      SET STEP

SET ECHO

Syntax: SET ECHO ON/*OFF*

Discussion: The SET ECHO command is a debugging tool that displays commands from a program as they are executed. Output from the command is intermingled with the normal screen display unless SET DEBUG is ON, in which case it is directed to the printer.

Tips: _____

1. The SET ECHO command is an excellent debugging tool, expecially when trying to determine whether conditional processing and/or looping structures are executing properly. It is helpful to SET TALK ON as well to provide additional information.
2. The display of the executed commands will generally scroll by too quickly to permit detailed study. Accordingly, use either Ctrl-NumLock or Ctrl-S to pause the display (pressing any key to continue). Alternatively, SET DEBUG ON to direct output of the ECHO command to the printer.
3. Since SET ECHO and SET DEBUG can both be set ON from within a program, it is often more efficient to isolate the problem to a particular section of code and set the parameters ON immediately before that section, rather than before running the entire program. Remember to set both parameters OFF at the end of the problem code and to eventually delete the commands altogether when debugging is finished.

Related Topics: SET DEBUG
SET DOHISTORY
SET STEP
SET TALK

SET ESCAPE

Syntax: SET ESCAPE *ON/OFF*

Discussion: The SET ESCAPE command determines whether pressing the Esc key will interrupt the command or program being executed. SET ESCAPE OFF disables the key so that it has no effect, except during full-screen commands (e.g., BROWSE and APPEND) which will still be terminated whether SET ESCAPE is ON or OFF. The specific effect of pressing the key when SET ESCAPE is ON depends on whether it is pressed from the dot prompt or during a program's execution.

Pressing the Esc key during the execution of a command from the dot prompt terminates the command, displays the message "***Interrupted***", and returns control to the dot prompt. Pressing the key during the execution of a program halts processing and displays the message "Cancel, Ignore, or Suspend". A choice of "cancel" causes the program to terminate and returns to the dot prompt, whereas "ignore" simply resumes execution. "Suspend" temporarily halts execution and returns control to the dot prompt to allow additional commands (DISPLAY HISTORY, DISPLAY MEMORY, and so on) to be entered to aid in debugging. The RESUME command may then be entered to continue execution at the point in the program where it was suspended.

Tips: _____

1. SET ESCAPE should be OFF at the beginning of a program so that a user is not returned to the dot prompt if the Esc key is inadvertently pressed (or if the user purposefully tries to interrupt a lengthy, but crucial process). Remember, however, to reset SET ESCAPE to ON at the end of the program.

2. `SET ESCAPE` should be ON during program development and debugging.
3. If `SET ESCAPE` is OFF, a program can be interrupted only by turning the computer off or by rebooting the system.

Related Topics: `RESUME`

SET EXACT

Syntax: `SET EXACT ON/`*`OFF`*

Discussion: The `SET EXACT` command determines whether two character strings have to be the same length to be considered equal. In both cases (`ON` and `OFF`), character strings are compared one character at a time, from left to right. When `SET EXACT` is `OFF` (the default), the two strings are considered equal as long as all the characters in the string on the right of the relational operator are identical to the characters in the same position in the string on the left, regardless of the length of the respective strings. For example, the commands

```
SET EXACT OFF
LIST FOR lname = "Sm"
```

will display records for Small, Smith, Smithson, and so on. In other words, any name beginning with "Sm" will be included, regardless of its length.

    `SET EXACT ON`, however, imposes the additional requirement that the strings have to be the same length to be considered equal. Hence, in the above example, no records would be listed unless someone had the unusual last name "Sm".

Tips:

1. The status of `SET EXACT` pertains to any command involving the comparison of two character strings. In other words, implicit comparisons in commands such as `SEEK` and `FIND` are affected in exactly the same way as are the explicit comparisons present in a FOR or WHILE clause.
2. Upper- and lowercase letters are treated as different characters, whether `SET EXACT` is ON or OFF. For example, the command

```
FIND MILLER
```

will not find "Miller" or "miller".

Related Topics: `FIND`
                             `LOCATE`
                             `SEEK`

SET FIELDS

Syntax: `SET FIELDS TO [<field list>/ALL]`
              `SET FIELDS ON/`*`OFF`*

Discussion: The SET FIELDS TO command limits the active fields in a database, effectively hiding the other fields from view. In general, other commands, whether from the dot prompt or a program file, can access only those fields included in the active field list.

The active fields are designated in a SET FIELDS TO command, with any subsequently issued SET FIELDS commands *adding* to (rather than replacing) the existing field list. For example, in the commands

```
SET FIELDS TO ssn,lastname
SET FIELDS TO initials
```

the first command establishes an *active field list* consisting of only the social security number and last name and the second command adds initials, so that the active list now contains all three fields.

The active field list applies to *all* open databases, regardless of which work area they are in; that is, there is a *single* field list applicable to all 10 work areas, as opposed to 10 individual field lists. *The active list must, therefore, comprise every field from every database that needs to be accessed.* Fields from different databases can be added to the active list in one of two ways, by

1. Including fields from nonselected databases with the file alias preceding the field name.

or

2. Selecting a work area and issuing a SET FIELDS command for the fields in that work area, then selecting a second work area and issuing another SET FIELDS command. The latter group of fields will be added to the existing field list.

The SET FIELDS ON/OFF command controls whether the field list is active. (A SET FIELDS TO command automatically sets SET FIELDS to ON.) A SET FIELDS OFF command deactivates the field list and returns to the default status (where all fields are active). The list remains inactive until either a SET FIELDS ON command (to activate the current list) or another SET FIELDS TO command (to add to the current list) is issued.

A CLEAR FIELDS command also returns to the default status where all fields are accessible. However, CLEAR FIELDS also cancels the effects of any previous SET FIELDS TO commands, so that the field list no longer exists.

Tips:

1. SET FIELDS TO, with no field list, removes *all the fields in the currently selected database* from the active list. (However, fields currently in the active list from databases in unselected areas remain active.)
2. Although fields from multiple files can be made active at the same time through one or more SET FIELDS TO commands, these commands do not establish a relationship between the files, nor do they check to see that a relationship has been established. A SET RELATION TO command must establish the proper relationships.
3. SET FIELDS TO ALL designates every field in the currently selected database as active.
4. A file alias must be used when referring to fields from an unselected work area, but is not needed when referring to fields in the currently selected work area.
5. DISPLAY STRUCTURE indicates all active fields for the currently selected DBF by placing a greater-than sign to the left of the field name.
6. Opening a new database in any work area turns off any active field list; that is, it implicitly issues a SET FIELDS OFF command. SET FIELDS ON is necessary to reactivate the list.
7. If a SET FIELDS ON command is inadvertently issued with no field list in effect, no fields will be accessible in any work area.

8. Certain dBASE commands ignore an active field list, proceeding as though all fields were accessible. APPEND and INSERT, for example, will ignore the field list when an index is active, whereas EDIT and BROWSE enable only the active fields to be accessed and edited. In essence, then, appending and/or editing records when a field list is active can be confusing and we suggest you avoid these operations when all fields are not accessible.

Related Topics: APPEND
                     BROWSE
                     CLEAR
                     DISPLAY STRUCTURE
                     EDIT
                     SET RELATION

SET FILTER

Syntax: SET FILTER TO [FILE <filename>] [condition]

Discussion: The SET FILTER command hides from view all records in the currently selected database that do not meet the specified filter condition. It is analogous to the SET DELETED command in that once a filter has been set, records not meeting the condition are treated as though they were not physically in the database. However, as with the SET DELETED command, a record not meeting the filter condition can still be processed if it is the current record or if it is explicitly referenced in a command, for example, EDIT RECORD 3.

A filter condition is established in one of two ways, either by explicitly specifying the condition in a SET FILTER command such as

    SET FILTER TO hiredate > CTOD("03/16/87")

or by opening a *query file* in which the filter condition was previously saved, for example,

    SET FILTER TO FILE hirespec

Using a query file assumes the existence of the file HIRESPEC.QRY on the default drive. It further requires the word FILE in the SET FILTER command.

The SET FILTER command is most useful when the same subset of records is to be processed by many different commands, for example,

Without filter condition:
    LIST FOR salary > 20000
    REPORT FORM employee FOR salary > 20000
    LABEL FORM employee FOR salary > 20000
    COPY TO mail.txt FOR salary > 20000 DELIMITED

With filter condition:
    SET FILTER TO salary > 20000
    LIST
    REPORT FORM employee
    LABEL FORM employee
    COPY TO mail.txt DELIMITED

The two sets of commands produce equivalent results. The second set, however, is easier to use and is also less susceptible to error because the condition is entered only once.

A SET FILTER TO command that specifies neither a condition nor a file name deactivates an existing filter condition, with all records once again accessible.

Tips: _____

1. Most dBASE commands respect the filter condition and process only those records meeting the specified condition. INDEX ON, REINDEX and ZAP are exceptions which ignore the filter condition and process *all* records in the currently selected database.
2. A filter condition can be built with any of the relational operators (=, <>, >, >=, <, <=) and/or any of the logical operators (.AND., .OR., .NOT.).
3. Only one FILTER condition can be in effect in a work area at one time, that is, issuing a second SET FILTER command deactivates the first filter condition. A different filter condition can, however, be in effect in each of the 10 work areas.
4. A filter condition can be stored in a memory variable and subsequently activated with macro notation, for example,

```
STORE "salary > 20000" TO mcond
SET FILTER TO &mcond
```

5. The SET FILTER command does not reposition the record pointer, even if the current record does not meet the filter condition; that is, the current record will be processed whether it meets the filter condition or not. (You may therefore want to display the current record and move the record pointer to a record meeting the condition before issuing any additional commands.)

Related Topics: SET DELETED

SET FORMAT

Syntax: SET FORMAT TO [<filename>]

Discussion: The SET FORMAT TO command opens an existing format file, which displays a previously designed data entry screen whenever an APPEND, EDIT, or INSERT command is issued. The custom screen appears in place of the input templates normally associated with these commands and is preferable because:

1. The custom screen is more attractive, is apt to contain more explicit prompting messages, and is certainly more oriented to the user.
2. Additional formatting and validating procedures are possible through the PICTURE and RANGE clauses.
3. Fields from related databases can be included in the same input screen.

The format file stays in effect (that is, it maps the screen whenever an APPEND, EDIT, or INSERT command is issued) until a CLOSE FORMAT or a SET FORMAT TO command with no file name is specified.

Tips: _____

1. The file specified in the SET FORMAT command is assumed to have an FMT extension unless otherwise indicated.

2. A format file consists of nothing other than a series of @...SAY...GET commands, and hence can be created with either MODIFY COMMAND or the non-document mode of a word processor. It is easier, however, to use the dBASE *screen generator* initiated by the CREATE SCREEN command.
3. If a format file includes fields from a database other than the currently selected database, those databases must be open and any necessary relationships established.
4. A READ command also activates an open format file, producing a problem in programs attempting to read memory variables while a format file is open. Be sure to close the format file before getting the memory variables.
5. A view file can contain a format file for the related databases, that is, opening the view file opens the format file as well.

Related Topics:
```
APPEND
CLOSE
CREATE SCREEN
EDIT
INSERT
MODIFY COMMAND
READ
SET VIEW
```

SET FUNCTION

Syntax: SET FUNCTION <expression> TO <character expression> [;]

Discussion: The SET FUNCTION command reprograms the 10 (or more) function keys available on a PC or compatible computer. The key to be reprogrammed can be specified as any valid numeric expression (a numeric field, memory variable, or constant, or an arithmetic expression). The command assigned to the key must be a character expression of 30 characters or less and be enclosed in quotes.

The function key may be set to execute the command immediately or merely to display the command at the dot prompt. Including a semicolon executes the command, whereas omitting it requires the user to press the Return key for execution. Consider:

```
SET FUNCTION 5 TO "USE solemp;"
SET FUNCTION 6 TO "MODIFY COMMAND"
```

Pressing the F5 key will open the SOLEMP.DBF file. Pressing the F6 key, however, will display MODIFY COMMAND at the dot prompt with the cursor positioned to the right of the command so that you can then enter the desired file name and press the Return key to execute the command.

Tips:

1. The F1 key *cannot* be changed because it is permanently set to bring up the Help Menu.
2. The default settings of the function keys can be changed by including an F<n> = command (where <n> is the key number) in the CONFIG.DB file. In this situation, no quotation marks should be used to delimit the command.

3. DISPLAY STATUS will list the current settings of the function keys. The default settings at the start of a dBASE session are:

```
F1      HELP;
F2      ASSIST;
F3      LIST;
F4      DIR;
F5      DISPLAY STRUCTURE;
F6      DISPLAY STATUS;
F7      DISPLAY MEMORY;
F8      DISPLAY;
F9      APPEND;
F10     EDIT;
```

4. Several commands can be assigned to the same function key by separating them with semicolons, for example,

```
SET FUNCTION 3 TO "USE solemp;SET INDEX TO"
```

Pressing the F3 key will open SOLEMP.DBF, then display SET INDEX TO at the dot prompt allowing the user to enter the index name. The Return key must be pressed to execute the latter command.

Related Topics: DISPLAY STATUS

SET HEADING

Syntax: SET HEADING *ON*/OFF

Discussion: The SET HEADING command determines whether a heading line is displayed in conjunction with the DISPLAY, LIST, SUM, and AVERAGE commands. If present, the heading will show the field names (and expressions) exactly as they were entered in the command, that is, if the command was typed in uppercase letters, the heading line will also be uppercase. The width of each column is determined by either the width of the field (as established by the file structure) or the width of the field expression, whichever is greater. If headings are not displayed (SET HEADING is OFF), the column width is determined by the field width.

Tips:

1. Complex field expressions are difficult to read when they appear in a heading line; SET HEADING OFF may be worthwhile in such instances.
2. It may also be advantageous to use a SET HEADING OFF command in a program which prints a listing with DISPLAY ALL or LIST as more descriptive headings can be created with an @...SAY or ? command.

Related Topics: AVERAGE
DISPLAY
LIST
SUM
@...SAY

SET HELP

Syntax: `SET HELP ON/OFF`

Discussion: The `SET HELP` command determines whether dBASE will display the question "Do you want some help? (Y/N)" if there is a syntax error at the dot prompt. The default status is `ON`, enabling you to answer `Y` to bring up the Help Menu or `N` to bypass the Help Menu and return to the dot prompt. `SET HELP OFF` precludes the offer of help, and returns immediately to the dot prompt after the error message has been displayed.

Tips:

1. The F1 function key will bring up the Help Menu regardless of the status of `SET HELP`.
2. The HELP.DBS file must be available (in the dBASE subdirectory on a hard disk drive or on the second dBASE disk in a floppy disk system) if help is to be provided. If the file is not present, the offer for help will still be made, but dBASE will be unable to produce the Help Menu.

Related Topics: `HELP`

SET HISTORY

Syntax: `SET HISTORY ON/OFF`
`SET HISTORY TO <numeric expression>`

Discussion: The `SET HISTORY` commands determine whether commands entered at the dot prompt are stored in history memory and, if so, the number of commands that can be held at one time. The default status is `ON`, which enables commands to be recalled, edited if necessary, and reissued.

`SET HISTORY OFF` prevents newly issued commands from being stored in history memory until such time as history is turned back on. However, commands already in memory can still be accessed and reissued.

The `SET HISTORY TO` command changes the number of commands that can be held in history memory from its default value of 20 to any integer between 0 and 16000. However, any subsequently issued `SET HISTORY ON` command automatically resets this value to 20, regardless of any value previously established with a `SET HISTORY TO` command.

Tips:

1. The `SET DOHISTORY` command will store commands executed from a program file in history memory and is an excellent debugging tool. Note, too, that when `SET DOHISTORY` is ON, it is usually necessary to increase the size of history memory.
2. If the `SET HISTORY TO` command inadvertently specifies a value less than the number of commands currently in history memory, all stored commands are lost.
3. The commands stored in history memory can be viewed with a `DISPLAY HISTORY` command.

Related Topics: DISPLAY HISTORY
SET DOHISTORY

SET INDEX

Syntax: SET INDEX TO <index file list>

Discussion: The SET INDEX TO command opens one or more existing index files (each with the NDX extension unless otherwise specified) associated with the currently selected database. Up to seven indexes can be listed, with the first designated the *master index*. The command

      SET INDEX TO lastname,location,title

opens three indexes, with LASTNAME.NDX established as the master index. The master index determines the logical sequence in which records in the database are accessed. The other indexes have no affect on how the records are accessed, but are only open so that they will be updated as the file is modified.

In other words, all open indexes are updated automatically when changes are made to the database (for example, when records are appended or deleted and/or changes made to the key fields). Closed indexes, on the other hand, are instantly outdated when the database is changed and will subsequently produce erroneous results. It is recommended, therefore, that all indexes associated with a particular database be open whenever file maintenance is done.

A CLOSE INDEXES, CLOSE DATABASES, or a SET INDEX TO command with no file list will close all open indexes.

Tips:

1. Existing indexes can also be opened by including the INDEX clause in the USE command, for example,

      USE file1 INDEX lastname,location,title

   In other words, the single USE...INDEX command is equivalent to the two commands

      USE file1
      SET INDEX TO lastname,location,title

2. A SET INDEX command first closes any open indexes, then opens the indexes specified in the file list.
3. A SET INDEX command repositions the record pointer to the first record of the master index.
4. Unless file maintenance is being done, it is neither necessary nor desirable to keep all indexes open. However, any index not open when the database is updated must be rebuilt with a subsequent INDEX ON or REINDEX command.
5. Keep the number of indexes associated with an individual database to seven or less, so that all indexes can be open when the file is updated. Realize also that the more indexes open during file maintenance, the longer it takes to process each change to the file.
6. Inadvertently opening an index whose key field is not found in the currently selected database produces an error message. However, opening an index associated with another

database that has a key expression appropriate for the current database will not produce an error message, just bizarre results.

Related Topics: CLOSE
INDEX ON
REINDEX
SET ORDER TO
USE

SET INTENSITY

Syntax: SET INTENSITY *ON*/OFF

Discussion: The SET INTENSITY command determines whether input templates are displayed in reverse video. The default status is ON so that reverse video is initially in effect and the templates are highlighted. SET INTENSITY OFF removes the highlighting, which means the input templates are no longer differentiated from the standard display area.

Tips:

1. SET INTENSITY and SET DELIMITERS should not both be OFF at the same time, as the input templates would no longer be differentiated on the screen, producing problems during data entry.
2. The SET COLOR command can change the colors of the reverse video (enhanced) area only as long as SET INTENSITY is ON. When SET INTENSITY is OFF, the enhanced area is the same color as the standard display area.

Related Topics: SET COLOR
SET DELIMITERS

SET MEMOWIDTH

Syntax: SET MEMOWIDTH TO <numeric expression>

Discussion: The SET MEMOWIDTH command determines the display width for memo fields specified in a LIST, DISPLAY, or ? command. (Any memo field not explicitly specified is not displayed.) The default width of 50 characters can be changed to any value between 8 and 255. Note, however, that setting a width larger than the display area (whether screen or printed page) causes the individual lines to wrap around, making the display difficult to read.

Related Topics: DISPLAY
LIST
?

SET MENU

Syntax: SET MENU *ON/OFF*

Discussion: The SET MENU command determines whether a menu showing the effects of the cursor control keys will be displayed in conjunction with full-screen commands (CREATE, APPEND, EDIT, and so on). The default status is ON, meaning that the menu is displayed.

Tips:

1. The F1 key toggles the menu on and off from within the full-screen mode regardless of the status of SET MENU.
2. The default setting of SET MENU can be changed by including a MENU = command in the CONFIG.DB file.

Related Topics: APPEND
BROWSE
CREATE
EDIT

SET ORDER

Syntax: SET ORDER TO <index number>

Discussion: The SET ORDER command selects one of the currently active indexes as the master index without closing any of the other active indexes. In particular it establishes as the master index, in the file whose *position* within the list of open indexes corresponds to the number specified in the SET ORDER command. For example, had the command

        USE file1 INDEX lastname,location,title

been used to open file1 and its associated indexes, the subsequent command

        SET ORDER TO 2

would establish LOCATION.NDX as the master index (because location was listed second) *without closing* the lastname and title indexes. Alternatively, you could issue the command

        SET INDEX TO location,lastname,title

to make location the master index, while keeping the other two open. (Omitting the lastname and title indexes in the SET INDEX command would have a very different effect because the omitted indexes would be implicitly closed.)

  The number specified in the SET ORDER command can be any valid numeric expression between 0 and 7, depending on the number of active indexes. If, however, the number specified is greater than the number of active indexes, an error message will be displayed.

Tips:

1. SET ORDER executes faster than SET INDEX because no indexes are opened or closed.
2. SET ORDER TO 0 causes the database to be processed in physical order, because no

master index is established. Note, however, that if ORDER is SET TO 0, *no indexes are updated* when changes are made to the database.

3. The SET ORDER command does *not* reposition the record pointer to the top of the file as does a SET INDEX command. The current record thus remains the current record.

Related Topics: SET INDEX
                     USE

SET PATH

Syntax: SET PATH TO <path list>

Discussion: The dBASE SET PATH command is different from a DOS PATH command because the latter searches only for files with BAT, COM, or EXE extensions, whereas the dBASE command searches for files of all types. Multiple paths may be specified and are separated by commas or semicolons, for example,

      SET PATH TO b:\soleil,b:\solstub

or

      SET PATH TO b:\soleil;b:\solstub

The SET PATH TO command (with no path list) deactivates any existing path, restricting future searches to the current subdirectory.

Tips:

1. The dBASE SET PATH command will *not* result in newly created files being stored in that subdirectory. In other words, the SET PATH command does *not* change the logged directory, but only provides an alternate place for dBASE to look for files not found in the current subdirectory.

   This can be circumvented by logging onto an application subdirectory *before* loading dBASE. You must, however, establish a PATH (while still in DOS) to the directory containing the dBASE *program* files so that DOS may find them. Consider:

      C> CD \USSTATES ——— *Changes path to application subdirectory*
      C> PATH \DBASE   ——— *Establishes path to dBASE program files for DOS*
      C> DBASE ———————— *Loads dBASE, while remaining in USSTATES subdirectory*

2. DISPLAY STATUS displays the current search paths.

3. A path must be specified in the dBASE DIR command to obtain a listing of files in other than the current subdirectory, for example,

      DIR b:\soleil;*.prg

4. dBASE does *not* recognize paths established with the DOS PATH command (except when using the RUN command, where the operating system actually takes control, searching the DOS path for the appropriate COM, EXE, or BAT file).

Related Topics: DIR
                     DISPLAY STATUS
                     RUN

SET PRINT

Syntax: `SET PRINT ON/OFF`

Discussion: `SET PRINT ON` directs all output normally displayed on the screen (except for the results of full-screen commands and text formatted with `@...SAY` commands) to the printer as well as to the screen. Included in the output sent to the printer are commands entered at the dot prompt, as well as the responses or messages that dBASE displays on the screen. Accordingly, specifying `SET PRINT ON` enables a printed record to be made of all commands issued and their results. `SET PRINT OFF` returns to the default mode, where output is displayed on the screen only.

Tips:

1. `SET DEVICE TO PRINT` must be issued to direct text formatted with `@...SAY` commands to the printer. (As indicated above, `SET PRINT ON` will not work in this instance.)
2. A `SET CONSOLE OFF` command, issued before a `SET PRINT ON`, will suppress the screen display while directing output to the printer.
3. The printer should be turned on and be on line, before issuing a `SET PRINT ON` command. If not, an error message will result.
4. Ctrl P acts as a toggle switch and can be used at the dot prompt instead of `SET PRINT ON/OFF`.

Related Topics: `SET CONSOLE`
`SET DEVICE`

SET PROCEDURE

Syntax: `SET PROCEDURE TO <filename>`

Discussion: The `SET PROCEDURE` command loads the designated procedure file into memory from where its individual procedures are available for other programs to use until the procedure file is closed. The advantage of a procedure file (containing a maximum of 32 procedures), over individual program files, is speed. Access to a procedure is nearly instantaneous because the procedure is already in memory. Access to a program, however, requires the program to be read from disk into memory before it can be executed.

Once open, a procedure file is closed with either a `CLOSE PROCEDURE` or `SET PROCEDURE TO` command with no file name specified.

Tips:

1. A procedure file has a default extension of PRG unless another extension is explicitly specified when the file is created.
2. Whenever dBASE encounters a `DO` command it looks first to memory, then to disk. Hence, if a procedure (in the open procedure file) and a program have the same name, the procedure will always be the one executed. You must, therefore, avoid using duplicate names for programs and procedures.

3. Only one procedure file can be open at a time. Opening a second procedure file implicitly closes the first one.

4. Although a single procedure file can contain up to 32 individual procedures, it still counts as only one open file. This helps to reduce the number of open files, and hence makes it easier to live within the limit of 15 open files at any given time.

5. The individual procedures in a procedure file should be separated with a blank line or a line of asterisks to make each module easily identifiable. In addition, comment each procedure as you would a program.

6. A procedure file is created the same way as an ordinary program, that is, with `MODIFY COMMAND` or the non-document mode of a word processor.

Related Topics: `DO`
`MODIFY COMMAND`

SET RELATION

Syntax: `SET RELATION TO [<key expression>/<RECNO()>/<Nexp> INTO <alias>]`

Discussion: The `SET RELATION` command establishes a link between records in the currently selected database and those in a second database open in another work area, so that moving the record pointer in the current database moves the record pointer to a corresponding record in the related database as well. The relationship can be based on a common field (the usual approach) or on record numbers. Either way, the command enables data from the two databases to be processed as though it were coming from a single file.

Consider, for example, a banking application that maintains two distinct files for accounts and customers. (One customer can have several accounts, but each account can only be associated with one customer.) Assume further that the bank is processing its monthly account statements and that the following commands are in effect:

```
SELECT 2
USE customer INDEX cust_id
SELECT 1
USE account
SET RELATION TO cust_id INTO customer
```

The `SET RELATION` command establishes a link between records in the currently selected database (ACCOUNT.DBF) with those in a dependent database (CUSTOMER.DBF). The link is based on a *common* field, that is, cust_id must exist in the file structure of both files. Henceforth, whenever the record pointer in the ACCOUNT.DBF file moves to a new account record, the record pointer in the CUSTOMER.DBF file is automatically repositioned to the corresponding customer record. [To establish the relationship, the dependent file (CUSTOMER.DBF) must be opened with an index whose key expression is the common field (cust_id).]

Once the relationship has been established, a field list can include entries from both files, making it appear as though the data were contained in a single file. For example, to produce a list of account numbers together with the corresponding customer names, use the command

```
LIST acct_id,acct_type,customer->name
```

Observe, however, that fields from the unselected file (CUSTOMER.DBF) are specified with the *file alias* before the field name.

Note, too, that the SET RELATION command moves the record pointer to the *first* matching record in the related file with no indication that other matching records (may) exist. Hence, additional coding is required to find the other records; for example, to list all accounts for a particular customer (GR0345), the following commands are necessary:

```
SELECT 2
USE account INDEX cust_id
SELECT 1
USE customer INDEX cust_id
FIND GR0345 ──────────────────────────────── Finds customer record
SET RELATION TO cust_id INTO account ──── Moves record pointer to first
                                             record with matching
                                             customer ID
SELECT 2 ─────────────────────────────── Makes ACCOUNT.DBF the
                                             active file
DO WHILE cust_id = account->cust_id──── Finds additional accounts
    DISPLAY name,account->acct_num,account->acct_type
    SKIP
ENDDO
```

The preceding code reverses the currently selected and related files from the earlier example; CUSTOMER.DBF is now the current database and ACCOUNT.DBF is the related file. A FIND command is used to find customer GR0345 in the customer file. The first account is then automatically identified through the established relation. The subsequent DO WHILE loop lists all other accounts for that customer.

A relationship can also be established based on record numbers rather than on a key expression. In that case, the related database is opened without an index and a common field need not exist. Now, whenever the record pointer moves to a new record in the currently selected database, the record pointer in the related file is repositioned at the record with the corresponding record number.

Issuing the command with no parameters (SET RELATION TO) deactivates the relationship and the record pointers once again move independently in the two files.

Tips:

1. A different relationship can be in effect for each of the 10 work areas, making an intricate network of related files possible. Only one relationship, however, can be in effect for any one area.
2. Relationships can be saved in a view (VUE) file, from where they can be reestablished with a SET VIEW command. (View files are created with a CREATE VIEW command.)

Related Topics: CREATE VIEW
JOIN
SELECT
SET VIEW

SET SAFETY

Syntax: SET SAFETY *ON*/OFF

Discussion: The SET SAFETY command determines whether dBASE will signal a warning before overwriting an existing file. The default status is ON and produces the message,

`"<filename> already exists, overwrite it?(Y/N)"`

A response of Y allows the file to be overwritten, whereas N cancels the command and returns to the dot prompt. If, however, SET SAFETY is OFF, the file is overwritten with no warning.

Tips:

1. SET SAFETY is normally OFF within a program because the intention is clearly to overwrite existing files. Moreover, the message produced by leaving SET SAFETY ON would clutter the custom screen and confuse the user.
2. As a precautionary measure, SET SAFETY should always be left ON at the dot prompt. Inadvertently specifying the name of an existing file in a command that creates a new file can lead to very unfortunate results.
3. The status of SET TALK does not affect the SET SAFETY message; the message appears whether SET TALK is ON or OFF.
4. The SET ALTERNATE TO command overwrites an existing file whether SET SAFETY is ON or OFF.

Related Topics: SET ALTERNATE
SET TALK

SET SCOREBOARD

Syntax: SET SCOREBOARD *ON*/OFF

Discussion: SET SCOREBOARD, in conjunction with SET STATUS, determines whether or not dBASE status indicators (Ins, Caps, Num, and Del) and error messages will be displayed, and if so, where. The effects of various ON and OFF combinations for the two commands is explained in the table below:

Status	Scoreboard	Result
ON	Immaterial	Status indicators appear on line 22 with error messages immediately below.
OFF	ON	Status indicators and error messages both appear on line 0.
OFF	OFF	Neither status indicators nor error messages appear at all.

Tips:

1. Either (or both) SET STATUS or SET SCOREBOARD should be ON at the dot prompt. In a program file however, they should both be OFF as they would otherwise interfere with custom screens.
2. The error messages affected by SET SCOREBOARD and SET STATUS pertain only to data entry (for example, an invalid character in a field name, data falling outside a specified range, and so on). These commands do *not* affect errors regarding command syntax.

Related Topics: SET STATUS

SET STATUS

Syntax: `SET STATUS` *`ON`*`/OFF`

Discussion: `SET STATUS`, in conjunction with `SET SCOREBOARD`, determines whether dBASE status indicators and error messages will be displayed, and if so, where. `SET STATUS ON` (whether `SET SCOREBOARD` is ON or OFF) displays the *status bar* on line 22 with the following information:

1. The current drive
2. The current database
3. The current record
4. The status indicators
5. The current command

Tips: _____

1. The status bar will appear during a `BROWSE` or `CREATE` operation and when the ASSISTANT is active, whether `SET STATUS` is ON or OFF.
2. The navigation and message lines are located on lines 23 and 24 (immediately below the status bar), and contain error, informational, and/or prompting messages. These lines are displayed (or not) with the status bar, depending on whether `SET STATUS` is ON or OFF.

Related Topics: `ASSIST`
`SET SCOREBOARD`

SET STEP

Syntax: `SET STEP ON/`*`OFF`*

Discussion: `SET STEP ON` is a debugging tool that temporarily halts program execution after each command line, displaying the command results with a prompting message. The user may choose to continue with the next command (by pressing the spacebar), suspend program execution (by pressing S), or terminate the program (by pressing the Esc key). Suspending execution returns control to the dot prompt and allows other debugging commands to be executed (`DISPLAY STATUS` or `DISPLAY MEMORY` for example), with control returning to the program when a `RESUME` command is issued.

Tips: _____

1. `SET STEP` is better used with `SET ECHO ON` and `SET TALK ON` because the command in isolation does not provide much insight into what is happening. Seeing the command (`SET ECHO`) first, and then its result, is much more helpful.
2. `SET STEP`, in conjunction with `SET DEBUG`, is extremely time consuming and should be used only with the most troublesome and complex problems.

Related Topics: SET DEBUG
                  SET ECHO
                  SET TALK

SET TYPEAHEAD

365

SET TALK

Syntax: SET TALK *ON/OFF*

Discussion: The SET TALK command determines whether or not an indication of the action dBASE has taken in response to individual commands is displayed on the screen. When SET TALK is ON, for example, dBASE responds to an INDEX ON command by reporting the number of records indexed, to a LOCATE command by indicating either the number of the found record or that the locate was unsuccessful. SET TALK OFF prevents these (and various other) messages from appearing.

Tips:

1. SET TALK ON is helpful and informative at the dot prompt. In the program mode, however, it disrupts custom screens and confuses the user.
2. SET TALK should be set ON when debugging a program to add to the information available for problem solving.
3. The SET SAFETY message ("Filename already exists, overwrite (Y/N)") is unaffected by the status of SET TALK.
4. dBASE error messages regarding problems in data entry and/or command syntax will appear regardless of the status of SET TALK.

Related Topics: SET ECHO
                 SET SAFETY
                 SET STEP

SET TYPEAHEAD

Syntax: SET TYPEAHEAD TO <numeric expression>

Discussion: The SET TYPEAHEAD command determines the size of the typeahead buffer which, in turn, controls the number of keystrokes that can be entered ahead of actual processing. The default value of 20 may be changed to any number between 0 and 32000. The typeahead buffer increases the speed of input from the dot prompt because a new command can be entered while the previous command is processing. In other words, any commands stored within the buffer are executed as soon as the previous commands are completed and no time is lost waiting for a new command to be entered.

Tips:

1. Any characters entered when the typeahead buffer is full are ignored (that is, lost). The bell will ring, however, if SET BELL is ON to warn that the buffer is full.

2. Setting SET TYPEAHEAD to zero disables the buffer; the buffer is immediately "full" and will not accept any typing while another command is being processed.
3. The typeahead buffer can become a liability within a program file since incorrect anticipation (by the user) of the next program input can produce erroneous results. Accordingly, disable the buffer entirely or use a CLEAR TYPEAHEAD command before each input is read.
4. The SET TYPEAHEAD command has no effect if SET ESCAPE is OFF, that is, the typeahead buffer can only be changed when SET ESCAPE is ON.

Related Topics: SET BELL
SET ESCAPE

SET UNIQUE

Syntax: SET UNIQUE ON/*OFF*

Discussion: The SET UNIQUE command controls whether an index entry is generated for every record in a database or only for those records with unique values of the key expression on which the index is based. By default, SET UNIQUE is OFF, so that an index contains an entry for *every* record in its associated database. When SET UNIQUE is ON, however, the resulting index includes only those records having a unique value of the key expression. In other words, any record that contains a duplicate of a key value that is already in the index is excluded from the index.

Indexes created with SET UNIQUE ON are used to obtain a list of the different key values that exist in a database. With extremely large databases, it is also useful in finding the starting location (the record number) of each of the different key values.

Tips:

1. Indexing with SET UNIQUE ON is equivalent to issuing the INDEX ON command with a UNIQUE clause.
2. A unique index retains its status when it is reindexed, or when changes are made to the database, whether SET UNQIUE is ON or OFF. Newly appended or edited records will be added to a unique index only if their key values do not already exist.
3. A unique index will not permit access to all the records in a database which contains duplicate values of the key expression. Therefore, it should not be opened as the master index unless it is specifically needed for its unique status.

Related Topics: INDEX
REINDEX

SET VIEW

Syntax: SET VIEW TO <filename>

Discussion: The SET VIEW command opens an existing view file, establishing the relational database environment specified in the view file. The appropriate database files and associated indexes are placed in their assigned work areas, relationships between the files are established, the field list (if present) is activated, the filter condition (if present) is established, and the format file is opened.

Tips:

1. A view file is unlike a regular file because once it establishes the environment it is no longer considered an open file. It therefore never needs to be closed. The files it opens, however, must be subsequently closed with appropriate CLOSE or CLEAR commands.
2. The DISPLAY STATUS command will show all environmental information.

Related Topics: CREATE VIEW
                       DISPLAY STATUS

SKIP

Syntax: SKIP [<numeric expression>]

Discussion: The SKIP command moves the record pointer forward or backward in the currently selected database, depending on whether the numeric expression is positive or negative. The command defaults to moving forward one record if no numeric expression is specified, otherwise it moves the specified number of records in the indicated direction. SKIP 10 and SKIP −5 move the record pointer forward 10 positions and backward five positions.

The record number indicating the new position of the record pointer is displayed on the screen immediately after the command executes as long as SET TALK is ON.

The SKIP command operates within the *physical* sequence of the records in the database, if no index is active. If an index is active, however, the command operates within the *logical* sequence according to the active index.

Deleted records are treated as if they were not physically present whenever SET DELETED is ON. In other words, if the record pointer is at record 3 and record 4 has been previously marked for deletion, SKIP +1 will reposition the record pointer to record 5. The same principle holds true when a filter condition has been established. Records not meeting the filter condition are treated as if they are not physically present.

Tips:

1. If the record pointer is on record 3 and a SKIP −7 is issued (assuming no index is active), the record pointer will be repositioned to record 1 and the BOF( ) function will be set to true. If, however, the record pointer is initially on record 1 and a backward SKIP is attempted, an error message indicating the beginning-of-file has been reached is displayed.
2. If the record pointer is on record 20 and a SKIP 10 is issued (assume a 25-record file), the record pointer will be repositioned to record 26 (the end-of-file marker) and the EOF( ) function set to true. If, however, the record pointer is initially on record 26 (the end-of-file marker) and a forward SKIP is attempted, an error message indicating that the end-of-file has been reached is displayed.
3. A SKIP command that moves the record pointer in the currently selected database will also move the record pointer in a related database (given that a relationship has been set).

4. The numeric expression can be a formula, constant, or numeric memory variable, for example, `SKIP 5*2`, `SKIP 10`, and `SKIP mnum`, are all equivalent (assuming mnum contains the numeric constant 10).

Related Topics: `BOF()`
`EOF()`
`GOTO`
`SET DELETED`
`SET FILTER`
`SET INDEX`
`SET RELATION`

SORT

Syntax: `SORT <scope> ON <field>[/A][/C][/D] [,<field>[/A]`
`[/C][/D]...] [WHILE <condition>]`
`[FOR <condition>] TO <filename>`

Discussion: The `SORT` command creates a copy of the currently selected database in which the records are physically reordered according to the specified key field(s). The newly sorted file is a database file in its own right and is assigned a default extension of .DBF (unless another extension is explicitly specified). The new file is completely independent of the file from which it was created.

Character, numeric, and date fields may be designated as keys (memo and logical fields may not be used) and reorder the file in alphabetic, numeric, and chronologic sequence, respectively. For example, the command

`SORT ON lastname TO alpha`

creates a new database file named ALPHA.DBF in which the records are sequenced alphabetically by last name, whereas the command

`SORT ON salary TO salary`

puts records in ascending numeric sequence of salary.

A 10-key maximum is permitted in the same `SORT` command. The individual keys need not be the same data type. The first field listed is the *primary key* within which records are sorted according to a *secondary key,* and so on. The command

`SORT ON location,salary TO locatsal`

creates a new file in which the records are first sequenced by location and then by salary within each location.

Unless otherwise indicated, all sorts are performed in *ascending* (low-to-high) sequence. This can be changed, however, by specifying one of the parameters as shown:

/A: Ascending order (default)
/D: Descending order
/C: Ignore the difference between upper- and lowercase letters (uppercase letters normally precede lowercase letters)

The ascending and descending parameters are mutually exclusive for the same key. Either one can, however, be combined with the /C parameter for use with character fields, for example,

`SORT ON loc/AC,salary/D TO locatsal`

A scope, FOR, or WHILE clause can be included to sort only a subset of records in the currently selected database to the new file, for example,

```
SORT NEXT 20 ON lastname TO newfile
```

Tips:

1. The sorted file can be processed only after it has been opened with a USE command.
2. A file cannot be sorted to itself or to any other open file.
3. Resequencing a large file with the SORT command is a time-consuming process which can be done more efficiently through indexing. (SORT is best used to create sorted *subsets* of the original database using the scope clause, or a FOR or WHILE condition.) If, however, it is essential that the physical and logical sequence of a file be made the same, index the file and then use the COPY command with the index as the master index. Erase the original file and rename the copy with the name of the original file.
4. If a filter condition is active, only those records meeting the specified filter condition will be sorted and copied to the new file. The same is true if SET DELETED has been set to ON; that is, records marked for deletion will not be copied to the new file.
5. If the SET FIELDS command has established a field list, all fields will still be copied to the new file whether they are included in the field list or not. In addition, any field, active or not, can be used as a sort key.
6. The SORT command repositions the record pointer to the end-of-file unless a scope of NEXT or a WHILE condition is used. In these two cases, the record pointer is repositioned one record below the last record processed.
7. If the source file contains a memo field, a copy of the DBT file will be automatically created for the new file and will have the same name as the sorted file, but with a DBT extension.
8. If the target file of the SORT command has the same name as an existing file and SET SAFETY is ON, dBASE will ask before overwriting the existing file. If, however, SET SAFETY is OFF, no warning will be given before the file is overwritten.

Related Topics: COPY
                  INDEX
                  SET DELETED
                  SET FIELDS
                  SET FILTER
                  USE

SPACE FUNCTION

Syntax: SPACE(<numeric expression>)

Discussion: The SPACE() function generates a character string consisting of the specified number of blank spaces. The expression in the function may be any valid numeric expression (that is, a numeric field, memory varible, constant, or arithmetic expression). The expression's value however, must result in a positive number between 0 and 254; if the number is negative or greater than 254, an error message will be displayed.

Tips:

1. The SPACE() function is often used to initialize a character type memory variable with

blanks, for example,

```
STORE SPACE(13) TO mlname
```

which is easier and more efficient than its equivalent

```
STORE '            ' TO mlname
```

2. The SPACE() function is used in a program to clear an individual line before mapping new text, for example,

```
@ 20,20 SAY SPACE(68)
```

Clearing an existing line is especially important if the new text is a shorter string than the text it replaces. A single @...CLEAR TO command can be used to clear a rectangular area of more than one line and is the equivalent of several individual @...SAY SPACE() commands.

Related Topics: @...CLEAR TO

STORE

Syntax: STORE <expression> TO <memvar list>
or
<memvar> = <expression>

Discussion: The STORE command initializes one or more memory variables, simultaneously creating the variables if they do not already exist. The expression is evaluated first, then the result is stored in the named memory variable. If it is an existing memory variable, any previous value is overwritten, and therefore lost.

The expression may be comprised of constants, fields, functions and/or other memory variables. The nature of the expression also determines the data type of the memory variable (character, numeric, date, or logical) as shown:

```
STORE 'hello' To mgreeting
STORE 10 TO mnumber
STORE CTOD('06/12/87') To mdate
STORE .T. TO mloop
```

A *numeric* memory variable is created by supplying a value consisting of only numeric digits. Numeric memory variables default to a length of 10 with no decimal places. (The assigned value may override this default if it is longer than 10 digits and/or explicitly includes decimal places.)

Character memory variables are created by enclosing the value in quotes, with the character string length determining the length of the memory variable.

Date memory variables are created by converting a character form of the date with a date conversion function. Date memory variables have a default length of eight.

Logical memory variables are created with a value of true or false set off by periods, and have a length of one.

Up to 256 memory variables can be active at one time, collectively taking a maximum of 6000 bytes in memory. (The amount of available memory can be increased or decreased with a MVARSIZ command in the CONFIG.DB file, but the number of memory variables is fixed at 256.)

Any PRIVATE or PUBLIC commands issued before the STORE command determine whether the memory variables are *local* or *global*. Local variables are available only to the program in which they were created and/or to its called programs. Global variables are accessible by both called and calling programs and are retained in memory after the program terminates.

Tips:

1. Several memory variables can be initialized in the same statement, for example,

```
STORE 0 TO mnum,mrow,mcol
```

2. A memory variable cannot be assigned a memo data type.

3. The name of a memory variable can consist of up to 10 characters. A common convention is to begin the name of all such variables with the letter "m" to indicate a memory variable. It is also helpful to assign names to related variables that have common prefixes so that they can be saved and/or released in groups with the use of a skeleton.

4. It is often necessary to create memory variables, with no particular initial values, so that other values may be input through subsequent GET statements. Assign a zero to numeric variables, a blank character string of the desired length to character variables, and a blank date to a date variable, for example,

```
STORE 0 TO mnumber
STORE SPACE(50) TO mcompany
STORE CTOD(' / / ') TO mdate
```

Logical variables, however, cannot be assigned a blank value and must be initialized to either true or false.

5. Additional examples are provided to indicate additional ways to initialize memory variables:

```
STORE TRIM(fname) + ' ' + TRIM(lname) to mname
STORE UPPER(mchoice) TO mchoice
STORE mprice * 1.15 TO mincrease
STORE mcounter + 1 TO mcounter
```

6. At no time should a memory variable be given the same name as a field in the currently selected database, as dBASE always assumes you are referring to the field in the file structure.

Related Topics:
```
DISPLAY MEMORY
@...SAY...GET
SAVE
RELEASE
RESTORE
WAIT
PUBLIC
PRIVATE
```

STR FUNCTION

Syntax: `STR(<numeric expression>, [<length>], [<decimals>])`

Discussion: The STR() function returns the character-string equivalent of the numeric expression specified in the function argument. The optional length parameter specifies the length of the character string (a default of 10 is assumed), whereas the optional decimal parameter indicates the number of decimal places (the default is zero). The length and decimal parameters themselves may be any valid numeric expression, that is, a numeric field, memory variable, constant, or an arithmetic expression.

The length parameter must take into account the total number of characters to be output, including a minus sign, decimal point, and the appropriate number of decimal places. If the length is smaller than the number of digits to the left of the decimal, dBASE returns asterisks rather than a character string; if the length can accommodate the digits to the left of the decimal, but not the decimal point or decimal places, the appropriately rounded integer will be returned. In any event, the number of decimal places must be less than the total length, or an execution error will result and no string will be returned.

Tips:

1. The STR() function permits numeric values to be concatenated with character strings in the same print statement, for example,

```
? 'Your raise is ' + STR(raise,7) + ' dollars'
Your raise is      750 dollars
```

A character-string display with leading blanks can be improved with the LTRIM() function as follows:

```
? 'Your raise is ' + LTRIM(STR(raise,7)) + 'dollars'
Your raise is 750 dollars
```

2. The STR() function is *necessary* to build an index based on a combination of character and numeric fields, for example,

```
INDEX ON location + STR(salary,6) To locsal
```

3. A numeric field can be converted to a character string and be spaced more attractively in a report form; for example, an entry for a column of

```
'     '+ STR(raise,6)
```

would place the salary amount five spaces from the beginning of the column. This can be used to center numeric values in a column.

Related Topics:
```
CREATE REPORT
INDEX ON
LTRIM()
VAL()
```

SUBSTR FUNCTION

Syntax:
```
SUBSTR(<character expression>, <starting position>,
       [<length>])
```

Discussion: The SUBSTR() function returns a portion (substring) of the specified character string, beginning with the character in the indicated starting position and ending with either the last character in the string (if no length is provided) or with the appropriate character as specified by the optional length parameter. Consider:

`SUBSTR('United States of America',1,6)`	United
`SUBSTR('United States of America',8,6)`	States
`SUBSTR('United States of America',18)`	America

The character expression can be a character field, memory variable, character expression enclosed in quotes, concatenated character expression, or the result of a function that returns a string. The starting position and length parameters can be any valid numeric expression (that is, a numeric field, memory variable, constant, or an arithmetic expression). The starting position must, however, be a positive integer and cannot be greater than the length of the original string. The length parameter can be greater than the number of characters between the starting position and the end of the character string, in which case, the substring ends with the last character in the string.

Tips:

1. The `SUBSTR()` function can be used to embed literal constants in a field for display purposes such as hyphens in a social security number. For example,

   ```
   SUBSTR(ssn,1,3) + "-" + SUBSTR(ssn,4,2) + "-" +
   SUBSTR(ssn,6)
   ```

   This expression can also be used as a content entry in either a report form or mailing label and results in displaying a social security number in the form 111-22-3333 as opposed to the form 111223333.

Related Topics: `STR()`

SUM

Syntax: `SUM [<expression list>][<scope>][WHILE <condition>]`
`[FOR <condition>][TO <memvar list>]`

Discussion: The SUM command computes the sum for numeric fields and/or arithmetic expressions involving numeric fields in the currently selected database. The command computes the total for *every* numeric field, unless an expression list is included in the command. Including the expression list restricts the computation to only those numeric fields specified.

   Every record in the database will be included in the computation unless the command contains a scope, FOR, or WHILE parameter. Thus, the command

   ```
   SUM salary
   ```

includes every record in the database, whereas the command

   ```
   SUM salary NEXT 10
   ```

includes only the next 10 records (the records included are the 10 beginning with the one at the current position of the record pointer). Similarly, the command

   ```
   SUM salary FOR location = '40'
   ```

computes the total salary amount for only those employees at location 40.

The results of the SUM command (the field names and their respective totals) are displayed on the screen immediately after the command is issued (as long as SET TALK is ON) but are not otherwise saved. To preserve the totals for future use, the TO clause must be specified with a valid memory variable included for each field summed.

Tips: ───

1. In the absence of an expression list, a sum is computed for every numeric field in the current database, whether it makes sense to do so or not. Thus, if an ID code is defined as a numeric field, a sum of the ID codes will be computed, even though it will be a meaningless number.
2. When using a TO clause to save multiple sums to memory variables, the sums are computed in the order that the fields are listed in the expression list and then assigned to the memory variables in the order of the memvar list. Thus, in the command

    ```
    SUM field1,field2 TO memvar1,memvar2
    ```

    the sum of field1 is assigned to memvar1 and the sum of field2 to memvar2.

Related Topics: AVERAGE
                    COUNT

TIME FUNCTION

Syntax: TIME()

Discussion: The TIME() function returns the system time as obtained from DOS, in the default format of hh:mm:ss. The system time is based on a 24-hour clock so that times between 1 p.m. and midnight are displayed as 13:00:00 to 24:00:00. The value returned by the TIME function is a *character* string that can be displayed in concatenated strings without conversion, for example,

```
? 'The present time is ' + TIME()
```

To use the time in arithmetic operations, it must first be converted to a numeric value with the VAL() function. dBASE does not provide time arithmetic as it does date arithmetic and, hence, a program must be written to compute time intervals if desired.

Tips: ───

1. Be sure to enter the time correctly when booting the system as that is the time used by the TIME function. (It is also the time stamped on all files created.)
2. The dBASE TIME function *cannot* be used to set the system time. (The DOS TIME command, can, however be accessed from within dBASE using a RUN command, for example, RUN TIME.)
3. An @...SAY TIME() command in a program will show the time when the screen was mapped; the time will *not* be updated until another @...SAY TIME() command is executed.

Related Topics: DATE()

@...TO

Syntax: `@ <row,col> [CLEAR] TO <row,col> [DOUBLE]`

Discussion: The `@...TO` command draws a continuous single (or double) line or box on the screen, or clears a rectangular area on the screen. The first set of ⟨row,col⟩ coordinates indicates the upper-left corner of the box, while the second set of coordinates designates the lower-right corner. Specifying the same row in both produces a horizontal line, whereas duplicate column coordinates produce a vertical line.

dBASE views the screen as consisting of 25 rows and 80 columns. Accordingly, the row coordinate can be any integer from 0 to 24, while the column coordinate must be an integer from 0 to 79. The CLEAR parameter is explained in the CLEAR command, elsewhere in the Programmer's Notebook.

A single line (box) is drawn unless the DOUBLE parameter is included in the command. Hence, the command

    @ 5,2 TO 5,78

produces a single line in row 5, whereas the command

    @ 5,2 TO 5,78 DOUBLE

draws a double line.

Tips:

1. The `@...TO` command is used primarily with program and/or format files to create attractive screen displays.
2. If the same box is used to frame the screen throughout a system, the `@...CLEAR TO` command should be used to clear text inside the box, rather than using the CLEAR command for the entire screen. This will eliminate the need to constantly redraw the box every time a new screen is mapped.

Related Topics: CLEAR
                   @...SAY...GET

TRIM FUNCTION

Syntax: `TRIM(character expression)`

Discussion: The `TRIM()` function strips trailing blanks from the specified character expression. The expression may be a character field, memory variable, character string enclosed in quotation marks, or a concatenated string expression. The function is especially useful when concatenating character fields to one another. For example,

Without TRIM function:

```
LIST lastname,initials TO PRINT
Arnold       JS
Baker        MJ
  .
    .
      .
Sugrue       PK
```

With TRIM function:
```
LIST TRIM(lastname) +', ' + initials TO PRINT
Arnold, JS
Baker, MJ
     .
       .
         .
Sugrue, PK
```

Tips:

1. The length of the trimmed character string is less than that of the untrimmed version, for example,

```
STORE 'Jessica     '     TO mname
? LEN(mname)
12 ─────────────────── dBASE response
? LEN(TRIM(mname))
7 ──────────────────── dBASE response
```

2. The `TRIM()` function can improve the appearance of report forms and/or mailing labels by using it in a content entry to concatenate character data. For example, to insert a comma immediately after the city name in a mailing label, use the expression:

```
TRIM(city) + ", " + state + "  " + zipcode
```

Related Topics:
```
CREATE LABEL
CREATE REPORT
LTRIM()
RTRIM()
```

UPPER FUNCTION

Syntax: `UPPER(<character string>)`

Discussion: The `UPPER()` function converts all lowercase letters in the specified character string to their uppercase equivalents. The argument may be a character string, character field or memory variable, or a concatenated string expression, as shown in the following table:

Function	Nature of the Argument
`UPPER("this is a string")`	Character string
`UPPER(lastname)`	Character field
`UPPER(memname)`	Memory variable
`UPPER("Today is" + DTOC(DATE()))`	Concatenated string

Tips:

1. The `UPPER()`, `LOWER()`, and `SUBSTR()` functions can be combined to convert the initial character in a field to uppercase and the remaining characters to lowercase,

```
    REPLACE lname WITH UPPER(SUBSTR(lname,1,1)) +
        LOWER(SUBSTR(lname,2))
```

A single REPLACE command can be used to make the substitution for every record in the currently selected database by specifying a scope of ALL.

2. Most systems allow the user to respond in upper- or lowercase, complicating the data validation process. Converting the response to a uniform standard (either uppercase or lowercase) and then testing for only one set of permitted responses solves the problem. For example, in a system in which A, B, C, or D or a, b, c, or d are valid, the following code would suffice:

```
    @10,20 GET response PICTURE 'A'
    STORE UPPER(response) to response
    IF response < 'A' .OR. response > 'D'
        @12,2 SAY 'Please respond with A, B, C, or D'
    ENDIF
```

Related Topics: LOWER()
                    SUBSTR()

USE

Syntax: USE [<filename>/?] [INDEX <index list>] [ALIAS
            <alias name>]

Discussion: The USE command opens an existing database file and up to seven associated index files, placing them in the currently selected work area. If the database file contains any memo fields, the associated memo file (.DBT) is automatically opened at the same time.

USE <filename> searches the default drive for a .DBF file with the specified file name. If the file exists on a drive other than the default drive, or in a subdirectory other than the logged subdirectory, the full drive specification and/or pathname must be used. Additionally, if the file was created with an extension other than .DBF, the extension must be included with the file name for the file to be found.

The USE ? form of the command can be used only when a catalog file is open and displays a menu of the catalogued database files. Once the desired database file is selected from the menu, it is opened for use in the currently selected work area.

Up to seven indexes can be opened and placed in the work area at the same time you open a database by using the INDEX <index list> option with the USE command. If more than one index is opened, the first index listed is the controlling (master) index and the others are listed only so that they will be updated if changes are made to the database. For example, the command

```
    USE solemp INDEX lname,ssn,salary
```

results in the file being accessed according to the logical order of the LNAME.NDX. SSN.NDX and SALARY.NDX will have no effect on file processing, but are opened so that they will be updated if records are added, edited, or deleted.

When the database file is opened without any associated indexes, the record pointer is positioned at record 1 (the first physical record). If, however, one or more indexes are opened with the file, the record pointer is positioned at the first record according to the logical sequence of the master index.

Up to 10 database files (DBF) can be open at any one time with each file placed in its own work area. There can, however, be only one database file per work area, and a given database file can be open in only one work area. Database files are assigned to a work area by SELECTing a work area and then issuing the appropriate form of the USE command. Thus, the command sequence:

```
SELECT 1
USE solemp INDEX lname,ssn
SELECT 2
USE location
```

places the SOLEMP.DBF in work area 1 along with its two indexes, while LOCATION.DBF is placed in work area 2. If no work area is explicitly specified (selected), the USE command opens the specified file in work area 1 and it becomes the currently selected work area.

An alias of up to 10 characters (the rules for an alias name are the same as for a field name) can be assigned to a file with the ALIAS option. The alias is a temporarily assigned name that is lost when the file is closed. A short, meaningful alias is particularly useful when the file name itself is difficult to remember as it may be used in place of the file name. Note that if no alias is explicitly assigned, the alias defaults to the file name.

The USE command, issued by itself with no parameters, closes the database file and its associated indexes in the currently selected work area.

Tips: _____

1. Should you forget which database file is assigned to which work area, the DISPLAY STATUS command will display the following information for each database file in use:

   Filename
   Work area number
   Alias
   Any database relations
   Open index files and their respective keys
   Open memo files (.DBT)

2. Since only one file can be open in a work area at one time, if a file is open in the currently selected work area and you issue a USE ⟨filename⟩ command to open another database file (without first selecting another work area) the first file (and any associated open indexes) is automatically closed and the second file assigned to the work area.

Related Topics: DISPLAY STATUS
                      SELECT
                      SET CATALOG
                      SET INDEX

VAL FUNCTION

Syntax: VAL(⟨character expression⟩)

Discussion: The VAL() function returns a numeric value equivalent to the character-type number specified in the argument. The VAL() function is used when arithmetic operations are to be performed on data that have been stored (for whatever reason) in character format.

Tips:

1. The VAL() function will return a numeric value with the appropriate number of decimal places as established by the SET DECIMALS command. (The full decimal value is used in arithmetic operations.)

```
SET DECIMALS TO 5
? STORE VAL('3.555678') TO mnum
3.55568                                    ——— dBASE response
SET DECIMALS TO 2
? STORE VAL('3.555678') TO mnum
3.56                                       ——— dBASE response
```

2. A numerical value of zero is returned for any character string beginning with other than a digit, zero, or a blank. If, however, the character string begins with a digit or blank, but contains a subsequent letter or special character, the digits are converted and the remaining characters are ignored. Consider the following examples:

Function	Numeric Equivalent
VAL("ABC")	0
VAL("ABC123")	0
VAL("123")	123
VAL("123ABC")	123

3. The TIME() function returns a character string (hh:mm:ss) rather than a numeric value, and cannot be used in a calculation unless it is first converted to a numeric equivalent. Remember, however, that dBASE does not provide time arithmetic as it does date arithmetic.

Related Topics: TIME()
STR()

WAIT

Syntax: WAIT [<prompt>][TO <memvar>]

Discussion: The WAIT command suspends processing while simultaneously displaying the default message, 'Press any key to continue. . .', in column 0 of the next available line. Compliance with the message (that is, pressing any key) causes dBASE to resume processing at the point where it was interrupted.

The prompt clause enables a custom message to be used in place of the default message. The prompt must be enclosed in quotes. In addition, the proper number of spaces must appear at the beginning of the prompt string if the message is to begin at any column other than 0.

Including the TO parameter stores the next keystroke entered into the specified memory variable, which is automatically initialized as a one-byte character field. This can be useful in a custom program as the following code demonstrates:

```
WAIT "Please enter choice: " TO manswer
DO CASE
     CASE UPPER(manswer) = 'A'
          DO addrec.prg
     CASE UPPER(manswer) = 'B'
          DO editrec.prg
          .
          .
          .
ENDCASE
```

If, however, the Return key itself is pressed immediately in response to the WAIT TO command, the length of the memory variable created is 0 rather than 1. The following code can therefore test for the Return key:

```
WAIT "Press return key to continue" TO manswer
IF LEN(manswer) = 0
     DO prog1.prg
ELSE
     DO error.prg
ENDIF
```

Tips:

1. User input associated with the WAIT command is limited to a single character, meaning that processing continues as soon as any key is pressed. Any extra keystrokes are stored in the typeahead buffer and can cause problems later in the program. It is good practice, therefore, to issue a CLEAR TYPEAHEAD command after a WAIT.

2. More sophisticated input menus which go beyond the one-character user response, enhance data validation capabilities, and improve the number and position of prompting messages are better produced with the @...SAY...GET and READ command combination.

3. The WAIT command can be used after error messages or important informational screens to give the user enough time to read the screen before processing continues.

4. The default message can be suppressed, with no message replacing it, by substituting a blank character string for the prompt message, that is, WAIT '   '. However, the user's input will still be collected and displayed on the next available line unless SET CONSOLE OFF is used as well. Consider:

```
SET CONSOLE OFF
WAIT '    '
SET CONSOLE ON
```

Related Topics:
```
READ
@..SAY...GET
CLEAR
```

YEAR FUNCTION

Syntax: `YEAR(<date expression>)`

Discussion: The YEAR() function returns a four-digit number corresponding to the year of the specified date expression. The argument in the YEAR() function may assume several different forms as shown in the following table:

Function	Nature of the Argument
`YEAR(hiredate)`	Date field
`YEAR(memdate)`	Date memory variable
`YEAR(DATE())`	DATE() function itself
`YEAR(CTOD("12/25/88"))`	CTOD() conversion function
`YEAR(DATE() + 10)`	Expression with date arithmetic

Tips:

1. The `YEAR()` function works only on date fields, that is, a character date may *not* be used as the argument unless it is first converted with the `CTOD()` conversion function.
2. The `YEAR()` function is often used in program files and/or report forms to display a date in a more attractive format. For example, given a date of 01/08/89, the command

   ```
   @ 20,20 SAY "Today is " + CMONTH(DATE()) + " "
   + STR(DAY(DATE()),2) + ", " + STR(YEAR(DATE()),4)
   ```

   returns the string "Today is January 08, 1989" (Note that the day and year must be converted to strings to be concatenated with the other character type data.)
3. The `YEAR()` function always supplies a four-digit value regardless of the status of `SET CENTURY`.

Related Topics: `CMONTH()`
 `CTOD()`
 `DATE()`
 `DAY()`
 `MONTH()`
 `STR()`

ZAP

Syntax: `ZAP`

Discussion: The `ZAP` command physically deletes every record from the currently selected database, leaving the file open and the file structure intact. It is equivalent to combining the `DELETE ALL` and `PACK` commands, except that it executes more quickly. It is *not* possible to recall records once a `ZAP` command has been executed.

Tips:

1. If `SET SAFETY` is ON, confirmation is requested before deleting the records. If `SET SAFETY` is OFF, however, the file will be `ZAP`ped with no warning.
2. Be sure you have a *current* backup copy of the file in question before issuing the `ZAP` command. If you are unsure of the backup, copy the file before you `ZAP` it.
3. The `ZAP` command is often used to clear a temporary work file.
4. Any open index files in the currently selected work area are automatically updated to reflect the fact that the associated database file has been cleared of all its records.

?

Syntax: ?/??

Discussion: The ?/?? command displays the value of an expression list. It may include literals, memory variables, and database fields. Execution of the command using a single ? begins with a carriage return and line feed so that the expression is displayed at the beginning of the next available line. The double ??, however, issues neither a carriage return nor a line feed, and thus displays the expression list starting at the current cursor position. For this reason, the ?? is used primarily within programs rather than from the dot prompt, where the display would overwrite the command line.

     The ? command can include an arithmetic, string, date, or logical operation as part of the expression list, in which case dBASE evaluates the operation, then displays the result. Some examples:

```
? salary * 1.10
? DATE() + 7
? lastname,salary
? 15*60
```

Tips:

1. The ? command with no expression list displays a blank line, that is, it skips a line in the output.
2. The ? command can be used to print the contents of a memo field by including the field name in the command. Use SET MEMOWIDTH to control the appearance of the display.
3. The data types of all fields in a *concatenated* expression list must be the same. Accordingly, the display of messages with numeric or date fields requires string and/or date conversion functions to be used, for example,

```
? 'Employee hired on: ' + DTOC(hdate)
? 'Current salary: ' + STR(salary,6)
```

4. The results of a ?/?? command will be sent to the printer if a SET PRINT ON command has been previously issued.
5. The ? can easily be used to test and debug a complex expression from the dot prompt before it is incorporated into a report or program, where it is more cumbersome to test and debug.
6. The ? command is best suited to displaying one line after another (sequential displays) with no special formatting. The @...SAY command is better suited to more sophisticated output.
7. The ? command can be used to evaluate a logical condition. For example, the command

```
? lastname = 'Scholl'
```

will return a .T., if the value of lastname is "Scholl", and an .F. if it is not. The command

```
? 3*3/4 > 2
```

evaluates the comparison, and returns a logical .T. since 9/4 is indeed greater than 2.

Related Topics: DTOC()   &—Macro Notation
         @...SAY...GET
         SET MEMOWIDTH   **383**
         SET PRINT ON
         STR()

---

*

Syntax: `* <comment>`
      or
    `NOTE <comment>`

Discussion: The appearance of an `*` (or the word `NOTE`) as the first nonblank character of a line, indicates a comment causing dBASE to ignore the entire line, for example,

```
***MAINMENU.PRG
***This program maps the main menu screen
```

Comments help to document a program. They are most useful to those involved in program maintenance as they help explain complex or unusual code.

Tips: _____

1. Don't over-comment, as too many comments are sometimes worse than no comments at all. Ill-chosen comments may be redundant with source code, or worse yet, obsolete or inconsistent (which happens when the program is changed but the comments are not). Do comment a program, but choose your comments carefully.
2. The choice between a `&&` or `*` to comment a program is one of personal preference, as one method is not necessarily better than the other. In general, the `*` is used to comment sections of code whereas the `&&` is used to explain an individual line of code.
3. The `*` (or the word `NOTE`) need not appear in column one, but can be indented the same number of spaces as the code it explains.
4. Every program should begin with comment lines that give, at a minimum, the name of the program, its function, the name of its author, and the associated called and calling programs.
5. A comment line can be continued to the next line by placing a semicolon at the end of the line and thus eliminating the need to begin the next line with another `*` or `NOTE`, for example,

```
* This program maps the screen and displays a choice;
  of report formats for printing or viewing on the;
  screen
```

Related Topics: `&&`

&—MACRO NOTATION

Syntax: `&<character memory variable>`

Discussion: A single ampersand (&) denotes the dBASE *macro* function, and is always followed immediately by a memory variable. Using the function causes dBASE to *substitute* the contents of the memory variable directly into the command in which it appears. For example, assume that the memory variable mreport contains the value "SALARY", and consider the command REPORT FORM &mreport. The macro function would substitute "SALARY" into the command in place of &mreport, effectively creating the command REPORT FORM SALARY. The concept may appear confusing at first, but once understood, the macro function provides increased generality within a program.

A second example is contained in the following code which generates one of several different reports based on a previously entered user response. The case structure stores a different index and report name into two different memory variables, after which macro substitution produces the desired report.

```
DO CASE
   CASE response = '1'
      STORE "location" TO mindex
      STORE "locrep" TO mreport
   CASE response = '2'
      STORE "salary" TO mindex
      STORE "salrep" to mreport
   .
   .
   .
ENDCASE
USE EMPLOYEE INDEX &mindex
REPORT FORM &mreport TO PRINT
```

Without the & in the above code, dBASE would search for an index named MINDEX.NDX and a report form named MREPORT.FRM. The macro function, however, instructs dBASE to look for the index and report form name as currently stored in the memory variables.

Tips:

1. The data stored in the memory variable associated with the macro function must be a character string.

Related Topics: STORE

&&

Syntax: && <comment>

Discussion: The appearance of double ampersands (&&) in a dBASE command indicates that the rest of the line is to be treated as comments; that is, as soon as dBASE encounters the &&, it ignores the rest of the line. For example,

```
@ 22,10 SAY SPACE(60)   &&Clears the message line
```

Comments help to document a program. They are most useful to those involved in program maintenance because they help explain complex or unusual code.

Tips:

1. Don't over-comment, as too many comments are sometimes worse than no comments at all. Ill-chosen comments may be redundant with source code, or worse yet, obsolete or inconsistent (which happens when the program is changed but the comments are not). Do comment a program, but choose your comments carefully.
2. The choice between a `&&` or `*` to comment a program is one of personal preference, as one method is not necessarily better than the other. In general, the `*` is used to comment sections of code whereas the `&&` is used to explain an individual line of code.

Related Topics:

Index

Index